VIETNAM AND CHINA
1938-1954

VIETNAM AND CHINA, 1938-1954

<<<<<<<<<<<<<<<<<<<<<<<<<<<<<<<<<<<<<<<<<<<<<<

By King C. Chen

<<<<<<<<<<<<<<<<<<<<<<<<<<<<<<<<<<<<<<<<<<<<<<

Princeton University Press, Princeton, N. J.   1969

This book has been composed in Linotype Caledonia

Printed in the United States of America
by Princeton University Press, Princeton, New Jersey

To the memory of my parents

Contents

List of Maps and Tables

Acknowledgments

◄◄

I STARTED this study in 1959—long before the Vietnam situation developed to the present stage. After the early draft of the manuscript was completed in 1962 I was busy with teaching and research projects for some time while waiting for additional Chinese materials from Taiwan. In the fall of 1966 I obtained the materials; then I resumed this work by doing further extensive research and rewriting the entire manuscript.

In the course of my study I have benefitted greatly from many scholars and friends. To Professors Vernon V. Aspaturian and A. Doak Barnett, I express my sincere appreciation for their criticisms and suggestions, which have proved very valuable. To Professor C. Martin Wilbur I extend my gratitude for his direct and indirect help. Informal conversations with Philippe Devillers, Dai Shen-yu, and Yin-maw Kau provided many insights into various problems of the subject. I am grateful to O. Edmund Clubb, Arthur Stein, Myron Cohen, and Lea E. Williams for their reading and commenting on parts or all of the manuscript. The late Bernard B. Fall read an early draft of the manuscript. I asked him in December 1966 to write a foreword for this book. His wife, Dorothy Fall, sent me a note saying that my request had been relayed to him in Vietnam and that it would take "several weeks" to hear from him. Shortly thereafter came the tragic news of his death. His passing was a great loss to the study of Vietnam.

I am indebted to Chiang Yung-ching (Taiwan) who was kind enough to allow me to use his entire unpublished collection of documents on Vietnam (and his earlier monograph, *Ho Chi Minh and China, 1941-44*), which contains a rich amount of never-published and very valuable materials from Taiwan; to General Chang Fa-k'uei (Hong Kong) for his interviews and correspondence; to Cardinal Paul Yupin (Taiwan) for his interview; to Generals Shao Pai-ch'ang

Acknowledgments

and Hou Chih-ming (Taiwan) for their correspondence and interviews; to Governor Huang Chieh of Taiwan for his not-for-sale memoirs; to Messrs. Vu Hong Khanh and Nghiem Ke To (Saigon) for their correspondence; and to Lui Fei-lung (Taiwan) for his constant help in obtaining data. I also extend my sincere appreciation to Mr. Roy A. Grisham, Jr. for his excellent editorial assistance and to Miss Karen Mollineaux for her help in drawing the maps. My thanks also go to those kind librarians and friends who helped me at the Library of Congress, the libraries of Columbia, Cornell, Brown and Harvard Universities.

I wish to thank the following publishers for permission to quote briefly from:

Lucien Bodard, *The Quicksand War: Prelude to Vietnam,* Boston: Little, Brown and Co., 1967.

Ellen J. Hammer, *The Struggle for Indochina,* Stanford: Stanford University Press, 1954.

Hoang Van Chi, *From Colonialism to Communism: A Case History of North Vietnam,* New York: Frederick Praeger, 1964.

To my wife, Grace Ho Chen, I owe a special debt for her constant encouragement and assistance throughout the years of research and writing.

King C. Chen

Providence, Rhode Island
April 1969

Introduction

HISTORY will undoubtedly record that no war with a foreign enemy has so widely divided the United States as had the American military engagement in Vietnam. In the great debate on the Vietnam war in the past, a question was often asked: why and how did the United States get involved in the war? Pondering the origins of the American involvement, one will logically turn to United States policy towards the Indochinese War (1946-1954) and even the earlier American role in the Vietnamese Communist movement under Ho Chi Minh (1944-1945). In a pattern unique to the West, the Vietnamese Communist movement was generated by the ideologies of nationalism and Communism, and combined the teachings of the Communist International with the peasant-based armed revolution of the Chinese Communist system. It was, however, only after the triumph of the Chinese Communist Party in the late 1940s that the Viet-Minh victory over the French in 1954 was made possible. An investigation of Sino-Vietnamese relations in the postwar decade, therefore, will enable us not only to evaluate the nature and significance of the Vietnamese Communist movement under the impact of the Chinese Communist revolution, but to analyze more meaningfully the distressing and perilous American engagement in Vietnam.

The Sino-Vietnamese relationship in the postwar decade was regarded as the continuation of century-old relations between these two countries. An examination of the pre-1945 records supports this view. Prior to the French conquest of Indochina, the interaction between China and Vietnam had established a pattern: when China was strong and magnanimous, Vietnam paid tribute to and imitated its northern neighbor; when China was aggressive, Vietnam resisted. With the coming of the French Vietnam suffered humiliation and exploitation at the hands of its conqueror, as China did from major world powers. The Chinese anti-foreign movement and republican revolution encouraged the Vietnamese independence struggle, and it was through the Chinese Communist revolution in the 1920s that the Communist movement in Vietnam began to take shape. During the Second Sino-Japanese War (1937-1945) China, sympathetic to the cause of Vietnam's independence, supported Vietnamese revolutionists, nationalists and Communists. Many Vietnamese Communist leaders besides Ho Chi Minh, such as Pham Van Dong, Vo Nguyen Giap, and Hoang Van Hoan, took refuge in China and made her a base for the revolution in their homeland.

The Chinese occupation in 1945-1946 was imposed on northern Vietnam by the Allied powers without previous consultations with either the French or the Vietnamese. The Viet-Minh, though unhappy with Lu Han's occupation forces, were able to strengthen themselves during the occupation period. Therefore, when the Chinese army left Vietnam in the summer of 1946, Giap's forces were strong enough to easily crush the Viet-Minh's arch rival, the anti-Communist Chinese-supported Dong Minh Hoi and the Vietnam Nationalist Party. But after the Indochinese war broke out, the most hopeful development for the Viet-Minh's resistance war was a stalemate in the isolated corner of northern Tonkin. One major reason was that the Viet-Minh had a neutral but sometimes hostile Nationalist China in the rear. The mistakes of the French policy to treat the nationalistic and popular Viet-Minh movement as a bandit group did not offer Ho Chi Minh any opportunity to win a major battle, to say nothing of the war.

The Communist victory in China not only tore down the Viet-Minh wall of isolation; it brought an end to the Viet-Minh's suffering dark days. It opened a new era of Sino-Vietnamese relations. The two Communist nations interacted at many different levels—ideological, political and diplomatic, economic, and military. Their relationship appeared to be much more dynamic and closer than that prior to 1949. In a tremendous effort to apply the Chinese revolutionary model to Vietnam, Ho's men successfully made use of Chinese aid, which led to the victory at Dien-Bien-Phu.

These developments raise many important questions. Did the Vietnamese revolutionists (both nationalist and Communist) turn to China for help because of historical tradition, geographical proximity, or ideological similarity? What were the policies of Nationalist and Communist China toward the Viet-Minh, and what was the Viet-Minh's response to them? To what extent did the Chinese Nationalists and Communists assist or intervene for the Viet-Minh Communists? Why were the Viet-Minh able to obtain Chinese military aid without inviting their massive military intervention, as happened in Korea? And what was the Soviet position on the Indochinese war and at the Geneva Conference? Above all, is there any difference in nature between Vietnam's relationship with the weak Nationalist China (1938-1949) and that with the powerful Communist regime in Peking (1950-1954)?

This book is intended to seek answers to these questions. Moreover, in view of the American involvement in Vietnam, it attempts to do more than this. During the extensive and destructive American air raids in North Vietnam from February 1965 to October 1968, aid to Hanoi from the Communist camp, especially from the Soviet Union and Communist China, became a vital factor in North Vietnam's continuation of the war. It is true that the agony of the war had grown to a significant dimension in the United States. It is equally true that American air strikes had brought a grim and extremely difficult situation to North Vietnam. Despite its public adamant statements, a settlement for South Vietnam through negotiations was, and is, believed to be the wish of Hanoi. And such a settlement is often conditioned by the attitudes of the Soviet Union and Communist China. With this background, this study also examines how the Viet-Minh came to the conference table for a settlement in 1954 and what the international implications were. In addition, an attempt is made to compare succinctly the situation of peace talks in 1954 with that in 1968.

Introduction

A NOTE on the documentation in the text is necessary. It is generally recognized that no study on foreign relations, particularly during a turbulent and revolutionary era, can be definite and complete unless archives are made available. Yet a rich amount of public documents and secondary materials can also provide valuable and fruitful insights into various aspects of domestic and foreign affairs; Western scholars have developed a rather sophisticated approach to using these sources for the study of Communist politics. In this work both sources, archives and public documents, are used. For the period 1938-1949 a sizable collection of archives from 1941 to 1948 have been used. The documents include field reports from those who were in charge of the affairs, reports on conferences, plans and programs of organizations and activities, cables and letters of correspondence. These sources, supplemented by my interviews, correspondence, and Chinese and Vietnamese publications, shed much light on what really happened between China and Vietnam in the 1940s and clarified many obscured and inaccurate points that have been maintained by some writers. It should be pointed out that the accuracy of the documents used in this book is borne out by several recent publications from Hanoi.

For the period 1950-1954 the documentation depends heavily on public documents and other primary sources. I went through the broadcasts from 1948 to 1954 from both the Viet-Minh and Communist China. Relevant broadcasts from Moscow were also studied. The *Survey of the China Mainland Press* and *Current Background* from 1950 to 1954 were examined; *Shih chieh chih shih, Jen min jih pao*, the Comintern journal, and major newspapers in Hong Kong during the same period were investigated. In addition, relevant issues of *Chieh fang jih pao* and *Hsin hua yueh pao* were searched. Although the early issues of the Viet-Minh publications such as *Su That, Cuu Quoc*, and *Nhan Dan* were not available for examination, their important articles and statements were broadcast at that time either in full or in excerpts by the Viet-Minh radio. It is true that not every item of Chinese or Vietnamese materials merits inclusion in the text, but some pieces are so valuable and revealing that Hanoi or Peking (particularly the former) will probably regret what it has stated.

VIETNAM AND CHINA
1938-1954

1. The Background

<<<<<<<<<<<<<<<<<<<<<<<<<<<<<<<<<<<<<<<<<<<<<<<<<<<<

"... We have sometimes been weak, and sometimes powerful, but at no time have we lacked heroes."

> — Emperor Le Loi's Proclamation in 1418, at the beginning of a 10-year war of independence against China

"Annam borders on China; her security concerns us. China's protection of that country should have no difference from that of Chinese provinces."

> — Tseng Chi-tse's suggestion to the Ch'ing government in 1881 for the protection of Annam against the French

1. HISTORIC TIES BETWEEN CHINA AND VIETNAM

VIETNAM is the only nation in Southeast Asia that has been under strong Chinese influence for a long period of time. Prior to the French conquest of Indochina, Chinese culture had been continuously introduced to and absorbed by Vietnam, making the country something of a miniature Chinese civilization. But the Vietnamese people had been in existence for several thousand years before they appeared in Chinese history, which is one of the most valuable original sources dealing with the Vietnamese and their relations with China in ancient times.[1] In the first book of the 25 dynastic

[1] While books in English on ancient Vietnam draw most of their materials from French sources, the French sources are heavily derived from Chinese and Vietnamese historical documents. For instance, Maurice Durand, an outstanding French scholar, has used Chinese and Vietnamese documents extensively in writing his well-known book on Vietnamese history. See *Texte et Commentaire du Miroir Complet de l'Histoire du Viet* (Hanoi: Ecole Française d'Extrême-Orient, 1950).

Also see Leonard Aurousseau's brief but outstanding work, "La première conquête chinoise des pays annamites," *Bulletin de l'Ecole Française d'Extrême-Orient*, Vol. 23 (Hanoi, 1923).

A Chinese historian, Ch'en Hsiu-ho, wrote a useful book on Vietnam's ancient history, people, culture, and relations with China. His work was based on both Chinese and Vietnamese histories, as well as his field studies in Vietnam. See *Yueh-nan ku shih chi ch'i min tsu wen hua chih yen chiu* (Study on Vietnam's Ancient History, People and Culture) (Kunming: Yunnan University, 1943). In Communist

histories of China, *Shih chi*, the Viet people were recorded as a people who had the custom of "tattooing their bodies and cutting their hair" to avoid attacks by the animals from the sea.[2] This was not denied by Vietnamese history. The custom was common in early times all over Southeast Asia among the Austro-Indonesian racial group, but the early Vietnamese did not belong to the Austro-Indonesians. They originated from a relatively late Mongolian attribution to an older Austro-Indonesian stock.[3] Scholars regard the early Vietnamese as one of several Viet groups of South China who resided in today's Szechuan, Yunnan, Kweichow, Kwangsi, Kwangtung, Fukien, Chekiang, and parts of Vietnam, Thailand, and Burma; they have a Chinese origin.[4] In

China, Ch'en wrote a Peking-approved brief survey of Sino-Vietnamese relations. See his *Chung-Yueh liang kuo jen min ti yu hao kuan hsi ho wen hua chiao liu* (Friendship and Cultural Intercourse of Sino-Vietnamese Peoples) (Peking: Chung-kuo ch'ing-nien ch'u pan she, 1957).

Another Chinese scholar, Li Cheng-fu, also wrote a book dealing with Vietnamese history and Sino-Vietnamese relations from the Ch'in dynasty to the Ming; he used Chinese sources entirely. See his *Chun hsien shih tai chih Annam* (Annam During the Chinese Chun-Hsien Period) (Chungking: Commercial Press, 1948).

In English there have been very few works on Sino-Vietnamese relations. For a survey see Harold C. Hinton, *China's Relations with Burma and Vietnam* (New York: Institute of Pacific Relations, 1958).

[2] *Yueh-wang Kou Chien shih-chia* (Biography of Kou Chien, King of Yueh), in *Shih chi* (Records of History) (Shanghai: Kai-ming Book Store, 1934), p. 146/0146.

[3] Pierre A. Huard and Maurice Durand, *Connaissance du Viet-Nam* (Paris: Imprimerie nationale, 1954), p. 43.

[4] Lo Hsiang-lin, a Chinese historian from Kwangtung, suggests that there were more than 16 Yueh groups (Viets) living in the areas from southeastern to southwestern China, and northern Vietnam, Thailand, and Burma. *Chung-hsia hsi t'ung chung chih Pai-yueh* (The Hundred Yueh in the Chinese People System) (Chungking: Tu li Publishing Co., 1943), pp. 88-188. Hsu Sung-shih, another Chinese scholar from South China, observes that the Vietnamese have a Chinese "blood relation." See his *Tung-nan-ya min tsu ti Chung-kuo hsueh yuan* (Chinese Blood Relations of the South Eastern Asiatic People) (Hong Kong: Ping On Book Co., 1959), pp. 140-46. Ch'en Hsiu-ho, *Vietnam's Ancient History*, pp. 48, 66-67, holds a similar view. Huard and Durand, *Connaissance*, p. 7, also indicate that the Vietnamese have a Chinese origin. Thus Chinese and French scholars are of a similar opinion in this aspect. However, Le Thanh Khoi, a Vietnamese

both Chinese and Vietnamese historical documents these Viets were called the "pai-Yueh"[5] (hundred Yueh), indicating that they consisted of numerous tribes living in various areas. And the early Vietnamese people and culture, as one scholar suggests, could well be a result of the development of the people and culture in southeastern and southwestern China.[6] As the Han people and culture moved to the south, Chinese cultural influence on the Vietnamese people became apparent.[7]

The beginning of Sino-Vietnamese relations was marked by the conquest of Ch'in Shih Huang Ti, who unified China and founded his empire in 221 B.C. From then on, Vietnam, either as a Chinese province or independent, was under Chinese influence for two thousand years. In view of the fact that China historically has spread her influence over Asia through two main levels, political-military and cultural, the Sino-Vietnamese historic ties should be discussed briefly.

When Ch'in Shih Huang Ti conquered Vietnam in 214 B.C., he met strong resistance and suffered many casualties. He established the counties of Kweilin (Kwangsi), Nanhai

---

historian, rejects this theory. See his *Le Viet-Nam, histoire et civilisation*, Vol. I (Paris: Editions du Seuil, 1955), pp. 86-87.

The legend of ancient Vietnam is interesting. It tells that the first king of the Viet people was the eldest prince in the fifth generation of the Chinese Yen Emperor, Shen Nung (the Divine Husbandman) who also appeared only in Chinese legends. Apparently what Vietnamese historians tried to account for is a Chinese origin of their people. For this reason, Vietnamese governments prior to the arrival of the French always claimed that China was the "Kingdom of the North," while Vietnam was the "Kingdom of the South." See Ch'en Hsiu-ho, *Vietnam's Ancient History*, p. 24.

[5] *Ibid.*, p. 18. The term "pai-Yueh" is still used in China, referring to the people of Kwangtung.

[6] *Ibid.*, p. 27.

[7] Sung-shih Hsu, *Yueh-chiang liu yu jen min shih* (History of the People of the Yueh River Valley) 2d ed. rev. (Hong Kong: World Book Store, 1963), pp. 148-55. In his book on the southward penetration of China's culture, peoples, and political control, Herold J. Wiens discusses some interesting aspects of the Yueh people and the state of Nan Yueh (Nam-Viet). See his book, *China's March Toward the Tropics* (Hamden, Conn.: The Shoe String Press, 1954), pp. 96-111, 133-41.

(Kwangtung), and Hsiang (Vietnam), and adopted the policy of sending Chinese criminals to mingle with the Yueh people who resided in these areas.[8] The Chinese also introduced farming implements and methods into Vietnam. Under the Chinese, the Vietnamese greatly improved their agricultural production by the use of the metal plough, the buffalo, and a more effective irrigation system. As a result, the wealth and population of Vietnam increased.[9]

Immediately after the death of the emperor, the Ch'in dynasty came to an end. Chao T'o, a newly inaugurated official of Nanhai, took both Kweilin and Hsiang counties by force and in 207 B.C. proclaimed himself the king of Nan Yueh (Nam-Viet), independent from Chinese rule. He voluntarily discarded the custom of the Han culture, calling himself Great Chief of the Man-Yi (barbarians), studied to copy the native custom, and promoted intermarriage between the Chinese and native peoples.[10] In 196 B.C., the Chinese Later Han dynasty recognized Nan Yueh as a vassal state.

A strong Han emperor, Wu Ti, took Nan Yueh in 112 B.C. and divided it into nine counties,[11] of which three (Chiao-Chih, Chiu-Chen, and Jen-Nan) were in what is now Vietnam. From 111 B.C. to A.D. 543 Vietnam was the Chinese province of Chiao-Chih. The governors and county chiefs were Chinese. Chinese political institutions were introduced; Chinese scholars, officials, as well as fugitives, were em-

[8] *Nan-Yueh Wang chuan* (Biography of the King of Nam Viet), in *Han shu* (History of the Former Han Dynasty) (Shanghai: Kai Ming, 1934), p. 315/0603. Ch'en Hsiu-ho, in disagreement with Leonard Aurousseau's assumption that Ch'in Shih Huang Ti had engaged in the Vietnam war for three years, argues convincingly that the Emperor took Vietnam in only one year as recorded in Chinese history and that it was done through the sea route from Canton to Da-Nang. See Ch'en Hsiu-ho, *Vietnam's Ancient History*, pp. 30-36.

[9] *Nan-Man chuan* (History of the Southern Barbarians), in *Hou-Han Shu* (History of the Later Han Dynasty) (Shanghai: Kai Ming, 1934), p. 256/0898.

[10] *Nan-Yueh-Wang chuan*, in *Han shu*, p. 315/0603. For Chao T'o's policy see Hsu Sung-shih, *People of the Yueh River Valley*, pp. 151-52. See also Wiens, *China's March*, p. 137.

[11] *Nan-Man chuan*, in *Hou-Han shu*, p. 255/0897.

ployed in the administration. During this period it appeared that the ruling group, with a minority of Vietnamese, constituted a new and privileged upper class.

150 years after Vietnam became a province of China, in A.D. 40, two Vietnamese sisters, Trung Trac and Trung Nhi, revolted against Chinese maladministration. They were only briefly successful. The revolt was put down by General Ma Yuan in A.D. 43, and stronger Chinese control was instituted.[12]

Successful governorship was found during the administration of Jen Yen in the Han dynasty and Shih Hsieh (or Si Nhiep, in Vietnamese) in the state of Wu of the Three Kingdoms—especially the latter. Shih Hsieh (A.D. 136-226, governorship, 187-226) not only protected the province from chaos during his time of rule, but also promoted education and kept people from unemployment. The whole province was prosperous.[13] The chaotic situation caused by the civil war in the Three Kingdoms resulted in an independent status for the remote Chaio-Chih.

In 264 the Wu state divided Chaio-Chih into Kuang-chow (Kwangsi and most parts of Kwangtung) and Chiao-chow (southwestern Kwangtung and northern Vietnam down to the 18th parallel).[14] The area of Chiaochow, except for Hoh-p'u and Chu-yai which belong to Kwangtung, is included in the territory of modern Vietnam.

As Vietnam's political relations with China remained close, the wealth taken by the Chinese was considerable. Besides its being a good source of taxation, the Chinese regarded Vietnam as a country of treasures from which they sought rare and precious items. A striking example was the Chinese adventure for treasures in 604 during the Sui dynasty. The emperor sent General Liu Fang, together with

---

[12] *Ma Yuan chuan* (Biography of Ma Yuan), in *Hou-Han shu*, p. 105/0747.

[13] *Wushu Shih Hsieh chuan* (Biography of Shih Hsieh, History of the State of Wu), in *San-Kuo chih* (History of the Three Kingdoms) (Shanghai: Kai-ming, 1934), p. 128/1042.

[14] *Ibid.* Chiaochow included five counties: Hoh-p'u, Chu-yai (Kwangtung), Chioa-chih, Chiu-chen, and Jen-nan (Vietnam).

more than 10,000 soldiers and a few thousand criminals, to attack Lin-I, then a district of Jen-Nan, where General Ma Yuan stationed his army.[15] The ruler of Lin-I resisted bravely but was defeated. Liu Fang's army looted the district of gold and other treasures before returning to China.[16]

Uprisings occurred occasionally in response to the weakness of Chinese rule, but none were successful. In 679, during the T'ang dynasty (617-907), the name of Chiaochow was changed to Annam. At first, the T'ang administration ruled more effectively than had previous dynasties, and brought parts of central Vietnam under Chinese rule. As the T'ang dynasty declined, revolt broke out. So strong was the rebellion that the Chinese rule was ended. Independent Vietnam recognized China's suzerainty by acknowledging herself as a tribute state of China. A new relationship was established; Vietnam agreed to send tribute missions once every three years, to adopt the Chinese calendar and court usages, and to report to China grave or urgent internal or external affairs. China, in turn, agreed to provide military protection on request and to allow Vietnam to govern herself.[17]

Ambitious and able rulers of China did not forget the earlier conquest of Vietnam. In 1284 and 1287 Mongolian soldiers twice invaded northern Vietnam, but were defeated in the Red River Valley. In 1407 the Yung-lo emperor of the Ming dynasty (1368-1644) reconquered Vietnam. The Chinese pao-chia (collective responsibility) system, Chinese dress, the conscription system, and heavy taxes were imposed on the Vietnamese. The Chinese also selected and sent more than 9,000 able Vietnamese to Peking for the purpose of serving the empire. In addition, Vietnamese were

[15] *Lin-I chuan* (History of Lin-I), in *Nan shih* (History of the Southern Dynasties) (Shanghai: Kai-ming, 1934), p. 187/2729.

[16] *Lin-I chuan*, in *Sui shu* (History of the Sui Dynasty) (Shanghai: Kai-ming, 1934), p. 191/2533.

[17] *Yi-man chuan* (Biography of the Savages and Barbarians), in *Sung shu* (History of the Sung Dynasty) (Shanghai: Kai-ming, 1934), p. 237/1653. See also Huard and Durand, *Connaissance*, pp. 15-16.

sent to the forests and the ocean for precious metals, stones, pearls, and elephant tusks for the Chinese invader.[18]

Two years after the death of the Yung-lo emperor in 1427, the Vietnamese won back their independence in a war that lasted 10 years. Thereafter, until the arrival of the French, Vietnam again acknowledged itself as a tribute state to China, paying tribute to Peking ranging from one to 12 years.[19]

As a result of the Sino-French agreement in 1885, following a war in Vietnam the preceding year between these two nations, China lost its control over Vietnam. Sino-Vietnamese political relations in the French colonial era became one aspect of the relationship between China and France.[20] And yet, Chinese economic activities and cultural influence in Vietnam had never ceased to exist.

[18] *An-nan chuan* (History of Annam), in *Ming shih* (History of the Ming Dynasty) (Shanghai: Kai-ming, 1934), p. 820/7906.

[19] Hosea B. Morse, *The International Relations of the Chinese Empire* (London: Longmans, Green and Co., 1910), p. 50. John K. Fairbank and Ssu-yu Teng, *The Ch'ing Administration* (Cambridge: Harvard University Press, 1961), pp. 151-52, 193-97. In the same period (1427-1883), Korea paid tribute to China almost every year, Liuchiu one to nine years (ended in 1877).

[20] A nearly complete collection of Chinese archives on Sino-French negotiations on Vietnam has been published by the Research Institute of Modern History, Academia Sinica, Taipei, dealing with Sino-French-Vietnamese triangular relations from 1875 to 1911. See Chung yang yen chiu yuan, chin tai shih yen chiu so (the Research Institute of Modern History, Academia Sinica), *Chung Fa Yueh-nan chiao she tang, 1875-1911* (Archives of Sino-French Negotiations on Vietnam), 7 vols. (Taipei, 1962). Of the many studies dealing entirely or partially with French Indochina, these are the most useful: Virginia Thompson, *French Indochina* (New York: Macmillan, 1937); André Masson, *Histoire de l'Indochine* (Paris: Presses Universitaires de France, 1950); D.G.E. Hall, *A History of South-East Asia* (New York: St. Martin's Press, 1955); John F. Cady, *The Roots of French Imperialism in Eastern Asia* (Ithaca: Cornell University Press, 1954); and Cady, *Southeast Asia: Its Historical Development* (New York: McGraw-Hill, 1964); Joseph Buttinger, *The Smaller Dragon: A Political History of Vietnam* (New York: Frederick Praeger, 1958); and Buttinger, *Vietnam: A Dragon Embattled*, 2 vols. (1967); Hoang Van Chi, *From Colonialism to Communism* (New York: Frederick Praeger, 1964); Donald Lancaster, *The Emancipation of French Indo-China* (London: Oxford University Press, 1961).

Chinese merchants had already built up a business empire in Vietnam before the French came. They secured a hold on Vietnam's commerce and banking, dominating rice and fish enterprises, while not a single farmer or fisherman was to be counted among them. They abided by the law and suffered from no management-labor struggles.[21] After the French assumed their colonial rule in Vietnam, the Chinese were exempted from military service by paying heavy taxes and their business was allowed to continue. The French realized that the Chinese merchants were indispensable to the Vietnamese economy. Furthermore, the French must have devised a way to use the Chinese to help rule Vietnam. Friction between Chinese and Vietnamese was welcomed by the French, for it reduced the antagonism of the two peoples toward French rule; the French were then able to act as peacemaker. The Vietnamese, in turn, admired Chinese business ability but disliked their domination.

As mentioned earlier, there were some basic cultural similarities in prehistoric China and Vietnam, a view that is borne out by modern archaeological discoveries. In 1924 French archaeologists discovered in Hoa-Binh (about 75 miles west of Hanoi) and Bac-Son (about 120 miles northeast of Hanoi) various items of both the earlier and later periods of the new stone age. While the items of the former period are strikingly similar to those from western China (the Szechuan area), those of the latter period differ merely in some minor respects.[22] S. V. Diselev (Isuliff), a Soviet archaeologist-historian, held a similar view. In early 1950, shortly before he came to lecture in China along with two other Russians, Diselev found, by reviewing the report on recent discoveries in Vietnam, some similarities between the Vietnamese items and those of the Shang (Yin) dynasty.[23]

---

[21] Thompson, *French Indochina*, p. 169.

[22] See the discussion in Ch'en Hsiu-ho, *Vietnam's Ancient History*, pp. 108-109.

[23] Chang T'ieh-hsien, "What Do We Learn from the Soviet Archaeologist-Historian?—A Brief Account of Diselev's Lecture Tour in China," in *Chin pu jih pao* (Progress Daily; formerly *Ta Kung Pao*; T'ientsin), May 20, 1950. At the invitation of the Sino-Soviet Friend-

It is asserted, therefore, that there were similar cultural features between western China and Vietnam as early as 3,000 B.C.[24] Subsequent to China's expansion into Vietnam, Chinese culture was exported to that country by political force.

Chinese philosophy, literature, language, arts, social rites, and religion gradually flowed into Vietnam after 207 B.C. The Chinese established schools, introduced marriage arrangements, and taught their literature to the Vietnamese.[25] Confucian teachings and Taoism came with the influx of Chinese scholars and officials. Buddhism entered Vietnam via China in the second century.[26]

Chinese culture in Vietnam was glorified by the educational efforts of the governorship of Shih Hsieh (187-226). His administration emphasized the studies of Chinese classics and the practice of social rites.[27] So grateful were the Vietnamese for his teachings that Shih was honored with the title, "the Founder of Studies."[28]

After the independence of Vietnam, Chinese culture not only continued to remain in Vietnamese society but became even more firmly rooted through its adoption by Vietnamese rulers. Schools for training civil servants were established in 1076, and examinations for selecting public officials were held in the form of literary competitions on the Chinese model.[29] The traditional Chinese belief that Chinese culture with Confucianism as its backbone is good for ruling a country must have also been found true by the rulers of Vietnam.

---

ship Association, Diselev's group toured widely in north, east, central-south, and southwestern China from March to May 1950.

[24] Ch'en Hsiu-ho, *Vietnam's Ancient History*, p. 109.

[25] *Nan-man chuan*, in *Hou-Han shu*, p. 256/0898.

[26] Le Thanh Khoi, *Vietnam*, p. 110.

[27] *Wushu Shih Hsieh chuan*, in *San-Kuo chih*, p. 128/1042.

[28] Nguyen-Van-Thai and Nguyen-Van-Mung, *A Short History of Vietnam* (Saigon: Times Publishing Co., 1958), p. 26.

[29] Vietnam began to hold the civil examination in the 12th century. See Li Cheng-fu, *Annam*, p. 179.

The Background

The Ming conquest of Vietnam (1407-1427) had a strong cultural impact on Vietnamese society. Teaching in the schools was conducted in Chinese only; local rites were replaced by the Chinese ones; Chinese literature flowed in; dress was changed to the Ming style; and local customs such as cutting hair and chewing the betel nut were prohibited. The Ming effort, obviously, was to Sinicize the Vietnamese.

Until the 19th century Confucian culture was profoundly rooted in Vietnamese society. Foreign missionaries invented and taught the Vietnamese *quoc ngu* (national language) at the turn of this century. But success required a long process.[30] So persistent was the influence of Chinese culture in Vietnam that even after the Ch'ing government had officially abolished the traditional civil examination in 1905, Vietnam's examination system lingered on for a few years. And, it is interesting to note, Ho Chi Minh's father, Nguyen Sinh Huy, was a famous scholar of Chinese studies; he passed the highest level of the examination and became a Pho Bang in 1901.[31]

From the preceding brief discussion it should be obvious that Sino-Vietnamese relations in the past were an enterprise of mutual interest. Politically and militarily China was for Vietnam an administrative tutor as well as an aggressor; economically China was a promoter and an exploiter; and culturally China was both teacher and indoctrinator.

Yet what is the result of the Chinese influence on Vietnam? Did the impact of Chinese culture help inspire the Vietnamese to modernize their country? It is true that the

[30] For instance, when *quoc ngu* schools were opened in 1906, the Vietnamese at first learned eagerly, but soon lost their enthusiasm. See Thompson, *French Indochina*, p. 468.

[31] Pham Van Dong and the Committee for the Study of the History of the Vietnamese Workers' Party, *President Ho Chi Minh* (hereafter Pham Van Dong, *President Ho*) (Hanoi: Foreign Languages Publishing House, 1960), p. 35. Pho Bang was the second laureate of the examination for the equivalent doctorate degree. It was during the Ch'ing dynasty that Vietnam established the Pho Bang title and adopted the written style of the Chinese "eight-legged essay" for examination. See Li Cheng-fu, *Annam*, p. 179.

Vietnamese learned China's techniques for civil administration, agriculture, education, literature, the arts, and so on. But more significantly, the Vietnamese rulers cherished the values and other characteristics of the Confucian state. The family system, the practice of ancestor worship, the social pattern, the semi-autonomous village administration, the central state authority, the mandarin bureaucracy, and even the concept of the Mandate of Heaven were all implanted and encouraged in Vietnam. In these circumstances Vietnamese intellectuals, following the Chinese gentry, developed a tendency which led them to the belief that the "man of letters" was more respectable than people of other walks of life, that moral force held a higher position than military power, and that the honors granted by the government were real honors. Above all, the barbarian Western civilization was regarded as inherently inferior to Confucianism. In order to be respectable Confucian gentry and earn high official positions through civil examination, Vietnamese intellectuals spent their youth and energy in studying the classics. After they attained some success in their scholarship, they, like most Chinese scholars, had already lost their originality, creativeness, and even health. And the nation, after generations, became a gentry-and-peasant state with little improvement in its political institutions, little innovation in its social system, and little progress in its technical fields. Consequently it took Vietnam a long time to win its independence from France and to modernize.[32] In this respect, Vietnam suffered the same fate as China at the hands of the Western powers.

2. VIETNAM AND MODERN CHINESE REVOLUTION

The French colonization of Indochina was a humiliating yoke which the Indochinese fought to throw off since the

[32] A contrast can be drawn between Vietnam and Japan. Japan originally learned various aspects of culture from China, but never adopted the Chinese civil examination system. Later Japan developed its own culture and succeeded in rapid modernization and complete independence from the West.

beginning of French colonialism there. Throughout the colonial period the responsibility for the fight against the French in Indochina was undertaken mainly by the Vietnamese. Before the end of the 19th century, the Vietnamese fought hard against the French in attempting to get rid of the foreign conqueror so their emperor could again independently rule their country. They did not have any particular modern ideas about political or social reforms. Their motive for fighting the French was the same as that of their ancestors who opposed the Chinese—independence. However, at the turn of the century the Vietnamese were profoundly influenced by events in China and Japan. They began to learn new Western ideas of political and social reforms and attempted to combine these with nationalist revolution.

The struggle for the self-strengthening[33] and modernization of China suffered a great setback immediately after the failure of the reform movement in 1898 led by K'ang Yu-wei and Liang Ch'i-ch'ao. The writings of the leaders of the Chinese reform movement, especially Liang Ch'i-ch'ao, stimulated the Vietnamese to read books by Rousseau, Locke, Montesquieu, and other modern philosophers in Chinese translations.[34] Moreover, as the Chinese republican revolution grew under the leadership of Sun Yat-sen, its

[33] The term "self-strengthening" (Tzu-ch'iang) was first suggested in 1860 by Feng Kuei-fen (1809-1874), a scholar from Soochow, and was made famous in the 1890s by Chang Chih-tung (1837-1909), a high official and moderate reformer in his time. For some of Feng's essays on self-strengthening see Ssu-yu Teng and John K. Fairbank, with E-tu Zen Sun and Chaoying Fang, *China's Response to the West: A Documentary Survey, 1839-1923* (Cambridge: Harvard University Press, 1954), pp. 50-55.

[34] After the failure of the reform movement both Liang Ch'i-ch'ao and his teacher, K'ang Yu-wei, escaped to Japan where Liang published periodicals beginning in November 1898 to disseminate reform ideas. His effective journalistic style made him a star of the Chinese press for several years. See Li Chien-nung, *The Political History of China, 1840-1928*, tr. and ed. Ssu-yu Teng and Jeremy Ingalls (Princeton: D. Van Nostrand, 1956), pp. 188-90, 205-208; and Joseph R. Levenson, *Liang Ch'i-ch'ao and the Mind of Modern China* (Cambridge: Harvard University Press, 1953), pp. 55-122.

influence resulted in the birth of a new concept of national independence and individual rights to freedom.

After 1902, China became an important base for the Vietnamese nationalist movement. That year Phan Boi Chau,[35] one of the most important leaders of the developing Vietnam nationalist movement, was the first man to direct revolution in his country from Canton. In the same year he went to Japan, where Chinese students were zealously engaged in revolutionary activity.[36] In Japan he met Liang Ch'i-ch'ao, through whom he was introduced to Sun Yat-sen. His acquaintance with Sun and others provided Chau with an opportunity to contact more Chinese revolutionists, to learn some of the techniques of revolution, and to obtain funds for his newly organized Vietnam Quang-Phuc Hoi (Association for the Restoration of Vietnam).[37]

Japan's victory over Russia in 1905 encouraged the Vietnamese nationalist movement. The myth of the white man's invincibility was dispelled, and anti-French sentiment grew

[35] Phan Boi Chau (1867-1940) was born in Nghe An, as was Ho Chi Minh. He spent many years in China, where he directed Vietnamese revolutionary movements and wrote a number of propaganda books and pamphlets. He was involved in many uprisings in Vietnam in the pre-World War I years. From 1902 to 1925, before his arrest by the French, he was the leader of the Vietnamese nationalist movement.

[36] Chinese students in Japan increased rapidly from 1902 to 1906. In 1902 there were 500; in 1904, 1,500; 1905, 8,000; and 1906 the figures jumped to 13,000. The most active ones at the time were Ch'en T'ien-hua, Huang Hsing, Sung Chiao-jen, Feng Tzu-yu, Wang Ch'ung-hui, Chang Shih-chao, Wu Chih-hui, Chang Chi, Wang Ching-wei, Ts'ai Yuan-p'ei, Chang Ping-lin, and Hu Han-min. For the above figures see Roger F. Hackett, "Chinese Students in Japan, 1900-1910," in *Papers on China* (Cambridge: Harvard University, May 1949), Vol. 3, p. 142. See also Feng Tzu-yu, *Chung hua min kuo kai kuo ch'ien ko ming shih* (A Revolutionary History before the Establishment of the Republic of China), 2 vols. (Chungking: China Culture Service, 1944), Vol. I, pp. 46-50; Marius B. Jansen, *The Japanese and Sun Yat-sen* (Cambridge: Harvard University Press, 1954), pp. 59-153; Li Chien-nung, *Political History of China*, pp. 200-28.

[37] Lu Ku, *Yueh-nan jen min fan ti tou cheng shih* (History of the Anti-Imperialist Struggle of the Vietnamese People) (Shanghai: Tung Fang, 1951), pp. 61-62. Lu Ku was on the faculty of Peking University when he wrote this book.

in Vietnam. In 1906 Prince Cuong De, another nationalist leader exiled in Japan, wrote letters in blood urging his fellow countrymen to rise against the French.

Vietnam, in return for China's serving as a revolutionary base, served as a base for the Chinese revolutionary movement in 1907 and 1908. After some uprisings directed by Sun Yat-sen were crushed by the Ch'ing government, Sun was forced to leave Japan and Hong Kong. He came to Hanoi with Huang Hsing, Hu Han-min, and others, where he established a temporary headquarters. From Hanoi and Lang-Son, Sun directed the Chen-nan-kuan uprising. The unsuccessful revolt of Hokow was also engineered in Vietnam.[38] It was under the protest of the Ch'ing government that the Chinese revolutionists were driven out of Vietnam.

After the success of the Chinese revolution of 1911 Phan Boi Chau, instead of promoting his original idea of a monarchical regime, favored a Vietnamese republic with Prince Cuong De as president. In Canton the following year, he united most of the nationalist groups into the League for the Restoration of Vietnam (Vietnam Phuc Quoc Dong Minh Hoi, or Phuc Quoc). A Vietnamese government in exile was soon organized in Canton.

It was also in Canton in 1914 that the Vietnamese revolutionists under Phan Boi Chau held a congress, in which a resolution to organize a "restoration army" against the French was passed. The plan was abortive, for Chau was put in prison by the Governor-General in Canton at the urging of the French. An uprising attempt was made on the Yunnan-Kwangsi-Vietnam border in 1917, which failed. In September of the same year the Kuomintang in Canton gained strength and organized a military government against the warlords in the north. The military government, with Sun Yat-sen as grand marshal, freed Phan Boi Chau.[39]

The period between the two world wars was one in which the Vietnamese revolution experienced both growth and

[38] Feng, *Revolutionary History*, pp. 100-29; Li Chien-nung, *Political History of China*, pp. 222-24.
[39] Buttinger, *Smaller Dragon*, p. 433.

decline. The tide of revolution, however it rose and fell, closely paralleled the Chinese situation.

After a series of setbacks for the Chinese republic, the Kuomintang decided to invite Soviet advisers, accept Chinese Communist requests to join the party on an individual basis, reorganize the party itself, and use Canton as its base for the unification of China. It sent Chiang Kai-shek to tour Russia, convoked its first party congress in January 1924, formed a military government, and established the Whampoa Military Academy. Then Soviet advisers, headed by Michael Borodin and General Vassily Bluecher (known as Galen), flowed in. Mao Tse-tung, Chou En-lai, and other Communist members took Kuomintang posts.[40] Canton became headquarters for Chinese revolutionists and the Mecca for Vietnamese nationalists. Young intellectuals came from Tonkin, Annam, and Cochin-China.[41] With Phan Boi Chau's

[40] Tan Ping-shan was appointed Chief of the Organization Department; Lin Tsu-han, Chief of Peasants (both in 1924); Mao Tse-tung, Chief of Agitprop; Chou En-lai, Chief of Political Affairs in the Army (both in 1925). Some other Communists served as secretaries in several departments.

Among many studies on the subject, covering the period 1924 to 1927, there are Harold R. Isaacs, *The Tragedy of the Chinese Revolution* (Stanford: Stanford University Press, 1951); Allen S. Whiting, *Soviet Policies in China, 1917-1924* (New York: Columbia University Press, 1954); Conrad Brandt, *Stalin's Failure in China, 1924-1927* (Cambridge: Harvard University Press, 1958); C. Martin Wilbur and Julie Lien-ying How, *Documents on Communism, Nationalism and Soviet Advisors in China, 1918-1927* (New York: Columbia University Press, 1956); Robert C. North, *Moscow and Chinese Communists* (Stanford: Stanford University Press, 1953); Conrad Brandt, Benjamin I. Schwartz, and John K. Fairbank, *A Documentary History of Chinese Communism* (Cambridge: Harvard University Press, 1950); Wang Chien-ming, *Chung-kuo kung-ch'an tang shih kao* (History of the Chinese Communist Party), 3 vols. (Taipei, 1965), Vol. I; Chiang Yung-ching, *Bao-lo-t'ing yu Wu-han Cheng ch'uan* (Borodin and the Wu-han Regime) (Taipei, 1963). The last two studies are based mainly on the materials in Taiwan.

[41] Tonkin (or Tongking, which, in Chinese, means "Eastern Capital," i.e. Hanoi) is used as the equivalent of today's North Vietnam (Bac Bo in Vietnamese, is "northern part"); Annam (An-nan in Chinese, is the "Pacific South"), as central Vietnam (Trung Bo in Vietnamese) is "central part"; Cochin-China is South Vietnam (Nam Bo in Vietnamese, "southern part"). After 1954 Tonkin and northern

arrangement, about 40 Vietnamese young men enrolled in the Whampoa Military Academy.[42] Its graduates played an important part in the Vietnamese resistance movement against the French, including the attack on Lang-Son in 1940.

Besides this, a revolutionary association, Tam Tam Xa (the Heart to Heart Association) was set up in 1923 by Ho Tung Mau, Le Hong Phong, and others. Inspired by the revolutionary atmosphere in Canton, the association in June 1924 sent Pham Hong Thai, a young Tonkinese student, on an unsuccessful mission to assassinate visiting Governor-General Merlin. Thai then committed suicide by jumping into the Pearl River at Canton. His tomb there frequently received homage from young Vietnamese.

In 1925, when the Vietnamese revolutionists were preparing to hold a conference in Canton for the organization of a new party, the Vietnamese Nationalist Party (Viet Nam Quoc Dan Dong), Phan Boi Chau was urged to come from Shanghai. But Chau, according to Hoang Van Chi, was drawn into a trap and sold out by Ho Chi Minh for 100,000 piasters in the French Concession in Shanghai.[43] He was arrested by the French police, immediately transferred to Hanoi, and sentenced to death. The Vietnamese strongly protested the sentence, and the French authorities were obliged to commute the sentence to confinement for life. Chau died in 1940 in Hue.

Annam became today's North Vietnam, while Cochin-China and southern Annam became South Vietnam.

[42] *Whampoa Monthly*, an official periodical of the academy, began publication in 1927 with the enrollment of the academy's sixth class. Enrollment figures from the first to fifth classes are lacking. The above figure is from a Chinese source in Taiwan. In other sources the figure varies from 30 to 60. See Hoang Van Chi, *From Colonialism to Communism*, p. 17; and Lu Ku, *Vietnamese Struggle*, p. 68.

[43] Hoang Van Chi, *Colonialism to Communism*, p. 18. Chi stated that Ho's followers later gave the following explanation of Ho's betrayal of Chau: Chau was too old to be of any further use to the revolution; his arrest would cause a strong sentiment of patriotism favorable to the revolution; and the money received from the French would serve the activities of the revolutionary movement.

The Background

The Vietnamese Nationalist Party (VNQDD) was finally founded in Hanoi in 1927. With Phan Boi Chau absent from the active political scene, Nguyen Thai Hoc, a teacher, became head of the party. It was the most important revolutionary organization in Indochina at the time.[44] Influenced by the Chinese Kuomintang, the party's organization was modeled on the Chinese party—it adopted the same name (nationalist party); it was based on the same doctrines (The Three People's Principles of Sun Yat-sen); and it was resolved to throw off French domination by force with Chinese aid.

It was at this time that Ho Chi Minh appeared in Canton.[45] Ho (alias Ly Thuy) came to the revolutionary city in December 1924 from Moscow, where he had served as a translator at the Soviet consulate. During this KMT-CCP cooperation period (1924-1927) the Soviet Union was on good terms with Kuomintang China.

Ho became the leader of the Communist movement in Vietnam upon returning to Asia from Moscow in 1924. Born in 1890 at Kim-Lien village, Nam Lien commune, Nam-Dan district in Nghe-An province, Ho's original name was Nguyen Sinh Cung. Later he was called Nguyen Tat Thanh (Nguyen-who-will-succeed).[46] His father, Pho Bang Nguyen Sinh Huy, a scholar and revolutionist, never served with the French colonial authorities in Indochina. Young Nguyen

[44] The other parties were (1) the League for the Restoration of Vietnam (the Phuc Quoc), (2) the Constitutionalist Party, (3) the Revolutionary Party of Young Annam, (4) the Vietnamese People's Progressive Party, and (5) the Scholar Party.

[45] While there is no attempt in this study to write a biography of Ho Chi Minh, his activities in China will be discussed in detail. For a general biography of Ho, see Jean Lacouture, *Ho Chi Minh* (Paris: Editions du Seuil, 1967); Bernard B. Fall, *The Two Viet-Nams: A Political and Military Analysis* (New York: Frederick Praeger, 1964), pp. 81-103. As of 1966 Hanoi had published several biographies of Ho. Among the useful are: Pham Van Dong, *President Ho*; Tran Dan Tien, *Glimpses of the Life of Ho Chi Minh* (Hanoi: Foreign Languages Publishing House, 1958); Hoai Thanh et al., *Hu pai pai* (Uncle Ho) (Hanoi: Foreign Languages Publishing House, 1962); Truong Chinh, *Hu chu hsi* (President Ho Chi Minh) (Hanoi: Foreign Languages Publishing House, 1966).

[46] See a list of his names in Chapter 2.

Tat Thanh first learned Chinese, then entered Quoc Hoc (national studies) College in Hue. In 1910 he gave up his study and taught at the Duc Thanh private school. One year later he went to Saigon, where he studied at a trade school for three months. In those days he was an admirer of Phan Dinh Phung, Hoang Hoa Tham, and Phan Boi Chau[47] (whom he betrayed in 1925).

In 1912 Ho left for Europe on the *Admiral Latouche-Tréville* as a kitchen helper. He then had the chance to visit Europe, some parts of Africa, and North America. From 1913 to 1917 he lived in London, working at the Carlton Hotel as a cook's helper under the famous French chef, Escoffier. During these years Ho made good use of his free time by studying English and joining the Overseas Workers' Union, a secret anti-colonial organization under Chinese leadership. In 1917 he went to Paris and identified himself as Nguyen Ai Quoc while working at a photography shop. Inspired by Woodrow Wilson's Fourteen Points, he went to Versailles in 1919 to deliver to the victorious statesmen his eight-point program for Vietnamese freedom and rights,[48] but none received him. During his stay in Paris he was busy working, reading, attending political meetings, and contributing articles to the Socialist organ, *Le Populaire*. Above all, he made friends. He was introduced to such leading Socialists as Marcel Cachin and Marius Moutet. Then

[47] Pham Van Dong, *Ho Chi Minh*, p. 37. Phan Boi Chau used to say that the young Nguyen Tat Thanh enjoyed reading some poems loved by Chau himself. See Hoai Thanh and Thanh Tinh, "His Native Village and His Childhood," in *Hu pai pai*, p. 13. The English edition of this book, *Hu pai pai*, is entitled *Days with Ho Chi Minh*.

[48] The eight points were: (1) General amnesty for Vietnamese political prisoners; (2) Equal rights between French and Vietnamese and abolition of the criminal court, an instrument of persecution of Vietnamese patriots; (3) Freedom of the press and freedom of thought; (4) Freedom of association and freedom of assembly; (5) Freedom of movement and freedom to go abroad; (6) Freedom to go to school and to open technical and vocational schools for the natives; (7) Substitution of the system of law for that of decrees; (8) There must be a Vietnamese representative near the French Government to settle issues concerning the interests of the Vietnamese people. See Pham Van Dong, *Ho Chi Minh*, pp. 41-42.

he became a delegate to the French Socialist Party Congress at Tours in 1920 and voted for the Third International and for Communism. From this moment on, he decided to take up the cause of international Communism. As Ho wrote later, the decision was made through patriotism: "At first, it was patriotism and not yet communism which made me put my trust in Leninism and in [the] Third International. Step by step, in the struggle and by combining theoretical study of Marxism-Leninism with practical work, little by little I came to understand that only socialism and communism can free the oppressed nations and toiling people in the world from slavery."[49]

In 1921 Ho became the editor of *Le Paria*, the organ of the Intercolonial Union created by Ho and other anti-colonial people from French Africa. According to a Communist-supported newspaper in Hong Kong, it was in 1922 that Chou En-lai met Ho Chi Minh in Paris. Chou was reported to have said that Ho had already become "a mature Marxist," while Chou had just joined the Chinese Communist Party.[50] That same year Ho attended the Fourth Comintern Congress in Moscow and was again sent by the French Communist Party the following year to Moscow to organize the Peasant International (Krestintern). In Moscow he was elected a member of the 10-man executive committee of the organization. Ho stayed in Russia after the conference and enrolled in early 1924 in the University of the Toilers of the East (or the Eastern Workers' University). His pamphlet, *French Colonization on Trial*, was probably written at this time, but was not published until 1925 in France.

Then Ho went to Canton as a Chinese translator at the Soviet consulate. His status was that of a Chinese national, but his task, as he was instructed by the Comintern, was to "build up and guide" the Communist movement in Indochina. While he officially used a Chinese name—Lee Suei (Ly Thuy in Vietnamese)—Ho took another name, Vuong

[49] *Ibid.*, p. 53.
[50] *Wen Hui Pao* (Hong Kong), November 2, 1956. See also Robert S. Elegant, *China's Red Masters* (New York: Twayne, 1951), p. 205.

Son Nhi (Wang Shan-yu in Chinese), or Mr. Vuong, for his activities among the Vietnamese. But when he delivered a speech on January 14, 1926 at the Second Congress of the Kuomintang in Canton, urging a worldwide anti-imperialist movement, which has never been made known before to the West, he used another name, Wang Ta-jen (Vuong Dat Nhan).[51] The use of Vuong Son Nhi was a clever but not secret device, for these three words (also three simple characters) are three parts of the character Suei (Thuy) in the Chinese ideogram. Without much difficulty many Vietnamese linked Ly Thuy with Vuong Son Nhi as the same person, and before long knew he was none other than the well-known Communist leader, Nguyen Ai Quoc.

Prior to Ho's arrival at Canton, the politically active Vietnamese there were mostly nationalists, including members of the popular Quang Phuc Hoi, under the leadership of Phan Boi Chau. Ho would have to either cooperate with or eliminate these nationalist elements before he could expand his Communist movement. The first move he made was to take over an existing revolutionary society, the Heart-to-Heart Society, which was founded in Canton in 1923 by Ho Tung Mau and Le Hong Phong who later became very close comrades of Ho.[52] Ho reorganized it as the Viet-Nam Cach Menh Thanh-Nien Dong Chi Hoi (Association of Vietnamese Revolutionary Young Comrades), or Thanh-Nien, to

[51] Ho's name, Vuong Son Nhi or Mr. Vuong, was first made known by Hoang Van Chi, *Colonialism to Communism*, p. 42. Chi's account has been confirmed by a recent Hanoi publication. According to Nguyen Luong Bang, Hanoi's first ambassador to Moscow, Mr. Vuong (or Comrade Vuong) was the name for Ho Chi Minh in Canton and Shanghai. See Nguyen Luong Bang, "The Times I Met Him," in *Hu pai pai*, pp. 48-83 passim. For Ho's speech at the KMT and his name, Wang Ta-jen, see the Kuomintang (comp.), *Records of the Second Congress of Kuomintang* (Canton, April 1926), pp. 97-100.

[52] Le Hong Phong, a Moscow-trained Communist, was a founder of the Indochinese Communist Party; he was arrested by the French in June 1939 and executed in September 1940. His wife was also arrested in July 1940 and executed the following month. See Lu Ku, *Vietnamese Struggle*, p. 75; Fall, *Two Viet-Nams*, p. 93. Ho Tung Mau was a member of the Chinese Communist Party when he was in China; he died in August 1951 in northern Vietnam.

train young revolutionists. In his second move, Ho in June 1925 eliminated from the political arena the most formidable opponent of his career, Phan Boi Chau, by using the French police in Shanghai, as previously mentioned. The "reward" of 100,000 piasters he obtained from the French was used for the activities of his Thanh-Nien. Ho also formed an Anti-Colonial League of Oppressed Peoples of the East, including members from Korea, China, Vietnam, India, Malaya, and Indonesia. An Annam branch of the league was organized to attract more anti-French Vietnamese. The Kuomintang's archives show that Ho used the alumni association of Moscow Sun Yat-sen University in Pai Yun Road, Canton, as the address of the Annam branch.[53]

In recruiting his followers Ho made good use of the opportunity provided by the Kuomintang-Communists' co-operation in Canton, by inviting Vietnamese sailors, workers, and a large number of French-expelled students to join his Special Political Training Class and the Thanh-Nien. Among them was Pham Van Dong, son of a scholar and today prime minister of North Vietnam, who later enrolled into the Whampoa Military Academy. Ho's Training Class was held in his Thanh-Nien on Wen Ming Road in Canton. The Kuomintang-Communist Peasant Seminar directed by Mao Tse-tung was nearby.[54] The Training Class maintained a close relationship with Mao's Peasant Seminar, and received some financial aid from the Chinese Communist Party. The training program included studies of Marxism-Leninism, Sun Yat-sen's doctrine, mass movements, and new revolutionary techniques. Ho wrote a pamphlet, "Road to Revolution," for a class text, and published a weekly paper entitled *Thanh-Nien* to disseminate anti-colonial and revolutionary ideas.[55] From June 1925 to April 1927, 88 issues of

[53] Chiang Yung-ching, comp., unpublished "Collection of Documents on Vietnam" (1966), hereafter, "Documents."

[54] Throughout 1926 Mao had trained 300 young men through his seminar, of whom 30 were from his native province, Hunan. With their assistance, Mao became the leader of the peasant movement in Hunan in 1926-1927.

[55] Nguyen Luong Bang, "Times I Met Him," pp. 51-53; Le Manh

the paper were published. After a training period of three or four months Ho selected some of the best-qualified men as his assistants, recommended some to enroll into the Whampoa Military Academy and to study in Russia, and sent the rest back to Indochina. Over a period of two years (mid-1925 to mid-1927) he trained and organized about 200 men who later became the major force of Vietnamese Communist revolution.

During his stay in Canton, Ho developed a two-stage revolutionary program for Vietnam. The first was to be a democratic bourgeois revolution with strong overtones of anti-colonialism and anti-feudalism; the second, a Communist revolution with the dictatorship of the proletariat. The origin of this program was at the Second Congress of the Third Communist International in Moscow in 1920, at which Lenin laid down, after compromising with M. N. Roy, a two-stage strategy for Communist revolution in Asia, particularly China.[56] In the case of China, the first stage of revolution was a movement of Nationalist-Communist cooperation against imperialism, feudalism, and warlordism; the second stage was to be a Communist revolution. Although the execution of this strategy in China resulted in a debacle for the Chinese Communist Party, the first stage of revolution was in high gear when Ho was in Canton. Since he was trained in Moscow and was a small cog in the machine in Canton, his two-stage revolutionary program for Vietnam was a well-planned strategy bearing a striking similarity to that for China. In execution, Ho had an almost perfect device. Those who were indoctrinated by Ho and had accepted his two-stage program were safe in working either outside or inside Indochina; those who did not accept

---

Trinh, "In Canton and Thailand," both in *Hu pai pai*, pp. 90-93; Truong Chinh, *President Ho*, pp. 7-8; Tran Dan Tien, *Hu Chih-ming chuan* (Biography of Ho Chi Minh) (Shanghai, August Publishing Co., 1949), p. 83.

[56] For a general discussion of this strategy see Whiting, *Soviet Policies*, pp. 42-58; and North, *Moscow and Chinese Communists*, pp. 18-20.

it risked their lives by staying in China or they had to return to their homeland. Many of the latter were arrested by the French upon their arrival in Vietnam because Ho revealed their names to the French police before their return. By this time a Nationalist-Communist split among the Vietnamese began to be felt in Canton, as well as Indochina.

The sudden but inevitable rift between the Kuomintang and the Chinese Communist Party in 1927 resulted in the departure of Borodin and other Soviet Communists for Moscow. Ho left China with Borodin via Chengchow and Outer Mongolia. Before leaving China, Ho appointed Ho Tung Mau (then a member of the Chinese Communist Party) to succeed him as leader of the Thanh-Nien, which continued to function until 1928 when Ho Tung Mau was arrested by the Kuomintang. It was then forced to move to Hong Kong where Lam Duc Thu took over the leadership.

After he left China, Ho Chi Minh was assigned in 1928 to Germany for a short mission. The following year he was sent to Thailand where about 20,000 Vietnamese lived in its northeastern area. Ho stayed at Phichit, Udon, Sakon, Nakhon, and other places, took the name Thau Chin, organized the Vietnamese into the Friendship Society, helped publish the "Friendship" paper, and spread revolutionary ideas in these areas and back in Vietnam.[57] He maintained connections with both the Thanh-Nien in Hong Kong and the short-lived Nan Yang (South Sea) Communist Party in Bangkok.

In the course of Vietnamese revolution, the Thanh-Nien was merely a transitional organization to a Communist party. When a congress of the Thanh-Nien was held in Hong Kong in May 1929, therefore, many delegates who came from Vietnam proposed organizing a Communist party—which was rejected. Already unhappy about the luxurious life of Lam Duc Thu, the leader in Hong Kong, the delegates from Vietnam returned home angry and disgusted. The following month they formed the Indochinese

[57] Le Manh Trinh, "In Canton and Thailand," pp. 94-106.

Communist Party in northern Vietnam. Fearful of losing influence, the members of the Thanh-Nien in Hong Kong and in southern parts of Vietnam organized the Annamese Communist Party. Soon thereafter, some members of the New Viet Revolutionary Party in central and southern Vietnam created the Indochinese Communist Union. These groups were opposed to one another and were vying for recognition from the Comintern.[58]

The Comintern sent Ho Chi Minh to Hong Kong to unite all the Communist parties. Ho convened a unification conference which resulted in the birth of the Vietnamese Communist Party in February 1930. Eight months later the party was enlarged and renamed the Indochinese Communist Party (ICP) which had links with the Comintern Far East Bureau, Communist movements in Thailand and Malaya, and the French Communist Party. Immediately after the Comintern had accepted this new organization, the central committee of the Chinese Communist Party encouraged its Indochinese comrades by sending them an open letter, saying: "Indochina is one of the most important links in the world chain of imperialism, and the Indochinese revolution is one of the decisive factors in the East."[59]

FOLLOWING Chiang Kai-shek's successful launching of the North Expedition, 1926-1928, the Kuomintang government in Nanking strived for reconstruction in the area it controlled and for further unification. To emulate the progress made in China, members of the Vietnamese Nationalist Party lost no time in mapping out their own revolution against the French. As a result, there was the "Yen-Bay Uprising" of February 1930 led by the nationalists with no participation from the Vietnamese Communists.[60] The re-

[58] Truong Chinh, *President Ho*, pp. 8-9.
[59] Virginia Thompson and Richard Adloff, *The Left Wing in Southeast Asia* (New York: William Sloane Associates, 1950), p. 43.
[60] One account given by Hanoi for the lack of participation was that the Vietnamese Communist Party had just been organized and was trying to make contacts with the Vietnamese Nationalist Party to establish an anti-imperialist front and dissuade the Nationalists from

volt, after a brief success, was severely suppressed. Hundreds of people were killed, and Nguyen Thai Hoc and 12 other party leaders were arrested and executed. After the revolt the French authorities instituted a harsh policy toward Vietnam, suppressing or crushing all opposition, serious or otherwise.

Among the Communists, members of the Vietnamese Communist Party were attracted by the events in China led by their Chinese comrades. From Mao's armed revolt in 1927 to 1930, the Chinese Communists had established several area Soviets[61] although they did not until November 1931 officially set up the Central Soviet, which was based mainly on Mao's Kiangsi-Fukien Soviet regime. Inspired by the plight of starving peasants in several villages of Nghe-An province in the spring of 1930, the Vietnamese Communists decided to imitate their Chinese comrades by leading the hungry peasants to revolt. The rebellion started on May Day 1930. Though it was soon put down, the Communists continued to struggle by setting up two months later the Nghe-An Soviet in the areas they controlled. It was the first and only Soviet that ever appeared in Vietnam before the Communists came to power. A lack of armed forces assured its destruction by the French with little difficulty. Ho Chi Minh did not participate directly in the revolt, but remained in Hong Kong. It was only made known in 1953, for the purpose of illustrating Ho Chi Minh's observation of democratic rule, that Ho voted against the proposal in 1930 for a peasant rebellion but followed the majority decision which upheld the original recommendation.[62] The Comintern gave no clear instruction as to whether a peasant revolt should

---

taking any blind action; before their connection was established, the Yen-Bay Uprising broke out. Apparently the newly born Vietnamese Communist Party was not ready to participate. See Le Manh Trinh, *In Canton and Thailand,* p. 106.

[61] The more important ones were the Kiangsi-Fukien Soviet (later the site of the Central Soviet), the Szechuan-Shensi Soviet, the Hunan-Kiangsi Soviet, the Hunan-Hupeh-Kiangsi Soviet, and the Shensi-K'ungsu Soviet.

[62] Hoang Van Chi, *Colonialism to Communism,* p. 52.

be undertaken. The Vietnamese, particularly their leader, were to bear alone the responsibility for the failure. This might well be a main reason for Ho's fall into disfavor with Stalin in late 1930s.

By 1931 the Kuomintang had made great progress against the Chinese Communists by defeating the Changsha Uprising (early August 1930), forcing the collapse of the "Li Li-san Line,"[63] and beginning its five military campaigns against Mao's Red Army.[64] Struggling for their own survival, the Chinese Communists were not able to aid the young Indochinese Communist Party. In Vietnam both nationalist and Communist armed revolts were completely eliminated. Some revolutionists were frustrated, some were converted. Even the old nationalist leader, Phan Boi Chau, announced his willingness to have "a loyal collaboration with France."[65] The Vietnamese revolution reached a low ebb.

From early 1930 to mid-1931 Ho Chi Minh was secretly active in Hong Kong and Shanghai. Then he was arrested in Hong Kong on June 5, 1931. A British lawyer defended him. The British authorities finally ordered that Ho be deported. With the lawyer's help Ho got secretly to Shanghai via Amoy.[66] The British *Daily Worker* reported his death from tuberculosis in Hong Kong, as did the French security police. Some stated that Ho simply managed to escape; others believed he was released because he promised to do secret work for the British police force.[67] In view of the fact that Ho used the same tactic of seeking his release in 1944

---

[63] After the failure of the Changsha Uprising, Li Li-san was forced to resign and his "Line" (political strategy) collapsed accordingly. In November 1930 he was ordered to go to Russia where he faced an international trial in the following month and was punished by having to "attend" the Bolshevik school in Moscow for a "few months," which turned out to be 15 years (1931-1945).

[64] The five campaigns ran: (1) December 1930 to January 1931, (2) April 1931 to May 1931, (3) July 1931 to September 1931, (4) January 1933 to April 1933, and (5) October 1933 to October 1934.

[65] Andrée Viollis, *Indochine S.O.S.* (Paris: Gallimard, 1935), p. 98.

[66] Nguyen Luong Bang, "Times I Met Him," pp. 66-67.

[67] Bernard B. Fall, *Two Viet-Nams*, p. 97.

by promising China to do anti-Japanese work in Vietnam, this suggestion may well be the true case.[68]

When Ho arrived at Shanghai in early 1933 the Chinese Communists in the city were under strong pressure from the Kuomintang. Time and again, Ho tried to make contact with the CCP members but failed. Unexpectedly Paul Vaillant Couturier, a member of the central committee of the French Communist Party, came to Shanghai. Ho grasped this rare opportunity by asking him for a meeting. Ho cleverly delivered a letter to him through Madame Sun Yat-sen, a long-time Communist sympathizer. Ho met Vaillant Couturier, through whom he reestablished the connection with his Chinese comrades. Finally Ho was put aboard a Soviet ship for Vladivostok, and then to Moscow.[69]

The Communist Party Ho established and left behind faced an extremely difficult situation under the strong French repression. Most Communist activists were arrested and sent to the prison at Poulo Condore. The central committee first took refuge in Thailand; later, in June 1934, it in effect ceased to function. It was replaced by two regional committees, one for the north and Laos, the other for the south and Cambodia. It was only in Cochin-China that Communist activities under the direction of Tran Van Giau (a graduate of the Eastern Workers' University in Moscow) and others could function with some effectiveness. Despite its almost ruined condition, the ICP still tried to maintain its relations with the Chinese Communist Party which was strongly opposed by Chiang Kai-shek.[70] As one French Communist reported after his investigation of the situation in early 1934, the ICP was subjected to fierce repression and persecution, but the blows had not crippled its fight. On the contrary, it kept struggling and lived "in close touch with the heroic Communist Party of China, whose glorious exam-

[68] See further discussion in the following chapter.
[69] Nguyen Luong Bang, "Times I Met Him," p. 67.
[70] In September 1932 the Chinese Communist Party was forced to move from Shanghai to Juichin, Kiangsi, capital of the Chinese Soviet under Mao Tse-tung, which was also under strong military pressure from the Kuomintang.

ple serves as a beacon to the Communist Parties of the East. . . ."[71]

In Moscow Ho Chi Minh studied at the Lenin School, an advanced institute for Communist leaders from various countries. After six months he graduated and enrolled in the Research Institute for Study of National and Colonial Problems. Meanwhile he worked at the Comintern. When the Seventh Congress of the Comintern was held in Moscow in 1935, the Indochina Communist Party sent two delegates, Le Hong Phong and Nguyen Thi Minh Khai. Le Hong Phong was elected a member of the Executive Committee of the Comintern. After the Congress ended (1936) they went back to Vietnam. According to Nguyen Khanh Toan, another student in Moscow at that time and Vice-Minister of Education in North Vietnam, Ho Chi Minh "could not return home" together with these two delegates because of existing "difficulties." So he stayed and continued to "study" at the Research Institute.[72] Nguyen Khanh Toan did not specify what the difficulties were and why Ho could not return to Vietnam. In view of the fact that Ho was not sent back to attend the First Congress of the Indochinese Communist Party, held in Macao in 1935,[73] that he was not elected a member of the Executive Committee of the Comintern, and that he "could not return" to Vietnam while Le Hong Phong and Nguyen Thi Minh Khai could, Ho's prolonged stay in Moscow for further studies, which he was not really interested in,[74] might well be a "punishment" for his failure in the early 1930s.[75]

[71] I. Milton Sacks, "Marxism in Viet Nam," in Frank N. Trager, ed., *Marxism in Southeast Asia: A Study of Four Countries* (Stanford: Stanford University Press, 1959), p. 135.

[72] Nguyen Khanh Toan, "Meeting Ho Chi Minh in the Soviet Union," in *Hu pai pai*, pp. 116-21.

[73] Truong Chinh, *President Ho*, p. 12.

[74] Nguyen Khanh Toan, "Meeting Ho," p. 121.

[75] It is no longer a secret that the ICP was under sharp criticism from the Comintern for its failure in the 1930-1931 period and that Ho Chi Minh (Nguyen Ai Quoc) was also under attack for failing to provide greater security measures to safeguard ICP members from arrest. See Sacks, "Marxism in Viet Nam," p. 127. While there is no

Relations between the Vietnamese revolutionary movement and China underwent little change from 1933 to 1935. On one hand, the Vietnamese Nationalist Party found it almost impossible to launch any armed revolt because of the French. On the other, the Indochinese Communist Party, besides suffering the same fate under the French as did the Nationalist Party, received almost no material aid from the CCP which had barely managed to escape the five extermination campaigns of the Kuomintang. It was not until 1936, after the "Popular Front" strategy had been adopted, that the Indochinese revolutionists were able to resume their activity. In the next two years some leftist leaders were released from prisons; newspapers run by the Communists or the nationalists were allowed to be published; there were strikes in Saigon, Hanoi, and Haiphong, and a mass rally of 50,000 people for the celebration of May Day 1938 was staged in Hanoi for the first time in Vietnamese history.[76] Meanwhile, the Chinese Communists launched a strong propaganda campaign for a "united front" and cooperation with the Kuomintang, the CCP, minor parties, and political groups against Japanese aggression.[77] With the Second Sino-Japanese War, in July 1937, Kuomintang-Communist cooperation materialized for the second time.

---

evidence to verify the above speculation that Ho Chi Minh was being punished by Moscow, it is relevant to cite Li Li-san's case here in order to understand Ho's possible fate in Moscow in this period. After Li Li-san's failure in China, the Comintern instructed the Chinese Communist Party on May 10, 1931: "We want him to attend the Bolshevik School here. We want him to understand the substance of his mistakes. This is not a thing to be completed quickly by doing it in a halfhearted way, but must be learned through daily work. . . . Comrade Li Li-san should stay here to study for a few months and to work with the Comintern in order to correct his mistakes." Cited in North, *Moscow and Chinese Communists*, p. 145. Also see Tso-liang Hsiao, *Power Relations within the Chinese Communist Movement, 1930-1934* (Seattle: University of Washington Press, 1961), p. 86.

[76] Truong Chinh, *President Ho*, p. 12; Lu Ku, *Vietnamese Struggle*, pp. 73-74.

[77] Some documents on the united front and Kuomintang-CCP cooperation may be found in Brandt, Schwartz, and Fairbank, *Chinese Communism*, pp. 242-53.

The Background

The war brought a closer Sino-Soviet relationship as well. Contrary to the United States' continuing to supply military materiel to Japan at a private business level, the Soviet Union, for both Chinese and Soviet interests against Japan, concluded a Sino-Soviet friendship pact in August 1937, and made three loans to Chungking by June 1939 totaling $250 million (in U.S. dollars).[78] In addition, a large number of Russian-made planes were delivered to China by Soviet pilots.[79] For the second time the Soviets enjoyed a good friendship with China.

In this friendly atmosphere Ho Chi Minh came to China from Russia.

[78] The first loan was $50,000,000, in March 1938; the second also $50,000,000 in July of the same year; the third was $150,000,000 in June 1939. See *China Handbook, 1937-1945* rev. ed. (Nanking: International Information Bureau, 1947), p. 209. See also Ch'eng Tien-fang, *History of Sino-Russian Relations* (Washington, D.C.: Public Affairs Press, 1957), pp. 213-14. Only half of the loans was granted to China.

[79] It was reported that a total of 1,000 planes were delivered to China and that about 2,000 pilots served in China from 1937 to 1939. See U.S. Department of State, *Foreign Relations of the United States*, 1939, III, p. 261.

2. Ho Chi Minh in China, 1938-1945

≪≪≪

> "One cannot blame me [a commander-in-chief of a war area in China] for my relations with Ho Chi Minh, because the Central Government in Chungking was at that time cooperating with the Chinese Communist Party and the Soviet Union."
> — General Chang Fa-k'uei to the author in 1960 in defense of his association with Ho Chi Minh during the war at Liuchow

> "I am a Communist, but my present concern is for Vietnam's freedom and independence, not for Communism. I give you a special assurance: Communism will not work in Vietnam in fifty years."
> — Ho Chi Minh to General Fa-k'uei at Liuchow in 1944 on the eve of his return to Vietnam

WHAT REALLY happened to Ho Chi Minh in China during the years 1938-1945 has been a matter of controversy. Philippe Devillers, who interviewed many Vietnamese after the Second World War, offers a good account of some aspects of Ho Chi Minh's whereabouts and activities from 1941 to 1944.[1] Hoang Van Chi, who participated in the resistance war against the French (1946-1954) firmly believes Ho's absence from China prior to 1941;[2] Harold R. Isaacs, who met Ho in Hanoi in November 1945, tells a brief story of him in China;[3] and Bernard B. Fall, who ably pieces together various sources, draws a general picture of Ho's activities in this period.[4] But some specific and significant events remain unclear, with many gaps yet to be filled. Was Ho Chi Minh in China in 1938-1941, if so, where was he and what did he do? What was the true reason for his arrest in China in 1942, and by whom (which authority)?

[1] Devillers, *Histoire du Viet-Nam de 1940 à 1952* (Paris: Editions du Seuil, 1952), pp. 96-113.
[2] Hoang Van Chi, *Colonialism to Communism*, p. 52.
[3] Isaacs, *No Peace for Asia* (New York: Macmillan, 1947), pp. 163-64.
[4] Fall, *Two Viet-Nams*, pp. 97-100.

Ho Chi Minh in China, 1938-1945

How did he succeed in being released from prison? What precisely did he offer to General Chang Fa-k'uei for his return to Vietnam? And what were the motives of General Chang in permitting and assisting Ho to return to Vietnam in the fall of 1944? In view of the fact that Ho's experiences during this period bear on his success in the establishment of a government in 1945, a thorough examination of this period is worthwhile. With some newly available Vietnamese sources, Chinese documents, interviews and other information, the story is reconstructed in this chapter.

1. FROM RUSSIA TO CHINA, 1938-1941

In the fall of 1938 Ho Chi Minh went to China from Russia.[5] One day before he left Moscow, he visited Nguyen Khanh Toan, at that time another Vietnamese Communist in Moscow. Ho did not inform Toan of his departure and left Russia in secret. Since the Soviet Union was assisting China by giving her Soviet aircraft and trucks, Ho reached Sian without difficulty. He then joined the Communist Eighth Route Army for disguise and went to Yenan from Sian. After a few months Ho (alias Ho Quang) went together with General Yeh Chien-ying to Chungking where he frequently visited Chou En-lai. According to Professor Franklin Lien Ho, a professor at Columbia University and then Deputy Minister of Economy of the Chinese government, who met Ho several times at Chou's residence in early 1939, the silent Ho was in a Sun Yat-sen uniform (which he wears today), and was introduced by Chou as "Comrade Hu" from Vietnam.[6] Then Ho went to Kweiyang and finally to Hengyang with Yeh Chien-ying, who had been appointed by Chungking to direct the Southwest

[5] Ho Chi Minh, "The Chinese and Vietnamese Revolutions," in *Vietnam Information Bulletin* (DRV) (Rangoon, August 9, 1961), p. 20. Nguyen Khanh Toan, "Meeting Ho," p. 122; Nguyen Luong Bang, "Times I Met Him," p. 67; Pham Van Dong, *President Ho*, p. 71.

[6] Franklin Lien Ho's letter to the author, dated July 13, 1967.

34

Guerrilla Training Class in Hengyang.[7] Yeh put him, as a Chinese Communist, in charge of party affairs. Before long he went to Kweilin, about 350 miles south of Hengyang (and 350 miles closer to Vietnam). Ho served as the club manager of a liaison office of the Eighth Route Army in Kweilin and concurrently as a radio operator.[8] Under the umbrella of the CCP, Ho, using pen name "P. C. Lin," was able to send back to Vietnam many short articles for publication in ICP's periodicals *Notre Voix* and *Le Travail.* Meanwhile he made reports to the Comintern containing suggestions for party policies and strategies he thought the ICP should follow. In his articles and reports he emphasized the importance of the development of the Indochinese Democratic Front,[9] cited the experience of the Chinese revolution, explained the significance of the struggle for democratic rights, freedom, and the legal status of the ICP, but refrained from demands for national independence.[10] It is clear that through his communications and directives Ho was skillfully helping to guide the Vietnamese revolution in the direction of international anti-fascism. His goal was somewhat different from the CCP's, but his strategy was similar to that of his Chinese comrades.

Ho was anxious to resume his connections with the Central Committee of the ICP. He wanted to slip back into

[7] Nguyen Luong Bang, "Times I Met Him"; Nguyen Khanh Toan, "Meeting Ho"; Ho Chi Minh, "Chinese and Vietnamese Revolutions," p. 20. According to General Ho Ying-ch'in, chief of staff of the Chinese Military Council during the war, the guerrilla training class was established in early 1939, and was one of two such training classes during the war. See Ho Ying-ch'in, *Military Reports during the Resistance War,* 2 vols. (Taipei: Wen Hsing, 1962), Vol. 1, pp. 205, 243, 326.

[8] Ho Chi Minh, "Chinese and Vietnamese Revolutions," p. 20.

[9] The Democratic Front, led by Pham Van Dong and Vo Nguyen Giap, was created in 1936 and was legally active in Tonkin. See Sacks, "Marxism in Viet Nam," in Trager, *Marxism in Southeast Asia,* p. 141.

[10] Vo Nguyen Giap, "Ho Chi Minh—Father of the Vietnam Revolutionary Army," in *Hu pai pai,* p. 159; Ho Chi Minh, *Selected Works* (Hanoi: Foreign Languages Publishing House, 1961), II, pp. 149-50.

Vietnam at the proper time. With the assistance of the Chinese Communists he got in touch with Hoang Van Hoan (first North Vietnamese ambassador to Peking, now a Politburo member of the Lao Dong Party) in Yunnan, through whom he reestablished communications with his party. At the end of 1939 the Central Committee sent a man to Lungchow, Kwangsi (about 570 miles south of Kweilin and 45 miles from the Vietnam border), to meet Ho there. But before Ho's arrival, the Vietnamese Communist had come and gone back to Vietnam because he ran out of money.[11] Disappointed but not frustrated, Ho tried to make a second arrangement through the Chinese Communists. This time he went to Kunming.

By now the Second World War had begun. To parallel the European military advance of Germany, Japanese troops landed at Ch'ien-hsien in southwestern Kwangtung in mid-November 1939, and from there advanced into Kwangsi, occupying Nanning on November 24. They stayed there for a year, presenting a threat to Liuchow, Kweilin, and Indochina. It was the Japanese army in Kwangsi that moved into northern Vietnam in September 1940.[12]

To prevent the Indochinese revolutionists from taking advantage of the war in Europe, the French imposed a rule of terror in Vietnam. Thousands of revolutionary elements, Communist and non-Communist, were arrested. Some were sent into exile, some to prison; some were executed, among them Le Hong Phong, secretary-general of the ICP and an alternate member of the executive committee of the Comintern. The ICP quickly shifted underground. More revolutionists fled to China, particularly Yunnan. Up to this point,

[11] Vu Anh, "From Kunming to Pac Bo," in *Hu pai pai*, p. 140; Ho Chi Minh, "Chinese and Vietnamese Revolutions," p. 20.

[12] According to Gen. Chang Fa-k'uei, the Chinese generals thought Japan's advance into Nanning was merely to cut off the Chinese supply line from Indochina and threaten the security of Kwangsi and Kweichow; they did not realize Japan's further plan to move from Kwangsi to Indochina and from there farther south in the Pacific. See Chang Fa-k'uei, *K'ang-chan hui-i lu* (Memoirs of the Resistance War), serialized in the *United Review* (Hong Kong), Chap. 6, July 6, 1962.

many Communists had already either resided or worked under cover in the area along the Yunnan section of the Indochinese Railroad, then a main international supply line of China. With the assistance of the CCP Kunming ICP elements had established their secret office and a liaison station and were publishing a newspaper.[13]

Also in Yunnan, the Vietnamese Nationalist Party took refuge, setting up its overseas headquarters in the city of Kunming. Because of its political and ideological alignment with the Kuomintang, the VNQDD was in a fairly good position for its activities. It set up party cells in I-liang, Kaiyuan, and Pise (Pisechai). Its members also lived in Kunming and along the Indochinese Railroad line. The party organized "Youth Corps," "Women Corps," "Phan Boi Chau Boy Scout," etc., and published a newspaper, the "Voice."[14] Its members could move freely and openly. The leaders, Vu Hong Khanh, Nghiem Ke To and Vo Quang Pham, maintained good relations with Chungking and Kunming and a fair relationship with other Vietnamese nationalist leaders in Kwangsi.[15] They were hostile toward the ICP.

The important ICP figures in Kunming at that time were Phung Chi Kien (alias Old Ly), who was in charge of the secret ICP branch and its publication, the *D. T. News*; Hoang Van Hoan (alias Ly Quang Hoa), who disguised himself as a tailor; and Vu Anh (alias Trinh Dong Hai), who served openly as a chauffeur at the Ying On Company, but secretly as a liaison officer of the ICP. As instructed by the ICP at home, Ho Chi Minh (alias Old Chen, or Old Tran)[16] went in February 1940 to see Vu Anh, through

[13] Giap, "Ho Chi Minh," p. 157.

[14] Report of the Central Investigation and Statistics Bureau (CISB), KMT, March 18, 1943, in "Documents."

[15] See more discussions of the VNQDD below.

[16] Throughout his life, Ho used numerous aliases. With some effort, I have composed the most complete list thus far of his names:

Nguyen Sinh Cung (1890-1900), Vietnam
Nguyen Tat Thanh (1900-1912), Vietnam
Ba (1912-1917), on ships and in Europe
Nguyen Ai Quoc (1917-1924), France and Russia

whom he met Phung Chi Kien (a Central Committee member killed in 1942) and Hoang Van Hoan. He took over leadership of the ICP branch at Kunming and improved the publication of the *D. T. News*, which began to be mailed back to Cao-Bang for local distribution.[17] All work was done in secret or near secret.

The Vietnamese Communists along the Yunnan section of the Indochinese Railroad had organized several party cells, from I-liang, Kaiyuan, Mengtsu, to Chihts'un (about 130 miles from Vietnam), covered by a legal organization, the "Vietnam Association for Support of China Against the Japa-

---

Nguyen O Phap (1923-1924), France and Russia
Ly Thuy (Li Jui, 1924-1927), China
Vuong Son Nhi (Mr. Vuong, or Old Vuong, 1924-1927), China
Wang Ta-jen (Vuong Dat Nhan, 1926), China
Tong Van So (Sung Wen-ch'u; Song Man-cho in Cantonese; Sung Meng-tsu; 1924-1927), China
Thau Chin (1928-1929), Thailand
Nguyen Ai Quoc (1930-1933), Hong Kong, Amoy, and Shanghai
Linov (1933-1938), Moscow
Lin (1934-1938), Moscow
P. C. Lin (1938-1940), China
Ho Quang (Hu Kuang, 1938-1940), China
Comrade Vuong (1939-1941), China
Mr. Tran (Old Chen, 1939-1940), China
Ho Chi Minh (1940-1941), China
Thu (Old Thu, 1941-1942), Vietnam
Vuong Quoc Tuan (Hoang Quoc Tuan, 1941-1942), Vietnam
Ho Chi Minh (1942-1945), China
Mr. Tran (Old Chen, 1944), China
Ho Chi Minh (1944 to date), Vietnam

Sources: Pham Van Dong, *President Ho Chi Minh*; Tran Dan Tien, *Hu Chih-ming Chuan* (Biography of Ho Chi Minh) (Shanghai: August Publishing Co., 1949) and *Glimpses of the Life of Ho Chi Minh*; Hoai Thanh et al., *Hu pai pai*; *Wen hui pao* (Hong Kong), September 7, 1953; Hoang Van Chi, *From Colonialism to Communism*; Fall, *Two Viet-Nams*; Chiang Yung-ching, comp., "Documents"; *Fei-ch'ing yen-chiu* (monthly, Studies of Chinese Communist Affairs), Vol. 8, No. 6 (1965); Taipei: Intelligence Bureau of the Ministry of National Defence; Franklin Lien Ho's letter to the author, dated July 13, 1967. *Records of the Second Congress of the Kuomintang* (April 1926).

[17] Hoang Quang Binh, "In Yunnan," in *Hu pai pai*, pp. 123-24; Vu Anh, "From Kunming to Pac Bo," pp. 140-43. *D. T. News* (Dang Ta) means "Our Party," "Struggle," or "Fight Against the French Devils."

nese." The front organization was the "Association for the Liberation of Vietnam." In order to understand and direct the activities of these party cells, Ho, accompanied by Phung Chi Kien, made a tour of inspection along the railway line in April 1940. They used the staff travel permit issued by the "Vietnam Association for Support of China Against the Japanese." They safely visited each cell and stayed with their men for awhile. During this tour, as recalled by one cell member, Ho acted as a man behind the scene and let Phung Chi Kien be the "front man" for their activities. They held discussions, opened small brief training classes for teaching their men Marxism-Leninism and training them for revolutionary activity. Ho urged them to support China against Japan by contributing money, and accepted their request for the establishment of relations with the CCP's members on the cell level.[18] After his tour Ho decided in mid-May 1940 to distribute propaganda papers along the railway from Kunming to the Vietnam border, to expose "the crime of the French-Japanese connivance" and urge the masses to support the Chinese in their war against Japan. Ho's tour was successful. He had significantly consolidated the ICP activities in Yunnan, disseminated new revolutionary ideas and techniques, and made broader contact with party cadres. Above all, he had gradually but firmly established an image of leadership among his men, although only two or three top members knew that this Old Chen was the famous Nguyen Ai Quoc.

In June Pham Van Dong (alias Lin Pai-chieh in Chinese, Lam Ba Kiet in Vietnamese) and Vo Nguyen Giap (alias Yang Huai-nan in Chinese, Duong Hoai Nam in Vietnamese) slipped into China at the ICP's instigation. They met Comrade Vuong (Ho) in Kunming.[19] Dong was a protégé of Ho in Canton in the 1920s. Giap, a long-time admirer of

---

[18] Hoang Quang Binh, "In Yunnan," pp. 125-32; Vu Anh, "From Kunming to Pac Bo," p. 143.

[19] Giap, "Ho Chi Minh," p. 155. According to Giap, when the ICP decided to send Dong and Giap to China, Dong was ill and Giap was teaching at the Thang-Long Private School; they were continually followed by the French police, but managed to slip into China.

Nguyen Ai Quoc, for the first time saw Ho, but immediately ascertained that Comrade Vuong and Nguyen Ai Quoc were the same.[20]

After these two men came, Ho decided to send them with Cao Hong Linh to Yenan to the Institute of Marxism-Leninism (the party school of the CCP). He also instructed Giap to study military affairs in the CCP capital. With Ho's guidance and recommendation the men reached Kweiyang, staying at the liaison office of the Eighth Route Army while waiting for transportation to Yenan. The Chinese comrades at this office asked warmly about Ho Quang (Ho) and treated the Vietnamese well.[21] Two weeks later, however, the Germans took Paris. Foreseeing an imminent change in the Indochinese situation, Ho held a meeting at which he made several decisions of far-reaching import. He decided to try to return to Vietnam and organize guerrilla forces there. "And once we have returned, we will have weapons," he optimistically said.[22] Then he canceled the Yenan trip of

[20] Giap, "Ho Chi Minh," pp. 158-59. Giap claimed that in 1926-1927, when he was a student in Hue, he with other students frequented the home of the imprisoned Phan Boi Chau and became good listeners to Chau's talks on the international situation. He heard of Nguyen Ai Quoc and his activities in Paris and Canton, and read his article, "French Colonization on Trial." In 1927 Giap joined the Tan Viet Party because he supported its "national revolution first and world revolution second" program. In the 1930s of the "democratic movement period," Giap worked for an ICP publication in Hanoi. They often received articles from abroad by "P. C. Lin." They knew the articles were written by Nguyen Ai Quoc, and published them. The articles were succinct, and dealt with the democratic movement in the world, the international situation, and Chinese revolutionary experiences. Giap was an admirer of Quoc and his writing.

[21] According to Vo Nguyen Giap, Ho got along well with the Chinese Communists, and taught them English and Russian while staying in Kweiyang; presumably this was when Ho went to Hengyang via Kweiyang. Giap, "Ho Chi Minh," p. 161. It became apparent that during 1938-1940 Ho used the name Ho Quang (Ho-who-is-bright) among the Chinese, and Comrade Vuong, or Old Chen, among the Vietnamese. In the Chinese name system, a man named "Kuang" (Quang in Vietnamese, meaning brightness or light) could well adopt "Chih-ming" (Chi Minh in Vietnamese, "enlightened mind") as his second name. Here we see the relationship between the two names of Ho Quang and Ho Chi Minh.

[22] Vu Anh, "From Kunming to Pac Bo," p. 144.

Dong, Giap, and Linh and called them back from Kwei-yang.[23]

But Ho Chi Minh's relations with Yenan were not cut off; on the contrary, they were strengthened. While canceling the trip of Dong's group, Ho sent an agent, Tran Van Hinh, who had just escaped from South Vietnam, to Yenan to establish new ties to meet the changing world situation. According to a Chinese source, a secret agreement was concluded in August 1940 which contained several basic items:

1. establish a "United Front of the Sino-Vietnamese people against Japan"
2. enlarge the Vietnamese Communist armed organization and begin guerrilla activities
3. unite the ICP with all political parties in an effort to set up a "United Front for National Independence"
4. make the goal of the ICP struggle "Anti-French Imperialism and Anti-Feudalism"
5. the ICP sends cadres to Yenan for training at the Resistance-Japan University
6. the CCP serves as representative of the Asian Information Bureau of the Comintern to guide the ICP, but offers $50,000 (Chinese dollars) per month to the ICP for its activities in China.[24]

After his mission Tran Van Hinh returned in the fall of 1940 to see Ho Chi Minh in Kweilin. As mentioned earlier, prior to the conclusion of the agreement Yenan had served

[23] Giap, "Ho Chi Minh," p. 162; Vu Anh, "From Kunming to Pac Bo," p. 144. Thus Giap never went to Yenan, as many writers have erroneously asserted. This Hanoi account is identical with a publication put out by the Intelligence Bureau of the Ministry of National Defence in Taipei. See Ch'en Kuang, "Five North Vietnamese Leaders," in *Fei-ch'ing yen-chiu* (Study of the Chinese Communist Affairs), Vol. 8, No. 6 (June 30, 1965), p. 94. But Giap did study in detail the strategy and tactics of the Chinese Communist army and wrote a pamphlet, "Chinese Military Affairs," which has probably never been published.

[24] The Sixth Section (information) of the Kuomintang, "Yueh kung yu Yueh-nan wen t'i ti chin hsi kuan" (Vietnamese Communist and Vietnamese problems—Today and Yesterday), in *Studies on Special Subjects*, 2 issues (Taipei, 1955), No. 21, pp. 12-13.

as a transit station for Vietnamese Communists from Moscow to Vietnam, and the CCP had given assistance secretly to the ICP in Chungking, Kweiyang, Kunming, and Kweilin. But the accord was a formal commitment between these Communist parties during the war.

The German victory over France brought a change in Indochina, as Ho Chi Minh had expected. Japan soon advanced into Vietnam. Japan had long accused the French of letting the Indochinese Railroad serve as a main supply line to China. Previous Japanese protests had forced the French to stop shipping armaments, but gasoline, trucks and some noncontraband items were still transported to China via the railroad. Three days after the fall of Paris on June 16, 1940 Japan presented an ultimatum to Gen. Georges Catroux, French governor of Indochina, demanding the end of all traffic to China through Haiphong, and asking to send a Japanese control mission to the Sino-Vietnamese border. France solicited help from the United States, but failed; General Catroux accepted the Japanese terms. On August 2 the Japanese sent another ultimatum to the new French governor, Adm. Jean Decoux, demanding that the Japanese be allowed to cross Tonkin and occupy Indochinese airfields. France turned again to the United States to no avail. The French began to negotiate with the Japanese in Hanoi on September 5. The negotiations were conducted by Generals Martin and Nishihara. Realizing the importance of Indochina to her war against Japan, the Chinese government instructed its ambassador to France, Wellington Koo, to give warning to the French government that China would not tolerate Japanese troops using Indochina to invade China. Before the French replied, China made a new proposal to France to the effect that Chinese troops move into Indochina from Kwangsi under Gen. Chang Fa-k'uei to help defend the French colony. The French rejected the Chinese offer on the grounds that they did not want a war with Japan, nor did they intend to offend Japan's ally, Germany. As the Franco-Japanese negotiations dragged on, Japan became impatient. Finally, on the afternoon of September 22nd, the French reluctantly concluded an agreement with Japan, allowing the Japanese to occupy three airfields (Phu-Tho, Lao-Kay, and Gia-Lam) and to station 6,000 troops in Indochina. On the same day, Admiral Decoux informed the Chinese consul-general in Hanoi that the French had signed the agreement and hoped that Chinese troops would not be moved to Vietnam for the time being. He hoped to prevent the Japanese from using such a troop movement as an excuse to increase their own forces.[25] But that same evening Japanese troops from southern Kwangsi and southwestern Kwangtung, ignoring the newly concluded French-Japanese accord, made a surprise attack on the French forces at Lang-Son and Dong-Dang. Contrary to his message only a few hours earlier, Decoux immediately talked to the Chinese consul-general in Hanoi, requesting Chinese troops to attack the Japanese from the rear.[26] But the Chinese did not move. The French lost about 800 men, and Dong-Dang fell on September 23; Lang-Son surrendered the following day, and Haiphong was bombed. Japanese troops moved from Kwangsi to Vietnam and completely cut off the Indochinese supply line. The Japanese attack also stirred up revolt in Vietnam.

The French concession to Japan was regarded by most Vietnamese and Chinese as French-Japanese collaboration against them. An enemy's friend is an enemy—France and Japan became no less than the common foe of China and Vietnam. This development offered a good reason for Ho Chi Minh to return to his country.

As the new situation in Indochina developed, Ho's men made contact with Ho Ngoc Lam,[27] a Vietnamese officer in the Fourth War Area in Kwangsi, who helped all Vietnam-

[25] Telegram from the Chinese consulate-general in Hanoi, September 22, 1940, in "Documents."

[26] Telegram from the Chinese consulate-general in Hanoi, September 23, 1940, *ibid.*

[27] Ho Ngoc Lam (Ho Hoc Lam) graduated from the Second Class of the Chinese Paoting Military Academy and served in the Chinese army for a long time. He joined the Independence Party and later became a leader of the Association for Vietnam Independence League

ese revolutionists (Communist or non-Communist) against the French. Lam, after talking with Truong Boi Cong[28] (a military officer also serving in the Fourth War Area), informed them that the time to return to Vietnam had arrived. Ho agreed with his men to "grasp" the opportunity.

It was apparent that Ho wanted to use the bridge of VNQDD and the Kuomintang for his return to Vietnam. He immediately sent his men to Liuchow and Kweilin. In Liuchow they saw Truong Boi Cong; in Kweilin, in the capacity of organizers of a liberation league, they got in touch with Li Chi-shen, a Kuomintang leader and Communist sympathizer,[29] who asked them to help draft a plan for "Chinese Troops to Vietnam" as preparation for the future moving of allied forces into that country. In October Ho also came to Kweilin, where he convened another important meeting. He proposed they move to the Vietnam border area and organize a broad united front; national unity could thereby be achieved to meet the new situation in Indochina. The front's name—Viet-Nam Doc Lap Dong Minh (Viet-Nam

organized in Nanking (1935) before the outbreak of the Second Sino-Japanese war. See "Short Biographical Sketches of the Members of the Preparatory Committee of the Vietnamese Revolutionary League" (hereafter "Short Biographical Sketches"), July 1942, in "Documents." See also Vu Anh, "From Kunming to Pac Bo," pp. 144-45; Kung-i Mei, *Yueh-nan hsin chih* (New Records of Vietnam) (Chungking: Chung Hua, 1945), p. 82. Mei, a Chinese-Vietnamese, trained by the Whampoa Military Academy, was working at the headquarters of the Fourth War Area during this time. His account could be comparatively dependable. Lam had contacts with the ICP as early as 1930. See Ho Chi Minh et al., *A Heroic People* (Hanoi: Foreign Languages Publishing House, 1960), p. 32.

[28] Truong Boi Cong also graduated from the Second Class of the Chinese Paoting Military Academy, served as a regimental commander in the Chinese army and as dean of the Chinese Military Academy at Nanning. In his service in the Fourth War Area at this time, he maintained good relations with Chang Fa-k'uei. See "Short Biographical Sketches," July 1942, in "Documents." Also the author's interview with Gen. Chang Fa-k'uei in New York on October 7, 1960 (hereafter Chang Fa-k'uei interview).

[29] Li Chi-shen, a leader of the Kuomintang Revolutionary Committee, became a vice-president of Communist China in October 1949. His official title in Kweilin was Director of Kweilin Office of the Chinese Military Council.

Independence League)—was thought more suitable than either the "Viet-Nam Liberation League" or the "Viet-Nam Anti-Imperialist League." It was to be called simply the "Viet-Minh," making it easy to remember.[30] Then they decided that the Viet-Nam Doc Lap Dong Minh Hoi (the Association for Viet-Nam Independence League),[31] previously formed in Nanking in 1935 by Ho Ngoc Lam and Hoang Van Hoan, should resume its activities. They elected Ho Ngoc Lam its director, Pham Van Dong deputy director.[32] It was a good choice, for Lam was the founder of the Association and had good relations with the VNQDD, ICP, and other nationalistic elements, while Dong could serve as a watchdog and actual controller.

In Vietnam, no sooner had the Japanese army moved into the country than there was revolt in Lang-Son. It was an anti-French rebellion led by the Phuc Quoc. Some pro-Japanese leaders of the insurgents such as Hoang Luong and Nguyen Phuc An, who were encouraged by their leader (Prince Cuong De) in Canton under the Japanese, hoped the Japanese would come to their assistance. But the Japa-

[30] Giap, "Ho Chi Minh," pp. 162-63.
[31] Viet-Nam Doc Lap Dong Minh Hoi, not to be confused with Viet-Nam Doc Lap Dong Minh (Viet-Minh) organized by Ho Chi Minh in 1941, was formed mainly by the members of the Viet-Nam Independence Party. It cooperated with the ICP in the common struggle for the independence of Vietnam. For a time it had some influence in Vietnamese rural areas. Ho Ngoc Lam was in charge, as previously noted. In searching sources for the Association's founding in Nanking, I found two solid pieces of evidence: (1) a letter from Nghiem Ke To to the author, March 31, 1969, stated that the Association was organized in late 1935 in Nanking by Ho Ngoc Lam, Hoang Van Hoan, Tran Chieu, Vi Chinh Nam, and Nghiem Ke To; (2) a *Yueh Sheng* (*Voice of Vietnam*) monthly published by the Association for Vietnam Independence Movement League in Nanking in March 1936 (first issue only) was listed in *Ch'uan kuo Chung wen ch'i k'an lien ho mu lu, 1833-1949* (United Index to All-China Chinese Periodicals, 1833-1949) (Peking: The Library of Peking, 1961), p. 1,089. This first issue is in the Nanking Library (the Library of Congress does not possess a copy). Undoubtedly the monthly was the organ of the Association. I assert, therefore, that the Association was the forerunner of Ho Chi Minh's Viet-Minh. See also Kung-i Mei, *New Records of Vietnam*, p. 82.
[32] Vu Anh, "From Kunming to Pac Bo," p. 145.

nese did not help and the revolt was quickly put down. The French tightened their rule in Lang-Son and Cao-Bang over both Communists and nationalists. Hundreds of insurgents and other Vietnamese revolutionists fled to China. The Lang-Son uprising was followed by a second revolt in November, which was participated in by the ICP at My-Tho in the south, and a third one in January 1941 at Do-Luong; both were crushed. During the revolt at Lang-Son a small unit armed by the ICP was born at Bac-Son, the first ICP guerrilla force. In February 1941 it was named the Vietnam National Salvation Army.[33]

The flow of Vietnamese revolutionists into China after the Lang-Son revolt attracted the attention of Gen. Chang Fa-k'uei, commander-in-chief of the Fourth War Area. With sympathy and support, Chang decided to receive and train the Vietnamese revolutionists. He first received a unit of the Phu Quoc army led by Hoang Luong and Nong Kinh Du. The French authorities asked Chang to return the men. Chang rejected the request and later set up a Vietnam Special Training Class in Liuchow for them.[34] Then he sent Truong Boi Cong to Chinghsi (about 600 miles from Liuchow and 65 miles from Vietnam) to organize a border work team for enlisting other political refugees.[35] Before they began work with the team they underwent a short period of training (cadre training class). Some Communists such as Le Quang Ba and Hoang Sam joined the team temporarily. On learning of Cong's activities in Chinghsi, Ho immediately sent three able men, Vo Nguyen Giap, Vu Anh and Cao Hong Linh, to Chinghsi. They were to cooperate publicly with Cong and encourage the young revolutionists in secret, particularly the Communists. In addition, they were instructed to pave the way for Ho's safe return.

After their arrival at Chinghsi in late November, Giap and his comrades maintained friendly relations with both

[33] Truong Chinh, *President Ho*, p. 15.
[34] Chang Fa-k'uei interview.
[35] Giap, "Ho Chi Minh," p. 163.

Cong and the Kuomintang in order to "use" them for their work in the border area.[36] They set up an office for the organization of a liberation league for which preparatory work was in progress in Kweilin and Liuchow. They cleverly succeeded in getting 40 young revolutionists from Cong's team and transferred them to two border villages of the Nung tribes. Meanwhile they informed Ho Chi Minh, who remained in Kweilin under the umbrella of the liaison office of the Eighth Route Army, of the progress they had made and advised him to come to Chinghsi. Ho, accompanied by Pham Van Dong, Phung Chi Kien, and Hoang Van Hoan, came via Nanning and Tientung—the same route over which he was escorted to Kweilin as a prisoner in 1942. He identified himself as a French-speaking Chinese reporter.[37] For security, he carried with him three identification papers dated 1940: (1) membership in the Young Chinese Newsmen Association, (2) Special Correspondent of the International News Service, and (3) Staff Travel Permit of the Headquarters of the Fourth War Area.[38] All these papers were marked with the bearer's name, "Ho Chi Minh." Thus Ho took his present name as early as 1940.

Ho arrived at Chinghsi in December and immediately set to work on two plans: opening a training class for the 40 newly transferred men, and sending Vu Anh back to northern Vietnam to select an absolutely secret and secure area for their revolutionary base. With the assistance of Pham Van Dong, Vo Nguyen Giap, Phung Chi Kien, and others, Ho started the training program from scratch. Finances were difficult. Even to support a group of 50 men for two weeks became a big problem. But Ho managed to overcome all difficulties and completed the training program. He then

[36] *Ibid.*, pp. 163-65.

[37] Vu Anh, "From Kunming to Pac Bo," p. 146.

[38] Report of Chang Fa-k'uei, January 23, 1944, in "Documents," which indicates that the identification papers Ho carried with him in August 1942 when he returned to China were marked with the year 1940. It is therefore my belief that Ho used the same papers in 1940 to identify himself as a "Chinese reporter," as Vu Anh recalled. Here Vu Anh's account is identical with the Chinese source.

sent the indoctrinated young men back to Vietnam. The training set an example to be followed by many training classes Ho conducted later.

In northern Vietnam Vu Anh selected Pac-Bo for Ho's base. It is a small border-hill village, hard for outsiders to reach, but easy for Ho to advance into Cao-Bang, Bac-Can, and Lang-Son. It was of great strategic importance. At this time the central committee of the ICP resumed direct contacts with Ho. Truong Chinh, Hoang Quoc Viet, and Hoang Van Thu secretly made their way into the Chinghsi area to meet him. In February 1941 Ho, having been away for 30 years, finally returned to his country.[39] He was to establish Pac-Bo as his "Chingkanshan!" Before Ho left China for Vietnam, he assigned Pham Van Dong, Hoang Van Hoan, and Vo Nguyen Giap to remain in Chinghsi and continue their activities with the nationalists there.

2. FROM CHINA TO VIETNAM, 1941-1942

In early 1941 Chinghsi, a small poor border city, suddenly became important. It was a temporary refuge of more than 700 Vietnamese revolutionists who in turn attracted many Vietnamese leaders from Liuchow, Kweilin, and Chungking. It became an unexpected gathering place for Vietnamese with different political faiths. To unite and consolidate their strength, they decided to establish a united organization, a decision that had its origin in 1940.

In the fall of 1940, after the Japanese had moved into Tonkin, Vietnamese nationalists in Liuchow exchanged views about organizing a "Vietnam National Liberation Committee" for a united front organization of all Vietnamese revolutionists against their common enemy. At the end of the year a preparation committee published a declaration in several newspapers in Kweilin, announcing its establishment. In the spring of 1941 some committee leaders such as Ho Ngoc Lam and Truong Boi Cong, selected Chinghsi as

[39] Vu Anh, "From Kunming to Pac Bo," pp. 146-47; Giap, "Ho Chi Minh," pp. 165-67.

the birthplace of the planned organization, a place to win the "mass" support from the several hundred newcomers and to arouse a stronger patriotic sentiment among the participants. Then the Vietnam Liberation League (or the Vietnam National Liberation League) was born in the late spring.[40] It included various parties and groups, with the Viet-Nam Doc Lap Dong Minh Hoi (founded in Nanking) as its nucleus.[41] The leading figures were Truong Boi Cong, Ho Ngoc Lam, Tran Bao, Truong Trung Phung, Pham Viet Tu, Tu Chi Kien,[42] Lam Ba Kiet (Pham Van Dong) Duong Hoai Nam (Vo Nguyen Giap), and Li Quang Hoa (Hoang Van Hoan).[43] In fact, Dong, Giap, and Hoan could well claim to be three original organizers, among others, since they saw Li Chi-shen in the fall of 1940 in their capacity as organizers of the liberation league (they set up a preparatory office in Chinghsi in late 1940).

The league set as its goal Vietnam's independence and freedom, but its pro-Chinese attitude was paramount. The preamble of its constitution stated its purpose: "To unite with those who treat us on an equal basis, especially the Chinese people, in an effort to defeat the French and Japanese imperialists in order to achieve Vietnam's independence, freedom and territorial integrity. To establish a Vietnamese republic of the people, by the people, and for

[40] Hsing Shen-chou, "Recent Developments of the Vietnamese National Movement for Independence," December 26, 1947, in "Documents." Hsing was then (1947) the head of the KMT office in Vietnam.

[41] Kung-i Mei, *New Records of Vietnam*, p. 83.

[42] According to the "Short Biographical Sketches" cited above, these men represented the following parties and groups: Truong Boi Cong (military man); Ho Ngoc Lam (Viet-Nam Doc Lap Dong Minh Hoi); Tran Bao (the Independence Party and Viet-Nam Doc Lap Dong Minh Hoi); Truong Trung Phung (VNQDD and Viet-Nam Doc Lap Dong Minh Hoi); Pham Viet Tu (Viet-Nam Doc Lap Dong Minh Hoi); Tu Chi Kien (Vietnam Association for Support of China against the Japanese).

[43] Nghiem Ke To's report, "A Short History of the Vietnamese Revolutionary Parties," August 16, 1942, in "Documents." To was a VNQDD leader working with the Chinese government. In his letter of March 31, 1969 to the author, To stated that Nguyen Hai Than was also a founder of the Liberation League.

the people in accordance with the spirit of the Three People's Principles, and to help China carry out its resistance-and-reconstruction policy based on the principle of Sino-Vietnamese mutual assistance."[44]

The league was the first united front, broad-base organization established during the war in China. From the above quotation it is apparent that no matter how perfect its program could be and how many parties it could include, its strong sentiment for allying with China was inevitable.

For a short time after its establishment, the Vietnam National Liberation League was active along the border. Giap and Dong used the opportunity to publish a propaganda newspaper for distribution in Chinghsi and northern Vietnam.[45] But internal troubles in the league soon developed. Ostensibly trouble developed out of ICP members' opposition to the participation of the "reactionary" Vietnam Democratic Party. Actually ICP members cooperated with the league in order to make good use of it, and their dispute with it was merely a matter of time. The league accepted the ICP's request to oust the Democrats. Soon thereafter a Democrat was murdered (presumably by ICP elements) and several other Democrats fled back to Vietnam. Then Pham Van Dong and Vo Nguyen Giap began to disseminate their pro-CCP views among the students of the Vietnam Training Class, claiming that only the CCP and not the KMT was truly assisting Vietnam's independence.[46] Their actions soon invited criticism from other members. As the dispute developed, Nguyen Hai Than[47] went to Chinghsi and reported to the local KMT office that Dong and Giap were Communists; the KMT immediately changed its atti-

---

[44] Kung-i Mei, *New Records of Vietnam*, p. 83.
[45] Giap, "Ho Chi Minh," p. 170.
[46] Nghiem Ke To, "Short History," August 16, 1942.
[47] Nguyen Hai Than (1878-1954?), from Tonkin, was trained in a Chinese military school and served in the Chinese army for more than 30 years. A friend of Phan Boi Chau, he claimed to be a successor to Chau. He made his residence in China after 1912. After the Chinese Communists came to Canton, he remained there, where he was reported to have died in 1954.

tude toward them.[48] Before long, Truong Boi Cong was taken into custody by Chinese authorities for working with ICP members who tried to turn the Vietnamese students against the KMT. Dong and Giap fled to Vietnam in January 1942.[49] After this incident the league virtually shut down.

As of early 1942 the several hundred Vietnamese in Chinghsi had split into several groups based mainly on their own choices: (1) more than a hundred young men and women remained at Chinghsi with the Border Work Team; (2) about 100 men enrolled in the Southwest War Area Personnel Training Class in Liuchow; (3) more than 300 went to Tachiao (near Liuchow) where General Chang Fa-k'uei set up a Vietnam Special Training Class for them; (4) approximately 40 joined the Political Work Team of the Fourth War Area, and (5) 20 enrolled in the Communication Training Class for technical training. There was a total of 702 young Vietnamese, including 36 women.[50] A few Communists and Communist sympathizers stayed in these groups, some of whom were taken back to Vietnam by Ho Chi Minh in 1944.

Up to this point, Ho Chi Minh had made substantial progress in northern Tonkin. To understand this fully, we should now look at Vietnam.

After his return in February 1941 Ho stayed in the Pac-Bo area in carefully chosen hideouts. His immediate task was to organize and develop "National Salvation Associations" (Cuu Quoc Hoi) of the youth, women, workers, farmers, intellectuals, etc. To arouse interest in the associations, Ho stressed the importance of developing political consciousness among the masses, which could only be accomplished by young revolutionaries engaging in propa-

[48] Giap, "Ho Chi Minh," p. 163; Giap gave no account of ICP's dispute with the league.
[49] Report from the Political Department of the Headquarters of the Fourth War Area, October 29, 1942, in "Documents." Cong was held, along with others, for a short time. See also Nghiem Ke To, "Short History," August 16, 1942.
[50] *Ibid.*

ganda. Ho sent out about 60 men and women for the job, which was a successful effort. National Salvation Associations sprang up in various places, and served as the foundation of the organization of the Viet-Minh. Meanwhile Ho directed the publication of a newspaper, *Vietnam Doc Lap Bao* (called *Viet Lap Bao,* or *Vietnam Independence News*). It wasn't a newspaper by modern Western standards; it was mimeographed, small, and simple, but its succinct vigorous style attracted the reader. It met the need to propagandize, and served as a means for mobilizing and organizing the people. In a few months the revolutionary movement in Cao-Bang grew radically.[51]

With the preparatory work done and the foundation laid, Ho convened the Eighth session of the Central Committee of the ICP at Pac-Bo in May 1941. Its participants were himself, Hoang Quoc Viet, Hoang Van Hoan, Hoang Van Thu, Truong Chinh, Phung Chi Kien, Vu Anh, and two others from central Vietnam.[52] It was a historic meeting. The leaders decided to continue preparations for an armed insurrection and to build guerrilla bases. They elected Truong Chinh as secretary-general. Most important, they resolved on May 19 (Ho's birthday) to organize the Viet-Nam Doc Lap Dong Minh (Viet-Minh).[53]

The establishment of the Viet-Minh is well known; so are

[51] Giap, "Ho Chi Minh," pp. 169-70; Pham Van Dong, *President Ho*, p. 74.

[52] Vu Anh, "From Kunming to Pac-Bo," p. 150.

[53] One earlier North Vietnamese source given by Hoang Quoc Viet when he visited China stated that the meeting place was in Kwangsi and not Pac-Bo. Viet said: "In May 1941, under the leadership of Comrade Ho Chi Minh, a conference was held in Kwangsi, China, with the participation of 50 delegates, representing all the revolutionary organizations; [it] decided to form a still broader united front, the Viet-Nam Independence League (Viet-Minh) to lead the national liberation struggle." (*New China News Agency* [NCNA], Peking, August 26, 1951.) This account may well be true because (1) Viet was a participant in the meeting, (2) he was simply telling the Chinese people of the fact of the Vietnamese revolutionary movement, and (3) Hanoi today wants to exhibit more nationalism in the establishment of the Viet-Minh, and therefore changed the conference place from Kwangsi in China to Pac-Bo in Vietnam.

its three basic goals—to expel the French and Japanese "fascists" and restore the independence of Vietnam; to ally with the democracies who fight against fascism and aggression; and to establish a Democratic Republic of Vietnam. Its political, economic, social, and cultural programs are also well known, and are covered by several studies.[54] But there are two points that have not been emphasized before and which deserve discussion. First, in his appeal to the Vietnamese people,[55] Ho stressed that the struggle of the Vietnamese people was almost entirely based on patriotism and nationalism; there was not a single word of proletarian dictatorship or Communist movement inserted in it. Compared with Mao's *New Democracy* (published in January 1940 when Ho was still in China), in which Mao stated categorically the CCP's leading role in both the "New Democratic" society and the proletarian-revolutionary society, Ho's approach was much more nationalistic and moderate than Mao's. Second, Ho highly esteemed the Chinese struggle against Japan and strongly urged the Vietnamese to "follow the heroic example of the Chinese people" to defeat the French and Japanese. Ho even borrowed the slogan popularly used by the Chinese at the time: "Those who have money give money," and "Those who can provide labor give labor."

After the Eighth session Ho's work was intensified. From May 1941 to January 1942 the ICP struggled on at least three fronts—the Hanoi-Haiphong area and the south, led by the Central Committee of which Hoang Quoc Viet, Truong Chinh, Hoang Van Thu, and others were in charge; in Pac-Bo of Cao-Bang, the revolutionary base led by Ho himself; and in China, where the fight was led by Pham Van Dong and Vo Nguyen Giap from Chinghsi. In addition, there were ICP activists in Lungchow and Yunnan.[56] Aided

[54] For instance, Devillers, *Histoire*, pp. 98-100.

[55] The appeal was printed in Lungchow, Kwangsi, in both Vietnamese and Chinese. For the English translation see Ho, *Selected Works*, II, pp. 151-54.

[56] Report of the Overseas Department of the KMT, March 15, 1943, in "Documents."

by Dong and Giap after January 1942, Ho's work was most significant. He conducted many military and political cadre training classes, almost one a month, with 50 to 60 trainees at a time. Later he set up the mobile training class in rural areas for smaller numbers of trainees and for only a few days. This type of class was devised especially for tribesmen and peasants who could not leave their work for long. In doing so, the Viet-Minh organization (based on various National Salvation Associations) and influence gradually spread into almost every part of the border area.[57] French-Vietnamese agents and forces often searched after them, but they disappeared ahead of time as mysteriously as the Viet Cong do today. Occasionally they clashed with the French, but most of the time chose to avoid a clash. The French were surprised to find in the forest large classrooms, a mess hall, and living quarters with a capacity of about 100 built by the Viet-Minh.

Despite difficulties and hardship, Ho took time to write and edit some training and propaganda pamphlets. His written contributions in this period were his "Guerrilla Warfare," "Experiences of Chinese Guerrilla Warfare," and a translation from the Chinese of the "History of the Communist Party of the U.S.S.R."[58]

By August 1942 Ho and his comrades had established many local self-defense units associated with the Viet-Minh. The Viet-Minh organization apparatus was built on the Salvation Associations from village to district to county to province and to interprovincial zones under the Viet-Minh. The network had spread, though only partially, to Cao-Bang, Bac-Can, and Lang-Son. The ICP set up party offices in various levels of the Viet-Minh to direct its activities, and party men were concurrently Viet-Minh leaders. The party, therefore, had an effective control over the front organization.[59] The pattern is similar to that of government-party relations in any Communist country today.

[57] Giap, "Ho Chi Minh," pp. 173-74.
[58] Truong Chinh, *President Ho*, p. 16; Vu Anh, "From Kunming to Pac Bo," pp. 151-52.
[59] Lu Ku, *Vietnamese Struggle*, p. 76.

Because its guerrilla forces could not develop rapidly with primitive weapons (such as knives, spears, old guns, and some captured guns from the enemy), the Viet-Minh decided to ask for aid from the Allies. The closest ally was China. Acting on the decision of the Viet-Minh, Ho departed for China in mid-August 1942.[60] His real motive was to request aid from the Kuomintang and, more important, from the Chinese Communist Party.[61] He planned to see the Chinese leaders in the capacity of the representative of both the Viet-Minh and the Vietnam Branch of the International Anti-Aggression Association which he set up in early 1942. Ho realized that since the Viet-Minh did not have direct relations with China, and the Association was only an international front organization, the Chinese might not let him pass through. Therefore he carried with him the three identification papers he used in 1940, plus his visiting card. On the card he had his name, "Ho Chi Minh," printed, along with his "profession," "journalist," and nationality, "Viet-Nam—Chinese resident."[62]

3. HO CHI MINH AND CHANG FA-K'UEI,[63] 1942-1944

The papers Ho carried did not serve as a passport for travel in wartime China. When he entered Kwangsi his identifica-

[60] Tran Dan Tien's *Biography of Ho Chi Minh*, p. 120. The biography was written in late 1947 by a pro-Communist—if not outright—reporter from Vietnam and translated into Chinese in 1949 before the CCP came to power. I have not seen an edition of the original version in any other language. It depicts many true and valuable aspects of Ho's story. In 1958 Hanoi published an excerpt from the book, entitled *Glimpses of the Life of Ho Chi Minh* (63 pages of the original 191), omitting all of the accurate and valuable sections. It is another dry, vague, official biography of Ho. Unless otherwise indicated, all subsequent references to this book are to the 1949 Chinese translation.

[61] Truong Chinh, *President Ho*, p. 16; Vu Anh, "From Kunming to Pac Bo," p. 152.

[62] *Ibid.*

[63] Chang Fa-k'uei (1896-) was born in Kwangtung and graduated from the Hupeh Military Academy. During the period of KMT-CCP cooperation in Canton (1924-1927) he had contacts with Soviet General Galen who served as a military adviser to the KMT army. As the commander of the Fourth Army Chang made his army well known as "Old Ironsides" during the years of the Northern Expedi-

tion papers, dated 1940, were considered outdated, and he was arrested as a Japanese-French spy by the local Chinese authorities at T'ienpao and immediately transferred to Chinghsi on August 29, 1942.[64] He was in Chinghsi's prison for about six weeks while the local authorities awaited instruction from the Kweilin office of the Military Council. Ho was removed to Kweilin in mid-October.

In Vietnam the ICP was shocked and depressed on learning mistakenly that Ho had died in the prison.[65] After they received Ho's secret message they worked for his release. They cabled for help from Sun Fo, son of Dr. Sun Yat-sen and president of the Legislative Yuan in Chungking, who had a few months earlier publicly advocated that the Allies

---

tion. Several top military leaders of Communist China today, such as Yeh Chien-ying, Yeh Ting, and Lin Piao, served in the Fourth Army as chief of staff, commander of a division and a battalion, respectively. At that time, the CCP persuaded Chang to join the party, but he refused. Although he is no longer officially a member of the KMT, he still claims to support it. In retirement in Hong Kong since 1949, he was reported to have tried in 1951-1953 to organize a "third force" without success. He visited the United States in 1960 after attending the Moral Rearmament Conference in Europe. In several speeches given in New York, Baltimore, Washington, Boston, and San Francisco, he urged the Chinese to fight against the Chinese Communists and restore the Republic of China to the mainland. He disagreed with the Nationalist government on Taiwan. Throughout his career he has been a controversial, left-of-center military leader. He is now (as of 1967) being interviewed in Hong Kong for an oral history project of Columbia University. His family name "Chang" (in English, not in French) has often been misspelled by Western scholars, including Bernard B. Fall, as "Chiang," which is quite different in meaning and writing in Chinese from "Chang."

[64] Report of Chang Fa-k'uei, January 23, 1944, in "Documents." According to this Chinese source, Ho was not arrested on the order of Gen. Chang Fa-k'uei. (General Chang denied absolutely this matter to me in an interview in October 1960.) Chang was the commander of the Fourth War Area (Zone), which included part of Kwangtung and the entire province of Kwangsi—not the governor of Kwangsi. The governor was Huang Hsu-ch'u who is now in Hong Kong.

[65] The misinformation occurred when a Vietnamese Communist was sent to inquire about Ho at Chinghsi prison; the officer of the prison indifferently answered: "Shih le, shih le" (yes, yes), which the Vietnamese nervously took for "Szu le, szu le," (dead, dead), and reported it to the ICP at home. Giap, "Ho Chi Minh," p. 176.

guarantee the independence of Vietnam, India, Korea, and the Philippines after the war.[66] Meanwhile they urged all Vietnamese in China and Vietnam under the ICP's control to write letters protesting and requesting Ho's immediate release.[67] Their cable to Sun Fo, sent in late October from Chinghsi, was delivered under the name of the Vietnam Branch of the International Anti-Aggression Association. It stated: "Our Association's representative Ho Khach Minh [sic], set off for Chungking to pay [his] respects to Generalissimo Chiang; [he] was arrested when he arrived at Chinghsi. Beg your cable to release him."[68]

On October 29 Sun Fo forwarded this cable to Wu Tieh-ch'eng, secretary-general of the Kuomintang. Wu first delivered a telegram to the Kwangsi provincial government at Nanning and then sent another on November 11 to Gen. Chang Fa-k'uei, asking Chang to repeat his instruction to the Kwangsi government, that it "examine" the case and "release" Ho.[69] In the meantime the ICP, again under the name of the Vietnam Branch of the International Anti-Aggression Association, sent on November 15 a long report from the "Sino-Vietnamese battlefront" to *Tass* in Chung-king. The report stated that "Ho Chi Minh," on behalf of the Vietnam Branch of the Association, was to go to Chungking to pay his respects to Generalissimo Chiang but was arrested at Chinghsi, that his arrest was a "very serious mistake" between China and the Vietnamese revolutionary party, that because of Ho's prestige and the importance of the Vietnam Branch of the Association, which had a membership of 200,000, Ho's arrest had increased resentment toward China among the Vietnamese revolutionists, and that although several members of the Association in China had appealed to the Chungking government for Ho's release, he was still imprisoned in Liuchow.[70] Apparently the

[66] *Chung yang jih pao* (*Central Daily News*, Chungking), March 23, 1942.
[67] Hoang Quang Binh, "In Yunnan," p. 133.
[68] The Vietnam Branch's cable to Sun Fo, in "Documents."
[69] Wu's cable to Chang, November 9, *ibid.*
[70] Report from the Vietnam Branch of the International Anti-

ICP wanted to get the matter in the open through *Tass* in order to create a favorable climate of opinion.

In Liuchow in December 1942 and January 1943, Chang Fa-k'uei and the Kweilin office of the Military Council cabled back and forth. Finally the Kweilin office instructed the political department of Chang's headquarters to handle the matter. As the cables traveled around Chinghsi, Chungking, Nanning, Liuchow, and Kweilin, so did Ho, except for Chungking. In his prison journey, he walked for about 400 miles before he reached a boat or train. He suffered from hunger, cold weather, illness, and harsh treatment; at times he almost collapsed. It was his strong willpower and optimism that kept him going. Although Ho did not consider himself a poet, he wrote more than a hundred Chinese poems to occupy himself.[71] This was the traditional way for Chinese intellectuals to serve their prison terms.[72] After eight months' hardship, Ho was finally transferred from Kweilin to Liuchow. The journey made him look 10 years older, appearing "as a demon gnawed by hunger."[73]

According to Gen. Hou Chih-ming, then acting director of the political department of the Fourth War Area in Liuchow, Ho was sent to Liuchow in May 1943.[74] The political

---

Aggression Association to *Tass* in Chungking, November 15, 1942, in "Documents." With the availability of this report and the cable from the same Branch to Sun Fo, I am able to clear up two points made by some scholars: (1) Ho Chi Minh was arrested on August 29, 1942, not "at the end of 1941" or in early 1942; (2) the name "Ho Chi Minh" was taken by Ho upon his own initiative and was not given by Chang Fa-k'uei when Ho was released by the Chinese general.

[71] Ho's poems were published as his *Prison Diary* by the Foreign Languages Publishing House in Hanoi. The poems, though not excellent in style, express Ho's feelings and experiences during his prison days.

[72] To name a few in the 20th century: republican revolutionary leader Wang Ching-wei in Ch'ing prison in 1910-1911; Kuomintang leader Liao Chung-kai in Ch'en Chiung-ming's prison in 1922; and Communist leader Ch'u Ch'iu-pai in the Kuomintang prison in 1935.

[73] Ho Chi Minh, *Prison Diary*, tr. Aileen Palmer, 1966, p. 86.

[74] Gen. Hou Chih-ming to the author, March 16, 1967. General Hou was appointed acting director of the political department in April 1943. Ho's case came under his jurisdiction until January 1944, when Gen. Chang Fa-k'uei took it over and assigned it to Hsiao Wen.

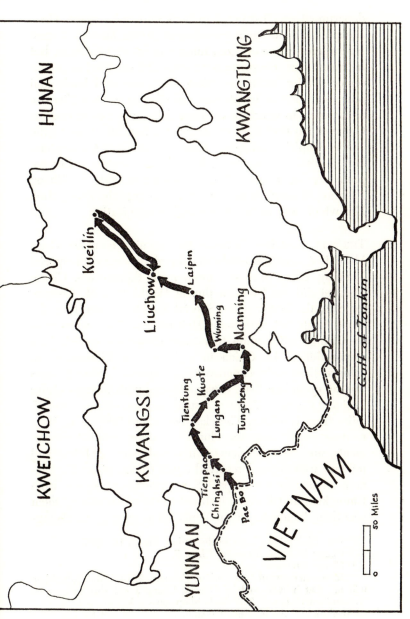

Ho Chi Minh's Prison Journey in China, 1942-1944

department was instructed to "look into and convert" Ho—a euphemism for light punishment. From May to August Ho suffered no more from hunger or harsh treatment, but he wasn't free. He presented to the Chinese the image of a senior scholar, polite but often silent. He read books and other materials as he pleased and often sent back Vietnam newspapers in which he enclosed messages. To impress the Chinese, Ho had shrewdly translated *San Min Chu I* (the Three People's Principles) into Vietnamese.[75] On September 10, 1943 he was freed. Ho lived for awhile under the protection of Hsiao Wen, an important aide to Chang Fa-k'uei. Meanwhile he was allowed to join the Dong Minh Hoi which was in the process of reorganization.

THE RELEASE of Ho Chi Minh, the organization of the Dong Minh Hoi, and the establishment of the Vietnam Special Training Class were the three main things Gen. Chang Fa-k'uei did for Vietnam during World War II. Chronologically the first was the Special Training Class, then the Dong Minh Hoi, and finally Ho's release. These were done on Chang's assumption that there should be no "shirking responsibility" by China in assisting the Vietnamese to achieve their independence.[76] The Special Training Class was set up in late 1941. It was affiliated with Chang's Cadre Training Corps in Tachiao, a small, narrow village about 15 miles from Liuchow. The class had about 500 young Vietnamese, mostly from the Phuc Quoc army, some leftist elements, and some students. They underwent political and military training and received equal treatment as did Chinese officers in the corps.[77] Some prominent figures from Chungking and Kweilin lectured to the class; among them was then Archbishop Paul Yupin.[78] On my way to Chung-

---

[75] Hou Chih-ming's letter to the author, March 16, 1967.

[76] Chang Fa-k'uei, *Memoirs*, Chap. 7.

[77] Chang interview

[78] In an interview in New York on February 2, 1961, the Archbishop told me that he was told by General Chang about this Vietnamese "revolutionary" group. The Archbishop gave a lecture in French on nationalism and the international situation. He also met Ho Chi Minh

king in early fall of 1943, I stayed in Liuchow for about a month and a half, visiting Tachiao and others.[79] According to Maj. Gen. Tseng Tien-chieh,[80] the director of the Training Corps, the Vietnamese in the Special Class maintained good discipline and worked hard.

The purpose in organizing the Dong Minh Hoi was to consolidate the Vietnamese revolutionary forces in China. As mentioned earlier, the Viet-Nam Liberation League had ceased to function in early 1942. Thereafter most of the Vietnamese revolutionists moved from Chinghsi to Liuchow. Although there were more than 20 leaders of several parties and groups, and 600 Vietnamese in Liuchow, they were divided in opinion and organization. The VNQDD members attributed the failure to achieve unity to the lack of cooperation from ICP elements and the incapability of the representatives of the Phuc Quoc, while others thought they lacked strong leadership. But the need for unity brought Vu Hong Khanh, Nghiem Ke To, and eight other VNQDD members from Kunming to Liuchow in June 1942. After a few days' discussion, the Vietnamese agreed to establish a Viet-Nam Cach Menh Dong Minh Hoi (Viet-Nam Revolutionary League).[81] They elected 19 preparatory members and founded the Dong Minh Hoi on August 10. To avoid repeating the mistake the Liberation League made in Chinghsi, at the very beginning they put their future organization under Chang Fa-k'uei's direction and excluded the ICP. The new organization included members of the Liberation League, the Phuc Quoc, the VNQDD, and some Chinese-Vietnamese.[82] But the scheduled founding date was

---

in Liuchow. After the war, when he learned about Ho and some Communist members in the class, he regretted giving the lecture.

[79] It was also at this time that I met Tien Han, a famous Communist playwright now purged by the CCP under the Cultural Revolution, at the political department in Liuchow.

[80] Tseng Tien-chieh graduated from the fifth class of the Whampoa Military Academy and joined the CCP in Kwangtung in 1949.

[81] Nghiem Ke To's report of August 16, 1942, in "Documents"; Vu Hong Khanh's letter to the author, dated May 30, 1969.

[82] Report of the Political Department of the Fourth War Area, July 28, 1942, in "Documents."

postponed until October 1 because of the strong opposition of Hoang Luong, a pro-Japanese leader of the Phuc Quoc. The reason for his opposition was that he "misunderstood the true intention of China's assistance to Vietnam's struggle for independence as a means to seize control of Vietnamese political power."[83] According to Chang Fa-k'uei, Hoang Luong, in an attempt to "undermine" the unity of the Vietnamese parties as well as the Sino-Vietnamese friendship, also spread the viewpoint that China was merely "using the Vietnamese revolutionists." Chang arbitrarily arrested Hoang and explained China's policy toward Vietnam to him.[84] With the obstacle to the organization gone, the founding conference of the new organization was held on October 1st. The conference passed a constitution, platform, working program, and resolutions. Its purpose was to unite all Vietnamese revolutionary forces, to ally itself with China and other anti-aggression democracies, and to gain Vietnam's independence and freedom.[85] In its platform it unequivocally stated, "down with French and Japanese imperialism." In its working program, the organization set forth a specific plan for propaganda, organization, training, and military preparation. Its last working item—the military—was intended to organize armed forces, request military aid from the Allies, and fight alongside the Chinese army.[86] Seven executive members were elected—Truong Boi Cong, Nguyen Hai Than, Vu Hong Khanh, Nghiem Ke To, Tran Bao, Nong Kinh Du, and Truong Trung Phung. Truong Boi Cong, Nguyen Hai Than, and Vu Hong Khanh were the standby members.[87] General Chang gave a subsidy

[83] Report of Chang Fa-k'uei, September 25, 1942, in *ibid.*
[84] *Ibid.*
[85] Constitution of the Viet-Nam Cach Meng Dong Minh Hoi, October 1942, in *ibid.* Also consult Chang, *Memoirs*, Chap. 7.
[86] The Working Program of the Dong Minh Hoi, Article 15, in "Documents."
[87] They also divided into seven work sections: Secretary, Nguyen Hai Than; Military, Truong Boi Cong; Organization, Vu Hong Khanh; Propaganda, Duong Thanh Dan; Training, Tran Bao; Finance, Nong Kinh Du; Public Relations, Nghiem Ke To. Report of the Politi-

of 100,000 Chinese dollars per month.[88] Lt. Gen. Liang Hua-sheng, head of the political department of the Fourth War Area, was appointed to serve as the director of the Dong Minh Hoi; he was replaced by Hou Chih-ming in May 1943.

The Dong Minh Hoi engaged in three activities after its establishment: the recruitment of membership; the publication of periodicals; and the setting up of offices in Tungh-sing, Chinghsi, and Lungchow, with a branch organization in Kunming.[89] But the newly organized Dong Minh Hoi was still unable to consolidate all of the Vietnamese revolutionary forces. First, its membership included only four or five parties and groups in exile in China; it excluded both the ICP and the Viet-Minh, who were working for the people's support in Vietnam. It therefore had little mass support in its own country. Second, the Dong Minh Hoi's leadership was weak and even corrupt. After embezzling some money from the Dong Minh Hoi, Nguyen Hai Than, who held at least the second most important position in the organization, left Liuchow for a long time, and the other six officers could find no way to discipline him. As General Chang commented, "The leading figures were still VNQDD men: Truong Boi Cong, Nguyen Hai Than, and Nong Kinh Du; but there was no one who really had the ability of leadership."[90] Third, although its important members were able to maintain the organization's façade, opinions remained divided. "Factions against factions, criticism against criticism; some of them enjoyed merely empty talks without any action; and a few of them did not even possess any quality as a revolutionist."[91] Fourth, it faced stiff resistance from the ICP in Kwangsi and Yunnan. In January 1943, when the

cal Department of the Fourth War Area, October 24, 1942, in "Documents."

[88] Chang Fa-k'uei interview.

[89] Report of the Political Department of the Fourth War Area, October 24, 28, 1942, in "Documents."

[90] Chang Fa-k'uei, *Memoirs*, Chap. 7. Strictly speaking, they were not VNQDD men, but nationalist leaders.

[91] *Ibid.*

organization sent Vu Hong Khanh to Kunming to organize a branch of the Dong Minh Hoi, in February Nghiem Ke To to Tunghsing (a border city in Kwangtung, a few miles from Vietnam's Mon-Kay), and Tran Bao to Chinghsi to establish working offices, ICP elements left no stone unturned in attempting to undermine the Dong Minh Hoi's activities.[92] The struggle in Kunming was particularly bitter; the ICP, through its front organization, the Liberation Association, first demanded the reorganization of the Dong Minh Hoi, then beat up a member of the Dong Minh Hoi.[93] As a result, the Dong Minh Hoi made little progress during the first year of its existence. "Disappointed" in its achievement, Chang Fa-k'uei decided to reorganize it.

It was at this time (fall 1943) that Ho Chi Minh was freed and comes into the picture vis-à-vis the Dong Minh Hoi.[94] How was Ho able to get out of prison and get the

[92] Report of the Overseas Department, KMT, March 15, 1943, in "Documents."

[93] The power struggle between the Nationalists and the Communists in Yunnan had been a problem for a long time. The Nationalists disliked ICP because they were Communists, while the Communists accused the Nationalists of being pro-French. When Vu Hong Khanh returned from an attempt to set up a Dong Minh Hoi branch in Kunming in January 1943, ICP elements headed by Duong Bao Son and Le Tung Son demanded the reorganization of the Dong Minh Hoi, with the approval of the Chinese government, as a condition of cooperation. Khanh refused, and set up without the participation of the ICP a branch organization on February 14. Duong Bao Son led 30 Communists and leftists in an unsuccessful attempt to disrupt the initial meeting; the failure was attributed to the mediation of a Chinese provincial official. On February 28 Duong Bao Son led three men to the VNQDD office, where they argued with Vo Quang Pham about an "insulting" report published by the VNQDD newspaper *Voice*. They beat up Pham before his neighbors could come to his rescue. (Report of the CISB, March 18, 1943, in "Documents.") This Chinese report is corroborated by a Hanoi source. The Hanoi report states that when Vu Hong Khanh organized the Yunnan branch of the Dong Minh Hoi, the ICP "resolutely refused to participate." See Hoang Quang Binh, "In Yunnan," p. 135. As of 1968 Le Tung Son was on the staff of the North Vietnamese embassy in Peking. Vu Hong Khanh's letter of May 30, 1969 also confirmed this point.

[94] Truong Chinh noted (*President Ho*, p. 16) that Ho was released from prison on September 10, 1943. Chang Fa-k'uei states in Chap. 7

go-ahead to participate in political activities in Liuchow?
One Chinese Communist source offered an answer.[95] In his
"confession" at the political department of the Fourth War
Area, Ho wrote a long essay analyzing the international situation, discussing the future of China's resistance war, and
arguing his own case. He said he had been held for two
years without trial, and asked that he be executed if guilty
or released if not. This bold request came to the attention of
Hsiao Wen,[96] a Communist sympathizer who was the deputy chief of the foreign affairs section of Chang Fa-k'uei's
headquarters; the section dealt solely with Vietnamese
affairs. Hsiao asked Chang's permission to talk with Ho.
Their talks were so congenial that they covered such subjects as the ICP and its popular leader Hoang (Vuong)
Quoc Tuan, whom they had not seen. Hsiao and Ho became
good friends. Hsiao asked Chang to write a petition for Ho
to Wu Tieh-ch'eng (Secretary-General of the KMT) and
Ho Ch'eng-chun (Executive Director of Military Laws
Department) in Chungking, suggesting that "Ho Chi Minh,
a man with fine qualities, honest and sincere, should regain
his freedom." Chungking approved the request and ordered
that Ho be "treated well."[97] Ho was released and worked in
the Dong Minh Hoi while maintaining "legal" contacts with
home under the protection of Hsiao Wen. By now Chungking had received a reliable report that Ho was an active

of his *Memoirs* that Ho joined the Dong Minh Hoi in the fall of 1943.
These two sources can clear up another point of disagreement: that
Ho was made head of the Dong Minh Hoi by China in February 1943.

[95] Liu San, "When President Ho Chi Minh Was in South China,"
Wen hui pao (Hong Kong), September 7, 1953. This article, judging
by its accuracy, must have been written by someone who had served
as a top aide to Chang Fa-k'uei in Liuchow at the time.

[96] Hsiao Wen, a native of Kwangtung, served first as Lieutenant-
general aide to Chang Fa-k'uei, then deputy chief of the foreign
affairs section, and finally the head of the office of the director for the
Dong Minh Hoi (director: Chang Fa-k'uei). A pro-Communist, Hsiao
was appointed a consultant to the Kwangtung provincial government
after 1950 (governor: Yeh Chien-ying).

[97] Liu San, "Ho Chi Minh in South China."

member of the Comintern.[98] The report was forwarded to Chang; but Chang still let Ho participate in the preparatory work for the reorganization of the Dong Minh Hoi. Why? According to Hou Chih-ming,[99] Chang was "surrounded" by Communists and pro-Communists such as his confidential secretary, Tso Hung-tao,[100] Chief of Staff Gen. Wu Shih,[101] and Hsiao Wen. These men had "influenced" Chang to protect and help Ho. But in his defense, General Chang said: "One cannot blame me for this because the Central Government in Chungking was cooperating with the Chinese Communist Party and the Soviet Union."[102] Another explanation is that Ho made a favorable impression on Chang Fa-k'uei. Chang, albeit well known for his peppery disposition, is a man who appreciates talent and ability. He viewed Ho as an "energetic and hard-working" man who had a "better knowledge" in world affairs [than other Vietnamese leaders] and who knew "Chinese, English, and French languages."[103] It was Chang's decision to include such a man and his followers in the Dong Minh Hoi so that they could cooperate with Vietnamese nationalists in a common struggle for the independence of postwar Vietnam.

Ho Chi Minh's participation in the Dong Minh Hoi did not help settle its internal quarrels and conflicts. The holding of a new conference after reorganization was first scheduled for September, then November, and finally postponed indefinitely. To Chang Fa-k'uei the lack of a new confer-

[98] Wang Chih-wu's report, September 22, 1943, in "Documents." Wang was a representative to Vietnam of the Chinese Overseas Department, and was stationed at Chinghsi.

[99] Hou's answer to the author. Hou was the director of the Dong Minh Hoi from May to December 1943.

[100] Tso Hung-tao, a Chinese Communist, became deputy secretary-general of the Kwangtung provincial government under Marshal Yeh Chien-ying (governor) in 1950.

[101] Wu Shih, a Chinese Communist, later served as deputy chief of staff of the Defense Ministry in Taipei, and was executed in 1950.

[102] Chang Fa-k'uei interview.

[103] Chang, *Memoirs*, Chap. 7. A Hanoi source said that although he disliked Ho's political views, Chang respected Ho. Hoang Quang Binh, "In Yunnan," p. 137.

ence was due mainly to the mediocre ability of its director, Hou Chih-ming, a loyal Kuomintang general who headed the political department. Partly to improve reorganization work and partly to get Ho Chi Minh involved in the organization, Chang wanted the Dong Minh Hoi out of Hou's hands. He "repeatedly" requested Chungking to appoint a well-known important man to replace Hou—himself. On a trip to Chungking for a conference in November 1943, Chang made a similar request on the grounds that Hou's prestige was "too low" for the job.[104] Chungking finally appointed Chang director and Hou deputy director, but put Hou in charge. Chang, however, was of "a different mind." He set up an office of the director and appointed Hsiao Wen to head it; then he made an "agreement" with Hou that Hou would not "inquire into this matter."[105] From January 1, 1944 on, Hsiao Wen was actually and exclusively in charge of both the Dong Minh Hoi and Ho's case.

It seems that Chang's assistance to Ho Chi Minh was well planned. Apparently it was initiated by Hsiao Wen. Only 23 days after Chang had officially become director, he decided to unleash Ho. In his report to Chungking (January 23, 1944) he commented favorably on Ho and suggested that he be allowed to return to Vietnam: "Ho Chi Minh has stayed in the Political Department [ever since his arrival]; [we] treat him with unusual politeness in order to convert him. Judging by his conversations and writings, he seems to have a good knowledge of *San Min Chu I* and understands well [our] resist-Japan policy. Being fifty, he is mature in thought. He claims that the Vietnam Branch of the International Anti-Aggression Association which he represents has the support of 200,000 people. . . . It seems that to let him continue to stay in China will not benefit us, and that to let him go back to Vietnam does us no harm."[106]

---

[104] As restated in Wu Tieh-ch'eng's letter, November 8, 1943, in "Documents."

[105] Hou's letter to the author.

[106] Chang Fa-k'uei's report, dated January 23, 1944, in "Documents."

Chungking did not veto Chang's suggestion, but Ho was not immediately released to go back to Vietnam, primarily because of strong opposition from the leaders of the Dong Minh Hoi.[107] To maintain Vietnamese unity, Chang delayed Ho's return.

Soon the preparatory work for the reorganization of the Dong Minh Hoi was completed. A meeting called the "Congress of Overseas Revolutionary Groups of the Dong Minh Hoi" was held from March 25 to 28, 1944; it was known as a reunification conference. The delegates were Truong Boi Cong, Nguyen Hai Than, Vu Hong Khanh, Nghiem Ke To, Truong Trung Phung, Tran Bao, Nong Kinh Du, Bo Xuan Luat, Tran Dinh Xuyen, Le Tung Son, Nguyen Tuong Tam, Nguyen Thanh Dong, Ho Duc Thanh, Ho Chi Minh, and Pham Van Dong. Totaling 15, they represented the Executive Committee of the Dong Minh Hoi (7), the Vietnam Special Training Class (3), the Association for the Liberation of Vietnam in Kunming (1), the Vietnam Liberation League in Lungchow (1), the Dai Viet Party (1), Vietnamese members of the Special Detachment in Nanning (1), and the Vietnam branch of the International Anti-Aggression Association (1).[108] The conference was punctuated by violent debates, particularly between the Nationalist and Communist delegates. According to Hsiao Wen's later report to the Kuomintang in Nanking, Ho spoke energetically in urging the "unification of all the parties and groups" and stressed that he would carry out the conference's resolutions to enter northern and central Vietnam.[109] The meeting passed resolutions and elected seven new executive members—Truong Boi Cong, Truong Trung Phung, Tran Bao,

[107] Tran Dan Tien, *Biography of Ho Chi Minh*, p. 126.

[108] Report of the Director of the Dong Minh Hoi, dated December 23, 1943, in "Documents." The Overseas Executive Department of the VNQDD reported on January 20, 1945 that this conference included (1) delegates from nationalist groups, (2) nonparty individuals, and (3) delegates from Communist groups. The report is in *ibid*. Devillers, *Histoire du Viet-Nam*, p. 109, names 13 of the above 15; Tran Bao and Nong Kinh Du were not included.

[109] Report of Hsiao Wen on November 1, 1946, in "Documents."

Bo Xuan Luat, Nghiem Ke To, Le Tung Son, and Tran Dinh Xuyen—and three control members—Nguyen Hai Than, Vu Hong Khanh, and Nong Kinh Du. Ho Chi Minh was given an alternate executive membership.[110] The following table indicates the party affiliation of the 11 new members:

TABLE 1

PARTY AFFILIATION OF THE 11 ELECTED MEMBERS OF THE DONG MINH HOI, MARCH 1944

Name	Affiliation
Vu Hong Khanh	VNQDD
Nghiem Ke To	VNQDD
Truong Trung Phung	VNQDD
Tran Bao	VNQDD, Independence Party
Truong Boi Cong	military
Nguyen Hai Than	old revolutionist
Bo Xuan Luat	Phuc Quoc
Tran Dinh Xuyen	Phuc Quoc
Nong Kinh Du	Phuc Quoc
Le Tung Son	ICP
Ho Chi Minh	ICP

Sources: see note 110.

Three important conclusions can be drawn from Table 1. First, the dominant influence still seemed to be that of the VNQDD; but among the four VNQDD leaders, only Vu

[110] Hsing Shen-chou, "Report on Vietnam," April 1944, in *ibid.* Also consult Tran Dan Tien, *Biography of Ho Chi Minh*, pp. 125-26. Ho, during his stay in China (1942-45), was never made "chief of the Dong Minh Hoi," nor was Nguyen Hai Than, as some writers have asserted. Than, however, was unhappy with the outcome of this election; Nguyen Tuong Tam (a Dai Viet leader who was jailed briefly by Chang Fa-k'uei prior to this conference because of his pro-Japanese attitude) was not even elected. From that time on, the two men were close friends, which explains why Nguyen Tuong Tam was made Foreign Minister in the 1946 Viet-Minh government, of which Nguyen Hai Than was named Vice-President.

Hong Khanh and Nghiem Ke To were diehards. Second, the membership of the Phuc Quoc was increased, as was its influence, due to the fact that the Phuc Quoc had substantial support from the 500 young officers in the Special Vietnam Training Class at Tachiao. If a Chinese or Allied military operation in Vietnam was to be carried out, these officers would certainly be the first to be called to duty. Third, the ICP's position was not strong, yet it made its influence felt. This was obviously a result of Chang Fa-k'uei's planning. With the able Le Tung Son on the executive Committee the ICP was soon to "turn the enemy's organization" into its own, which was what Ho Chi Minh had planned to do.[111]

It has been reported that at this time the Dong Minh Hoi, under the direction of Chang Fa-k'uei, had set up in Liuchow a Provisional Republican Government of Vietnam headed by Truong Boi Cong, and that Ho Chi Minh was merely given a ministerial post.[112] According to Chang, the Dong Minh Hoi had never established such a regime under him, nor had there ever been a provisional government in Liuchow.[113] However, there were attempts to institute such a government by another group of Vietnamese. Chinese sources show that this group in Liuchow headed by Vo Phi (Vo Bang Duc), a man with a vague background, submitted reports to the Chinese authorities in Liuchow and Chungking, claiming establishment of a preparatory committee for a provisional government of Annam, and requesting Chinese aid. They promised that once they were granted Chinese loans, which they "guaranteed" with future taxes and railroad incomes, they would immediately establish a provisional government and organize a strong army.[114] Vo Phi later used an "official" seal engraved with Chinese characters of the "Annam Republic" in requesting and soliciting

[111] Hoang Quang Binh, "In Yunnan," p. 135.
[112] Devillers, *Histoire*, p. 109; Fall, *Two Viet-Nams*, p. 100.
[113] Chang Fa-k'uei interview.
[114] Report of the Preparatory Committee for the Republican National Government of Annam, November 4, 1942, in "Documents."

financial support.[115] The Chinese at first suspected the group's activities and later jailed some of its members in Nanning on charges of swindling.[116] The so-called Vietnam Provisional Government never came into being. The Vo Phi group was only a few Vietnamese drifting in China during the war without any significant political belief or action.

CHANG FA-K'UEI's effort to direct the reorganization of the Dong Minh Hoi had two objectives. One was to help the Vietnamese revolutionists achieve their independence. The other was to prepare for China's future military advance into Vietnam in collaboration with the Allied forces. It was the "expectation of a great plan" of Chang Fa-k'uei that the Vietnamese revolutionary forces would be mobilized to cooperate with the Chinese from within Vietnam in a joint effort against Japan.[117] Previous suggestions for an Allied military operation in Indochina had been made in the United States and in China. In the United States the suggestion was first presented in late 1941 by Lt.Gen. Hugh A. Drum who was the first candidate for a mission to China. Drum found that he and Secretary of War Stimson were "in accord about the desirability of a thrust across Thailand and Indochina to take the Hanoi-Haiphong area and open a supply line to China."[118] His plan, however, did not meet with the approval of Gen. George C. Marshall and he was not chosen to go to China. A second suggestion was submitted by Gen. Joseph W. Stilwell in July 1942, recommending attacks on Burma and Indochina by an Allied force based in China or India. In the Burma attack a force

[115] Report of the Overseas Department of the KMT, April 4, 1943, in *ibid.*

[116] Chang Fa-k'uei interview with author, and his report, February 3, 1944, in "Documents."

[117] Chang Fa-k'uei, *Memoirs*, Chap. 7.

[118] General Drum thought that his suggestion was, "a plan of operations, mainly American, from without China to within China for the purpose of securing adequate lines of supply by which to build up in China a theater with adequate bases, air and ground, from which to attack Japan." See Charles F. Romanus and Riley Sunderland, *Stilwell's Mission to China* (Washington, D.C.: Department of the Army, 1953), pp. 67-68.

composed of one United States division, three British divisions, two Chinese divisions from India, and 12 Chinese divisions from Yunnan, would attack Burma and aim for Rangoon. In the Indochina attack a force of nine Chinese divisions would advance from Yunnan and Kwangsi and head for Hanoi and Haiphong.[119] The Indochina part of Stilwell's plan was not carried out although the Burma part was, in 1943.

In China the Kweilin Office of the Military Council under Li Chi-shen drafted in the fall of 1940 a military plan for Vietnam to which Vo Nguyen Giap gave a helping hand. One month after the Cairo conference of November 1943[120] Gen. Chang Fa-k'uei received instructions from Chungking, asking him to work out a plan for "entering Vietnam" and to begin preparation for such an undertaking. This Chang did immediately. According to the plan three armies were to advance into Vietnam. One army would move from Chinghsi to Cao-Bang, then advance south together with troops coming in from Yunnan; a second army would move from Lungchow to Lang-Son; and a third would proceed from the border to northern Lang-Son. All three armies were to join at Hanoi. Meanwhile the Chinese were to encourage and assist Vietnamese revolutionaries in Vietnam to create unrest through propaganda, and to supply munitions for revolts from within.[121] To achieve genuine cooperation from the Vietnamese, Chang was anxious to include all Vietnamese forces, nationalist and Communist, in the reorganized Dong Minh Hoi; this was part of his "great plan." To make the plan more realistic and get acquainted with the terrain, he held military staff travel maneuvers along the Sino-Vietnamese border in the spring of 1944. By the end of the spring, it seemed that Chang's plan was well

[119] *Ibid.*, p. 183.
[120] At the Cairo conference President Roosevelt offered Indochina to Generalissimo Chiang Kai-shek. See the discussion below in this chapter.
[121] Chang Fa-k'uei, *Memoirs*, Chap. 7.

underway, and the possibility of an Allied military operation looked good.

The French were emphatically opposed to a Chinese military advance into Vietnam. In the early fall of 1943 rumors were abroad in Vietnam that Chinese troops would attack the Japanese in Indochina in October. The French ground forces commander, General Mordant, sent a representative to meet secretly with the head of the Chingsi office of the Fourth War Area, Ch'en Pao-ts'ang, and express the difficulty the French were having with the Japanese in Indochina, while actually warning against a Chinese attack on Vietnam.[122] In the meantime, M. H. Hoppenot, a representative of General de Gaulle's Committee of Liberation to Washington, sent a memorandum to the Department of State on October 20, 1943, expressing strong opposition to a Chinese attack on the Japanese in Tonkin because it "would have the immediate effect of causing the whole Indochinese population to rise against the Allies." He also said, "For the Annamites, the Chinese . . . represent the hereditary enemy."[123] The following day Hoppenot went to see Adolf A. Berle, Jr., Assistant Secretary of State, repeating the statement he had made the day before, saying: "If Chinese troops attacked there, plainly there would not be any support from the French. . . ."[124] But the Chinese were counting not on French support, but on Vietnamese, both nationalist and Communist. Furthermore, should such a Chinese attack take place, both the Chinese and Vietnamese, operating under Chang Fa-k'uei's "great plan," would not be sorry to see both the Japanese and the French go.

Staying in Liuchow with Hsiao Wen's protection, Ho Chi Minh must have been informed, at least partially, about what Chang was prepared to do in Vietnam. To ride the

[122] Report from Wang Chih-wu, November 4, 1943, in "Documents."

[123] Department of State, *Foreign Relations of the United States, Diplomatic Papers, 1943, China* (Washington, D.C., 1957), pp. 882-83.

[124] *Ibid.*, pp. 883-87 passim.

mounting tide of China's interest in Vietnam, Ho seemed to have employed dual tactics in dealing with the Chinese. On the one hand, he appeared to be very cooperative, sincere, even obedient toward Chang and Hsiao Wen.[125] Ever since he came to Liuchow and joined the Dong Minh Hoi, Ho had cordially and frequently sought advice on various problems from Hsiao Wen,[126] completed his translation of *San Min Chu I* into Vietnamese, and was soon to present his "Outline of the Plan for Activities of Entering Vietnam."[127] On the other hand, he exhibited—albeit merely by claiming—his strength in Vietnam, and persuaded the Chinese to work step by step in his favor against other Vietnamese groups, particularly the VNQDD. In this respect, Ho had convinced Chang and Hsiao of his party's overwhelming support (200,000 people), had inserted ICP influence into the Dong Minh Hoi, and now, through Hsiao Wen, was to make ICP members in Kunming share the leadership of a reorganized Yunnan branch of the Dong Minh Hoi and strike a blow against diehard VNQDD groups.

ICP-VNQDD rivalry in Yunnan was an old issue. The ICP never cooperated with the VNQDD in founding a Dong Minh Hoi branch there. And the situation had changed, because now Ho Chi Minh and Le Tung Son, the leaders of the ICP, had joined forces and were sharing minor leadership of the Dong Minh Hoi in Liuchow. It was decided at the reunification congress of the Dong Minh Hoi in Liuchow in March that the original VNQDD-led Dong Minh Hoi branch in Yunnan and the Association for the Liberation of Vietnam (the ICP's association)[128] should be reorganized into a new Yunnan branch of the Dong Minh Hoi.

[125] Chang interview with author. Chang said that Ho was cooperative and always accepted Chinese advice or demands.

[126] Liu San, "Ho Chi Minh in South China."

[127] See the discussion below.

[128] Chinese sources give differing names for this association—"Association of Vietnamese People for Liberation," "Association for the Liberation of Vietnam"; the latter is the same as that given by Hanoi. See Pham Van Dong, *President Ho*, p. 73.

Preparatory reorganization work began in April and was ready for the conference by early June. The Committee members reported to Director Chang Fa-k'uei who sent Hsiao Wen, in the capacity of the head of the Office of the Director, to Kunming to supervise the meeting.[129] The conference was held on July 2, 1944 at the Vietnam Club in Kunming. Attention was obviously focused on the election of new officers. Both the original Dong Minh Hoi branch and the Association nominated six candidates apiece. The election was another power struggle between the VNQDD and ICP. The result was election of five executive members, of which the ICP elements controlled three, and three control members, of which the VNQDD had two.[130] A table below shows the party affiliation and strength of the eight elected members:

TABLE 2

PARTY AFFILIATION OF EIGHT ELECTED MEMBERS OF THE YUNNAN BRANCH OF THE DONG MINH HOI, JULY 1944

Name	Affiliation
Pham Viet Tu (Standing Exec.)	ICP
Ly Dao (Standing Exec.)	ICP
Pham Minh Ton (Exec.)	ICP
Duong Tu Giang (Standing Exec.)	VNQDD*
Dang Dinh Cuong (Exec.)	VNQDD
Ha Thanh Dai (Control)	VNQDD
Ly Xuan Lam (Control)	VNQDD
Duong Bao Son (Control)	ICP

* Soon joined ICP.
Source: see note 130.

In Table 2 one can easily see that the ICP had gained the upper hand. They occupied two seats on the three-man

[129] Chang Fa-k'uei's letter to Wu Tieh-ch'eng, June 6, 1944, in "Documents."

[130] Report of the Office of the Director of the Dong Minh Hoi, August 7, 1944, in "Documents."

Standing Executive Committee and three seats on the five-man Executive Committee, which was more powerful and active than the Control Committee. Furthermore, the only VNQDD Standing Executive member, Duong Tu Giang, soon left the VNQDD to join the ICP. Consequently the ICP, in effect, now controlled the reorganized Yunnan branch.

The incident involving Duong Tu Giang brought more troubles for the VNQDD. Giang had earlier secretly negotiated with a British liaison officer named Whitehead in Kunming for cooperation from the British. The British agreed to exchange money and weapons for VNQDD political and military intelligence.[131] For one reason or another, the agreement was revealed by Giang in the summer of 1944. The revelation angered party leader Nghiem Ke To, who dismissed Giang. The ICP took advantage of the situation by asking Giang to join their association, which Giang did. To doublecross Nghiem Ke To, Giang showed the VNQDD-British negotiation documents to Hsiao Wen, and said that "the VNQDD collaborated with the British-French imperialists." Hsiao did not like the "British-French imperialists" nor Nghiem Ke To, who had opposed the reorganization of the Yunnan branch. On August 4, 1944 Hsiao arbitrarily had Nghiem Ke To and his assistant, Vo Quang Pham, arrested at Tunghsing, where they were working for the Dong Minh Hoi. Hsiao also threatened to arrest Vu Hong Khanh and his associates.[132] The Kuomintang in Chungking immediately ordered Hsiao to release To and not to go any further.[133] But To and his followers were not released until December after the Japanese attacked Liuchow.[134] Hsiao Wen's action was probably designed to weaken the VNQDD; the arrest of Nghiem Ke To

[131] Report from Hsing Shen-chou, September 1, 1944, in "Documents."

[132] Nghiem Ke To's report, January 30, 1945, in *ibid*; and Vu Hong Khanh's letter of May 30, 1969.

[133] Letter of the Central Secretariat of the Kuomintang to Hsing Shen-chou, October 21, 1944, in *ibid*.

[134] Nghiem Ke To's letter to the author, March 31, 1969.

was merely a means to that end. In any event, after the two capable VNQDD leaders, Nghiem Ke To and Vu Hong Khanh, had been disgraced by Hsiao Wen, the influence of the VNQDD in the Dong Minh Hoi declined, while that of the Phuc Quoc and ICP increased. Hsiao Wen's high-handed arbitrary action against the VNQDD and his tight control over the Dong Minh Hoi caused, in To's words, "unspoken grievances" to many Vietnamese.[135]

Five days after Nghiem Ke To was arrested by Hsiao Wen (August 9, 1944), Ho Chi Minh was set free by Chang Fa-k'uei and allowed to return to Vietnam. Two important questions about these events are: (1) What was the significance of the timing of Ho's release and return to Vietnam? (2) What did Ho actually offer Chang for his freedom?

To the first question, the answer can be found in three aspects. First, Chang Fa-k'uei had decided as early as January 1944 to permit Ho to go back to Vietnam. He delayed Ho's departure because of the opposition of some members of the Dong Minh Hoi in Liuchow. With Ho's participation in the reorganized Dong Minh Hoi, and particularly with the disgrace of the VNQDD leaders, the rest of the Dong Minh Hoi officers were no longer in a position to openly and effectively oppose Ho's return. Second, Ho had laid the foundation in the Liuchow and Kunming organizations of the Dong Minh Hoi for "turning the enemy's organization into our organization," and had realized that the VNQDD leaders had been dealt a blow by the Chinese. If there was to be an Allied military operation in Vietnam requiring the cooperation of the Dong Minh Hoi, Ho's men were ready. Third, a Japanese attack on Kweilin and Liuchow was imminent[136] after the loss of Hengyang, an important city in the defense of Kweilin, to the Japanese on August 8, 1944. To reduce his burden in the impending battle, Chang simply carried out his earlier decision to let Ho go.

[135] Nghiem Ke To's report, January 30, 1945, in "Documents."
[136] Chang Fa-k'uei recalls that the Japanese attack actually began on September 2, 1944; see Chang, *Memoirs*, Chap. 8.

The second question—what Ho had offered Chang for his release—is a controversial one. Philippe Devillers, basing his conclusions on interviews with Vietnamese then living in China, wrote that Ho was released from the prison and sent back home because of his promise to send intelligence information to China from Vietnam.[137] A West German source asserts that Ho was released at the request of American representatives in Chungking.[138] In the Chinese file, Ho did submit to Chang an "Outline of the Plan for the Activities of Entering Vietnam," offering his collaboration with future Chinese and Allied military operations in Vietnam and projecting a detailed plan for revolutionary activity. It is my contention that Ho for the third time in his career employed his old tactic—offering to serve his "enemy" for the return of his freedom—to get permission to leave China. The first time, he reportedly offered to serve as an agent provocateur in France for the French Sûreté in the years after the First World War.[139] The second time, in 1932, Ho promised to work for the British police force in Hong Kong.

In Ho's "Outline," which was reported to Chungking by Chang Fa-k'uei on August 9 (the date Ho left Liuchow), there were seven major sections.[140] In the first section Ho claimed that his plan was for the following purposes:

(1) to spread the determination of the Chinese government in helping [achieve] national liberation of Viet-Nam

(2) expand the organization and strength of the Viet-Nam Cach Menh Dong Minh Hoi

(3) prepare for collaboration from within with Chinese and other Allied troops entering Viet-Nam

(4) strive for the complete independence and freedom of Viet-Nam

[137] Devillers, *Histoire*, p. 105.
[138] As cited by Fall, *Two Viet-Nams*, p. 99.
[139] *Ibid.*, p. 89.
[140] Ho Chi Minh, "Outline of the Plan for the Activities of Entering Vietnam," in "Documents." See also Chang Fa-k'uei interview.

Ho had skillfully placed China's interests above Vietnam's. The first item implied that the Chinese, not the French nor the Japanese, were the true friends of the Vietnamese, and therefore a closer Sino-Vietnamese relationship was intended. The second seemed to suggest that Ho would remain loyal only to the Dong Minh Hoi and would not expand the strength or organization of either the Viet Minh or ICP. The third met China's (and the Allies') needs, just as Chang Fa-k'uei had expected. The fourth seemingly put Vietnam's final goal after Chinese interests, but it also indicated that what Ho was truly fighting for was the *complete* independence of his country—a word not used by any other Dong Minh Hoi leader.

The second major section was a five-point program of activities that Ho was to carry out:

(1) to lead a group of cadres secretly to the Vietnam border area that parallels an area running from Lung-chow to P'ingmeng; look into the situation and prepare for activity

(2) secretly set up a short-term training class at Tungh-sing to train a group of reliable and able men in the methods and techniques of revolutionary activities

(3) send a group of trained personnel into Vietnam to propagandize secretly and openly (when armed), in order to mobilize the people

(4) unite with political parties and groups in Vietnam and urge them to join the Dong Minh Hoi; prepare for a national congress, and engage in practical revolutionary activity

(5) establish guerrilla bases [and forces]

These points constituted a specific and practicable program of preparation, training, propaganda, and organization.

To initiate the first item, Ho asked 18 young Vietnamese, in the Border Work Team or the Special Training Class, to go back with him.[141] Possibly able and pro-Communist,

[141] The 18 were: Duong Van Loc, Vi Van Ton, Hoang Quang Trao, Hoang Kim Lien, Pham Van Minh, Hoang Si Vinh, Nong Van Muu,

these men had undergone three years of training under Chang Fa-k'uei; then they were turned over to Ho. They were not necessarily "sold out," but the move was certainly a success for Ho. Furthermore, the border area proposed by Ho obviously was suggested with the idea of using it as his sanctuary in case of emergency. In such a redoubt Ho's forces, once established, could not be wiped out by the French or the Japanese operating out of Indochina.

Under item 2 Ho proposed that the short-term training class at Tunghsing should be limited to 15 men for a period of 15 days. The training would include quality and qualification for revolution; propaganda methods; organization techniques; and how to maintain secrecy. The funds for training were to be shared by the Chinese and the Vietnamese revolutionaries (Ho's followers).

As for the third item, Ho added that propaganda personnel should above all be those who had been trained; then they could recruit others. They must operate both secretly and openly. To propagandize publicly, the men must be equipped with arms, the more the better. If necessary, a propaganda team would organize and lead acts of sabotage. In this respect, we now see that Ho's establishment of the armed-propaganda unit in December 1944—the forerunner of the Liberation Army of North Vietnam today—was a plan Ho had conceived before he returned to Vietnam in August 1944.

In the important fourth item Ho listed the parties and groups with whom he would cooperate after he returned: the VNQDD, ICP, Constitutional Party, Viet-Minh, Youth Anti-Imperialist League, Women's Liberation Organization, and the national salvation organizations for the peasants, workers, and students. He excluded the Royalist and Dai Viet Parties; presumably the former was against Ho's principle of establishing a democratic republic and the latter

---

Hoang Gia Tien, Truong Huu Chi, Le Nguyen, Hoang Nhan, Nong Kim Thanh, Hoang Thanh Thuy, Ha Hien Minh, Le Van Tien, Duong Van Le, Do Trong Vien, Do Lac.

was pro-Japanese. On the surface, it looked like there were nine different parties and groups Ho would invite to join with the Dong Minh Hoi. Actually there were only two, the VNQDD and the Constitutional Party, that held a different political faith from the Viet-Minh; the rest were either ICP, Viet-Minh, or their front organizations. Should these nine groups join the Dong Minh Hoi, Ho would undoubtedly be able to control the entire organization.

Perhaps the most important and intriguing proposal was Ho's fifth item, to establish guerrilla bases and forces. He suggested the building of two medium-sized bases in the Sino-Vietnamese border area. The bases were to be fairly close together so they could cooperate easily. Each would have a guerrilla unit of 300 guns (carbines and pistols); in addition, several platoons totaling 400 guns would be organized for hit-and-run attacks in wartime and propaganda in time of peace. Ho asked for a large amount of weapons and medicine: 1,000 guns (short hand-operated automatic) and ammunition, 4,000 grenades, 6 machineguns, and 15,000 quinine tablets. He promised to build strong bases within six months after receiving the weapons, explaining in detail why he wanted small weapons and only 1,000 of them—for secrecy and portability.

All of the above proposals would not work without money. Ho asked for 50,000 Chinese dollars and 25,900 piasters without specific explanation. The amount was not large; Ho had realized he needed to be realistic, and had deliberately made the request small. Finally, he made several requests on his own: (1) a letter from Director Chang Fa-k'uei to all patriotic parties and groups; (2) a certificate of appointment of Ho's mission from the Dong Minh Hoi; (3) a military map of Vietnam; (4) a travel permit (with a longer time limit);[142] (5) propaganda materials such as "The Records of Japanese Atrocity"; (6) a pistol for self-defense; and (7) some money for traveling expenses.

It is now clear that Ho did not offer to provide Chang

---

[142] This request could have been made after the bitter experience of his arrest in Chinghsi in 1942 because of an outdated travel permit.

Fa-k'uei with military intelligence from Vietnam. His offer to collaborate with Chinese and other Allied troops was a promise for future operation that looked doubtful at the time. Ho pinned his hopes on achieving a guerrilla force with more than two bases and 1,000 guns.[143] If this request were rejected completely, Ho could still attain a minimum achievement—safe passage from Chang Fa-k'uei. And the certificate of appointment by the Dong Minh Hoi, another item he surely could get, would also serve as a helpful tool in Ho's organization and consolidation of patriotic forces in Vietnam.

According to Gen. Chang Fa-k'uei, before Ho left Liuchow he was granted a travel permit, certificate, Chang's letter, a military map, propaganda materials, medicine, and 76,000 Chinese dollars (for travel expenses, subsidies, and a training fund).[144] Although Chang Fa-k'uei never provided Ho with the weapons and munitions he had requested, Ho had obtained considerably more than the minimum. Furthermore, the 18 men were turned over to him.

Before he left Liuchow on August 9, Ho said to Chang: "I am a Communist, but my present concern is for Vietnam's freedom and independence, not for Communism. I give you a special assurance: Communism will not work in Vietnam in fifty years."[145] This statement was apparently intended to fool Chang. Above all, who would really care during the wartime what happened to Vietnam in 50 years?

To Hsiao Wen Ho expressed gratitude for his assistance, and said: "What I have told you [about Vietnam and the Vietnamese revolutionary movement] is 99 per cent true; there is only one per cent that I did not tell you." What was the one per cent? Ho did not elaborate nor did Hsiao ask.

---

[143] A guerrilla unit with more than 1,000 operable guns was not a small force to begin with. When Mao Tse-tung organized his peasant guerrilla force at Chingkanshan in 1927, he had only about 1,000 men with a few hundred old guns!

[144] Report of Chang Fa-k'uei, August 9, 1944, in "Documents"; and Chang interview with author.

[145] Chang, *Memoirs*, Chap. 7.

It was one of the things Ho kept secret from Hsiao.[146] But Hsiao thought it might concern the identity of Hoang (Vuong) Quoc Tuan, the leader of the Vietnamese Communist movement.[147]

One month after Ho had returned to Vietnam the Chinese received reports confirming that he was the famous Nguyen Ai Quoc, but this confirmation did not cause Chang Fa-k'uei to regret releasing Ho. Basically there are three aspects of Chang's motives, defense, and release of Ho. First, Chang's attitude toward Ho was formulated mainly by his pro-Communist staff, particularly Hsiao Wen. Because of his left-of-center political line, Chang had tolerated some Communists and Communist sympathizers serving at his headquarters. This was what I learned in Liuchow in 1943.[148] and what was borne out by Gen. Hou Chi-ming's account. A policy established by those who served with the Communist regime in Kwangtung immediately after its establishment would undoubtedly work in Ho's favor. It is not surprising,

[146] Maintaining secrecy has become a habit with Ho, which he himself has admitted. When he talked to Bernard Fall in July 1962 in Hanoi, Ho said he liked "to have a little air of mystery" about himself. See *Ho Chi Minh on Revolution*, ed. Bernard B. Fall (Frederick Praeger, 1967), p. 354.

[147] Liu San, "Ho Chi Minh in South China."

[148] It seemed that to influence Chang Fa-k'uei and Li Chi-shen was a strategy of the Chinese Communist Party, though there was no evidence to verify this. The author got this impression by learning from some officers at the political department in Liuchow and from a friend, Liang Chia (Liang Ching-fu, a disguised Communist), who taught at the Chung-cheng High School established by Gen. Liang Hua-shen (director of the political department until May 1943) and who had close friends serving as aides to Chang. There had been much talk in the political department, such as "Tien Han has come to Liuchow," "The Commander-in-Chief [Chang Fa-k'uei] is now also for a new democratic government in a post-war China," "Li Chi-shen has made great progress and is now reading Tolstoy's *War and Peace*," and others. Liang Chia became an instructor at Kweichow University in 1944, and worked in Chungking under Sun Fo in early 1945. Late in 1945, after Japan had surrendered, he became a political commissar of a Chinese Communist guerrilla unit (division level) in Kwangtung. His political news might well be a reflection of CCP's strategy for Chang Fa-k'uei and Li Chi-shen in the later years of the war.

therefore, that Chang appeared to be a defender and helper of Ho. Second, Chang intended to use Ho, rather than the other Dong Minh Hoi leaders, to fulfill the "expectation" of his "great plan." Because of the proximity of his War Area to Vietnam and his frequent contacts with Vietnamese emigrés, Chang was probably the only leader during the war who ever thought of or made known the problem of future collaboration between Vietnamese revolutionists and Chinese troops. As the Allied forces steadily advanced in Europe and the Pacific, Chang's plans and preparation for entering Vietnam were in readiness.[149] If the plan became reality, the only Vietnamese force that could cooperate with the Chinese would not be the nationalists of the Dong Minh Hoi, who had no mass support, but that of Ho Chi Minh. With his "Outline" and his determination to return to Vietnam, Ho impressed Chang (and Hsiao) that he could move effectively. Therefore his position overshadowed that of any other Dong Minh Hoi leader. As Hsiao Wen said in replying to questions at a Kuomintang discussion meeting in 1946, Ho was the only one among the Dong Minh Hoi leaders who could carry out the organization's resolution to return to Vietnam from China at that difficult time.[150] Thus Chang's original hope for the fulfillment of his great plan by the Vietnamese shifted from the nationalists to Ho Chi Minh. Third, Chang expected postwar China to remain a Kuomintang-led nation, asserting that if Vietnam could obtain her independence through Chinese aid, "an independent Vietnam, under Ho or otherwise, will be a friendly nation to China and under China's influence."[151]

Ho sought to capitalize on Chang's (China's) interest in Vietnam. In doing so, he dealt only with Chang and Hsiao. Ho had assessed the political situation in Liuchow and endeavored to take advantage of it. His efforts, including

[149] Chang, *Memoirs*, Chap. 8.

[150] Hsiao Wen's replies to questions on Vietnam raised by the Secretariat of the KMT, November 1, 1946, in "Documents."

[151] Chang interview. Devillers, *Histoire*, p. 109, argues that an independent Vietnam receiving Chinese aid would in effect be a Chinese satellite.

the translation of *San Min Chu I*, the participation of the Dong Minh Hoi, and the submission of his Outline, were intended to influence Chang and Hsiao. Ho had convinced the Chinese general and his aide that he would be cooperative, even obedient. In his association with the Dong Minh Hoi, Ho deliberately set out to "turn the enemy's organization" into his own. Here, Ho was using the same tactic the Comintern had used in China in 1924-1927 to secure KMT-CCP cooperation: "Ally but do not merge, cooperate but prepare to fight."[152] His promise to collaborate in the future with Chinese and other Allied troops in Vietnam was made in the hope that they would expel the French puppet regime and the Japanese invader from his country. By now there was a lot of talk among the French in Indochina that the Americans were going to land troops on the Indochinese coast as they had in North Africa.[153] Ho must have learned of the rumor from home. To pave the way for such a historic collaboration, it was necessary to cooperate in advance with the Chinese, who were prepared to bring Ho's forces to the Allied side. Ho well knew that Chang was using him, yet Ho was also using Chang. Who would exploit whom the most was a matter that only time could tell. Up to this point, however, one thing was certain: Ho had succeeded in changing his status from that of a prisoner to an ally!

4. Tonkin, Kunming, and Paise, 1944-1945

When Ho Chi Minh left Liuchow in August 1944, he took 16 young Vietnamese with him. They crossed into northern Vietnam (Tonkin) from Chinghsi on September 20.[154] Pham Van Dong (alias Lam Ba Kiet) and Vo Nguyen Giap (alias Duong Hoai Nam) came to Chinghsi to welcome Ho.[155] In

[152] Whiting, *Soviet Policies*, p. 50.

[153] Ellen J. Hammer, *The Struggle for Indochina* (Stanford: Stanford University Press, 1954), p. 35.

[154] Report of Hsing Shen-chou, September 25, 1944, in "Documents." In his Outline Ho had requested 18 men. Apparently Hsing did not know of Ho's request, and therefore gave no reason for the number 16.

[155] Liu San, "Ho Chi Minh in South China." Giap stated, "Ho Chi

his Outline Ho had estimated 15 days for the journey to Lungchow. Given five extra days for his trip from Lung-chow to Chinghsi and Tonkin, he spent 20 additional days in the whole journey, presumably for meetings with his men in Lungchow and Chinghsi, and the training class in Tungh-sing, as he had suggested.

In the absence of Ho Chi Minh from September 1942 to September 1944, the Viet-Minh, under the de facto leader-ship of Pham Van Dong and Vo Nguyen Giap, had made progress in their armed forces and in the occupied areas. Like all Communist rebels, the Viet-Minh engaged in dual struggle of legal and illegal activities, open and under-ground movements according to circumstances. Meanwhile, they were active in the Sino-Vietnamese border area. According to Chinese files, the main Viet-Minh leaders active in the border area were Vo Nguyen Giap, Pham Van Dong, Hoang Van Hoan, Hoang Quoc Hon, Le Quang Ba, and Tran Son Hong; in Lungchow were Tran Thieu Hung and Bui Quoc Thanh.[156] Their propaganda among the Viet-namese claimed that they were true patriots and that those who sought foreign assistance (Chinese aid) were "Viet Gian" (traitors to Vietnam).[157] Yet they themselves, led by Ho Chi Minh, solicited Chinese and later American assist-ance. One Chinese source states that in the fall of 1943 Hoang Quoc Hon, Le Quang Ba, and Tran Son Hong went to Ko-ma and P'ing-meng (two small Chinese border towns) to promote Communism and purchase at a high price arms and ammunition. Some men were persuaded to partici-pate in their activities, and a local bandit leader, Huang Ya-ch'ang, joined them.[158] In northern Tonkin they urged the Vietnamese to associate with the Viet-Minh, gained sup-port from the people, and enlarged their control in the area.

Minh," p. 179, that he and Vu Anh were selected to welcome Ho at Pac-Bo.

[156] Report of the Overseas Department, KMT, March 15, 1943, in "Documents."

[157] *Ibid.*, April 24, 1943.

[158] Wang Chih-wu's report, September 22, 1943, in "Documents."

They did this with persuasion when the people were responsive and coercion when they resisted.[159]

According to Vo Nguyen Giap, their program picked up momentum.[160] After Ho had left for China in 1942, their southern activity continued; the farther south they went the more youthful support they gained. Soon they met Chu Van Tan's force[161] and a company of the Bac-Son Salvation Army. Wherever they went they established local organizations and armed units. By the end of 1943 they had established transportation and communication lines in the Cao-Bac-Lang area and laid the foundation for an advance into the plains.

But the French immediately moved to block the Viet-Minh's progress. Beginning in early 1944 "white terror," as Giap called it, was imposed on the people in northern Tonkin. A considerable number of guerrilla fighters and Viet-Minh supporters were killed, and the Viet-Minh temporarily retreated underground.[162] But the will to resist grew stronger in hiding. Meanwhile, among the French, with the Allied forces advancing steadily in Europe and Asia by July 1944, the hope of restoring their prewar position in Indochina grew. If the Allies could land a force on the Indochinese coast, the French were prepared to cooperate with them against the Japanese.[163] French-Japanese antagonism was becoming more apparent each day. Under these circumstances, it seemed to the Viet-Minh leaders that the time for a large-scale uprising had come. In July they held a cadre conference, convened by the Cao-Bac-Lang Inter-Provincial Committee, to discuss the question of armed revolt exclusively. After an emotional and enthusi-

[159] Hsing Shen-chou's report on Vietnam for the latter half of 1944, in *ibid.*

[160] Giap, "Ho Chi Minh," pp. 176-77.

[161] Chu Van Tan's force was one of the gangs in the border area that merged with the Viet-Minh army. Tan was the first national defense minister in Ho's regime, and is now a vice-chairman of the Standing Committee of the National Assembly in Hanoi.

[162] Giap, "Ho Chi Minh," pp. 177-78; Report of the Overseas Department, KMT, August 9, 1944, in "Documents."

[163] Hammer, *Struggle for Indochina*, pp. 34-35.

astic discussion, they decided to launch an insurrection in Cao-Bang province.[164] A second meeting was to be held to discuss the practical, specific problems involved, such as timing, long-term guerrilla warfare, regaining lost territory. At this juncture came the news of Ho's return, and the meeting was postponed until his arrival.

At the second meeting Ho studied the situation and made two decisions. One was his veto over the decision about the Cao-Bang insurrection. The other was to establish an armed propaganda unit. Concerning his first decision, Ho explained that the insurrection would be based only on the situation in the provinces of Cao-Bang, Bac-Can and Lang-Son, and not on that of the country as a whole, that there were no insurrection units in other parts of the country which could take part in the immediate future, and that if the insurrection were launched under these conditions the "imperialists" would concentrate their forces for swift retaliation. Ho's assessment of their strategy was: "The period of peaceful development of the revolution is now over. However, the time for general insurrection of the entire people has not yet come. Therefore, if our activity is limited to the political sphere only, it will not be strong enough to advance the movement. But if the general insurrection is launched immediately, we will be driven to a deadlock by the enemy. The struggle has moved from a purely political form to a military one, but for the time being the political form is still more important than the military one."[165]

As for his second decision, Ho thought the setting up of an armed propaganda unit meant that political activities were more important than military activities, and that fighting was less important than propaganda. Since resistance was to be waged by all the people, they had to mobilize and

---

[164] Giap, "Ho Chi Minh," p. 179; Pham Van Dong, *President Ho*, p. 78. Giap stated that their conclusion was: "On the basis of the situation in the world, in the country, and the situation of the revolutionary movement in Cao-Bac-Lang provinces, it can be said that conditions are ripe for starting guerrilla warfare in these provinces."
[165] Pham Van Dong, *President Ho*, p. 79; Giap, "Ho Chi Minh," p. 180.

arm the whole nation, and the propaganda unit was established for dual struggle: to propagandize in time of peace and fight in time of war.[166] This was what Ho had suggested to Chang Fa-k'uei in his Outline. As a result, a Vietnam People's Propaganda Unit for National Liberation, consisting of 34 men, was organized on December 22, 1944, under the command of Vo Nguyen Giap. It later became the core force of the scattered armed units and was one of the predecessors of the Vietnam People's Army. The unit soon went into action, and in a few days won two battles in the Cao-Bac-Lang border area.[167]

After Ho's return to Vietnam, Chungking received frequent reports on Viet-Minh activities. They indicated that the Viet-Minh appeared to be considerably more active since Ho (Nguyen Ai Quoc) had returned home, that elements of the Viet-Minh in Kunming had asked Chang Fa-k'uei for permission to go back to Vietnam, and that ICP units had clashed with French-Vietnamese forces in Cao-Bang province.[168] In its first victory, the armed propaganda unit of the Viet-Minh killed more than 70 of the enemy.[169] They meanwhile intensified their propaganda in northern Tonkin, distributing leaflets urging the Vietnamese and free French to join in expelling the French "fascists" from Vietnam.[170] Ho had proved himself an effective leader of the Viet-Minh, which had carried out precisely the strategy and tactics he had decided on.

While making good progress in his own country, Ho did

[166] Pham Van Dong, *President Ho*, pp. 79-80; Vo Nguyen Giap, *People's War, People's Army* (New York: Frederick Praeger, 1962), p. 79.

[167] Ho had told Giap that within a month of its establishment the unit had to win a military victory for propaganda purposes.

[168] Cables from Hsing Shen-chou, October 1, 16, December 1, 1944, in "Documents." The identification of Ho as Nguyen Ai Quoc was first made by Hsing in his cable of October 1, 1944.

[169] Cable of Hsing Shen-chou, January 7, 1945, in *ibid.* The Viet-Minh disguised themselves as French-Vietnamese soldiers and attacked the enemy by surprise. Giap did not account for the enemy casualties or the disguise.

[170] Cables from Hsing Shen-chou, January 14, February 18, 1945, in "Documents."

not neglect his Chinese "ally." In a letter to Hsiao Wen he showed warm friendship. Ho said he was busy and had to make frequent inspections at various places, and that his only wish was an early victory of the resistance war so that he could build a cottage (or hut) in a scenic area and enjoy a scholarly life with Hsiao Wen[171]—a nice way to fool the Chinese!

Another ally, which was paramount in Ho's mind, was the United States. Up to 1946 the Viet-Minh's goodwill toward the U.S. was unquestioned. As recalled by an American OSS (Office of Strategic Services) lieutenant who parachuted into Ho's headquarters in the Tonkin jungle in May 1945, Ho and his men had an "unrestrained affection for all Americans." Ho also seriously asked the lieutenant about the language of the American Declaration of Independence.[172] While he might not know the exact story of Indochina at the Cairo Conference in 1943, and what Franklin D. Roosevelt had proposed for his country, Ho had learned that the Allied leaders at Cairo were determined to let Korea regain her independence after the war and that Americans were concerned about the postwar fate of Indochina. His establishment of relations with the OSS in Kunming confirms this.

Before the end of his life Roosevelt pondered for at least two years the future of Indochina. Should Indochina be returned to France? Should Indochina be given to China as a victory prize? Should Indochina be given her independence, but before that be placed under international trusteeship? Characteristically Roosevelt cast aside the consideration that Indochina should be returned to the French. He wrote to Secretary Hull on January 24, 1944: "France has had the country—thirty million inhabitants—for nearly one hundred years, and the people are worse off than they were at the beginning." He was of the opinion that the people of

[171] Liu San, "Ho Chi Minh in South China." Here, in the Western sense, cottage seems to be a peasant's house; but it was a poor scholar's living and study place to the Orientals.

[172] Robert Shaplen, "The Enigma of Ho Chi Minh," *Reporter*, January 27, 1955, p. 11. Shaplen interviewed some OSS men who had either known Ho in person or communicated with him in 1944-1945.

Indochina were entitled to something better than colonial status, and told the British ambassador in Washington, Lord Halifax, the same month, "Indo-China should not go back to France."[173] At the Cairo Conference Roosevelt asked Chiang Kai-shek whether Chiang wanted Indochina. Chiang declined, saying the Indochinese "are not Chinese. They would not assimilate into the Chinese people."[174] When asked his opinion on the future of Indochina, Chiang thought Indochina should not go back to the French who, in the hundred years they had been there, had done nothing about educating the people for self-government nor improving their welfare. Roosevelt asked Chiang for his view on an independent Indochina through international trusteeship, an idea Roosevelt had thought of as early as March 1943.[175] He suggested to Chiang that a trusteeship for Indochina would consist of "a Frenchman, one or two Indochinese, and a Chinese and a Russian . . . and maybe a Filipino and an American." Chiang supported the suggestion. Later, at Teheran, Stalin also approved of the plan; but Churchill disapproved because he was worried about the effect it would have on the British colonies in Southeast Asia. Hull, who preferred continued French tutelage to trusteeship, nevertheless supported Roosevelt's view in regard to an independent Indochina.[176] As recalled by Gen. Albert C. Wedemeyer, Roosevelt, despite the disagreement with Churchill, still clung to his view a month before his death, and "was going to do everything possible to give the people in that area [Indochina] their independence."[177] De Gaulle would certainly not agree to it in 1943, although his French

[173] Cordell Hull, *The Memoirs of Cordell Hull*, 2 vols. (New York: Macmillan, 1948), Vol. II, p. 1,597.

[174] Samuel I. Rosenman, comp., *The Public Papers and Addresses of Franklin D. Roosevelt, 1944-45 Volume, Victory and the Threshold of Peace* (New York: Harper, 1950), p. 562.

[175] Roosevelt expressed this view to Anthony Eden, British Foreign Secretary, in March 1943 when Eden went to Washington for a meeting. Hull, *Memoirs*, II, p. 1,596.

[176] *Ibid.*, p. 1,598.

[177] Albert C. Wedemeyer, *Wedemeyer Reports* (New York: Henry Holt, 1958), p. 340.

Committee of National Liberation in North Africa had issued a declaration on December 8, 1943, promising "a new political status" for those Indochinese "who have affirmed their national sentiments and political responsibilities." Unless France acted quickly and effectively in regaining Indochina from the Japanese, her position there would be jeopardized. The French provisional government had encouraged the resistance movement against the Japanese in Indochina, and the French in the colony had talked much of possible American landings, but Admiral Decoux, who understood the weakness of the French forces on hand, warned the provisional government in France that any offensive against the Japanese should be avoided in order to prevent a Japanese takeover.[178] Moreover, Decoux, who realized that China was prepared to send troops into Vietnam, proposed Sino-French negotiations several times from the fall of 1944 to the spring of 1945, to the Fourth War Area headquarters and the Foreign Ministry in Chungking. He hoped that such negotiations would lead to a treaty that would include French concessions to China as well as Chinese agreement to the return of the French colonial power in Vietnam.[179] China did not accept the French proposal for negotiations.

Ho probably did not know any details of Allied planning for Indochina; but he realized that the United States was more sympathetic toward the Indochinese independence movement than the other Western Allies. He therefore hoped to obtain support from the United States, as well as from China. To prepare for an Allied military operation in his country he wanted to establish relations with the American military authorities nearby, i.e., in China. Then a golden opportunity came. In late 1944 an American aircraft was shot down over Cao-Bang and its pilot, Lieutenant Shaw, parachuted into the hills. The Viet-Minh spirited him

[178] F. C. Jones et al., *Survey of International Affairs, 1939-1946: The Far East, 1942-1946* (London: Oxford University Press, 1955), pp. 30-31.
[179] Hsiao Wen, "Report on French-Vietnamese Situations," November 1, 1946, in "Documents." For details see the next chapter.

to safety and took him to see Ho on the Sino-Vietnamese border. Ho took the opportunity to escort Shaw to Kunming. After they entered China, the Chinese warmly received the American and sent him to Kunming by plane, but did not see the need to let Ho accompany him. Ho decided to continue his trip separately.[180] With the travel permit issued by Chang Fa-k'uei, Ho, in a Chinese army uniform and accompanied by two men, made the trip as an inspection tour to several ICP cells along the railroad, as he had done in 1940. One of his men recalled that Ho stayed at I-lang for a week. He explained the Vietnamese revolutionary situation and urged his men to return home for revolutionary struggle.[181]

When Ho arrived in Kunming the American pilot had returned to the United States. But Ho got in touch with the Office of Strategic Services in that city. According to Geoffrey Moorhouse of the *Manchester Guardian*, Charles Fenn, then a captain of the OSS and now (1968) in Ireland, recalled that Ho was recruited by the OSS as one of 35 agents working with Fenn.[182] As Agent 19 with the code name of Lucius, Ho was instructed to pick up information about Japanese troops in Indochina, note trends in agriculture, and report on typhoons, floods, and other disasters. Besides this, Ho wished to see Gen. Claire L. Chennault, commander of the "Flying Tigers." Fenn took Ho to see the general who asked Ho whether the Viet-Minh would be willing to organize a rescue team in Vietnam for Allied pilots who had been shot down. Ho agreed to do so. General Chennault put Fenn in charge[183] and gave Ho a photograph signed by the general. Ho also asked for arms and ammunition from the OSS. At first the request was rejected because Ho refused to pledge that any arms he received would be used only against the Japanese and not against the French. But Ho kept on trying. As recalled by Paul L. E. Helliwell,

[180] Tran Dan Tien, *Biography of Ho Chi Minh*, pp. 128-29.
[181] Hoang Quang Binh, "In Yunnan," pp. 134-38.
[182] Moorhouse, "He Knew Ho as OSS Agent 19," in *Providence Journal* (supplied by *Los Angeles Times–Washington Post* News Service), June 26, 1968.
[183] Tran Dan Tien, *Biography of Ho Chi Minh*, p. 130.

then an OSS chief in Kunming, Ho went secretly four times to the office between late 1944 and early 1945 (Charles Fenn met Ho three times). Finally Ho was given six .38 caliber revolvers and 120 rounds of ammunition.[184]

After having made contact with General Chennault and the OSS, Ho left for Kwangsi to visit the Dong Minh Hoi. This time he went to Paise instead of Liuchow because Liuchow had fallen into Japanese hands on November 11, 1944.[185] Paise is a small but strategically important city in southwestern Kwangsi, about 80 miles east of Yunnan, 150 miles north of Vietnam, and 400 miles west of Liuchow. Chang Fa-k'uei moved his headquarters there after Kweilin and Liuchow were occupied by the Japanese. Ho saw Chang in Paise in early 1945,[186] and met there with a few Dong Minh Hoi leaders. He learned that within six months after he left Liuchow the Dong Minh Hoi had undergone great changes. The organization's leaders—Nguyen Hai Than, Truong Boi Cong, Nghiem Ke To, Vu Hong Khanh, Nong Kinh Du, and Tran Bao—had left the Fourth War Area for either Yunnan or Kweichow. The Vietnam Special Training Class had only 140 men staying in Paise. The Dong Minh Hoi had in fact ceased to function,[187] although Le Tung Son, Bo Xuan Luat, and Truong Trung Phung were still on the scene. The change was due mainly to the Chinese defeat in Kwangsi; the policy of Hsiao Wen toward the VNQDD leaders had also had an effect. One thing remained unchanged: Viet-Minh elements were still active along the border.

When the Japanese took over in Indochina on March 9, Ho Chi Minh was in China. The Chinese reaction to the

[184] Shaplen, "The Enigma of Ho Chi Minh," p. 13.
[185] Tran Dan Tien, *Biography of Ho Chi Minh*. Chang Fa-k'uei, *Memoirs*, Chap. 8. The Japanese attack on Kweilin and Liuchow began in early September 1944 and ended on November 11, when Liuchow fell. General Stilwell visited Kweilin and Liuchow during this period, which resulted in the shipment of new arms and ammunition to the Kweilin garrison.
[186] Chang interview.
[187] Hsing Shen-chou's report, December 17, 1944, in "Documents."

takeover was intensified preparation for moving into Vietnam. On March 14 Chang Fa-k'uei received orders from Chungking, to be ready for such an eventuality. Chang's plan centered on three points: (1) to fight shoulder to shoulder with the French as allies; (2) to give positive assistance to the Vietnamese revolutionaries; and (3) to let the Vietnamese revolutionaries announce their independence and establish a new regime after the expulsion of the Japanese from Vietnam.[188] In late March Gen. Ho Ying-ch'in, commander-in-chief of the Chinese army, came to Kunming from Chungking to organize two new armies for Vietnam, under the command of Generals Lu Han from Yunnan and Chang Fa-k'uei from Kwangsi, respectively. Hsiao Wen went to Kunming on March 30 to ask General Ho to let him lead an armed foreign affairs section, of which he had been the chief since its establishment, to advance into Vietnam ahead of the armies. General Ho approved his request, but gave him some advice, if not a warning, in regard to his past policy toward the VNQDD.[189]

While in China Ho Chi Minh must have learned of Chang's plan. To monopolize Chang's future aid to the Vietnamese revolutionaries, Ho attempted to turn the Dong Minh Hoi into his own organization. With the absence of most of the Dong Minh Hoi's leaders, Ho and Le Tung Son found a good opportunity to reorganize the association to meet the new situation in Vietnam. They planned to convene a new congress, and sent for five Viet-Minh delegates from Tunghsing, including Hoang Quoc Viet, Dang Viet Chau, and Duong Duc Hien. Although they failed to hold the congress because of a lack of participation by other parties, they did succeed in establishing an "Action Committee of the Dong Minh Hoi" on April 12 over the opposition of Bo Xuan Luat. Seven committee members were elected: Le Tung Son, Ting Truong Duong, Ho Chi Minh, Trinh Kiem, Hoang Quoc Viet, Nguyen Van Giang, and

[188] Report from Chang Fa-k'uei, September 17, 1946, in *ibid.* Chang did not go to Vietnam.
[189] Yeh Hsiu-feng's report, May 26, 1945, in *ibid.*

Bo Xuan Luat.[190] But Bo Xuan Luat was still strongly opposed, on the grounds that except for him all of the other members were ICP men.[191] Two days later (April 14), Hsiao Wen returned from Kunming. He regarded the organization and election of the "Action Committee" as "illegal," and ordered it disbanded. He arbitrarily nominated six for a new "Action Committee"—Truong Trung Phung, Bo Xuan Luat, Le Tung Son, Vu Kim Thanh, Ho Chi Minh, and Tang Ke Ban. Chang Fa-k'uei appointed Truong Trung Phung, Bo Xuan Luat, and Le Tung Son the Standing Committee members, with Phung as its chairman.[192]

The rapid advance of the Allies in Germany stimulated the Chinese to increase their activity on the Sino-Vietnamese border. On May 2, one day after Russian forces entered Berlin, the Action Committee was set up in Tienpao (about 50 miles north of Chinghsi). Hsiao Wen's armed Foreign Affairs Section had moved down from Paise to the Chinghsi area, as had the Special Class just renamed the "Action Brigade," under the command of the Action Committee. On May 11 the Action Brigade, consisting of 115 men with full equipment and divided into three units led by Bo Xuan Luat (50 men), Le Tung Son (10), and Truong Trung Phung (55), entered the border area. Their areas of operation in Vietnam were assigned separately: Luat's unit on the right at Tra-Linh, Son's in the center at Soc-Giang (Viet-Minh-controlled), and Phung's on the left at Bao-Lac.[193] Besides the Brigade, two other units entered Tonkin. One was led by ICP member Ho Duc Thanh from Lungchow, the other by Vu Kim Thanh, a nationalist, from Tunghsing. It seemed that the Vietnamese revolutionaries in China were returning or preparing to return to Vietnam. A Chinese advance into Indochina was imminent. As Hsiao Wen told Hoang Quoc Viet, the Chinese army was soon to liberate

---

[190] Hsing Shen-chou's report, May 25, 1945, in "Documents."
[191] *Ibid.*   [192] *Ibid.*

[193] Hsing Shen-chou's reports, May 6, 13, 25, 1945, in *ibid.* Chang Fa-k'uei, *Memoirs*, Chap. 7, says that in the spring of 1945 he sent the Special Class men back to Vietnam from Paise with full military equipment.

Indochina; the Viet-Minh should give all possible assistance to the Chinese entering Indochina. Hsiao also proposed that the VNQDD, Dong Minh Hoi, and Viet-Minh "work with the Allies."[194] Realizing the vital importance of control over the internal situation in the future power struggle against the nationalists, the Chinese, and the French, Ho Chi Minh rushed back to Vietnam, accompanied by Hoang Quoc Viet's party.

Ho's visit to China in late 1944 and early 1945, which was little known to the West, was another success. He had established relations with the OSS and with General Chennault in Kunming; cooperation with the OSS was to begin in May 1945.[195] Second, Le Tung Son was made a standing member of the Action Committee and was leading a fully armed unit of the Action Brigade (the former Phuc Quoc Army) back to Vietnam. Third, and most important, he had secured accurate information about the movement of Chinese troops into Vietnam, and particularly about Chang Fa-k'uei's plan, which obviously had some bearing on his decision about Vietnam's declaration of independence and the establishment of a rival regime before the arrival of the Chinese. Here was a tug of war between Ho and the Chinese general; while Chang wanted the Chinese to take a direct hand in helping Vietnam obtain her independence, Ho was to present the Chinese with the fait accompli of an independent Vietnam without Chinese aid for the Chinese to recognize and support.

Up to this point, one cannot help asking, what was the policy of Chungking (the central government of China) toward Vietnam; was Chungking in complete accord with Chang Fa-k'uei's policy toward the Vietnamese revolutionary movement? According to the analysis of Hsing Shen-chou, who was in charge of Vietnamese affairs in the KMT, Chungking at the time did not have any established policy for Vietnam, although the Chinese leaders were in favor of

[194] Hoang Quoc Viet, "Our People, A Very Heroic People," in Ho Chi Minh et al., *A Heroic People* (Hanoi, 1960), p. 251.
[195] See the following chapter.

97

a postwar Vietnamese government chosen by the Vietnamese people. Taking a careful view of the French provisional government, which China recognized on October 23, 1944, and of the various Vietnamese revolutionary forces, Hsing held a different opinion from that of Chang Fa-k'uei. He observed that France was a Chinese ally who was to return Vietnam and that the incompetent leadership of the various Vietnamese parties in China had caused many to join the Viet-Minh, which was merely using China as a means to strengthen itself. The Viet-Minh, Hsing asserted, would eventually turn against China. In these circumstances, to assist the present Vietnamese revolution China could "make France an enemy on the one hand, and [bring exploitation] by the [Vietnamese] Communists on the other. It would do us nothing good but a great harm."[196]

[196] Hsing Shen-chou, "Plan for Relations with Vietnam," November 14, 1944, in "Documents." What Hsing Shen-chou reported here, that "Chungking at that time did not have any established policy for Vietnam," was true. As recalled by Vu Hong Khanh in his letter of May 30, 1969 to the author, the Chinese Nationalist government, because of its own wars and problems with external and internal enemies, "had never formulated a policy for Vietnam." On several occasions local leaders (e.g. Hsiao Wen and Lu Han) distorted or even ignored Chungking's favorable attitudes toward the Vietnamese nationalists.

3. The Birth of the Democratic Republic of Vietnam and the Chinese Occupation, 1945-1946

≪≪≪≪≪≪≪≪≪≪≪≪≪≪≪≪≪≪≪≪≪≪≪≪≪≪≪≪≪≪≪≪≪

"I believe the doctrine of *San Min Chu I*; China's national policy is Vietnam's policy. . . . I will accept Chinese orders and guidance, and I offer my life to assure you that there will be no more anti-Chinese actions from the Vietnamese people."
— Ho Chi Minh to Hsiao Wen in 1945 after Hsiao and the Chinese Nationalist Army occupied Hanoi

"It is better to smell the feces of the French for a little while than to eat Chinese excrement all of one's life."
— Ho Chi Minh to Paul Mus in 1947 following the Chinese occupation

By March 1945 internal and external events had taken a very encouraging turn for the Vietnamese revolution. The famine of 1944-1945, which cost about two million lives from Quang-Tri to Tonkin, increased apathy and resentment toward French rule. The Viet-Minh had established guerrilla bases and "people's regimes" in six provinces, Cao-Bang, Lang-Son, Bac-Can, Tuyen-Quang, Phu-Tho, and Thai-Nguyen. The Allied armies were closing in on Berlin. The Americans had landed on Luzon and were soon to reoccupy the whole of the Philippines. Finally, on March 9, 1945, the Japanese suddenly moved in force in Indochina, which turned the Viet-Minh to the Allied side against their common enemy, Japan.

The March 9 incident was well planned by the Japanese. Within 24 hours, and with only token resistance in Hanoi and Lang-Son, the Japanese disarmed the French and disbanded the French colonial government. Most of the French were sent to prison camps, including Admiral Decoux. Generals Sabattier and Alessandri and their troops got through the Tonkin mountain areas and fled to China.[1]

---

[1] For a good account of the French side see Fall, *Two Viet-Nams*, pp. 55-59.

Birth of Republic of Vietnam

On March 11 the Japanese put Emperor Bao Dai at the head of a puppet regime and appointed Tran Trong Kim to organize a cabinet. Bao Dai proclaimed the "immediate abolition of the treaty of protectorate signed with France" in 1886, and he declared the independence of Vietnam. He also expressed his determination to cooperate with Japan in the Greater Co-prosperity Sphere in Southeast Asia.[2]

Prompted by the incident, the Central Standing Committee of the ICP met in emergency session at Dinh-Bang village (Bac-Ninh province) from March 9 to 12, with Ho Chi Minh absent from the meeting. The committee issued a directive, "The Japanese-French Conflict and Our Action," urging its members to give a strong push to the revolutionary movement because of the new situation.[3] Meanwhile, the Viet-Minh issued a similar declaration on March 15, attacking the Japanese and the Tran Trong Kim government and calling on the people to "organize demonstrations, processions and strikes . . . destroy all communication and transport facilities . . . launch surprise attacks on their isolated outposts and ambush their patrol units. . . ."[4] It also publicized a program expressing its determination to establish a democratic republic upon the defeat of Japan and announcing future political, social, economic, cultural, and educational reforms.[5] Soon thereafter several massive demonstrations occurred in Tonkin and there was renewed guerrilla fighting. In response to the call of the Viet-Minh hundreds joined the Liberation Army. Local revolutionary regimes mushroomed. The advancing Liberation Army and the National Salvation Army joined forces in the Tan-Trao

[2] *A Chronicle of Principal Events Relating to the Indo-China Question, 1940-54* (Peking: Shih-chieh chih-shih she, 1954), p. 6. Hereafter, *Chronicle.* Also *Ta Kung Pao* (Chungking), March 12, 1945.

[3] Truong Chinh, *President Ho*, pp. 16-17.

[4] *Factual Records of the Viet Minh August Revolution*, p. 20, cited in Hammer, *Struggle for Indochina*, p. 99.

[5] Hsiao Yang, *Chieh fang chung ti Yueh-nan* (Vietnam in Liberation) (Shanghai, Ch'ung lien, 1951), pp. 13-14.

area.[6] Guerrilla forces were making good progress in their southward advance. They were able to guard their original jungle bases in Cao-Bang and Bac-Son and advanced to the plain in Thai-Nguyen, heading for Hanoi.

To make known to the world her determination to return Indochina to the status of a colony, the French provisional government issued a declaration on March 24, announcing that Indochina "was destined" for a special place in the French Union, that the colony would have its own federal government and its own military forces within the defense system of the French Union, and that the future federal government, which would comprise five countries (Tonkin, Annam, Cochin-China, Laos, and Cambodia), would enjoy an autonomous economy and democratic liberties.[7] It became clear that the provisional government intended not only to restore its former colonial rule after the war but to divide Indochina into five countries. But the division of three countries (Tonkin, Annam, and Cochin-China) simply could not be accepted by almost all Vietnamese, particularly those associated with the Viet-Minh. This was the thorny problem created by the French which later prevented Franco-Vietnamese negotiations from reaching a final agreement.

The Viet-Minh ignored the French appeal. To step up the tempo of its guerrilla operations it convoked a Bac-Ky military conference at Hiep-Hoa (in Bac-Giang) on April 15, at which Vo Nguyen Giap and other leaders decided to set up various war regions in the six liberated provinces and to map out future operations.[8]

[6] Giap, "Ho Chi Minh," pp. 183-84; Truong Chinh, *President Ho,* p. 17.
    [7] The declaration is in Allan B. Cole, ed., *Conflict in Indochina and International Repercussions: A Documentary History, 1945-1955* (Ithaca: Cornell University Press, 1956), pp. 5-7.
    [8] Giap, "Ho Chi Minh," pp. 184-86; Truong Chinh, *President, Ho,* p. 17.

Birth of Republic of Vietnam

1. THE AUGUST REVOLUTION

No sooner had the news of Germany's surrender on May 7 come to the Viet-Minh jungles than the message of Ho Chi Minh's return from China reached Vo Nguyen Giap and other ICP leaders.[9] Giap rushed north to welcome Ho. It was the first time they had met since the establishment of the armed propaganda unit in December 1944. Ho briefed them on the "favorable outside situation," and told them the immediate task was to select an ideal liaison headquarters, one from which they could easily contact foreign countries, the jungle area in the north, and the plain in the south. There was much to be done.[10] Before long they selected Tan-Trao, a village in the jungle of Tuyen-Quang province, and Ho moved in at once.

It was at Tan-Trao, from May to August, that Ho directed the completion of receiving American units from China for the establishment of an underground mission that would help Allied personnel escape from Japanese-held territories, changing the decision of the Bac-Ky military conference, and convening the ninth session of the ICP Central Committee and the first Viet-Minh people's congress.

The first American unit arrived in May, shortly after Ho had returned to Tonkin. They walked from the border to Ho's headquarters, accompanied by 50 Viet-Minh. Soon several units parachuted into the area.[11] The Viet-Minh received them warmly and assigned 350 men to protect and work with them. They built a small airfield, studied the terrain, and discussed military and international problems. Ho himself spent some of each day with the Americans. Immediately after the Japanese surrender, Ho, on behalf of his National Liberation Committee, asked the Americans to

[9] Giap, "Ho Chi Minh," p. 184; Truong Chinh, *President Ho*, p. 17; Tran Dan Tien, *Biography of Ho Chi Minh*, p. 140. As was discussed in Chapter 2, Ho was active in Kunming and Kwangsi from late 1944 to early 1945. During this period Ho, according to Hanoi's accounts, was absent from Viet-Minh activities at home until May 1945.
[10] Giap, "Ho Chi Minh," p. 185.
[11] Tran Dan Tien, *Biography of Ho Chi Minh*, pp. 140-41.

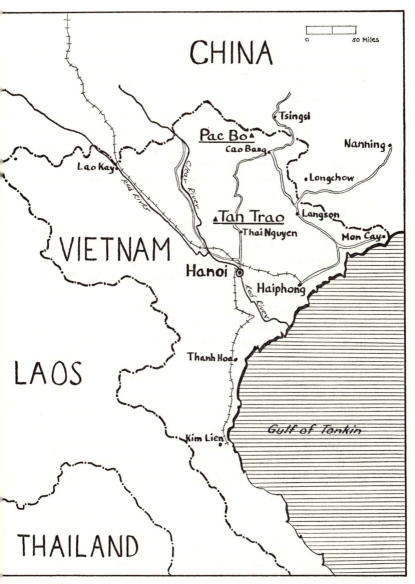

Pac-Bo and Tan-Trao (Ho Chi Minh's Revolutionary Bases),
1941-1945

wire messages to the Allies, requesting the "United Nations to realize their solemn promise" by granting Indochina "full independence."[12] Without a doubt Ho and his men urgently needed American help and wanted to cooperate with the West, especially the United States and France.

On June 4 Ho revised the decision made by the April 15 military conference: the various war regions were merged into one "liberated area" under the control of the Viet-Minh; meanwhile, the various armed units were unified in a "Liberation Army" under the command of Giap.[13] Then Ho ordered intensified preparations for the convention of the two meetings, despite the difficulties of transportation for the delegates.

The political significance of the convention of a people's national congress at this militarily critical moment was not fully understood by some Viet-Minh leaders who observed the situation from a purely military viewpoint. But Ho insisted on the convention, saying, "even if a portion of delegates could not come on time, the meeting would have to be held as scheduled."[14] To Ho the congress was not only to make his future independence government "legitimate," but, more urgently, to isolate the incoming Chinese-sponsored Dong Minh Hoi from the people's support. The return of the Dong Minh Hoi and the VNQDD with the Chinese army was even more pressing than the defeat of Japan. To offset their Chinese backing, the only effective way was to alienate them from the people while strengthening the Viet-Minh's position among the populace. To understand the situation of the Dong Minh Hoi and VNQDD, let us turn to China.

Hsiao Wen's Foreign Affairs Section and the Dong Minh

[12] See Robert Shaplen, *The Lost Revolution: The U.S. in Vietnam, 1946-1966* (New York: Harper & Row, 1966), pp. 29-30.

[13] Truong Chinh, *The August Revolution* (Hanoi: Foreign Languages Publishing House, 1958), p. 11; *Chronicle*, p. 7.

[14] Giap, "Ho Chi Minh," p. 185. It took some delegates over a month to reach Tan-Trao. See Tran Dan Tien, *Biography of Ho Chi Minh*, p. 143.

Hoi (including the Action Brigade) had moved to the Tien-pao-Chinghsi area. In early July Hsiao Wen attempted to convene a national congress of Vietnamese revolutionists. Some original Dong Minh Hoi leaders in Chungking, Kwei-yang, and Kunming, such as Truong Boi Cong, Tran Bao, Vu Hong Khanh, and Nghiem Ke To, were opposed to the meeting, but Chang Fa-k'uei regarded them as "swindling and reactionary" politicians who "had no support from the people and dared not return to Vietnam."[15] The main reason for their opposition was that they had planned to return to Vietnam with Lu Han under the banner of the VNQDD rather than Chang Fa-k'uei or the Dong Minh Hoi. Because of their refusal, the congress was not held.

By early July the Action Brigade of the Dong Minh Hoi had already entered Vietnam, occupying Bao-Lac and Soc-Giang and beginning to appear active in some parts of Cao-Bang, Bac-Can, and Thai-Nguyen provinces. A Chinese major general, Ma Wei-yo, was sent by Chang Fa-k'uei to Bao-Lac to direct the brigade.[16] Ho Chi Minh did not want the brigade to advance into Tonkin, and ordered, directly or indirectly, his forces in various places to either attack or kidnap them, a tactic also used by the Viet Cong today against Saigon's officials in the countryside. Hsiao Wen warned Le Tung Son (still with the Dong Minh Hoi) and asked Ho to come to Chinghsi for talks, but Ho did not go. In early August the Viet-Minh was reported to have adopted a policy of "allying with the United States against China,"[17] which indicated that a good Viet-Minh–American relationship was developing.

As the Viet-Minh was stepping up its preparation for the congress, Ho Chi Minh fell ill. At one point he was dying. He called in Vo Nguyen Giap and Pham Van Dong, talked to them, saying that no matter how costly it was, "we must win independence!" He reportedly left his will with the two

[15] Hsing Shen-chou's report, July 8, 1945, in "Documents."
[16] *Ibid.*, June 24, 1945.   [17] *Ibid.*, July 15, August 5, 1945.

men.[18] This indicates that Dong and Giap had become Ho's "close comrades in arms" as early as 1945.

On August 13 and 14 the Central Standing Committee of the ICP held its ninth session. The news of the Japanese surrender stimulated a heated discussion on two questions: to seize power, if they could, before the Allied forces came, or negotiate with the French, if they could not, then win independence from the French through revolutionary struggle.

Ho, still not completely recovered, was of the opinion that even if the Viet-Minh was weak, the immediate task was to stir up a revolutionary high tide and establish a nationwide liberated area. At the end of the meeting, an insurrection committee was established, which issued the order for the launching of a general insurrection.[19]

Events in the following two weeks moved rapidly. On August 15 the insurrection committee talked in Tonkin with the royal delegate from Hue, and urged the Bao Dai government to give way to the revolutionary forces. The negotiations, revealed in 1965, were unproductive.[20] On August 16 the Viet-Minh national congress was held at the temple of Tan-Trao. It was attended by over 60 delegates from various national minorities and political groups. Ho Chi Minh was introduced to the congress; most of the delegates were meeting him for the first time. After a day of reports and discussions, a National Liberation Comitee (Provincial Government of the Democratic Republic of Vietnam) was established. Ho was its president. In addition, the Viet-Minh adopted a significant policy with three objectives: (1) to disarm the Japanese before the arrival of the Allied forces in Indochina; (2) to wrest power from the Japanese and their puppets, and (3) as the people's power, to welcome the Allied forces.[21] On August 17 Ho and his staff of the

[18] Giap, "Ho Chi Minh," p. 187; Nguyen Luong Bang, "The Times I Met Him," p. 62.

[19] *Ibid.*, pp. 64-65; Truong Chinh, *August Revolution*, p. 12.

[20] *Vietnamese Studies*, No. 7: *Pages of History, 1945-1954* (Hanoi: Vietnamese Studies, 1965), pp. 31-32.

[21] Truong Chinh, *August Revolution*, p. 13.

Liberation Committee were sworn into office, and the delegates rushed back to their posts.

On the same day, Viet-Minh forces under Giap attacked the city of Thai-Nguyen. An American officer assisted Giap in "liberating" it.[22] The victory greatly enhanced the prestige of the Viet-Minh. Almost at the same time, Ho, on behalf of the National Liberation Committee, sent messages through the Americans to the Allied powers, asking for support of Vietnam's independence. According to Robert Shaplen, the messages reached Léon Pignon, who later became a high commissioner of Indochina, and Jean Sainteny, who was soon to serve as the representative of the French high commissioner, Admiral d'Argenlieu, for northern Vietnam. They replied vaguely to Ho that they were willing to negotiate. No definite date and terms of the messages were reported.[23] A Chinese source fills in the gap. On August 18, 1945 Ho sent the French his message, which contained five conditions:

(1) the French government recognizes the Vietminh government; (2) the Viet-Minh recognizes French sovereignty in Vietnam within five to ten years; after that, the French government grants independence to Vietnam; (3) in these five to ten years, Vietnam enjoys internal autonomy; the French government can appoint personnel to serve at various administrative agencies as directors against foreign invasion; (4) the French government enjoys priority in Vietnamese industry and commerce; and (5) the French may serve as advisers to [Vietnamese] diplomacy.[24]

Checked against the French-Vietnamese agreement of March 6, 1946, the conditions must have served as basis for discussion in their 1946 negotiations.[25]

[22] Tran Dan Tien, *Biography of Ho Chi Minh*, p. 147.
[23] Shaplen, *Lost Revolution*, pp. 29-30, 40-41.
[24] Hsing Shen-chou's report, October 10, 1945, in "Documents."
[25] See the discussion of the March 6, 1946 agreement in section 4 below.

In addition, Ho wrote a letter to Capt. Charles Fenn, expressing his friendship with the Americans and including a prediction that future Vietnamese-American relations would be difficult. It reads (original form):

> The war is finished. It is good for everybody. I feel only sorry that all our American friends have to leave us so soon. And their leaving this country means that relations between you and us will be more difficult.
>
> The war is won. But we small subject countries have no share, or very small share, in the victory of freedom and democracy. Probably, if we want to get a sufficient share, we have still to fight. I believe that your sympathy and sympathy of the great American people will be always with us.
>
> I also remain sure that sooner or later, we will attain our aim, because it is just. And as our country gets independent, I am looking forward for [sic] the happy day of meeting you and our other American friends either in Indo-China or the USA! I wish you good luck and good health.[26]

As the letter shows, there is little doubt that Ho not only was friendly toward the OSS and the United States, but wished the war had lasted longer so that the Vietnamese could have achieved their independence before the Americans went home. Comparing this with the American involvement in Vietnam in the 1960s, one can only say that the present Vietnam tangle is an American failure to take the opportunity.

While the French gave no definite reply to Ho's demands, local, emotional demonstrations in favor of independence occurred throughout Tonkin and Annam. The Viet-Minh, claiming the support of the Allies, made impressive propaganda gains among the people. It also employed terrorism against prominent nationalists and anti-Communist officials. Pham Quynh, leader of the People's Progressive Party and

---

[26] Moorhouse, "He Knew Ho as OSS Agent 19."

former minister of interior of Bao Dai, was murdered in Annam for his attempt to contact the French. Ngo Dinh Khoi, former governor of Quang-Ngai province and a brother of Ngo Dinh Diem, was also killed in Annam for his anti-Communist attitude. The Viet-Minh won over Phan Ke Toai, Viceroy of Tonkin under the Japanese. Toai had a close relationship with the Dai Viet, the opponent of the Viet-Minh in Hanoi.[27] His defection provided the Viet-Minh with information about the strengths and weaknesses of the Dai Viet which was also attempting to seize power, information that enabled the Viet-Minh to take over Hanoi on August 19.

Immediately after the Tan-Trao conference Hoang Quoc Viet and Cao Hong Linh were sent to South Vietnam, where Viet-Minh influence was weak, to seek coordination and cooperation. Ho Chi Minh gave instructions on their departure: "Go in haste to south Vietnam, don't lose one single day." They met Nguyen Khang at Hanoi, Nguyan Tao and Le Viet Luong at Thanh-Hoa, Nguyen Chi Thanh at Hue, Le Van Hien at Da-Nang, Tran Qui Hai at Quang-Ngai, Nguyen Van Nguyen, and others at Saigon. Wherever they went, they saw the "August electric current" of demonstrations and meetings for independence. But one question was asked constantly: "Who is Ho Chi Minh?"[28]

Once the Japanese attempted to help the Dai Viet gain power, but the Dai Viet showed no capacity for doing so. The resignation of the Tran Trong Kim cabinet on August 7 created a power vacuum that needed to be filled urgently. With no effective central government, the situation became still more favorable to the Viet-Minh. In Hanoi and other big cities in Tonkin, there were almost daily demonstra-

[27] After Japan surrendered, a group of Japanese officers in Hanoi offered to help the Dai Viet seize power. The leaders of the Dai Viet went to ask for cooperation from Viceroy Phan Ke Toai who, more impressed by the program and power of the Viet-Minh, fled and joined the Viet-Minh. Toai was rewarded with a ministerial position in Ho's government after 1947.

[28] Hoang Quoc Viet, "Our People, A Very Heroic People," in *Heroic People*, pp. 254-62.

tions, with the Japanese looking on. On some occasions the Japanese sold arms through private channels to the Viet-Minh. And there were rumors in Hanoi that the Viet-Minh was a creation of the Japanese. In Annam the Japanese either gave arms to the Bao Dai government, which clashed occasionally with the Viet-Minh, or simply burned their weapons. In other parts of Vietnam, the Japanese handed over equipment to the Viet-Minh. The situation was confusing. Finally, when the insurrectional forces headed by Viet-Minh cadres led mass demonstrations in Hanoi on August 19, they were joined by local Bao An (security) forces and police detachments. They quickly occupied public buildings and took over the entire city.[29] As recalled by Pham Van Dong in 1952, the Japanese defeat by the Soviet army in Manchuria in August 1945 apparently had served as a strong encouragement to the "August Revolution" in Hanoi.[30]

Developments in Tonkin attracted the attention of the whole nation, and particularly that of Bao Dai. Encouraged by the events, the Emperor on August 18 sent a special letter to General de Gaulle, urging him to recognize Vietnam's independence so as to safeguard French interests in Indochina.[31] Despite Bao Dai's appeal, Jean Sainteny, French representative for northern Vietnam, arrived in Hanoi on August 22 in an American military plane. Col. Henri Cedile, French representative for southern Vietnam, was air-dropped and taken to Saigon by the Japanese.

On August 22 Emperor Bao Dai was to ask the Viet-Minh to form a new cabinet. But a student meeting in Hanoi on August 21 changed his decision. The meeting, dominated by left-wing intellectuals, issued a resolution calling for the abdication of Bao Dai and the installation of a republican regime led by the Viet-Minh.[32] Some officials around the

[29] Truong Chinh, *August Revolution*, p. 14.

[30] Pham Van Dong, "The Seventh Anniversary of the Resistance War of the Democratic Republic of Vietnam," in *World Culture* (Peking: Shih-chieh chih-shih she), No. 34 (August 30, 1952), p. 8.

[31] The letter is in Cole, *Conflict in Indochina*, pp. 17-18.

[32] See Devillers, *Histoire*, p. 137.

Emperor supported the demand. Under these pressures Bao Dai abdicated on August 24 and became citizen Vinh Thuy; the Liberation Committee accepted the abdication.[33] The people hailed his "democratic spirit" and the entire nation seemed to appear unprecedentedly united.

In the south Admiral Decoux, who was still in captivity at Loc-Ninh, asked the local Japanese commander, General Tsuchihashi, to release him and other imprisoned French officials in order to prevent the triumph of the forces of the Viet-Minh. The Japanese general replied that he was unable to act without higher orders. The admiral, therefore, was not given the opportunity.[34] The Japanese now no longer made any effort to stop the Viet-Minh movement. On August 25, one day before Hoang Quoc Viet reached Saigon, the Viet-Minh set up a southern provisional executive committee led by Tran Van Giau. Thus the Liberation Committee had institutionally spread all over Vietnam.

Ho Chi Minh secretly entered Hanoi. To meet the new situation, the Liberation Committee held a long meeting, discussing Ho's proposal that the independence government include non-Viet-Minh people. Several cabinet posts were offered to non-Viet-Minh. After the meeting the committee issued a proclamation to the people (August 28), announcing that national power was in the hands of the Liberation Committee which was to be reorganized to include all patriots regardless of party affiliation.[35]

On September 2, 1945 the Provisional Government of the Democratic Republic of Vietnam[36] was sworn in at Hanoi's

---

[33] A three-member Viet-Minh delegation headed by Tran Huy Lieu (the other two members were Nguyen Luong Bang and Cu Huy Can) was sent to Hue to attend the ceremony of Bao Dai's abdication.

[34] Jones, *Survey*, p. 35.

[35] Tran Dan Tien, *Biography of Ho Chi Minh*, pp. 147-48; *Chronicle*, p. 8.

[36] The cabinet of 1945 was as follows:

President	Ho Chi Minh	Viet-Minh (Communist)
Foreign Affairs	Ho Chi Minh	Viet-Minh (Communist)
Interior	Vo Nguyen Giap	Viet-Minh (Communist)
Finance	Pham Van Dong	Viet-Minh (Communist)
Propaganda	Tran Huy Lieu	Viet-Minh (Communist)

Birth of Republic of Vietnam

Ba-Dinh Square.[37] 500,000 people attended the ceremony. Ho Chi Minh, as president of the government, proclaimed the independence of his country and read its declaration of independence. The first sentence of the document, as we well know today, was from the Declaration of Independence of the United States, the language of which Ho had sought from OSS men in the jungle a few months before. Ho did not deliver a speech, but unexpectedly asked a simple question after having read the declaration: "My fellow countrymen, have you fully understood?" His kind voice and friendliness gave a warm and father-like image to the people who immediately felt close to their new leader.[38] This image, which Bao Dai and Ngo Dinh Diem lacked, has been welcomed overwhelmingly by the people of North Vietnam.

After Ho's proclamation Vo Nguyen Giap, Interior Minister and chief of the Viet-Minh army, issued a statement dealing with the Viet-Minh, military, political, economic, financial, cultural, educational, and foreign affairs. In the area of foreign relations Giap emphasized Vietnam's relations with China and the United States, saying:

> China is the nearest nation to us, from [a] geographical as well as economical and cultural point of view.
>
> The Chinese, living up to now in this country, have undergone untold miseries from the French, then from

National Defense	Chu Van Tan	Viet-Minh (Communist)
Labor	Le Van Hien	Viet-Minh (Communist)
Education	Vu Dinh Hoe	Democratic Party
Youth	Duong Duc Hien	Democratic Party
Justice	Vu Trong Khanh	Democratic Party
Economy	Nguyen Manh Ha	Catholic
Health	Pham Ngoc Thach	nonparty (later Communist)
Social Welfare	Nguyen Van To	nonparty
Public Works	Dao Trong Kim	nonparty
(Supreme Political		
Advisor: Bao Dai)		

[37] Before the inauguration an OSS officer went to see Ho and told Ho he did not have a uniform for the ceremony. Ho took off his and gave it to the American.

[38] Tran Dan Tien, *Biography of Ho Chi Minh*, p. 156.

the Japanese oppression. . . . They have acclaimed and supported the independence of Vietnam, and the Vietnamese Government will defend their rights. . . .

The United States of America . . . has paid the greatest contributions to the Vietnamese fight against fascist Japan, our enemy, and so the Great American Republic is a good friend of ours.

The democratic nations sincerely hope for the liberation of the lesser powers and they are of the same opinion as Chiang Kai-shek that "the end of the World War must bring with it the end of Imperialism because Imperialism is the cause of war."[39]

The important fact was that the United States, through the OSS and other units, had helped the Viet-Minh against the Japanese. The OSS files for 1944-1946, which are in the custody of the Central Intelligence Agency, are not yet available to the public.[40] The discussion thus far has indicated the Americans' active role in the Viet-Minh's coming to power. The Chinese Nationalists assisted only the Dong Minh Hoi and VNQDD which were confined to the border area. There is no evidence of any Chinese Communist aid to the August Revolution. And Moscow, though realizing the strategic value of Indochina,[41] did not take a part in the insurrection,[42] despite the fact that the Viet-Minh had made good use of the Soviet Union's name to promote its influence

[39] Cole, *Conflict in Indochina*, pp. 26-27.

[40] A letter to the author from Joseph C. Godwin, assistant to the director of the CIA, dated July 26, 1967, states: "It has been determined that these [OSS] records must be kept classified in the interests of national security. . . . They are not available for scholar's research and probably will not become available in the foreseeable future."

[41] At the Yalta Conference in February 1945, President Roosevelt and Marshal Stalin exchanged views on Indochina. "Stalin . . . thought Indochina was a very important area." *New York Times*, March 17, 1945.

[42] Charles B. McLane, *Soviet Strategies in Southeast Asia; An Exploration of Eastern Policy under Lenin and Stalin* (Princeton: Princeton University Press, 1966), pp. 266-67.

in Saigon.[43] It is thus no wonder that the French said: "It was largely America who 'made' Ho Chi Minh."[44]

But Vietnam's independence, as pointed out by the Central Committee of the Viet-Minh on September 2, 1945, "remains quite fragile. To win back power is difficult, but to keep it is more difficult still."[45] Upon assuming power the Viet-Minh found its state treasury almost empty (only 1,250,720 piastres remained, half of which were old worthless bank notes);[46] its food crisis remained serious; the army was weak compared with those of France and China; and it had no experience in administration, particularly financial affairs.[47] Above all, the Chinese army was coming. Ho and his cabinet discussed at length how to deal with the Chinese. He repeatedly urged his followers to be patient. He declared: "Our present policy is that followed by Kau Tjian, but perseverance does not mean submission."[48]

[43] A leaflet published by the ICP on August 17, 1945, stated: "The authorities and the French population of Indochina must remember that the powerful ally of their country, the U.S.S.R, is also the guide and hope of the Indochina Communist Party and "the Viet-Minh. . . ." Cited in Sacks, "Marxism in Viet-Nam," p. 154.

[44] Lucien Bodard, *The Quicksand War: Prelude to Vietnam*, tr. and with an introduction by Patrick O'Brian (Boston: Little, Brown, 1967), p. 222.

[45] *Vietnamese Studies*, No. 7, p. 39.

[46] *Ibid.*; Ho Chi Minh et al., *Yueh-nan min chu kung ho kuo shih nien lai ti ch'eng chiu* (The Achievements of the Democratic Republic of Vietnam in the Past Ten Years) (Peking, *World Culture*, 1956), p. 53; hereafter, *Achievements*.

[47] On September 3, 1945 Ho held the first cabinet meeting after independence, and said: "We all are not familiar with the Administrative skill. . . ." (Tran Dan Tien, *Biography of Ho Chi Minh*, p. 157.) Truong Chinh remarked that one of the weaknesses of the August revolution was the Viet-Minh's failure to seize the Bank of Indochina. See Truong Chinh, *August Revolution*, pp. 37-38.

[48] Nguyen Luong Bang, "The Times I Met Him," p. 72. Kau Tjian (Kou Chien), King of the Yueh State (Viet) of ancient China on the southeast coast, failed in his first fight against the King of the Wu State. He retreated to Huichi, Chekiang and adopted a policy of training and preparation for 10 years. He finally defeated Wu in 473 B.C. What Ho is referring to here is Kou Chien's policy of the 10 patient years.

2. THE CHINESE OCCUPATION AND THE VIET-MINH

It was decided at the Potsdam Conference in July 1945 that Indochina would be divided at the 16th parallel, to facilitate the disarming of the Japanese. The Chinese army was given the opportunity and authority to occupy the area north of the parallel, the British that to the south.[49] France, because of her weak position among the Allies, was not in a position to refuse the decision on her colony. As Jean Sainteny has observed, the occupation given to China was in compensation for the Soviet occupation of Manchuria agreed on at the Yalta Conference.[50] General MacArthur managed to direct the Japanese Emperor to issue an order, General Order No. 1. Item (a) of the order stated: "The Japanese Commanders and all ground, sea, and auxiliary forces within China (excluding Manchuria), Formosa, and French Indochina north of 16 degrees north latitude surrender to Generalissimo Chiang Kai-shek."[51]

For the Chinese, Generalissimo Chiang Kai-shek announced August 24, 1945 that, apart from dispatching troops to accept Japan's surrender north of the 16th parallel in accordance with the decision of the Allied powers, China "definitely does not have any territorial ambition in Vietnam." China hoped that "the Vietnamese people would gradually reach independence in accordance with the provisions of the Atlantic Charter."[52] This moderate position underlined Chinese policy toward postwar Vietnam.

Since the Japanese had surrendered, the Chinese did not see any need to send Chang Fa-k'uei's and Lu Han's armies to Vietnam as originally planned. Chang was assigned to Canton. The change was welcome news to the French.

---

[49] See Herbert Feis, *Japan Subdued: The Atomic Bomb and the End of the War in the Pacific* (Princeton, 1961), pp. 79-83.

[50] Jean Sainteny, *Histoire d'une Paix Manquée, Indochine, 1945-47* (Paris, 1953), p. 50.

[51] Feis, *Japan Subdued*, p. 139.

[52] *Chung yang jih pao* (*Central Daily News*, Kunming), August 25, 1945. A brief summary also appeared in the *New York Times* on the same date.

According to Hsiao Wen, Chang's replacement by Lu Han was to the French, "the revival of hope in despair."[53] A French return to Vietnam (Indochina) now became not only possible but probable. General Chang transferred his Foreign Affairs Section to General Lu Han,[54] with its name changed to the Section for Overseas Chinese Affairs, still headed by Hsiao Wen.[55] From then on Hsiao's position was less powerful than before.

The Allied units in Yunnan, which tried to enter Vietnam either before or with Lu Han's army, were those of France and the United States. The French groups and personnel included a military mission headed by Jean Sainteny, a group representing the Ministry of Overseas France headed by Jean de Raymond (later commissioner in Laos and Cambodia), a unit led by Léon Pignon (later high commissioner of Indochina), and a group under General Alessandri who, with his unit of 5,363 French and Vietnamese soldiers, evacuated from Indochina in March 1945. Except for Sainteny, who was flown to Hanoi by an American aircraft on August 22, they were semi-openly blocked from an early return to Indochina by either the Chinese or Americans or both.

Three American groups went to Hanoi on their own in August and September. An OSS unit led by Maj. Archimedes L. Patti went in late August. Major Patti, with the permission of General Wedemeyer, took Jean Sainteny to Hanoi and later took Vo Nguyen Giap to see Sainteny.[56]

[53] Hsiao Wen's report, dated November 1, 1946, in "Documents." Hsiao said the French in Saigon were of the opinion that if China sent Generals Chang Fa-k'uei, Ch'en Ch'eng, or Pai Ch'ung-hsi to Vietnam, Vietnam would eventually go to China, and all efforts to achieve a French return would be in vain.

[54] Lu Han, a graduate of the Military Academy of Yunnan, is a professional soldier. During the occupation of Vietnam he was appointed to serve as Governor of Yunnan after the "Kunming Incident" of October 5, 1945. He is now a powerless member of the National Defense Council in Peking.

[55] Chang Fa-k'uei said to me in an October 1960 interview that the Chinese government "should have assigned" him to go to Vietnam because he and Hsiao Wen had known the Vietnamese leaders well and had dealt with Vietnamese affairs since 1941.

[56] Sainteny, *Histoire*, p. 86.

Birth of Republic of Vietnam

Gen. Philip E. Gallagher, who later had an important part in settling the Sino-French financial dispute, arrived in September as the head of the American military mission. And a group led by Colonel Nordlinger occupied itself with the needs of prisoners of war. Ironically the French in Kunming, prior to the Potsdam Conference, were more enthusiastic about keeping the United States out of Indochina than in defeating Japan in Vietnam,[57] while after the conference the Americans tried to block the French from an early return to Vietnam.[58] Realizing that the United States would be more aggressive in helping Vietnam achieve independence than would China, General de Gaulle preferred a Chinese rather than American occupation of Vietnam.[59]

The Chinese government in Chungking organized a Vietnam advisory group consisting of a representative from each of the Ministries of Finance, Foreign Affairs, Military Administration, Economy, Communications, Food, and the Kuomintang. It was headed by Shao Pai-ch'ang (Military Administration). The group represented the Chinese central government, dealing mainly with nonmilitary affairs in occupied Vietnam in cooperation with Lu Han's forces.[60]

[57] Shaplen, *Lost Revolution*, p. 41.

[58] For instance, Major Patti informed Jean Sainteny in Kunming that the Potsdam agreements made no mention of French sovereignty over Vietnam, and therefore the French no longer had any right to intervene in Vietnamese affairs. See Sainteny, *Histoire*, pp. 91-124, passim.

[59] Jean Decoux, *A La Barre de L'Indochine, 1940-45* (1949), p. 345; in Jones, *Survey*, p. 35.

[60] The members of the group were: Shao Pai-ch'ang (Military Administration), Chu Hsieh (Finance), Ling Ch'i-han (Foreign Affairs), Chuang Chih-huan (Economy), Cheng Fang-heng (Communications), Ma Ts'an-yung (Food), and Hsing Shen-chou (Kuomintang). A book by Chu Hsieh, *Yueh-nan shou hsiang jih chi* (Diary of Accepting the [Japanese] Surrender in Vietnam) (Shanghai, 1947), with some documents inserted, is probably the only published and dependable Chinese source for the occupation. Chu, German-educated and a professor in Chungking during the war, is also a writer and historian. Since 1950 he has served as a member of the Chinese History Compilation Commission in Peking. Shao Pai-ch'ang, a Pao-ting Military Academy graduate and educated in Germany, is now in Taiwan.

Meanwhile the Chinese government formulated a 14-point policy for the occupation, based on the statement by Generalissimo Chiang of August 24, 1945. Its major points were:

(1) to confer and maintain close contact with the delegations of the American Military and French Missions

(2) to invite the French representative to attend the ceremony of accepting surrender

(3) all the communication and industrial enterprises in Vietnam should be kept in operation until after negotiations between the Occupation Headquarters and the French

(4) for military security and transportation convenience the Indochina Railway and all seaports should be placed under temporary military control

(5) the French Mission should ask the Vietnamese [government] to provide food and transportation for the needs of the occupation army; the Chinese Foreign Ministry will negotiate with the French for agreements on liquidation

(6) to disallow those French who have been hostile toward the Chinese government or have slaughtered Chinese in Vietnam, to return to Vietnam

(7) to maintain a strictly neutral attitude toward Franco-Vietnamese relations.[61]

It became clear that the policy of the Chinese government was to carry out a merely military occupation in Vietnam. The Chinese government maintained a strictly neutral position on Vietnam's political future.[62] Several issues concerning China, France, and Vietnam that were pending would be settled through diplomatic negotiations. The Chinese government had no intention and made no attempt to foster a Chinese-inspired, Chinese-dominated, and anti-

[61] *Ibid.*, pp. 2-4.

[62] Gen. Shao Pai-ch'ang, in a letter of July 7, 1967, answering questions from the author, confirmed that the Chinese government did maintain a neutral policy toward Vietnam.

French regime in Vietnam. But the Chinese policy suggested some implications: First, it did not acknowledge at all the establishment of the Viet-Minh regime and the self-imposed independence of Vietnam. Second, it recognized French sovereignty over Vietnam (Indochina), and therefore reverted Vietnam's "independence" position to a colonial status under the French. Third, it was prepared for a French return. Strictly speaking, it was the reverse of the position held by Generalissimo Chiang Kai-shek and President Roosevelt from later 1943 to early 1945. Apparently it was formulated from the overall outlook of world situation (including the position of China's ally, France) rather than from the revolutionary stand of the Vietnamese people. It did not contain a favorable position for the Viet-Minh. In theory China was willing to help Vietnam achieve independence; in reality China was reluctant to commit herself to the Vietnamese situation because Vietnam's independence was complicated by the power conflict among the Allies. Vietnam was not Korea, and the Chinese could not act in Vietnam as the Soviet Union could in Korea. The entire situation must have been taken into consideration when the policy was formulated; hence, the neutral policy.

Lu Han disagreed with the policy of the central government. He held a more aggressive view, and asserted that the 14 points were unsuited to the Vietnamese situation. He preferred a long period of occupation, along with placing Vietnam under China's trusteeship while supporting and assisting the Vietnamese to obtain their independence.[63] Lu Han's vigorous attitude toward Vietnam and hostile one toward France, which were contrary to the position of the Chinese government, had been consistent throughout the occupation period. Obviously Lu Han, viewing the Vietnamese situation from a corner of China—Yunnan—was not as well informed about the international situation as the policy-makers in Chungking were. The central government was planning to return Vietnam to France after securing a French agreement on the Vietnamese section of the Indo-

[63] *Ibid.*, p. 10.

china Railway and Haiphong port. Under this circumstance, the best thing for China to do would be to evacuate her troops immediately after disarming the Japanese and not interfere in Franco-Vietnamese affairs.

THE ALLIED occupation forces entered Vietnam in August and September. In the south British troops arrived September 12. The weak Viet-Minh, in cooperation previously with the United National Front (including the Cao Dai, the Hoa Hao,[64] the old Phuc Quoc, and the Struggle Group of the Trotskyites), tried hard to deal with the British. On September 23 the French, with British help, took over Saigon by force. The meager Viet-Minh forces were driven to the countryside. The cooperation between the Viet-Minh and the Front soon vanished.[65] The Viet-Minh have not controlled Saigon since. The French-Vietnamese conflict was underway.

In the north the Chinese, totaling 152,500 men under General Lu Han, began to move in from Yunnan and Kwangsi in late August.[66] Lu Han arrived in Hanoi one week after the Viet-Minh had declared independence. General Alessandri on August 11 received permission from Gen. Ho Ying-ch'in, commander of the Chinese army, to let his French-Vietnamese soldiers accompany Chinese troops into Vietnam. Lu Han did not carry out the order.[67]

[64] I have seen frequent reports on the Cao Dai and the Hoa Hao in recent years. The Cao Dai is a religious group with a strong political character. Founded at Tay-Ninh, Cochin-China in 1926, it is a religion of many faiths—Taoism, Buddhism, Confucianism, and Christianity. After 1935 the religion led a strong nationalist drive among officials, landlords, students, and peasants. It was pro-Japanese and anti-French, formerly had its own armed forces (20,000 men in 1954), and is still influential in South Vietnam. For its history and ideology see Gabriel Gobron, *History and Philosophy of Caodaism* (Saigon, 1950) tr. Pham-Xuan-Thai. The Hoa Hao, founded in 1939, is a Buddhist group with an armed force of approximately 5,000 in 1954. During the war it was pro-Japanese. It has been much less influential than the Cao Dai.

[65] See Hammer, *Struggle for Indochina*, pp. 106-27.

[66] Chu Hsieh, *Diary*, pp. 1, 41-42, 103. The forces were the 53rd, 60th, 62nd, and 93rd Armies, and the 23rd, 39th, and 93rd Divisions.

[67] Devillers, *Histoire du Viet-Nam*, p. 152.

As seen by Chu Hsieh, the situation in Vietnam was most unfavorable for the French. The Vietnamese were hostile, the Japanese cool. It was through the Americans that the French hoped to have the Japanese to guard French officers and their concentration camps against Viet-Minh attacks. But the Americans were unenthusiastic in helping the French restore colonial rule. In Hanoi slogans such as "We would rather die than be slaves," "Don't negotiate with the French," and "Independence or death" were seen all over the city. The national flags of the United States, Great Britain, the Viet-Minh, China, and the Soviet Union were streaming in the wind, but not a single French one. The French were well aware of the situation; the only thing they could do was to wait and see.

The Chinese were not welcome by the Viet-Minh either. Prior to the arrival of Lu Han, the Viet-Minh had mapped out its policy and tactics toward the Chinese army.[68] In a 1965 Hanoi publication, its policy was made known: "With regard to the Chiang Kai-shek troops, it was necessary to avoid clashes, underline their mission which was to disarm the Japanese troops, prevent their acts of aggression, check their acts of intervention in the internal policy of the country; in case they attacked the national sovereignty, it was necessary to stand ready to launch an unarmed opposition, to mobilize the masses to demonstrate, in a word to 'oppose a political struggle to them.' "[69]

This was precisely what the Viet-Minh had done to the Chinese forces. In some cities Viet-Minh forces had even come in conflict with the Chinese army. On September 5, as the Chinese were entering the city of Cao-Bang, the Viet-Minh mobilized the people to demonstrate against the Chinese, then asked the Chinese to allow the Viet-Minh to share the occupation of the city. The Chinese refused and armed conflict broke out. More than 340 Viet-Minh and their weapons were captured by the Chinese. Viet-Minh forces also attacked and harassed the Chinese in Lao-Kay and

[68] Nguyen Luong Bang, "The Times I Met Him," p. 72.
[69] *Vietnamese Studies*, No. 7, p. 42.

Yen-Bay.[70] Meanwhile they organized the merchants from Bac-Giang to Hanoi for a strike to last several days whenever and wherever the Chinese army arrived.[71] But when the news of the French takeover of the south reached the north, and there was a public outcry against the British and French, the Viet-Minh changed to a friendly attitude toward the Chinese.

Regarding the Dong Minh Hoi and the VNQDD, the Viet-Minh's tactics were: "to isolate them before the masses of the people, utilize the forces of the masses as a means of pressure to enable the government to repress the counter-revolutionaries, and in case tangible proofs could be adduced against them, to proceed to wipe out their forces step by step. In case they received the support of their masters, it was necessary to neutralize them gradually; compromises might also be reached while safeguarding the revolutionary power."[72]

The Viet-Minh carried out exactly what it had planned. The "best way" to isolate the Dong Minh Hoi and the VNQDD from the people was to hold general elections, and, in Ho Chi Minh's words, "the earlier the better."[73] The Viet-Minh government announced on September 8, 1945, before the arrival of the Chinese and the Vietnamese nationalists, that general elections would be held on January 6, 1946. It was a good decision, for if the Viet-Minh won the elections, which it was sure to do, it would not only isolate the Dong Minh Hoi and VNQDD from the people but also obtain the recognition of the legitimacy of its regime from the Chinese, French, and Americans.

On August 20 Dong Minh Hoi leaders Nguyen Hai Than, Nong Kinh Du, Truong Trung Phung, Bo Xuan Luat, Le Tung Son, and others, together with a few hundred men, entered Vietnam under Hsiao Wen's command.[74] They

[70] Nguyen Luong Bang, "The Times I Met Him," p. 73.

[71] Hsing Shen-chou's report, October 1, 1945, in "Documents."

[72] *Vietnamese Studies*, No. 7, p. 43.

[73] *Ibid.*; Nguyen Luong Bang, "The Times I Met Him," p. 74.

[74] Truong Boi Cong died in China in July 1945.

arrived in Hanoi on September 16. Two days later Ho Chi Minh went to see Hsiao Wen to emphasize (1) that he would "obey" Chinese orders and accept direction and (2) that he "offered" his life as a "guarantee" to assure Hsiao that there would no longer be any anti-Chinese actions or words from the 2,500,000 Vietnamese people. Ho also said his provisional government would be willing to accept the participation of other parties.[75] It is clear that Ho, though cooperative with the Chinese, had won acceptance of his government from China, over other political parties.

The armed unit under Vu Kim Thanh, which sought to enter Vietnam from Tunghsing, as already mentioned, had by mid-August developed into an army of more than 1,000 men with 700 guns. On September 1 (one day before the establishment of the Viet-Minh regime), Thanh set up a "National Provisional Government of Vietnam" at Mon-Kay (a border city facing China's Tunghsing) with Nguyen Hai Than as its president (at the absence of Than, Thanh served as acting president). After learning that Than had arrived in Hanoi, Thanh on October 6 secretly went to the Viet-Minh capital via Haiphong to see him.[76] Meanwhile, there was another armed group at Lang-Son led by Nong Quoc Long (son of Nong Kinh Du) that was supporting Nguyen Hai Than.[77] It seemed that Than, because of his connections with China, could rally a good number of nationalists behind him. But Hsiao Wen persuaded Than and his supporters to cooperate with Ho Chi Minh for a united "opposition to the French." At this point, the Viet-Minh tactfully neutralized its hostile attitude toward the Dong Minh Hoi. On October 23, 1945 the Viet-Minh persuaded Vu Kim Thanh and some of the Dong Minh Hoi to sign a "cooperation declaration" with the Viet-Minh. The document announced that the two parties, at their unification conference, had decided to unite and support the provisional government in the interest of a "common struggle against the

[75] Chang Fa-k'uei's report, September 17, 1946, in "Documents."
[76] Hsing Shen-chou's report, October 15, 1945, in *ibid.*
[77] Hsiao Wen's report, November 1, 1946, in *ibid.*

French aggression in order to defend the liberty and independence of the Democratic Republic of Vietnam."[78] But apart from Vu Kim Thanh, the other signatories of the Dong Minh Hoi were either ICP or pro-Viet-Minh under Hsiao Wen's control. None was an original Dong Minh Hoi leader. Thus Nguyen Hai Than complained to Chungking about Hsiao Wen's intervention: "After I have returned to Vietnam, all the anti-Vietminh elements, partisan or non-partisan, rallied under the banner of the Dong Minh Hoi; but Mr. Hsiao Wen urged Vietminh members Le Tung Son, Truong Trung Phung, Ho Duc Thanh, Bo Xuan Luat and others, to organize a phony Dong Minh Hoi splitting the Vietnamese revolutionary strength."[79]

Soon after the signing of the "cooperation declaration" Vu Kim Thanh realized he was caught in a Viet-Minh trap. He found out that the Viet-Minh was employing a dual policy against him—to cooperate with him politically in Hanoi and attack him militarily in his occupied areas of Hai-Ninh and Vinh-Yen.[80] In anger, Vu Kim Thanh withdrew from the Viet-Minh.

Conflicts between the Viet-Minh and the VNQDD occurred simultaneously in north and northwestern Tonkin. In Lao-Kay, Yen-Bay, and Phu-Tho Viet-Minh forces clashed with the VNQDD and Dai Viet under Vu Hong Khanh, Vo Quang Pham, and Nguyen Tuong Tam, then retreated.[81] When the VNQDD reached Hanoi its leaders published "Vietnam News" denouncing the Viet-Minh as a Communist party that intended to Communize Vietnam. Nguyen Hai Than and his men were apprised of the denunciation. Ho Chi Minh found it necessary to compromise with

[78] *Ch'ing nien jih pao* (a Chinese paper; *Youth Daily News*, Hanoi; Thanh-Nien in Vietnamese), October 25, 1945. The signatories were Ting Truong Duong, Truong Trung Phung, Le Tung Son, Bo Xuan Luat, Ho Duc Thanh, Vu Kim Thanh, Duong Thanh Minh (DMH); Nguyen Luong Bang, Duong Duc Hien, Nguyen Van Ba, Hoang Huu Nam, Nguyen Cong Bac (VM).

[79] Nguyen Hai Than's report, February 15, 1946, in "Documents."

[80] Vu Kim Thanh's report, October 26, 1945, in *ibid.*

[81] Hsiao Wen's report, November 1, 1946, in *ibid.*

them; his approach was through the Chinese. But, to what extent would the Chinese, now headed by Lu Han and not Hsiao Wen, help or hinder?[82] Let us now turn to the occupation authorities.

As pointed out earlier, Lu Han disagreed with the Chinese occupation policy and disliked the French colonial personnel. With a view to assisting the Chungking government in formulating a more realistic policy for the occupied Vietnam, Lu Han conferred on September 22 with all of the Chinese personnel, military and civilian, seeking suggestions for Chungking. They decided to send Shao Pai-ch'ang and Ling Ch'i-han to Chungking to report on the situation in Vietnam and seek an up-to-date policy.

In comparison, Lu Han was not as hostile to the Viet-Minh as he was to the French. At the Japanese surrender ceremony on September 28 the Viet-Minh officials were invited to attend, but the French were not—in defiance of the occupation policy. General Alessandri, just arrived from Yunnan for the ceremony, was not allowed to attend because of his "unclear position."[83] Alessandri asked to raise the French flag, which was also refused on the grounds that disturbances, as had occurred in Saigon during the surrender ceremony, might also occur if the French flag were raised. In anger Alessandri left the ceremony. Moreover, in a proclamation issued on the same day, Lu Han warned "the enemy of Vietnam" that if he dared to cause any trouble or to stir up bloody tragedy, Lu Han would severely punish him according to laws "regardless of their race and religion."[84] With the Japanese defeated and disarmed and the Americans and Chinese on good terms with the Vietnamese, the "enemy of Vietnam" could only be the French.

[82] According to Shao Pai-ch'ang, Hsiao Wen was disgraced with Lu Han. At one time Lu Han intended to arrest Hsiao. Shao's letter to the author.

[83] Chu Hsieh, *Diary*, p. 19. To Lu Han, the "unclear position" of General Alessandri was his service with the Vichy regime and co-operation with the Japanese in Indochina, although the French general had purged himself of his Vichy taint by serving with General de Gaulle after March 9, 1945.

[84] *Ibid.*, p. 21.

Before the two men sent by Lu Han returned from Chungking, Gen. Ho Ying-ch'in arrived at Hanoi on October 1. General Ho's main concern was the discipline of the Chinese army, but he also maintained an interest in the Viet-Minh and the French. Lu Han gave a dinner on October 1 in his honor; both General Alessandri and Ho Chi Minh were invited. On October 4, at a conference convened by General Ho, a few important items, among others, were decided on:

(1) to complete, before October 31, the acceptance of surrender and the disarming of Japanese troops
(2) to complete, before November 10, the concentration of the disarmed Japanese
(3) to be careful in dealing with the Vietnamese Provisional Government, while maintaining a friendly position. Formal governmental communications with it should be avoided[85]

Ho Ying-ch'in's position regarding the Viet-Minh was also moderate. But Lu Han expressed different views. He offered Ho Ying-ch'in three alternatives for the political future of Vietnam: (1) support the present regime (Ho Chi Minh's government) and defend internationally its position on securing Vietnam's freedom and independence; (2) place Vietnam under international trusteeship for a period of time and then grant her independence, or (3) return Vietnam to the French after both China and Vietnam have secured from France the most favorable conditions.[86] It became clear that Lu Han preferred an independent Vietnam under the aegis of China. But after the "Kunming Incident" of October 5 he was appointed to serve concurrently as governor of Yunnan, replacing Lung Yun.[87] He spent most of his time

[85] *Ibid.*, pp. 30-31.
[86] Hsing Shen-chou's report, October 15, 1945, in "Documents."
[87] Lung Yun (1888-1962) was a cousin of Lu Han. A graduate of the Yunnan Military Academy, he was the ruler of Yunnan until 1945. After the "Kunming Incident" he was transferred to Chungking and then Nanking, serving as director of the military Advisory Board, a powerless office under President Chiang. He escaped from Nanking

in Kunming during the occupation period, too preoccupied to take any significant and independent part in Vietnam.

Three days later Ling Ch'i-han returned to Hanoi with a message from Chungking which was summarized by Chu Hsieh into four points:

(1) take a stand of non-intervention in regard to the Viet-Minh, but the Chinese army should firmly control the railway and seaports
(2) evacuate the occupation forces immediately after completing the disarmament and repatriation of the Japanese armies
(3) take over no Vietnamese civilian offices
(4) not take over the Bank of Indochina[88]

The reaffirmation of the neutral policy of Chungking further blocked Lu Han from acting freely toward the Viet–Minh. Yet his pro–Viet-Minh position must have been made known to Ho Chi Minh since the latter was a frequent visitor of Hsiao Wen's in Hanoi.[89] Realizing that the Chinese must first be pleased before a compromise with the VNQDD and Dong Minh Hoi could be made, Ho handled them carefully. He purchased arms from the Chinese with the gold he collected from the people during the "gold week" campaign in September,[90] issued directives that the chief enemy of Vietnam was "aggressive French imperialism," and repeatedly assured Shao Pai-ch'ang and Hsing Shen-chou that

---

to Hong Kong in 1948 and went to Peking in 1949, where he held the post of vice-chairman of the Defense Council. During the "one hundred flower" period in 1956-1957, he accused the Soviets of looting in Manchuria in 1945-1946. As a result he lost his position. One of his sons, Lung Shen-wu, was a division commander in Lu Han's occupation army in Vietnam, while his other son, Lung Shao-wu, gave his support to the Chinese Communists in early 1948. Vu Hong Khanh's letter of May 30, 1969 states that Lu Han's pro–Viet-Minh position was well known.

[88] Chu Hsieh, *Diary*, p. 35.

[89] Liu San, "Ho Chi Minh in South China." Shao Pai-ch'ang said that Hsiao Wen received gifts from Ho and always defended Ho. (Shao's letter to the author.)

[90] Nghiem Ke To's letter to the author, March 31, 1969.

he respected China, believed the philosophy of *San Min Chu I*, and was not a Communist.[91] He invited Nguyen Tuong Tam to serve as foreign minister, Nghiem Ke To as deputy foreign minister, Vu Hong Khanh as chairman of the military council, and Vu Kim Thanh as army commander.[92] At a cabinet meeting on November 5, 1945 Ho proposed sending a governmental delegation to Chungking to pay their respects to Generalissimo Chiang; but the Chinese government declined the request.

Ho next made a surprising move. After a meeting November 9 to 11, the ICP issued a resolution proposing to dissolve the party. A communiqué was issued to explain the decision:

> In order to destroy all misunderstanding, domestic and foreign, which can hinder the liberation of our country, the Central Executive Committee of the Indochina Communist Party in meeting assembled on November 11, 1945, has decided to voluntarily dissolve the Indochina Communist Party.
>
> Those followers of Communism desirous of continuing their theoretical studies will affiliate with the Indochina Association of Marxist Studies.[93]

It would be naive to assume that the ICP was actually dissolved. It merely went underground[94] to prepare for the fight with the Chinese. On November 12 the ICP held a secret cadre meeting at which two items for dealing with the Chinese army were decided on:

> (1) If the Chinese impose an armed repression, [we will] call for strikes by all the workers, if necessary, destroy the electric and water plants, employ terrorism and disturb social order.

[91] Shao-Pai-ch'ang's letter to the author.
[92] Hsing Shen-chou's report, June 23, 1946, in "Documents."
[93] Hsing Shen-chou's report, November 20, 1945, in *ibid.* Also see Sacks, "Marxism in Viet Nam," p. 158.
[94] *Vietnamese Studies,* No. 7, p. 43.

(2) If the Chinese forces and the reactionaries, Nguyen Hai Than, Nghiem Ke To, and Vu Hong Khanh, would cause the loss of our power, we will carry out a "scorched-earth" policy and instigate the peasants and workers to rebel.[95]

With a showdown policy for the ICP ready, Ho began to negotiate with the Dong Minh Hoi and VNQDD, which had already solicited Chinese pressures on Ho. For a month, from mid-November to mid-December, the negotiations yielded no result. At first, as Shao Pai-ch'ang recalled, the nationalists asked for the presidency and six ministerial seats in the government.[96] Ho refused, and offered three ministerial posts, plus a political advisory group headed by Nguyen Hai Than. This the nationalists rejected. As the negotiations dragged on, armed conflict, including kidnapping and terrorism, between these two parties went from bad to worse. To maintain security and civil order under the occupation and to help settle the disagreements, the Chinese were asked to intervene. The occupation headquarters called for a meeting on December 19 which was attended by the Viet-Minh, the Dong Minh Hoi, VNQDD, and the Chinese. After several meetings a final agreement was reached and a communiqué expressing cooperation was issued on December 26 with the signatures of Ho Chi Minh, Nguyen Hai Than, and Vu Hong Khanh. It announced:

(1) The Provisional Coalition Government will be established on January 1, 1946.
(2) The VNQDD should occupy 50 seats and [the] Dong Minh Hoi 20 seats in the future National Assembly.
(3) Ho Chi Minh will be the President and Nguyen Hai Than Vice-President.

[95] Hsing Shen-chou's report, November 20, 1945, in "Documents." See also Vu Hong Khanh's letter of May 30, 1969 to the author.

[96] Shao Pai-ch'ang's letter to the author. On November 23, 1945 the Chinese Communist *Hsin hua jih pao* (Chungking) published the news that the Viet-Minh and the VNQDD had agreed on a ceasefire and unification for independence.

(4) The division of the ministerial posts in the coalition cabinet is: the Viet-Minh 2, the VNQDD 2, the Democratic Party 2, the Dong Minh Hoi 2, and non-party 2. The Defense and Interior Ministries will be headed by the two nonparty members.

(5) Both sides (the Viet-Minh and the VNQDD-DMH) exchange the lists of captured and kidnapped personnel and release them before December 28.

(6) Independence first, unification first! From now on both sides [will] stop mutual attacks and settle differences by sincere negotiations.[97]

The leaders of the Dong Minh Hoi and the VNQDD in Hanoi were to hold high governmental positions.[98] General elections were held on January 6, 1946 as scheduled. The Viet-Minh claimed a victory consisting of 97 per cent of the popular vote, giving it 300 seats in the Assembly, but kept its promise to give 50 seats to the VNQDD and 20 to the Dong Minh Hoi. Ho Chi Minh's tactics of isolating his opponents from the people were successful and enabled the Viet-Minh to claim it had mandate of the people. The Chinese could only extend their congratulations to Ho. Ho continued to express his sincere willingness to cooperate with China and

---

[97] Hsing Shen-chou's report, December 26, 1945, in "Documents."

[98] The cabinet of the Provisional Coalition Government of January 1946 was:

President	Ho Chi Minh	VM (Communist)
Vice-President	Nguyen Hai Than	DMH
Foreign Affairs	Nguyen Tuong Tam	VNQDD (Dai Viet)
Economy	Chu Ba Phuong	VNQDD
Health	Truong Dinh Tri	DMH
Agriculture	Bo Xuan Luat	DMH (Phuc Quoc)
Finance	Le Van Hien	VM (Communist)
Education	Dang Thai Mai	VM (Communist)
Justice	Vu Dinh Hoe	Democrat (VM)
Public Works	Tran Dang Khoa	Democrat (VM)
Interior	Huynh Thuc Khang	Independent
National Defense	Phan Anh	Independent (Socialist)
Military Council	Vo Nguyen Giap	VM (Communist)
	Vu Hong Khanh	VNQDD

Meanwhile, Nghiem Ke To and Nong Kinh Du were made deputy-ministers, and Vu Kim Thanh vice-chairman of the Military Council.

accept Chungking's direction. The newly elected National Assembly met on March 2, 1946. The prearranged coalition government headed by Ho Chi Minh was sworn in, but Nguyen Hai Than had left Hanoi for China. At its cabinet meeting on March 4 the government adopted a pro-Chinese policy in foreign relations. Ho's pro-China attitude was so convincing that some Chinese personnel in Hanoi thought a better relationship between the Chinese government and Ho was in effect. Before and after the Sino-French agreements of 1946 were published (March 1), Shao Pai-ch'ang, in the capacity of the chief of the Vietnam Advisory Group, twice urged Ho to negotiate immediately with the French for a satisfactory settlement before the Chinese departed. At this point, China was genuinely sympathetic toward Ho's Vietnam.[99]

Yet friction between the VNQDD and the Viet-Minh was not over; this was only a brief lull. On the same day of the general elections (January 6), more than 10 VNQDD men were killed in northern Tonkin. In February there was sporadic fighting in Yen-Bay, Phu-Tho, Lang-Son, Phuc-Yen, and Viet-Tri. With the imminent departure of the Chinese army, the Viet-Minh forces under Giap could afford to defy the Chinese and violate the December 23 agreement by eliminating the VNQDD armed units bit by bit. In the scramble for power between the Vietnamese Communists and nationalists, it was soon obvious that the Chinese effort to establish the Vietnamese nationalists had failed.

A final point should be made here. At a television interview (NBC) on May 14, 1967, C. K. Yen, vice-president and premier of the Republic of China in Taiwan, was asked by Stanley Swinton of the Associated Press, who was in Hanoi in 1946, to explain how Ho Chi Minh was put in power by

[99] Chu Hsieh, *Diary*, pp. 99, 101. Shao Pai-ch'ang, in a letter to the author, defended the Chinese sympathy and assistance to Ho Chi Minh as an expediency to meet the needs of the Vietnamese people. After the departure of the Chinese army the weakness of the VNQDD and the error of French policy offered opportunities for the rise of the Viet-Minh.

Free China (the Republic of China).[100] It seems the question is not *how* Ho was put in power by the Chinese, but *whether* he was. As the above discussion shows, Ho had already established his regime by the time the Chinese occupation forces had arrived in Hanoi, and the Chinese intervened in favor of the Vietnamese nationalists, not Ho Chi Minh; they significantly weakened Ho's power thereby. China was not in a position to wrest power from Ho completely, for the Vietnamese nationalists were weak and without mass support. Moreover, Americans in Hanoi at the time of the State Department's involvement in American policy-making,[101] favored Ho over the nationalists or a return of the French. Many factors combined that were favorable to Ho's regime. One wonders whether Ho was put in power by the Republic of China at all.

3. THE CHINESE OCCUPATION AND THE FRENCH

The Chinese occupation of Vietnam was an unhappy event for the French. Treatment of the subject in French and English have accused the Chinese of taking advantage of the occupation, while Chinese publications have been critical of French colonialism. Both the Chinese and French governments should bear responsibility for the failure to make prior arrangements in several issues that caused trouble during the occupation.

The question of whether the French should provide the Chinese occupation forces with funds for military expenditures (including food) was difficult to agree on. If the French should, then how? Had the policy-makers in both Chungking and Paris been realistic enough to take the issues seriously for a timely settlement, the troubles could have been avoided.

As mentioned above, the Viet-Minh government found only about 1,250,000 piasters in the state treasury when it

[100] See *Meet the Press*, (Washington, D.C.: Merkle Press Inc., May 14, 1967), p. 4.

[101] See Donald Lancaster, *The Emancipation of French Indochina* (London: Oxford University Press, 1961), p. 143.

took over. The Bank of Indochina, which the Viet-Minh did not take over, had 175,000,000 piasters. In view of the fact that the budget of the Indochinese government for 1944-1945 was merely 285 million piasters,[102] the allocation of approximately 96 million piasters per month to the Chinese for military occupation expenses was a great burden to the French.

The food situation was on the verge of disaster. According to the estimates of the Viet-Minh, the 1945 autumn harvest was poor; it "hardly sufficed to feed eight million persons for three months."[103] To avoid new nationwide starvation, the Viet-Minh government in September 1945 launched an "All-Out Campaign against Famine." The arrival of the Chinese army of 152,500 men certainly increased the difficulty of food supply. Fortunately the problem was gradually alleviated by supplies from Saigon, although the French tried time and again to delay shipments to the north.[104]

The exchange rate between Chinese currency and the piaster was another issue that should have been settled before the occupation took place. The unilateral Chinese decision on the rate, which was in favor of the Chinese bank note, created a golden opportunity for the military to reap the benefits through legal or illegal commercial channels between Hanoi and Kunming.

As soon as the Chinese moved into Vietnam they dismantled the French military fortifications along the Sino-Vietnamese border, quickly disarmed the Japanese army, concentrated the disarmed Japanese at the seaport area for repatriation, and secured their control over the Indochina Railway and seaports. The Chinese residents in Hanoi were heartened by the arrival in the city of their own army. Crowded with Chinese, Vietnamese, and some Japanese and Americans, Hanoi became an internationally important city.

[102] Chu Hsieh, *Diary*, pp. 13-16, 67-68.
[103] *Vietnamese Studies*, No. 7, p. 44.
[104] Hsing Shen-chou's report, Oct. 27, 1945, in "Documents"; Chu Hsieh, *Diary*, pp. 55, 61, 78.

The French welcomed Chinese negotiations on Vietnam with them, for it was a sign of Chinese recognition of French sovereignty over Indochina, but they did not want the arrival of the Chinese army. The problems of military expenditures and the exchange rate caused great difficulty for the French mission headed by Sainteny. Upon his arrival Lu Han asked the French-controlled Bank of Indochina to advance 15,000,000 piasters for urgent military needs.[105] Then he requested through the Chinese Advisory Group about 95,935,000 piasters for monthly expenditures.[106] Meanwhile his headquarters raised the exchange rate between the piaster and the Chinese gold-unit dollar from 1-to-1, to 1.5 piasters to 1 gold-unit.[107] This tripled the value of Chinese money in Hanoi. While a fixed exchange rate was necessary since the Chinese army had brought in 1,200,000,000 Chinese dollars in bank notes, the increase was made by Lu Han's arbitrary decision rather than by an adequate foreign exchange rate. In early October the Chinese government in Chungking took up the two financial problems with the French embassy there, but no agreement was reached. As the negotiations in Chungking continued off and on financial needs compelled the Chungking government to decide on November 2 on the maintenance of the increased exchange rate on a temporary basis, and to authorize Lu Han to borrow 40 million piasters monthly from the Bank of Indochina. The account would be liquidated by future Sino-French agreements.[108]

On November 14 Chinese occupation authorities conferred with Sainteny's French Mission. The Chinese, in accordance with the aforesaid decision by their government, demanded that the French make two decisions:

[105] Chu Hsieh, *Diary*, p. 23.

[106] *Ibid.*, pp. 24, 41. Lu Han requested 210,000,000 piasters, but the Chinese Financial Ministry cut it to 95,935,000.

[107] Sainteny, *Histoire*, p. 149; *Vietnamese Studies*, No. 7, p. 201; Chu Hsieh, *Diary*, p. 25. The gold-unit (kuan-chin) was then a new bank note valued at 20 times the old Chinese currency. Both notes were in circulation.

[108] *Ibid.*, pp. 40, 48-49.

(1) The Bank of Indochina and the Sino-French Bank provide daily 600,000 piasters for the exchange of the gold-unit. The daily exchange limit per person is 50 gold-unit dollars.

(2) The Bank of Indochina advances 40,000,000 piasters monthly to the Chinese army for urgent needs. The account will be liquidated by future Sino-French negotiations.[109]

The French thought it would be difficult to carry out the demands. On the Chinese side, Chu Hsieh, Shao Pai-ch'ang, and Ch'en Hsiu-ho explained their needs and Chungking's decision; then the deputy chief of staff of the occupation army insisted that the French accept the request. Sainteny had no other choice, and indicated his willingness to accept, while offering some views on technical aspects of the exchange issue.[110]

November 20 was the scheduled first day for exchange. But the preceding day the Chinese were informed by the French that the Bank of Indochina (under the control of the French) could not carry the exchange service for the Chinese government. On November 20 the Sino-French Bank, which was taken over by the Chinese from the Japanese but with the French management, also informed the Chinese that the French mission had ordered it to make no exchange services. But the Chinese insisted the exchange be carried out by the Sino-French Bank. Worse still, Sainteny announced the same day that the proclamation, which was issued by the French authorities in Saigon on November 17 to the effect that all 500-piaster bank notes were no longer good in circulation, was applicable to north of the 16th parallel.[111] This was an attempt to devaluate the

---

[109] *Ibid.*, p. 54.   [110] *Ibid.*, pp. 54-55.

[111] *Ibid.*, pp. 57-58. The reason for the invalidation of the 500-piaster notes was that the Japanese authorities had issued 250 million piasters during the war without an official French signature. The total value of the notes in circulation was 627 million piasters. The French authorities under Admiral d'Argenlieu ordered the recall of all 500-piaster notes with no compensation for the above-mentioned 250

Chinese gold-unit under the pretext of "reforming" the finances of Indochina. The Chinese, to maintain the value of the gold-unit and protect the interests of Chinese residents and the northern Vietnamese who held at least half of the total value of 600 million piasters,[112] declared that the 500-piaster notes were still good. The contradictory measures of the two parties caused a great fluctuation to the financial market in Hanoi. In accusing the French of breaking the November 14 agreement, the Chinese sent a strong protest to Sainteny, demanding a satisfactory reply by November 26. Otherwise they would withdraw their guards at the banks.[113]

Ho Chi Minh watched the Sino-French confrontation closely and sought to exploit it. On November 26, before the French gave their reply, the Viet-Minh organized a mass demonstration in front of the Bank of Indochina, demanding the exchange of 500-piaster notes for ones of smaller value. During the afternoon the demonstrators encircled the Bank in protest against the French. At four o'clock shots rang out from the windows of the Bank, the masses responded, and the Chinese guards joined in the fighting. Some Vietnamese were killed, and the French were blamed. The following day the banks were closed. Vietnamese merchants and workers went on strike, refusing to sell food to the French.

Returning from Saigon, Sainteny gave his answer on the morning of November 27:

(1) The French will advance 40,000,000 piasters monthly.
(2) The French government does not want to take the

---

million, but with a discount of 30 per cent for the remaining 377 million piasters, which were issued with the official French signature.

[112] Tran Dan Tien, *Biography of Ho Chi Minh*, p. 172, said that the invalidation of the 500-piaster notes brought "bankruptcy" to hundreds of thousands of Vietnamese and Chinese families. Truong Ching, *August Revolution*, p. 37, stated that the French rejection of the 500-piaster notes placed more difficulties on the Viet-Minh's financial condition.

[113] Chu Hsieh, *Diary*, pp. 58-60.

gold-unit exchange service; if the Chinese army needs more money, the French could advance 15,000,000 more piasters.

(3) The invalidation of the 500-piaster notes is a financial policy of the French government; no change will be made.[114]

However, when on November 28, the Chinese asked the Bank of Indochina to reopen and advance the 15,000,000 additional piasters offered by the French, the managers of the bank refused. To pour oil on the flames, Sainteny informed the Chinese on November 29 that the French could not advance the 15,000,000 piasters unconditionally. The Viet-Minh–sponsored strikes went on, and the financial market became chaotic. To settle the financial crisis the Chinese came to grips with the French by arresting two French managers of the Bank of Indochina for their refusal to cooperate. The situation was truly strained. The French were searching desperately for a solution.

American General Gallagher, at the request of Sainteny, served as a mediator in the dispute. After a three-day conference General Gallagher expressed the opinion that Sainteny, who had failed to consult with the Chinese occupation authorities about the announcement of the invalidation of the 500-piaster notes which had caused the financial crisis, should bear responsibility for the dispute.[115] Then he himself offered to ask Ho Chi Minh to end the Vietnamese strike and boycott against the French. With new concessions from Saigon, a final agreement was reached on December 4:

(1) The French, with no conditions attached, will advance 15,000,000 more piasters monthly to the Chinese.

(2) The 500-piaster notes will still be valid north of the sixteenth parallel.

(3) The change of 500-piaster notes for smaller-value

[114] *Ibid.*, p. 64.   [115] *Ibid.*, p. 70.

ones will be carried out. For the people (Vietnamese, French, and Chinese), the limit is 15,000,000 piasters per month in total; for the Chinese soldiers, the change will be made only by the request of official letters.[116]

The financial dispute was over. The strikes ended and the Bank of Indochina reopened on December 6. Relations between the French and the Chinese gradually improved. Yet General Gallagher's efforts to bring about a settlement, and his amicable relations with Ho Chi Minh at the time, became the object of French accusations of American help to the Viet-Minh.[117]

The third item of the agreement on the rule for the Chinese forces, however, was a loophole through which Lu Han's army made great profits.[118] Chu Hsieh told the inside story. The military, in cooperation with Chinese merchants on occasion, forced the bank to change notes, operated a black market, and smuggled gold-units from Kunming to Hanoi. For example, in December 1945 the 21st Division of the army at Nghe-An forcibly borrowed 750,000 piasters from the Nghe-An branch of the Bank of Indochina. In January 1946 the 22nd Division at Haiphong demanded that the local branch of the bank exchange 700,000 gold-units daily for the piaster notes. On February 17, 1946 military headquarters sent an official letter to the Bank of Indochina in Hanoi, requesting small change of 16,000,000 pias-

[116] *Ibid.*, pp. 72-74. A North Vietnamese source (*Vietnamese Studies*, No. 7 [1965], pp. 201-202) gives a brief similar account, but makes no mention of Chinese and American efforts to bring about a settlement. Later, at the conclusion of the Sino-French agreements on February 28, 1946, the French government agreed to advance monthly to China 60,000,000 piasters (from September 1945 to February 1946), for military occupation expenses which were to be counted as part of Japan's reparations to France.

[117] On October 17, 1945, a Vietnamese-American Friendship Association was founded in Hanoi. General Gallagher and his officers attended its first meeting.

[118] Shao Pai-ch'ang recalled (letter to the author) that Lu Han's army took advantage of the occupation to make great profits through legal and illegal commercial channels.

ters worth of 500-piaster notes! It was reported that most of the 500-piaster notes had been purchased from the black market where a note was valued at 400 piasters or less.[119] The Vietnam Advisory Group, as a nonmilitary agent responsible for political, financial, and social stability, was disgusted with the military's behavior. Moreover, the three to five times difference between Chinese currency and the piaster in Kunming and Hanoi presented a fantastic opportunity for profit-making to Chinese businessmen, who often served as agents for high military officers.[120] Every flight of Chinese Airlines from Kunming to Hanoi brought in a great number of gold-units, once as high as 60,000,000.[121] Small merchants acted independently or in cooperation with lower ranking military officers, and used cars and trucks to smuggle merchandise and gold-units overland to Vietnam from China with the Chinese national flag for protection.[122] Lu Han's men bought up the big hotels, shops, and houses.[123] Some soldiers sold arms to the Vietnamese through private channels, and small weapons were smuggled into Indo-china from Kwangtung and Kwangsi.[124]

The notorious behavior of the army was reported to Gen. Ho Ying-ch'in, who ordered an investigation and the dismissal of the commander of the 21st Division. But the orders did not completely halt the military scandals.[125] As a result,

[119] Chu Hsieh, *Diary*, pp. 83, 86-87, 89, 91-92.

[120] Based on French, Chinese Nationalist, and Chinese Communist sources, the differences between the Chinese and Vietnamese banknotes were as follows: Hanoi, one gold-unit = 1.5 piasters; Kunming, one gold-unit = 0.29 to 0.5 piaster. Sources: Sainteny, *Histoire*, p. 149; Chu Hsieh, *Diary*, pp. 25, 43, 63; Mai Lang, *Chan tou chung ti hsin Yueh-nan* (The New Vietnam at War) (Shanghai: New Vietnam Publishing Co., 1948), p. 46. Mai Lang (Pai Mai-lang) was a Chinese Communist in Vietnam during the Chinese occupation period.

[121] Chu Hsieh, *Diary*, p. 63. This amount equalled 90,000,000 piasters in Hanoi at the time.

[122] Hsing Shen-chou's report, December 7, 1945, in "Documents."

[123] Isaacs, *Tragedy*, p. 169.

[124] *New York Times*, April 1, 1947.

[125] Chu Hsieh, *Diary*, p. 83. The scandals in Lu Han's army were reaffirmed in 1953, though not in detail, by Gen. Huang Chieh, Governor of Taiwan in 1968. See *Chung yang jih pao* (Taipei), July 24, 1953.

the Chinese gold-unit was devaluated, the honest businessmen in Hanoi suffered,[126] and the misbehavior of the occupation army was made known internationally.

There were other issues pending between the Chinese
and the French. The first was the Indochina Railway. Thor-
oughly aware of the importance of the railway and the
seaport of Haiphong, China wanted complete control of the
Yunnan section of the railroad that was on Chinese territory.

The second issue was the status of the 500,000 Chinese
residents in Indochina, most of whom lived in Hanoi, Haiphong, Saigon, Cholon, and Phnom Penh. As the major
business community, they played an important role in the
economic life of Indochina and held much property in the
cities. Although the 1935 Treaty of Nanking had classified
them as "foreigners" with a privileged position, the Chinese
still suffered from legal discrimination, heavy taxation, and
severe administrative restrictions.[127] As a victorious ally,
China was anxious to improve their position.

The third issue was French extraterritoriality in China.
The other powers, such as Great Britain and the United
States, had already yielded their similar special rights in
1943. China expected France to renounce hers through
negotiations.

The Chinese occupation of Vietnam placed China in an
advantageous position for bargaining with the French.
Negotiations started in Chungking in September 1945, and
went on for several months. During the negotiation period
foreign and domestic factors contributed to the early departure of the Chinese occupation army and the conclusion of
a Sino-French accord. The first was the French takeover of
Saigon on September 23, 1945. From there they reimposed
their rule on southern Vietnam, Cambodia, and Laos. The

[126] Hsing Shen-chou's report, December 7, 1945 in "Documents";
Chu Hsieh, *Diary*, p. 63.

[127] For the text of the Sino-French Treaty of 1935 in both French
and Chinese, see the Ministry of Foreign Affairs, Republic of China,
Treaties between the Republic of China and Foreign States (1927-
1957) (Taipei: China Engraving & Printing Works, 1958), pp. 113-
21.

return of the French to the greater part of Indochina indicated that the north would sooner or later be handed over to the French. Another factor was the evacuation of French and British troops from Lebanon and Syria after "the Syria-Lebanon case" was brought up in the Security Council in early February 1946. The case hinted at the possibility that foreign troops would have to leave occupied soil one way or another. The third factor, which might have directly and effectively influenced the negotiations, was the strong demand of Chinese students in February 1946 for the withdrawal of Soviet troops from Manchuria. The implication of the demand was that Chinese troops should also leave Vietnam. The fourth and most urgent was the Chinese Communist rebellion. In February 1946 a few thousand "empty-handed" Communists in Manchuria under Lin Piao turned the area into a Communist stronghold with a well-equipped "United-Democratic Army" of a hundred thousand men. After Gen. George Marshall was sent to China in late December 1945 to mediate the KMT-CCP civil war, a ceasefire was temporarily agreed upon; but the situation, especially in Manchuria, remained strained. The Kuomintang government in Nanking was anxious to reach an early settlement with the French on the above-mentioned issues so it could transport the bulk of its army from Vietnam to Manchuria and deal with its rival there.

Negotiations were stepped up in late February. On February 28, final agreements were reached. Wang Shih-chieh, the Chinese minister of foreign affairs, and Jacques Meyrier, French ambassador in Chungking, signed the agreements.[128]

According to the agreements, the relief of the Chinese occupation army would begin between March 1 and 15 and be completed by the 31st. The procedures for carrying out the operation were to be worked out by the Chinese and French military staff in Chungking. The French government renounced all extraterritorial and related rights in Shanghai, Tientsin, Hankow, and Canton. The Chinese and French would share rights to travel, reside, and carry on

[128] See Appendix III.

commerce in all the territories of France and China. Other rights concerning these two countries and their people were also based on mutual equality.

In regard to the Indochina Railway, the agreement of October 29, 1903 concerning the rail line was terminated. Although the Chinese government did not succeed in obtaining a Sino-French joint management of the Vietnam section of the railway and Haiphong port, the Chinese section of the rail line, from Kunming to Hokow, was transferred to China by "advanced repurchase."

The status of the Chinese in Vietnam was improved. Their traditional rights and exemptions in Indochina were continued, particularly those relating to taxation, real estate, establishment of primary and secondary schools, etc. They also enjoyed the right, which was no less favorable than that enjoyed by the nationals or any third most-favored nation, to travel, reside, and engage in business. Taxes, particularly the capitation tax, could not be heavier than that imposed on the Indochinese. Furthermore, they enjoyed the same treatment in legal proceedings and the administration of justice as enjoyed by the French.

Another accord was on international transit. It was provided that the French government would reserve a special zone in Haiphong for the free transit of merchandise to and from China. In this zone Chinese customs authorities were to be responsible for customs supervision. Merchandise coming to the zone from China via the Indochina Railway would be exempt from all transit duties or taxes.

The Chinese obtained a good price from the French for the agreement to evacuate their occupation forces. But Lu Han, who came back to Hanoi in mid-March, still expressed deep dissatisfaction with the accords.[129] Ironically, no sooner had the French yielded their special rights in China than the Chinese secured special rights from the French in Vietnam. This was the first time since the West had gone into China that China had concluded an "unequal treaty"

[129] Chu Hsieh, *Diary*, p. 111.

with a foreign power. In international affairs the ending of military occupation in a foreign land is always costly. In comparison, the price the French and Vietnamese paid for the Chinese occupation in Vietnam was much lower than what the Chinese had paid for the Soviet occupation in Manchuria.[130]

As soon as the Sino-French treaty was published (March 1) the situation in Hanoi worsened. The Vietnamese learned that the French forces would reoccupy northern Vietnam, and apprehension grew. Anti-French sentiment turned into complaints against China.[131] Within a week many people left Hanoi. The Viet-Minh strengthened its military positions. Hanoi was nearly deserted.

The French intended to move into Hanoi by March 9; the timing was meant to be symbolic revenge for the humiliation they had suffered from the Japanese one year earlier. Also, they could now negotiate with the Viet-Minh from strength. The French military mission asked that its troops be allowed to land at Haiphong on March 6. At a Sino-French military conference on the evening of March 4, Gen. Raoul Salan presented (incorrectly) a decision by an earlier Sino-French staff meeting in Chungking, that Chungking had agreed to a French landing at Haiphong on March 6.[132] Without consulting the Vietnam Advisory

---

[130] It is interesting to compare the cost of the Chinese occupation in Vietnam and the Soviet in Manchuria. The cost of the Chinese occupation has never been officially estimated or published. However, according to various sources, the amount may have run more than 500,000,000 piasters. Chu Hsieh, *Diary*, pp. 23, 83, 91-92, 113-14; Sainteny, *Histoire*, p. 148. The cost of the Soviet occupation in Manchuria was estimated as follows: $3,000,000 (U.S.) in gold bullion stocks and 500,000,000 Manchurian yuan were issued by the Soviet authorities; 70 per cent of machine plants, 50 per cent of food factories, 50 per cent of steel plants, 25 per cent of food processing plants, and 16 per cent of the coal mines were destroyed or the machinery was removed. See Department of State *Bulletin*, March 17, 1946, pp. 448-49, December 22, 1946, pp. 1,154-55; *United States Relations with China* (1949), pp. 601-603; *New York Times*, November 27, 1945, February 27, March 13, April 9, 26, 1946; *Ta Kung pao* (Shanghai), March 4, 5, 1946.

[131] Chu Hsieh, *Diary*, p. 100.

[132] *Ibid.*, p. 103. On March 8 the Vietnam Advisory Group received

Group the Chinese military authorities granted the French request.

On the morning of March 5, when the Advisory Group learned of the impending French landing, Shao Pai-ch'ang and other members of the Advisory Group were surprised and divided in opinion, for French–Viet-Minh negotiations had not then been concluded. If the French landed at Haiphong the Viet-Minh would resist—a war situation for which the Chinese would be responsible. At this difficult moment a cable from Chungking stated that since China's acceptance of the Japanese surrender in Indochina was by order of the Far East Supreme Commander for the Allied Forces, the removal of Chinese forces from the area should first be reported to General MacArthur's headquarters. The cable might not have been intended to prevent the French from landing at Haiphong on March 6, but the Vietnam Advisory Group now urged the military authorities to order the Chinese army at Haiphong not to let the French land on that date. Meanwhile the Advisory Group advised Ho Chi Minh to negotiate immediately with the French. Both the French and Chinese liaison officers were prevented from flying to Haiphong to give the landing order.[133]

But the French force, in six warships near Haiphong, was ordered to land at the seaport early on the morning of March 6. The Chinese refused to allow them to land. Fighting started at 8 A.M. and lasted for two hours. A Chinese arms depot on the docks was blown up; one French warship was sunk and two sailed off after being damaged.[134] The French apologized and promised to pay for the damage. After a cease-fire agreement in the afternoon the Viet-

a cable from Chungking, stating that the Chinese government did not agree to a French landing on March 6.

[133] Chu Hsieh, *Diary,* p. 102.

[134] *Ibid.,* pp. 102-108. Shao Pai-ch'ang (letter to the author) stated that two French warships were sunk, with 500 casualties. Bernard Fall merely stated that the Chinese depot was hit and exploded, and did not mention the French casualties. See Fall, *Two Viet-Nams,* p. 73.

namese in the city demonstrated in the streets, celebrating the Chinese preventing the French from landing.[135]

But the French landed at Haiphong the next day. On March 18 a French force of 1,076 men under General Leclerc occupied Hanoi, bringing with them truckloads of weapons for rearming the French prisoners to be released. The Chinese had agreed to the French occupation of Haiphong on March 22, Hanoi on the 23rd, Nam-Dinh and Da-Nang March 24 to 26. Because of the limited size of the French force, some areas, such as Thanh-Hoa, were handed over directly to the Viet-Minh by the Chinese. These Viet-Minh areas later became Viet-Minh strongholds against the French.

4. A THREE-FRONT BATTLE

If one asks about the most difficult political-military battle Ho Chi Minh has ever fought in a given time, the answer should not be the Indochinese war (1946-1954), nor the present war with the United States, but the three-front battle against the Chinese, French, and Vietnamese nationalists in 1945-1946, particularly 1946. As the Viet-Minh journalist Tran Dan Tien said in 1947: "This was the most difficult time for Ho."[136] Alert and skillful, Ho demonstrated tactics of maneuverability and flexibility, and played one enemy against another.

Throughout the Chinese occupation Ho repeatedly told Hsiao Wen, Shao Pai-ch'ang, Hsing Shen-chou, and others that he believed the doctrine of *San Min Chu I*, that he needed Chinese friendship, that the Chinese government's policy of fighting for complete independence and freedom was his government's policy, that he was not carrying out the Communist program, and that the first enemy of the Vietnamese was French colonialism. Not a word was offensive to the Chinese. Realizing the keen interest of the Chinese occupation authorities in protecting Chinese residents,

[135] Chu Hsieh, *Diary*, p. 108.
[136] Tran Dan Tien, *Biography of Ho Chi Minh*, p. 171.

his men agitated a Chinese-Vietnamese anti-French movement in Hanoi. On January 3, 1946 a Chinese newspaper
in Hanoi, *Ch'ing nien Daily News*, published a special edition on a Saigon incident the previous month in which some
Chinese were killed by the French. Chinese youths held
emotional meetings and organized mass demonstrations
against the French. Viet-Minh newspapers fanned the
flames. On January 10 and 11 Chinese and French clashed
in the streets; and the Viet-Minh helped the Chinese. Not
until later did the Chinese youths realize that they had
played into the Viet-Minh's hands.[137]

While the Viet-Minh leaders showed their most cordial
and respectful side to the Chinese north of the 16th parallel,
their followers in the south took advantage of the Chinese
occupation. They displayed the Chinese national flag on
vehicles and boats, which carried personnel, arms, and
merchandise from place to place. Their terrorists pinned on
their clothes badges with Kuomintang's symbol and Chiang
Kai-shek's portrait as a sign of protection and support from
China.[138] The French, without any knowledge of the Viet-
Minh activity, complained of illegal activities by the Chinese in the south.

As noted earlier, a Chinese source has pointed out that
the Franco-Vietnamese negotiations began secretly as early
as August 18, 1945. The goal of the five conditions presented
by Ho at that time was Vietnam's independence, while the
Viet-Minh regime was willing to accept the French as
advisors "against foreign invasion." Who else but China
would be the foreign invader? It became clear that Ho had
begun to play the French against the Chinese before the
Chinese occupation took place. As is well known today, a
Franco-Vietnamese agreement based on Ho's five conditions was signed March 6, 1946.[139] The agreement provided
that the Viet-Minh agreed to accept the French army in

[137] Chu Hsieh, *Diary*, p. 88; Ling Ch'i-han's report, January 24,
1946, in "Documents."
[138] Hsing Shen-chou's report, December 7, 1945, in *ibid.*
[139] Text in Cole, *Conflict in Indochina*, pp. 40-42.

place of the Chinese forces, while the French government recognized Vietnam as a "free state," having its own government, parliament, army and treasury, and belonging to the Indochinese Federation and to the French Union. While Ho was glad to see such a replacement, it must have been an unspeakable pain for him to accept the return of French colonialism.

Ho Chi Minh's compromise with the French in March 1946 greatly disappointed his people. At a rally of some 100,000 in front of the Hanoi City Theatre on March 7, both Vo Nguyen Giap and Ho had to explain eloquently and emotionally to the audience why they "welcomed" the return of French colonial rule. Giap told the rally that there were three solutions to the Vietnamese situation: a long war of resistance leading to a final victory, a short war for a better settlement, and negotiations. The Viet-Minh could not choose the first or the second because the international situation was unfavorable to them, and to do so would bring about the complete destruction of the Viet-Minh's strength. The only way out, Giap said, was to negotiate with the French.[140] Ho was more emotional in attempting to calm the restive crowd, a tactic he used for serious issues. He said: "I, Ho Chi Minh, have always led you on the road to liberty. I have fought all my life for the independence of our Fatherland. You know that I would prefer death rather than to betray our country. I swear to you that I have not betrayed you."[141]

In fact, Ho himself was not satisfied with the agreement. As he said to Sainteny after the conclusion of the accord: "I am not happy about it, for after all, it is you who have won; you know well that I wanted more than that. . . ."[142] What the French had really won was that, with the agreement on the evacuation of the Chinese forces and the conclusion of the Franco-Vietnamese accord, the Vietnamese problem had been changed from an international issue to

[140] Devillers, *Histoire*, p. 229. [141] *Ibid.*, p. 231.
[142] Sainteny, *Histoire*, p. 167.

an internal problem. The French once again had a free hand in Indochina.

The VNQDD and Dong Minh Hoi bitterly attacked the Viet-Minh. They propagandized the accord as "an act of treason."[143] Nguyen Hai Than, already unhappy with his ceremonial position, used the ineffectiveness of the position as an excuse to protest against the Viet-Minh. He resigned from the vice-presidency and left for China in early March. To forestall any attacks Than and other nationalists might make in China on the Viet-Minh, Ho decided at a cabinet meeting on March 8, 1946 to send a mission to Chungking. He appointed a VNQDD leader, Nghiem Ke To, then deputy foreign minister, who still worked for China, to head the three-man delegation, accompanied by Bao Dai. (He also sent a delegation to Paris for a final agreement.) The delegation to China reached Chungking on March 23rd and returned to Hanoi on April 13th. It conveyed Ho's long-standing views to the Chinese government. Ho looked to China for guidance, and his government would endeavor to build up its army for future resistance against French colonialism.[144] After the visit Bao Dai was advised by Ho to stay in China temporarily, but he soon left for Hong Kong, where Vietnamese nationalists had begun to work for the restoration of his power against Ho.

The most revealing of Ho's tactics to play off the Chinese against the French were his suggestions to the Chinese military authorities in Hanoi in late March. Realizing the dissatisfaction of the people with the March 6 Franco-Vietnamese agreement and the weakness of his position, Ho proposed:

(1) The Chinese military authorities give strong pressure to the French for early negotiations to reach an early formal agreement with Vietnam.

[143] *Vietnamese Studies*, No. 7, p. 51.
[144] Nghiem Ke To's report, March 22, 1946; Hsing Shen-chou's report, April 14, 1946, in "Documents"; and Nghiem Ke To's letter to the author, March 31, 1969.

(2) The Chinese army leaves Vietnam only after the conclusion of the formal French-Vietnamese agreement.

(3) Before leaving the Chinese army hands over to the Vietnamese the building of the military occupation headquarters which was the palace of the former French High Commissioner and symbolizes the authority of governing Vietnam; if it is handed over to the French, it will have great ill effects on the psychology of the people.

(4) The Chinese occupation authorities help the Vietnamese government prevent the French from holding a military review.[145]

Ho was attempting to belittle the strength of the French army, on one hand, and strengthen the Viet-Minh's position for future French-Vietnamese negotiations, on the other. He talked to Hsiao Wen on May 16, 1946 of his "Three Principles of National Policy": (1) to adopt a pro-Chinese line; (2) not to surrender to France, and (3) not to carry out the Communist program for 50 years. Ho explained to Hsiao that Communism was unsuitable to the industrially backward Vietnam, that his government was not a Communist government, and that the main policy of his government was the same as China's as announced by Generalissimo Chiang—"People first, nation first."[146] Ho had tried his best to gain China's friendship and support before he went to France for negotiations.

The task of negotiating with the French was much more complex and difficult than dealing with the Chinese. Ho knew that the French would not grant Vietnam independence status, yet he had to try for a settlement leading to independence. Because of French determination to return colonial rule to Indochina, all of his efforts were in vain and the negotiations were doomed.

It is not necessary to discuss in detail the unsuccessful

[145] Hsing Shen-chou's report, April 6, 1946, in "Documents."
[146] Hsiao Wen's report, June 29, 1946, in *ibid.*

French-Vietnamese negotiations from April to September 1946, since they have been well explored by other writers. In a nutshell, the Gordian knot was the issue of South Vietnam. The French, favoring a separate state of South Vietnam, never wanted to settle the issue together with that of North Vietnam. The Viet-Minh insisted that Vietnam was one, and the issue should be settled that way. When Ho Chi Minh left Hanoi for France on May 31, he said to the people in typical oriental fashion: "Our brothers in Nam Bo are citizens of Vietnam; rivers may dry up and mountains erode away, but this truth will remain for ever."[147] Yet on June 1, 1946, one day after Ho left Vietnam, the French authorities in Indochina officially announced the establishment of the "Republic of Cochin-China" to be headed by Nguyen Van Thinh. Worse still, a delegation from the new republic was sent to Paris by the French for a separate conference with the French. After the failure of the Fontainebleau Conference (July to September 1946), the modus vivendi, signed in the late evening of September 14,[148] was concluded only after Ho Chi Minh had made a desperate request. He said to his French counterparts, Marius Moutet and Jean Sainteny, "Don't let me leave this way. Give me some weapon against the extremists."[149] By "extremists" he apparently meant those nationalists, particularly the VNQDD and Dong Minh Hoi, who were opposed to a French-Vietnamese settlement. Although the modus vivendi was concluded, the issue of South Vietnam remained unsettled; both parties would have to renegotiate a final settlement in early 1947.

The Chinese did not wait for a final French-Vietnamese settlement, as Ho had requested; they evacuated their troops completely in June. Only a skeleton staff was left in Hanoi. Inside Vietnam the Viet-Minh now had only one

[147] Truong Chinh, *President Ho*, p. 53. *Vietnamese Studies*, No. 7, p. 53.
[148] For text of the modus vivendi see Cole, *Conflict in Indochina*, pp. 43-45.
[149] Sainteny, *Histoire*, p. 209.

immediate enemy: the VNQDD and Dong Minh Hoi. To settle the problem of internal disunity, the Viet-Minh sponsored the loosely organized Lien Viet (League for the National Union of Vietnam); it was composed of 27 leaders, and was a broader organization than the Viet-Minh, including members of the Viet-Minh, the Dong Minh Hoi, the VNQDD, the Democratic Party, the Socialists, and independents. One of the organization's objectives was a unified administration and army. But the leaders from the Dong Minh Hoi and VNQDD refused to merge their local administrations and armies into the Lien Viet on the grounds that they would be taken over by the Viet-Minh. The refusal deepened the conflict between the two parties and the Viet-Minh. The Viet-Minh used the refusal as a pretext to launch a military campaign against them. With the Chinese leaving, leaders of the Dong Minh Hoi and VNQDD such as Nguyen Tuong Tam[150] and Vu Hong Khanh felt insecure in Vietnam; they left Hanoi for the China border area in late May and June. Ironically the Viet-Minh cooperated with the French against its own fellow countrymen by agreeing to a French takeover of Bac-Giang which was under nationalist control. Meanwhile its army attacked nationalist forces in various places—Vu Kim Thanh's unit (under Nguyen Hai Than) at Mon-Kay; Vu Hong Khanh's and Nghiem Ke To's units in Phu-Tho, Yen Bay, and Lao-Kay; Nong Quoc Long's unit (under Nguyen Hai Than) in Lang-Son; and Nghiem Cam Sanh's unit (under Nghiem Ke To) in Dinh-Lap. In a period of nine days, from June 18 to 26, the Viet-Minh army took Lang-Son, Phu-Tho, Vinh-Yen, and Yen-Bay. Vu Hong Khanh and his 600 men withdrew to Lao-Kay, while Nghiem Cam Sanh's unit moved to Mon-Kay. Giap's army had defeated the main force of the two nationalist parties. The French assisted the Viet-Minh because they regarded the two nationalist parties as more anti-French than the Viet-Minh.

---

[150] Nguyen Tuong Tam, then Foreign Minister, was supposed to head the Viet-Minh delegation to France; instead he left for China. Hanoi's sources said that he fled with public funds.

Back in Hanoi the Viet-Minh continued to exert political pressure on the nationalists. After a meeting of the Lien Viet on June 25, the Viet-Minh (represented by Nguyen Luong Bang and Vo Nguyen Giap) decided to cooperate with the Democratic Party and dissident VNQDD members in issuing a declaration urging all Vietnamese to unite under the government for the reconstruction of the country.[151] On July 13 Hanoi police made a massive, surprise raid on the VNQDD. They arrested more than 120 and searched and took over quarters of the VNQDD organ, *White Star News*. At the same time, the Viet-Minh encouraged some dissident VNQDD members to issue a statement accusing Vo Hong Khanh of betraying the VNQDD and announcing their intention to reorganize the party.[152]

At this point the VNQDD and Dong Minh Hoi still could not cooperate with each other; a power struggle between them was going on. After his (VNQDD) unit had moved to Mon-Kay, Nghiem Cam Sanh forced Vu Kim Thanh (Dong Minh Hoi) to leave for China while taking over Thanh's force. On August 10 Sanh counterattacked the Viet-Minh from Mon-Kay and captured Tien-Yen. The Viet-Minh was alarmed and immediately offered them money to negotiate. As Giap reported to the cabinet meeting on August 13, 1946, the problem presented by Sanh's forces would soon be settled by money through the mediation of a Chinese major general in Hanoi.[153] On August 27 a cease-fire was arranged.[154] Giap took over the equipment of Sanh's unit, which had been supplied mostly by the Chinese Nationalists and with which he equipped a larger army. By now the only remaining VNQDD force was that of Vu Hong Khanh in the Lao-Kay area. It fought against both the French and the Viet-Minh. Even after the Indochinese war had begun, it did not cooperate with the Viet-Minh. It

[151] Shang Hsing-i's report, July 12, 1946, in "Documents."
[152] Nghiem Ke To's report, August 13, 1946, in *ibid.*
[153] *Ibid.*
[154] *Chieh fang jih pao* (Liberation Daily, Yenan), September 1, 1946.

simply struggled for survival in the corner of northern Tonkin.

By the end of August 1946 the Chinese occupation forces had completely withdrawn and the VNQDD and Dong Minh Hoi armies had been eliminated. The only remaining problem was the French. A three-front fight had become one front, which, as time proved, could only be settled by military means.

GENERALLY speaking, the Chinese occupation had achieved its aims by maintaining a neutral policy, transferring forces to North China and Manchuria, and settling old issues with the French. But there were ill effects, also. To Lu Han the neutral occupation policy was unrealistic and almost without any significance. Since his views on occupation did not prevail, he arbitrarily carried out a policy for occupied Vietnam. This was an old problem of Chinese politics—local authorities disagreed with the central government on policy. The French realized the possibility of the disagreement but were not sure about it. As a result, Lu Han offended Alessandri at the surrender ceremony, let his soldiers misbehave against the order of the central government, and ordered (through his headquarters) his own 60th Army at Haiphong to remain neutral while the 53rd Army (the central government's army) was battling French warships on March 6, 1946.[155]

To the VNQDD and Dong Minh Hoi the policy and the occupation were disappointing. Although Nguyen Hai Than's demand for replacing the Viet-Minh regime with the Dong Minh Hoi was unjustifiable, the request for more aid made by Nghiem Ke To and Vu Hong Khanh was not favorably received. China tried to decrease her assistance to the nationalists, but could hardly purge herself of the charge that she had nurtured the nationalist parties in an attempt to turn Vietnam into a Chinese satellite. When the nationalists were defeated militarily by the Viet-Minh and

[155] Chu Hsieh, *Diary*, pp. 103, 107.

Nghiem Ke To was imprisoned by the French in Hanoi,[156] the VNQDD and DMH semi-openly complained of Chinese "desertion."

The French had successfully exploited the Chinese neutral policy; they returned to North Vietnam peacefully. The occupation had also avoided a "massacre of the 30,000 Frenchmen north of the sixteenth parallel."[157] But for once the French were so angry at the Chinese that they said they would not accept an ultimatum-form financial demand and that they would appeal to Moscow, Washington, and London for justice.[158] Clinging to the sentiments and privileges they had enjoyed as colonialists in Indochina, the French were disgusted with the Chinese presence despite the merits of the occupation.

The Viet-Minh tried its utmost to use the Chinese against the French and nationalists while strengthening its own forces. Its friendly attitude won much sympathy from the Chinese. Its tactics proved highly successful. Publicly Viet-Minh leaders expressed their appreciation and sincerely thanked "President Chiang . . . together with General Lu Han and all top-ranking officers and officials of the Chinese occupation forces."[159] Privately they scolded China. As Ho Chi Minh later told Paul Mus: "It is better to smell the feces of the French for a little while than to eat Chinese excrement all of one's life."[160]

[156] Nghiem Ke To was imprisoned by the French on the excuse of "protection" immediately after the outbreak of the French-Vietnamese war (the Indochinese war) in December 1946, and was not released until early 1948. Nghiem Ke To to the author, March 31, 1969.

[157] Sainteny, *Histoire*, p. 159.   [158] Chu Hsieh, *Diary*, p. 61.

[159] Vo Nguyen Giap, *One Year of Revolutionary Achievement; Report to the Viet-Nam People at Hanoi* (Bangkok: Viet Nam News Publication, 1946), p. 7. This message was delivered on September 2, 1946, to celebrate the first anniversary of the establishment of the DRV.

[160] Lauriston Sharp, "Paradoxes in the Indochinese Dilemma," *The Annals of the American Academy of Political and Social Science* (July 1954), p. 91.

4. Chinese Influence: Decrease and Increase, 1946-1949

"We are realizing the People's Three Principles of Asia's great revolution, as stated by Dr. Sun Yat-sen, though the French reactionary colonialists mistook them for the 'class principle' of Karl Marx."

> — Ho Chi Minh to a foreign newsman in July 1947, three months after the Kuomintang army had captured Yenan

"The Vietnam people and army not only would heartily welcome but would also actively support the Chinese Liberation Army, should the latter deem it necessary to pursue the remnant Kuomintang elements in Vietnam."

> — Viet-Minh radio in January 1950 after a Kuomintang army of 30,000 men had retreated to Vietnam in December 1949

WHEN HE left for France in late May 1946, Ho Chi Minh chose Interior Minister Huynh Thuc Khang to serve as acting president. Khang was a veteran nonparty nationalist and good scholar of Han studies. Before his departure Ho advised Khang, ". . . you must keep calm before all eventualities and you will be able to thrash out every question" ("yi pu pien ying wan pien" in the Chinese version)—a typical Oriental attitude which Chinese leaders often took in difficult times.[1] When he returned to Vietnam in October 1946 Ho found events had developed mostly in his favor. The Chinese army was gone; the armed forces of the VNQDD and Dong Minh Hoi were practically eliminated; a Socialist party had been founded in Hanoi; and Viet-Minh–French cooperation against their common "foe"—the VNQDD and Dong Minh Hoi—seemed going well except in the south. He further learned that if foreign and domestic situations had turned against the Viet-Minh the Socialist Party and the Lien Viet would have cooperated to lead the government with a moderate program. All this, however,

---

[1] Nguyen Luong Bang, "The Times I Met Him," p. 78.

was done by Vo Nguyen Giap and other Viet-Minh leaders, not by Huynh Thuc Khang. Giap's power had greatly increased; he had become the virtual president in Ho's absence. In the ceremonies marking the first anniversary of the independence of the DRV (Democratic Republic of Vietnam) on September 2, 1946, it was Giap and not Khang who delivered the only long policy speech on the achievements of the one-year-old Viet-Minh regime.

While hoping that a peace settlement with France could eventually be worked out, so that he would be able to persuade the people to accept the modus vivendi of September 14, Ho was realistic enough to adopt a moderate policy toward France after his return home. In a proclamation of October 23, 1946 he urged his people to be moderate and cooperative with the French, asked both the French and Vietnamese to stop fighting, and prohibited acts of reprisal. On October 29 he asked Giap to issue a cease-fire order in the south.[2] The statement and order might not have been made out of "sincerity," as Ho claimed they were; yet cooperation with the French, designed to promote independence, was necessary for the militarily weak Viet-Minh.

To get approval of his agreement with France and to complete his regime's constitutional façade, Ho convened the second session of the National Assembly on October 28, 1946, with 291 members present.[3] The 95 members of the Viet-Minh and the Marxist group constituted the largest single block in the Assembly. When they were joined, as

[2] *Vietnamese Studies*, No. 7, p. 93.

[3] The party affiliation of Assembly seats in its October-November session:

Party affiliation	Total delegates	Present delegates
Viet-Minh	80	80
Marxist Group	15	15
Independents	90	90
Socialist Party	24	24
Democratic Party	45	45
VNQDD	50	20
Dong Minh Hoi	20	17
Total	324	291

they always were, by the delegates of the Democratic and
Socialist Parties, they became the majority. The remaining
delegates from the VNQDD and Dong Minh Hoi (totaling
37) could hardly cooperate with the 90 independents in any
significant opposition to the Viet-Minh. Besides, there were
pressures from the regime; heavily armed police were always in evidence at the Assembly, and the homes of some opposition delegates were searched. Therefore Ho had no difficulty in putting through his modus vivendi. The Assembly
gave him a vote of confidence, and "requested" him to
reshuffle the cabinet since some members had left their
posts. The new men in the cabinet were either Viet-Minh
or from its associated parties, except for the Ministries of Interior and Health. The government had become virtually
a one-party regime.[4] On November 8 the Assembly adopted
a constitution by a vote of 240 to 2, thus enabling Ho to put
his government on a constitutional basis. By now, the Viet-
Minh had taken a firm control over the cabinet, the Assembly, and the military.

One of the reasons for the reorganization of the regime
was to facilitate Franco-Vietnamese cooperation. On the
surface a new phase of cooperation had begun; in essence
there was an undercurrent of conflict between the two parties. One example should suffice. The new constitution
provided that the territory of Vietnam, composed of Bac-bo
(northern Vietnam), Trung-bo (central Vietnam), and
Nam-bo (southern Vietnam), "is one and indivisible." But

[4] The cabinet of November 1946:

President	Ho Chi Minh	Communist
Foreign Affairs	Ho Chi Minh	Communist
National Defense	Vo Nguyen Giap	Communist
Finance	Le Van Hien	Communist
Labor	Nguyen Van Tao	Communist
Education	Dang Thai Mai	Communist
Agriculture	Cu Huy Can	Communist
Interior	Huynh Thuc Khang	Independent
Health	Truong Dinh Tri	VNQDD
Economy	Phan Anh	Socialist
Justice	Vu Dinh Hoe	Democrat (VM)
Public Works	Tran Dang Khoa	Democrat (VM)

Admiral d'Argenlieu retorted on November 12: "Nam-bo being French territory, only the French Parliament can decide on its status." Moreover, immediately after the self-confessed puppet Nguyen Van Thinh,[5] President of the Cochin-Chinese Republic, hanged himself on November 11, 1946, Admiral d'Argenlieu appointed Le Van Hoach, a leader of the Cao Dai, to form a new government. This move indicated French determination to keep Cochin-China separate from northern Vietnam at all costs. Disagreement and conflict amounted to a general war following the "Haiphong Incident" of November 20.

The port of Haiphong was under the control of the French navy. On November 20 a Chinese junk loaded with contraband attempting to reach port to unload supplies for the Vietnamese, was seized by a French patrol boat. Viet-Minh soldiers on the shore fired on the French ship. There was shooting in the nervous city, which continued off and on for two days, when local authorities reached an agreement. However, Admiral d'Argenlieu, who then was in Paris, decided to teach the Vietnamese a "lesson." He obtained authority from the French government to cable General Valluy, his deputy in Saigon, who then ordered Colonel Debès in Haiphong to suppress any Vietnamese resort to arms. On November 23 Colonel Debès delivered an ultimatum to the local Viet-Minh authorities, demanding the withdrawal of Viet-Minh forces from the Chinese quarter of the city within two hours. When the time was up, the French moved into the quarter and the French cruiser *Suffren* opened fire on the rest of the city. The attack caused heavy casualties among the civilians who tried to flee the city.[6]

Although the Viet-Minh government had been surprised by the ruthless French move, and although the situation in Haiphong remained strained, Ho tried to avoid open con-

[5] Nguyen Van Thinh told his friends before he died, "I am being asked to play a farce." *New York Times*, November 11, 1946.

[6] The total casualties were approximately 20,000, including 6,000 deaths.

flict with France. According to a Hanoi source, he had made at least four appeals to the French for a cease-fire before the war broke out on December 19.[7] The French did not heed Ho's appeals. They merely reinforced their military forces throughout Vietnam. Hundreds of French soldiers moved into Hanoi and occupied government buildings. The situation in the capital grew tenser. *Su That* (The Truth), the organ of the Association of Marxist Studies, urged a hard line toward the French on November 26. It stated that the modus vivendi of September 14 "was the last concession. Any new concession will harm national sovereignty and the supreme interests of the nation. . . . We must oppose violence [with] violence. . . ."[8] The Viet-Minh government removed its regular forces from the city, and their place was taken by the aggressive Tu Ve (the militia). The French demanded the disarming of the Tu Ve. On December 19 the Viet-Minh, after refusing the demand, decided to launch a surprise attack on the French. Ho Chi Minh made the decision at 11 a.m. When the French learned of the plan through a Eurasian agent at 6 p.m., Sainteny tried to persuade Ho to call off the assault, but it was too late. At 8 p.m. the Hanoi power station was blown up as the signal for a general attack on French military posts and installations. Sainteny was wounded when his armored car hit a mine. The following day Ho issued an appeal to the people to wage a "resistance war." "We would rather sacrifice all than lose our country," he declared. "We are determined not to be enslaved." Thus the Indochina war had begun. It is fair to say, while the Viet-Minh had taken the initiative in preparing for the general assault, the return of French colonialism was the fundamental cause of the war.

AT THE beginning of the war the French were superior in several aspects. Militarily the Viet-Minh armed forces, which

[7] December 6, 15, 18, and 19. Ung Van Khiem, "Ten-year Struggles and Diplomatic Victories," in Ho Chi Minh et al., *Achievements*, p. 31.

[8] As cited in *Vietnamese Studies*, No. 7, p. 58.

were estimated at less than 50,000, were no more than a poorly trained guerrilla unit with inadequate equipment and little battle experience. The French had approximately 20,000 well-equipped French troops. The Kuomintang government in Nanking extended no military assistance to the Viet-Minh, and Mao Tse-tung's army was a thousand miles away fighting the Kuomintang forces in Manchuria and northern China. The French controlled the money supply by controlling the bank which the Viet-Minh had failed to seize during the August Revolution. Furthermore, Paris supported the war with a billion francs a day. The Viet-Minh had even greater difficulties in supplying the meager rations of food and salt[9] daily in the areas they occupied. Internationally the Vietminh was cornered in a very isolated area in northern Tonkin. The French Communists first remained aloof, then in 1947 merely voiced their support of the Viet-Minh but extended no material aid. Moscow, though sympathetic to the Viet-Minh's cause, made no commitment or assistance.[10] The war, however, quickly simplified Ho's political problems. The dissident and radical elements could no longer accuse him of selling out Vietnam. In the name of the "resistance war," he won many converts. Numerous independent intellectuals joined the Viet-Minh for the same reason. The people were polarized into two categories, the patriots and the Viet Gian (traitors to Vietnam). Those who supported the Viet-Minh resistance movement were "patriots"; those who did not were "Viet Gian." In Viet-Minh–controlled areas fighting spirit was high; hundreds of thousands of the people in the French-controlled areas secretly supported the Viet-Minh. The French-Vietnamese side lacked such popular support. As seen in late 1946 by Hsiao Wen, the morale of the Vietnamese was

[9] In many places in Vietnam and China (mostly the inland areas), the problem of storing salt is no less serious than that of rice. At the outbreak of the war, the Vietminh barely managed to ship 20,000 tons of salt from the coast area to various inland provinces, mostly to Viet-Bac (Ho's stronghold during the Indochina war). Nguyen Luong Bang, "The Times I Met Him," pp. 81-82.

[10] McLane, *Soviet Strategies*, p. 274.

high and the war could last a long time, but the Viet-Minh lacked financial resources. They anxiously hoped for international support, particularly from China.

While the fighting in Hanoi was going on, Ho was willing to negotiate with the French for peace terms acceptable to the Viet-Minh. During a visit by French Socialist Overseas Minister Marius Moutet to Indochina in December 1946 and early January 1947, Ho's radio broadcast messages requesting negotiations with France through a Ho-Moutet meeting. Moutet and d'Argenlieu received the messages but made no favorable response. Morover, Moutet paid a secret one-day visit to Hanoi. Instead of meeting his old friend Ho Chi Minh for possible peace talks, he issued a statement to the effect that before any negotiations could be made, "it is necessary to have a military decision. I am sorry for the necessity, but one cannot commit with impunity such madness as the Viet-Minh have done."[11] Obviously the French authorities did not want to negotiate with the Viet-Minh at this moment.

With superior military strength the French adopted a strategy of "rapid fighting for quick decision," as observed by the Viet-Minh. They planned first to occupy the major cities and main transportation lines and then spread out to the rural areas, hoping to reconquer Vietnam in five or six weeks.[12] But the Viet-Minh countered the strategy with its "long-lasting war." The fight in Hanoi lasted for two months, a surprise to the French. Before his forces left the capital in mid-February 1947 Ho appealed to the Vietnamese, urging them to destroy anything of value to the French. This tactic was in fact a scorched-earth policy similar to that used in some parts of China against the Japanese in 1937-1945, and which, as was mentioned previously, was adopted by the Viet-Minh in November 1945 against a possible

[11] *Le Monde*, January 5, 6, 1947.
[12] Tran Haoi Nam, *Yueh-nan jen min ti chieh fang tou cheng* (The Struggle for Liberation of the Vietnamese People) (Peking: Shih chieh chih shih she, 1954), p. 18. Tran Hoai Nam serves (May 1969) as the chief spokesman of the delegation of the National Liberation Front to the Paris Peace Talks.

Chinese takeover of Vietnam. Although the policy Ho asked for did not work out as effectively as he had expected, the Vietnamese generally were not cooperative toward the French. Moreover, the morale of the French, who were spread thin already, was low. They could control only the cities, while the vast countryside remained in the Viet-Minh's hands. The situation became one of stalemate, bearing a close similarity to the Japanese bogging down in China in 1937-1945.

Since a settlement with the Viet-Minh by military or political means was not in sight, the French looked for an alternative. It was Admiral d'Argenlieu's idea to seek a "Bao Dai solution" to counteract the Viet-Minh. But the solution took a long time to materialize. D'Argenlieu was replaced by Emile Bollaert on March 5, 1947. In May Bollaert sent his political adviser, Paul Mus, a French scholar, with a peace plan to offer Ho Chi Minh. Even Mus objected to the plan. And Ho found it unacceptable. He told the Vietnamese people about it and urged them to fight on. In the spring the French Communists, who had been in the French cabinet since November 1945, were ousted from the coalition government. The French in Indochina employed a hard-line policy by launching the largest offensive of the war against the Viet-Minh. The resistance war became increasingly difficult to Ho Chi Minh. As a guide for their difficult and isolated struggle, Ho and his men developed a strategy for the war.

1. THE THEORY OF RESISTANCE WAR

It is well known now that the Viet-Minh's theory of war was modeled on Mao Tse-tung's military thought. But it should be pointed out that its development was in the main due to the analogy between Vietnamese and Chinese problems in the political, economic, social, and cultural fields rather than a simple copying of the Chinese Communist leader.

Chinese Influence, 1946-1949

Apart from some fundamental similarities between the two nations, as they were compared in the first chapter, the Vietnamese revolutionary war shared most of the four characteristics of the revolutionary war in China as analyzed by Mao in 1936: (1) the uneven development of China's political and economic conditions, (2) the stronger military power of the enemy, (3) the weakness of the Communist army, and (4) the leadership of the Communist Party and the agrarian revolution.[13] Only the first item was not true of the Vietnamese war. Vietnamese social conditions, particularly in the rural areas, were almost identical with those in China. For instance, prior to the Chinese Communist revolution the gentry were fully responsible for rural (village) administration. The central government had no direct contact with individuals, peasant or scholar. Each village was a unit considerably isolated from the state. As an old Chinese proverb says, "the mountains are high and the Emperor far away." In Vietnam the rural areas were ruled by a council of notables. Each village was encircled by a bamboo hedge. Similarly, the imperial government had no direct contact with individuals in the village. And an old Vietnamese proverb says, "The power of the Emperor stops at the bamboo hedge." But since the revolutionary war began in these two countries, "armed adolescents have replaced" the peaceful gentry and councils of notables.[14] The isolation of the rural areas from the central authorities provided both the CCP and the Viet-Minh with an excellent opportunity to develop their armies and revolutionary bases. This was one of the basic reasons for the growth and development of Mao Tse-tung's army. With the similarities, plus the traditional Vietnamese inclination to look to China, the

[13] Mao Tse-tung, "Problems of Strategy in China's Revolutionary War," in *Selected Works* (Peking: Foreign Languages Press, 1965), Vol. I, pp. 196-98.

[14] A good account of Vietnam's rural politics is given by Paul Mus, "The Role of the Village in Vietnamese Politics," *Pacific Affairs* (September 1949); also his "Viet Nam: A Nation Off Balance," *Yale Review* (June 1952).

Viet-Minh's learning of military theory from Mao seems natural.[15]

Ho wrote a pamphlet in 1941-1942 entitled *Experiences of the Chinese Guerrilla Warfare* based mainly on Mao's works, *Strategic Problems of China's Revolutionary War* and *Strategic Problems in the Anti-Japanese Guerrilla War*. Ho's writing, together with a Viet-Minh pamphlet, *Experiences of the Anti-Japanese War*, were widely distributed in north and south Vietnam as a guide to the Viet-Minh's strategy. It was reported in 1954 that shortly after the Indochinese war began, the pamphlet *Experiences of the Chinese Guerrilla Warfare* became indispensable in encouraging the continuation of the fighting in the south where conditions were extremely difficult for the Viet-Minh.[16]

The task of writing about the resistance war was done basically by Truong Chinh, then secretary-general of the ICP, and not Ho Chi Minh or Vo Nguyen Giap. From March 4 to August 1, 1947 Truong Chinh published a series of articles in the review *Su That* (The Truth), which appeared in a booklet form in September 1947 as *The Resistance Will Win*. Truong Chinh's work fully reflected "the party's policy of guiding the long-lasting resistance war,"[17] and was regarded by Giap as "an important contribution to the thorough understanding of the Resistance War line and policies of the Party"[18] at the time. After the Chinese Communist army reached the Vietnam border in late 1949, Giap and others flavored the theory with a more proletarian character.

Within the limits of the theory developed by Truong Chinh in 1947, but revised and published in 1960, a com-

---

[15] Mao Tse-tung himself was ambitious from the very beginning to export his military thought, especially on guerrilla warfare. He said: "We must point out that the guerrilla campaigns being waged in China today are a page in history that has no precedent. Their influence will not be confined solely to China in her present anti-Japanese war but will be world-wide." *Mao Tse-tung on Guerrilla Warfare*, tr. Samuel B. Griffith (New York: Frederick Praeger, 1961), p. 65.

[16] *Jen min jih pao*, January 1, 1954.

[17] Nguyen Luong Bang, "The Times I Met Him," p. 79.

[18] Giap, *People's War, People's Army*, p. 102.

parison between Chinh's and Mao's views should be revealing. Truong Chinh's work is based primarily on Mao's *On
New Stage* and *On Protracted War*.[19] Two significant features of Truong Chinh's writing typify his and Mao's
theoretical relationship—the characteristics of the war and
strategy, tactics, and "forms of the war."

The characteristics of the resistance war: The Vietnamese
resistance war against the French was a "just and progressive war," Truong Chinh declared, while the aggressive
war of the French colonialists was unjust, reactionary, and
imperialistic. The resistance war was also a revolutionary
war with the character of a national liberation, of democracy, freedom, and world peace[20]—a view expressed by
Mao throughout *On Protracted War*. There Mao asserted
the Chinese resistance war was a revolutionary one against
Japanese imperialism; it was sacred, just, progressive; its
aims were for national liberation and perpetual peace in
China and the whole world.[21]

It was also a people's war, Truong Chinh asserted. Since
the overwhelming majority of the Vietnamese people were
peasants, it was "in fact a peasant war led by the working
class."[22] Mao developed his views on a peasant war as early
as 1927, when he began his leadership of the peasant-
worker army. But the terms "people's war" and "people's
army," heard so often today, were first used unequivocally
in 1945 when Mao demanded that the Kuomintang government organize a coalition government.[23] Mao and Truong
Chinh emphasized the significance of close cooperation
between the army and the masses of the people. In practice
the outstanding examples were the Hwai-Hai battle in
1948-1949,[24] in which each of Mao's soldiers was supported

[19] Hsiao Yang, p. 71; see also the citation in Truong Chinh, *The
Resistance Will Win* (Hanoi: Foreign Languages Publishing House,
1961), p. 105.

[20] *Ibid.*, pp. 31-34.

[21] Mao, "On Protracted War," *Selected Works*, II, pp. 148-50.

[22] Truong Chinh, *Resistance*, p. 33.

[23] Mao, "On Coalition Government," *Selected Works*, III, pp. 263-
67, 295-97.

[24] For the Hwai-Hai battle see O. Edmund Clubb, "Chiang Kai-

by five peasants on the average, and the battle of Dien-Bien-Phu, where many peasants were mobilized to support the Viet-Minh army.

Inferior in equipment, training, and battle experiences, but superior in manpower, morale, and knowledge of the terrain, the advocacy of a "long-lasting war" was a logical conclusion. Truong Chinh insisted that the whole "resistance must be to prolong the war." He explained in full why the war must be protracted, and tried to justify his argument by citing three resistance wars: the Vietnamese Tran dynasty against the Mongol invasion for 31 years; the Later Le dynasty against the Chinese Ming army for 10 years; and China's opposition to Japanese invasion for eight years.[25] He admitted that the Viet-Minh would suffer loss of territory and people, great suffering by the people, economic blockade, and possibly even outside intervention. But the French would have their difficulties—economic, the opposition of the Vietnamese, and the loss of a large portion of their army. A long drawn-out fight could break the French colonialists, first economically, then militarily. Apparently the Chinese resistance war and Mao's thesis of protracted war strongly influenced Truong Chinh. While Mao's theory is too well known to be repeated here, it should be pointed out that his thesis of a protracted war was under development long before it matured in 1938. On July 16, 1936, when he was interviewed by Edgar Snow, Mao visualized a war against Japan that could possibly be painfully long, and advocated a strategy of protracted fighting to gradually destroy Japan's power, economically

---

shek's Waterloo: The Battle of the Hwai-Hai," *Pacific Historical Review* (November 1956), pp. 389-99.

[25] Truong Chinh, *Resistance*, pp. 35-37. Today the North Vietnamese still propagandized their victories over the more powerful Mongols and the Ming army. They emphasize the theory of "people's war," a protracted struggle against the United States, and do not intend to deny its similarity and relationship with the Chinese thesis as expressed by Lin Piao in his essay, "Long Live the Victory of People's War." See Harrison E. Salisbury's reports, *New York Times*, December 30, 1966 and January 17, 1967.

and militarily. This view was also held by most of the high-ranking Kuomintang generals in 1936-1937.[26] It was this strategy and conviction that was to carry the Viet-Minh through the difficult period of 1948-1949.

It is interesting to find that even the pattern of interlocking forces described by Truong Chinh was also learned from Mao. In such a pattern the regular army, militia, and guerrilla forces fought together. The French advanced deep within Viet-Minh territory, and the Viet-Minh attacked deep within French areas. The war had "the characteristics of two combs whose teeth are interlocked" in the delta, the rice fields, the mountains, and the plain.[27] Mao said in *On Protracted War* that, "One of the special features of this war is the interlocking 'jigsaw' pattern which arises from such contradictory factors as the barbarity of Japan and her shortage of troops, on the one hand, and the progressiveness of China and the extensiveness of her territory, on the other." The forces extended deep into the enemy's occupied areas and into the enemy's rear.[28] Because of the large territory main forces and guerrilla units could operate in different areas. As a whole, the situation presented "a remarkable spectacle of pincers around the enemy" from interior and exterior lines.

The resistance war was a war without battlefronts, yet everywhere there was a front. It was a war of scorched earth. It was a war of encirclement. "The enemy encircled us in the center of the city, and we encircled the enemy in the suburbs," Truong Chinh stated. "Our guerrilla bases in the enemy-held regions can appear to be mere enclaves surrounded by the enemy. But all these guerrilla bases . . . form a huge net encircling the enemy in return." Throughout the world, Truong Chinh went on, the enemy appealed to imperialist forces to encircle the Viet-Minh. But together with "the democratic, progressive, peaceful forces the world

[26] Edgar Snow, *Red Star over China* (New York: Random House, 1938), pp. 85-91. Mao's view was, of course, fully discussed in "On Protracted War."

[27] Truong Chinh, *Resistance*, pp. 63-65.

[28] Mao, *Selected Works*, II, 145-46.

over . . . we are encircling the aggressive French colonialists." This was the "mutual encirclement."[29] Mao described
the entire nation as a huge battlefield; the front was everywhere; there was "no rear, nor . . . a battle line." It was
destructive and even ruthless. Its pattern was encirclement
and counterencirclement. At a special point or city, the
Chinese were strategically encircled by the enemy, but
formed a counterencirclement against the enemy's advance.
Mao believed that in the world context the Allied forces of
peace were counterencircling the world enemy of Japan,
Germany, and Italy,[30] an explanation Truong Chinh had
applied so well to the Vietnamese situation.

Strategy, tactics, and war forms: Although the Viet-Minh's
strategy and tactics are not unusual today, the brief discussion here is intended to explain what the Viet-Minh had
learned from Mao and why North Vietnam is using the
same strategy against the United States today.

Truong Chinh wrote that their long resistance would pass
through three stages—contention, equilibrium, and general
counteroffensive.[31] Vo Nguyen Giap agreed with this view.[32]
At the beginning (the first stage), the enemy forces were
stronger than the Viet-Minh's; the enemy's strategy was
offensive and the Viet-Minh's defensive; but the Viet-Minh's
tactic was constant attack. During this period the Viet-Minh
engaged in positional warfare in the streets of the cities
(battles in Hanoi, Nan-Dinh, and Hue), then withdrew to
the countryside. As this process went on, the form of positional warfare gave way to guerrilla and mobile warfare.
The stage of equilibrium was a period in which the

[29] Truong Chinh, *Resistance*, pp. 65-67.

[30] Mao, *Selected Works*, II, 146-47. This pattern of encirclement is
no doubt the earlier view of Mao's recent thesis of the encirclement
of the city by the countryside, as expressed by Lin Piao in 1965. Its
origin, however, should be traced back to September 1930 after the
collapse of the "Li Li-san Line." Since then the theory has gained
greater acceptance. See Chiang Kai-shek, *Soviet Russia in China: a
Summing Up at Seventy* (New York: Farrar, Straus, and Cudahy,
1957), p. 60.

[31] Truong Chinh, *Resistance*, p. 70.

[32] Giap, *People's War*, pp. 46-47.

strength of the Viet-Minh forces gradually equalled that of the enemy. While the enemy's strategy remained defensive the Viet-Minh prepared for a general counteroffensive. Guerrilla warfare was the most widely used; mobile warfare came next; and positional warfare played an auxiliary role. Part of guerrilla warfare turned into mobile warfare. It was "a relatively long . . . stage." The Viet-Minh moved from an inferior position to a superior one.

In the final stage of a general counteroffensive, the Viet-Minh's strategy was an offensive one, while the enemy's was a defensive withdrawal. A counteroffensive was made possible by the increase in strength of the Viet-Minh and the increasing weakness of the enemy, such as the demoralization of its forces, the exhaustion of the French economy and finance (in Vietnam, then France), and the opposition to the war by the French people. The Viet-Minh had reached only the threshold of the third stage at the time of the battle of Dien-Bien-Phu.

The strategy, tactics, and guerrilla aspects of Mao's protracted war are too well known to be discussed in detail here. In short, Mao divided the war into three stages. The first covered the period of the enemy's strategic offensive and the Chinese defensive. The second was the enemy's consolidation and the Chinese preparation for a future counteroffensive. The third was the counteroffensive which led to victory. The first stage was short and the second long. Guerrilla warfare was the main way of fighting. After a long period of fighting, attrition, and preparation, the Chinese grew stronger and the enemy weaker. Then Mao's army engaged the enemy in decisive fighting for the final victory.[33] In fact, the Sino-Japanese war did not reach the third stage. Mao had more accurately applied this strategy to his rebellion against the Kuomintang.

Truong Chinh was the leading theoretician of the Viet-Minh. Vo Nguyen Giap was preoccupied with military affairs, and Le Duan, whose ability in theoretical writing was recognized by his co-prisoners on Condore Island, had

---

[33] Mao, *Selected Works*, ɪɪ, 136-45.

not yet become an outstanding figure in the party. In reading Truong Chinh's work, one senses the meagerness of its philosophical background. This was basically due to the fact that the unstable war situation made a serious theoretical study impossible. But even this simple theory proved to be necessary for the Viet-Minh to follow in the difficult period 1947-1949. After the Chinese Communists reached the Vietnam border in late 1949, encouraging events brightened the thesis, and the influence of Truong Chinh, as well as that of Communist China, gained a significant dimension among the Viet-Minh.

2. THE DECLINE OF NATIONALIST CHINESE INFLUENCE

The Chinese government in Nanking was maintaining its neutral policy toward Vietnam. The main consideration was its relationship with France and its civil war with the Chinese Communists. Theoretically Nanking was sympathetic to Vietnam's independence movement inspired by nationalist sentiment; practically it sided with France. This position was similar to that of the United States at the time.

The increasingly burning issue of the civil war reduced much of Nanking's sympathy for the Viet-Minh. In January 1946 Gen. George C. Marshall achieved a cease-fire agreement between the Nationalists and Communists. But on April 15, within 24 hours of the departure of Soviet forces from Changchun in Manchuria, Chinese Communist troops attacked the city and seized it in direct violation of the cease-fire accord.[34] The result was attacks and counterattacks, negotiations and further negotiations, truce and further truce. Marshall's efforts turned out to be a complete failure; he left China in December, blaming both the "reactionary" group in the Kuomintang and the "dyed-in-the-wool" Communists who had no sense of compromise for peace but were determined to gain power by all means. The civil war was running apace; both sides saw no

[34] Department of State, *United States Relations with China* (1949), p. 149.

prospect for peace. In these circumstances the best the Nanking government could do in regard to Vietnam was keep the Viet-Minh separated from the Chinese Communists while remaining aloof from the implications of the Franco-Vietnamese conflict.

One of the Chinese government's direct concerns in Vietnam was the life and property of Chinese residents. Since the Haiphong incident and the ensuing fighting there and in Hanoi, the Viet-Minh had stationed the bulk of its forces in the Chinese quarter against the French. The purpose was twofold: to avoid heavy damage being inflicted on the Vietnamese quarter, and to force Chinese residents to side with the Vietnamese against the French. As a result, the Haiphong incident alone caused about 500 deaths among the Chinese, with more than 500 missing, wounded, and arrested (by both the French and the Viet-Minh). The loss of property exceeded 40 million piasters.[35] As the war continued, Chinese property in Haiphong and Hanoi was either destroyed or heavily damaged. Thousands were homeless. They fled to Ha-Dong, Vinh-Yen, Thai-Nguyen, Bac-Can, and Cao-Bang. Some continued to flee to Yunnan and Kwangsi. The Viet-Minh, primarily to win the Kuomintang's sympathy and assistance to its cause, took the opportunity to give aid to the Chinese refugees. According to a report from Duong Thanh Dan, vice-chairman of the executive committee of the Sino-Vietnamese Cultural Assocation in Vietnam who participated in the Viet-Minh relief program, the Viet-Minh sent food to the refugees in Nam-Dinh, Thai-Binh, Ha-Dong, and other cities. The Chinese requested that Duong Thanh Dan go to China on their behalf, to urge the Chinese government to give assistance. The Viet-Minh government decided to

[35] See the report prepared by a Chinese committee in Haiphong by Hai-fang hua ch'iao shan hou wei yuan hui (Chinese Reconstruction Committee of Haiphong), *Yueh-nan Hai-fang hua ch'iao sun shih pao kao shu* (Report on the Loss of the Chinese Residents at Haiphong, Vietnam) (Haiphong, 1947); also see *Chung yang jih pao* (Nanking), January 18, 1947. *Chieh fang jih pao* (Yenan, December 18, 1946) reported more than 100 deaths and wounds, 300 missing, and a property loss of 100,000,000 piasters.

send to China a delegation of four members (including Duong Thanh Dan), headed by Nguyen Duc Thuy, representative of the ministries of foreign affairs and national defense. The delegates carried the Viet-Minh relief program into Ha-Dong, Vinh-Yen, Thai-Nguyen, Bac-Can, and Cao-Bang in January 1947, and explained to both the Chinese and local Viet-Minh leaders the Viet-Minh government's policy toward China. They planned to leave for Nanking in the late spring, and ask China for "effective aid" to Chinese refugees. They further hoped that if close Sino-Vietnamese cooperation could be developed, it "could prevent the radical Yenan elements from slipping into the Vietnamese government in an attempt to split [Chinese and Vietnamese] activities, on one hand, and avoid the danger of losing southwestern China to French imperialism, on the other."[36]

The Viet-Minh delegation did not go to China as scheduled because of a French offensive, the largest up to then, in March 1947. The French succeeded in occupying principal cities and towns in Viet-Bac (Ho's stronghold), but did not defeat the Viet-Minh main force. As the war spread, the number of Chinese refugees increased. Many fled to Yunnan and Kwangsi, and sent their own representatives to Nanking for aid. They were, of course, eyewitnesses to the fighting in Vietnam. As they told reporters of a Chinese newspaper sympathetic to the Viet-Minh cause, they were very impressed by the determination and bravery of the Vietnamese fighters. The French Expeditionary Corps under General Valluy were superior to the Viet-Minh army in equipment but inferior in morale; they dared not push into Viet-Minh areas, and were often forced to abandon points they had previously occupied.[37] It seemed that they were in store for a long drawn-out war—as predicted by Truong Chinh.

[36] Report of Duong Thanh Dan, March 15, 1947, from Canton, in "Documents." Dan left for Canton by himself, while Nguyen Duc Thuy's delegation was still in northern Tonkin. Dan is now in Hong Kong.

[37] *Ta kung pao* (Shanghai), June 28, 1947.

Chinese Influence, 1946-1949

Ho Chi Minh made his people fight as a heroic people,[38] and the Viet-Minh made Ho the god of its independence war. Vietnamese heroic fighting was admirable. They were engaged in an isolated war, a war without an ally. Inferior to France militarily, diplomatically, and financially, the Viet-Minh's only superior and effective weapon was its cause: nationalism. Internally, Ho assiduously argued that Vietnamese nationalists and independents join the Viet-Minh coalition in a common fight for Vietnam's independence. No Communist program or appeal was ever publicized before 1949. Externally, Ho appealed directly and indirectly to Asian nations, particularly China, asking for understanding and aid.

In Vietnam numerous nonparty intellectuals joined the Viet-Minh simply for Vietnam's independence. The example of a distinguished engineer, Nguyen Duy Thanh, well explains the general attitude of many nationalists toward the Viet-Minh: "In the beginning, the [Viet-Minh] Communists did not openly profess their particular ideology. The common programme of the coalition was to get rid of the French rule, with the help of the Chinese, and attain independence. This was a popular programme and, therefore, gained the support of the masses."[39] After he had associated himself with the Viet-Minh, Thanh, like many others, was appointed to a government position; Thanh was made chairman of the Committee for National Production and Industries. There was indeed a "broad national unity" as claimed by a Viet-Minh writer in an article in the Cominform organ in Bucharest. The writer said: "The government of the resistance movement, headed by Ho Chi Minh, is a government of broad national unity. Besides representatives of the working people, there are in the

[38] In their writings on the August Revolution, Ho, Hoang Quoc Viet, and others emphatically stated, "Our people are a heroic people." See Ho et al., *Heroic People*.

[39] Nguyen Duy Thanh, *My Four Years with the Viet-Minh* (Bombay: Democratic Research Service, 1950), p. 18. This pamphlet was written after his defection in 1949.

173

government representatives of the intellectuals, the Catholics and the national minorities."[40]

But after the engineer realized what the real political coloration of the Viet-Minh was, he broke with the regime after he was sent to India (1949) as head of the Viet-Minh information mission in India. He denounced the Viet-Minh as a Communist party, revealed that many nationalists were held by force in the Viet-Minh, and forecast that the regime would enslave the people.[41] Yet how many nationalists with the Viet-Minh had the chance to defect if they wished to? Even if they had, by the time of their defection they had already helped carry the Viet-Minh to a point where the regime had gone through its darkest days and was ready to welcome the Chinese Communists on the border!

Ho shuffled his cabinet in the summer of 1947 when the news of a peace movement under Bollaert was much in the air and the "Bao Dai solution" was gradually taking shape. Ho broadened the bases of participation by non-Communists who supported his policy, and removed "all vacillating, pro-imperialist and bureaucratic elements."[42] He dismissed two of his most trusted lieutenants, Pham Van Dong and Vo Nguyen Giap, from the cabinet, and eliminated VNQDD minister Truong Dinh Tri and others.[43]

---

[40] Van Bo, "Vietnam People Defend Their Liberty and Independence," in *For A Lasting Peace, For a People's Democracy* (Bucharest: Organ of the Information Bureau of the Communist and Workers' Parties), November 1, 1948, p. 7.

[41] S.R. Mohan Das, *Ho Chi Minh—Nationalist or Soviet Agent?* (Bombay: Democratic Research Service, 1951), p. 12.

[42] Van Bo, "Vietnam," p. 7.

[43] The cabinet of the summer of 1947 was organized as follows:

President	Ho Chi Minh	Communist
Finance	Le Van Hien	Communist
Labor	Nguyen Van Tao	Communist
Foreign Affairs	Hoang Minh Giam	Socialist
Economy	Phan Anh	Socialist
Public Health	Hoang Tich Tri	Socialist
Education	Nguyen Van Huyen	Independent
Interior	Phan Ke Toai	Independent
National Defense	Ta Quang Buu	Independent
Public Works	Tran Dang Khoa	Democrat

Ho's efforts to cope with the difficulties of the war were not limited to the governmental structure. In social, economic, and educational affairs, his regime made strenuous efforts for improvement. It urged the people to increase industrial and food production, reduced land rents by 25 per cent (the original land program of the Kuomintang), and intensified the teaching of Quoc Ngu (national language). The policy of "reconstructing the country while resisting the enemy," which was adopted by the Chungking government in 1937-1945, was put into effect. On the anniversary of the first six months of his resistance war, Ho said in a broadcast that under the "reconstruction and resistance" policy, the longer the Viet-Minh fought, the stronger it grew.[44]

In foreign affairs Ho appealed to Asian nations. A few weeks after the start of the war he requested all the Asian peoples to aid the Viet-Minh.[45] At the Asian Relations Conference, held in New Delhi in March and April 1947, which was also attended by Nationalist China, the Viet-Minh delegates denied that they had received any help from Russia.[46] In a joint statement of April 4, the Viet-Minh and Indonesian delegations urged that:

(1) Asian Members of the United Nations should put the issue of colonialism in general and the issue of Viet Nam in particular on the Security Council agenda.

(2) Asian nations should recognize immediately the governments of the Indonesian Republic and the Viet Nam Republic.

(3) Asian nations should act jointly to force the withdrawal of foreign troops from all parts of "occupied" Asia.

Justice	Vu Dinh Hoe	Democrat
Veterans and Invalids	Vu Dinh Tung	Catholic

[44] *Ta kung pao* (Shanghai), June 21, 1947.

[45] *Chung yang jih pao* (Nanking), January 20, 1947.

[46] F. C. Jones, "Indochina," in *Survey of International Affairs, 1947-48*, ed. Peter Calvocoressi (London: Oxford University Press, 1949), p. 387.

(4) Joint efforts by Asian countries should make it impossible to send Dutch and French reinforcements to Indonesia and Viet Nam.

(5) Asian nations should send immediate medical aid and volunteers to Asian "battlefields."[47]

The reaction to the statement from the participants was disappointing. Jawaharlal Nehru, then an Indian delegate, informed the Viet-Minh delegation that it would be extremely difficult for India to give any actual support to Vietnam.

Ho kept an eye on the turbulence in China. After General Marshall returned home the fighting seesawed back and forth. The Kuomintang government decided to convene the National Assembly, draft a constitution, and hold general elections in order to complete its constitutional façade. The Chinese Communist Party refused to participate in the constitutional process, and the government launched a large-scale operation against the CCP at Yenan for the first time. The Kuomintang army captured the CCP capital in March 1947, but missed capturing Mao Tse-tung by only a few hours. Meanwhile it defeated Mao's army in several battles in Shantung and Manchuria. The military might of the Kuomintang reached its peak in 1947, while the Communists retreated temporarily.

Watching the development of the Chinese situation closely, Ho, like many other observers, was probably under the impression that Chiang Kai-shek's army would defeat Mao's main force in the very near future. Under strong military pressure from the French, and with no intention of making an enemy in his rear, the Viet-Minh leader continued to hope for the establishment of good relations between his regime and Nanking. In the summer of 1947 Ho told one foreign correspondent: "We are realizing the People's Three Principles of Asia's great revolution, as stated by Dr. Sun Yat-sen, though the French reactionary

[47] *Ta kung pao* (Shanghai), April 6, 1947; and *New York Times*, April 6, 1947.

colonialists mistook them for the 'class principle' of Karl Marx."[48] The statement was not a surprise to those familiar with Ho's tactics; he had made similar claims before. What was different this time was that the statement was made in the absence of the Chinese authorities, which might well indicate an attempt by Ho to show goodwill toward Kuomintang China. A mission sent by Ho in the fall confirmed this.

In August 1947, one month after Ho had shuffled his cabinet, he sent a telegram to the Kuomintang in Nanking, stating his plan for sending a goodwill delegation to visit China. The mission might also have been devised to cover up Chinese Communist activities in Vietnam.[49] The Kuomintang welcomed the mission and expressed sympathy for Vietnam's independence fight, but hoped that the Viet-Minh would cooperate with other political parties and groups in order to attain independence in a joint effort. Meanwhile the Kuomintang, intending to serve as a mediator for the various political parties, cabled Bao Dai and Nguyen Hai Than in Hong Kong, inviting their representatives to Nanking for a conference with the Viet-Minh.[50] The Kuomintang position remained neutral.

Ho selected a delegation of seven members headed by Nguyen Duc Thuy, which was scheduled to leave Cao-Bang for China on October 10, a Chinese national holiday. But a new French campaign started on October 7 and delayed the mission's departure. In the campaign the French mobilized more than 50,000 soldiers and all their planes and armored vehicles. The largest offensive under General Valluy, it succeeded in occupying many cities in Viet-Bac, including Bac-Can, Lao-Kay, Lai-Chau, and Cao-Bang. The French almost captured Ho Chi Minh, and again did not defeat the Viet-Minh main force.

[48] *Bulletin* of the Vietnam-American Friendship Association, New York, July 7, 1947, in Thompson and Adloff, *Left Wing*, p. 42.
[49] See more discussions on Chinese Communist activities in Vietnam below.
[50] Chang Shou-hsien's report, November 1947, in "Documents."

Amid the French offensive, which lasted until early December, Ho asked Nguyen Duc Thuy to go on to China and await the other members in Chinghsi. Thuy was Ho's trusted man, serving as chief of the Chinese Section and Acting Deputy-Minister in the Foreign Affairs Ministry. He acted according to Ho's instructions, but when he arrived in Chinghsi he was arrested by the local authorities because he was a Viet-Minh Communist. It should be pointed out here that at the time there were local Chinese Communists active in the Hundred-Thousand Hills area along the Kwangsi-Kwangtung border.

One could attribute Thuy's imprisonment to Ho's hasty and incomplete preparations for dealing with the Chinese local authorities, since Kuomintang headquarters had no intention of arresting his delegate. Obviously hastiness was caused by the sudden and formidable French offensive. Mindful of his mission to China, Thuy agreed to write a letter to the Viet-Minh regime, urging its expulsion of Chinese Communist elements from Vietnam. In the meantime, he signed a statement with the Chinghsi authorities that included three items:

(1) Both parties sincerely hope that China and Vietnam will establish friendly relations.

(2) The Viet-Minh assures China there will be no hatred against Chinese residents in Vietnam despite [the fact that] some Chinese have been employed to work for the French military forces.

(3) China will not regard the Viet-Minh as a supporter of the Chinese Communists and will, accordingly, show no hatred against the Viet-Minh despite [the fact that] some Chinese Communists have entered Vietnam.[51]

Thuy was kept in Chinghsi for a few months. Neither Ho Chi Minh nor the Kuomintang in Nanking knew his whereabouts until February 1948 when Ho received a letter from

[51] Nguyen Duc Thuy's letter of February 4, and Ho Chi Minh's letter of April 5, 1948, in "Documents."

him. The local Chinese authorities in Chinghsi retained Thuy until the Viet-Minh executed the terms he had agreed on. Thus his arrest not only dampened Ho's "goodwill" toward the Kuomintang, but committed Ho to carry out (nominally, of course) Thuy's agreement with the Chinese. According to a news report from *Chung yang jih pao* in Kweilin, Ho himself seems to have put some pressure on the local Chinese Communists. The report said: "The Vietnam regime has recently ordered the people in its occupied Ha-Quang, Tra-Linh . . . areas to destroy their houses before April 30 and move along with the army. . . . Since their defeat at P'ingmeng, the Chinese and Vietnamese Communists, because of the shortage of food and munitions, have occupied respective areas for recruitment and supplies. They have internal disagreement and conflict. The Chinese Communists . . . feel difficult in their position and show the possibility of moving to other areas or surrendering to the Kwangsi government."[52]

Nguyen Duc Thuy did not continue his visit to Nanking, apparently on Ho's orders. He returned to the Viet-Minh-occupied area in the late spring of 1948. His abortive mission was Ho's last attempt before the Chinese Communists came to power to appeal to the Kuomintang. The gradual victory of the Chinese Communists in 1948 encouraged Ho to await further developments in China, which, with his great patience, he was so adept at. In October 1948 Chinese Nationalist commanders in Mukden defected to the Communists, and the whole of Manchuria was soon taken over by Lin Piao's army. Thereafter the military situation turned rapidly in favor of the Communists. Ho now saw no need to appeal to the Kuomintang.

WHILE THE French were working on the "Bao Dai solution," many leaders who either disliked the Viet-Minh or struggled for personal political power gradually switched their support to Bao Dai. They were former mandarins, leaders of the Dong Minh Hoi, the VNQDD, the Catholic League,

[52] *Chung yang jih pao* (Kweilin), May 7, 1948.

179

the Cao Dai, the Hoa Hao, the Buddhists, the Democratic-Socialist Party, and others.[53] From these groups came Nguyen Hai Than, Nguyen Tuong Tam, Tran Trong Kim (premier in early 1945), and Nguyen Van Sam (from the Democratic-Socialist Party). They played an important role in the first half of the "Bao Dai solution" movement (1947-1948). The leading role in the second half (1948-1949) shifted to Nguyen Van Xuan, Ngo Dinh Diem, and others. During the first half a National Union Front was established (early 1947) as the counterpart of the Viet-Minh. The Front was headed by Nguyen Hai Than who used the same old tactic of soliciting aid from China and making use of Chinese influence.

Nguyen Hai Than's advanced age and long residence in China severely limited his ability to be a modern political leader of Vietnam. While criticizing Ho Chi Minh for being too confident in and relying too much on the French Communists, Than himself made a similar error with China. In January and February 1947 he repeatedly informed Nanking of his plan:

(1) To unite with all nationalists of the Dong Minh Hoi, VNQDD, the Catholic groups and other units, and establish a new government headed by Nguyen Vinh Thuy (Bao Dai).

(2) The new government will negotiate and cooperate with the Viet-Minh for unity.

(3) The new government will negotiate with the French for a semi-independent status as that of British Dominions.

(4) The new government wishes to obtain support from China, the United States, and the United Nations.[54]

Than explained that a French–Viet-Minh settlement,

[53] The Vietnam Democratic-Socialist Party was an anti–Viet-Minh group, while the Vietnam Democratic Party was pro–Viet-Minh.

[54] Nguyen Hai Than, "The Current Situation of Vietnam," February 10, 1947, and his "Memorandum" of February 1947, in "Documents." Vu Hong Khanh's letter to the author states that at that time the VNQDD supported Nguyen Hai Than's plan.

either military or political, was impossible and unacceptable to the nationalists; both sides (France and the Viet-
Minh) would have to depend on the nationalists with whom
he was uniting to be a new force. Than's plan was imprac-
tical, however. First of all, the "nationalists" were not disciplined members of a solid political group; they were
disunited and disputatious leaders of many political units.
How cooperative and united they would be under the
leadership of Bao Dai and Nguyen Hai Than was ques-
tionable. Second, a status of modified independence would
certainly disappoint many genuine nationalists who had
fought in various ways for complete independence. Third,
whether the French and Viet-Minh would really negotiate
with the new government was doubtful, since the latter was
to be led by a former emperor and a pro-Chinese leader
without the support of the military or the people. While
the French in all probability, did not want to see the re-
emergence of Chinese domination in Vietnamese affairs,
the Viet-Minh would at all costs eliminate any political
forces competing with Ho Chi Minh.

But Nguyen Hai Than went ahead with his plan. In
March 1947 he and Nguyen Tuong Tam flew to Hong Kong
from Canton to meet with Bao Dai and leaders from South
Vietnam. The same month they announced the establishment of the National Union Front with a southern branch
in Saigon and a northern one in Hanoi. On April 1, 1947
the Front's spokesman in Hong Kong declared that it was
opposed to French domination and to the Viet-Minh regime,
would fight as a group of "nationalists," would support the
restoration of Bao Dai, and claimed to have guerrilla forces
in Vietnam equipped with arms purchased mostly from
the Chinese army during the occupation.[55] On May 5 the
Front's president, Nguyen Hai Than, declared a similar
view in Canton, that the Front was against the Viet-Minh
and for Bao Dai's return to Vietnam, but that the armed
units of the Dong Minh Hoi and VNQDD had evacuated
to the border areas in China and had surrendered their

[55] *New York Times*, April 1, 1947.

weapons to the Chinese local authorities. Once the situation became favorable, he continued, the armed forces would return to Vietnam.[56]

The southern branch of the Front in Saigon, under Nguyen Van Sam, was making good progress. Sam established contacts with various parties and groups, as well as the Cochin-Chinese government. He intensified propaganda activities and gained support. On May 17 a formal proclamation was published in Saigon, attacking the Viet-Minh government as a Communist regime, supporting Bao Dai as the leader to conciliate and unify all the Vietnamese political parties and forces, and asking France to recognize the unity and independence of Vietnam.[57] On August 16 it succeeded in holding a southern conference in Saigon attended by delegates from the Dong Minh Hoi, VNQDD, Democratic-Socialist Party, National Youth Corps, religious groups, and armed units. It resolved to strengthen the organization of the Front and to urge Bao Dai to form a new national government.[58] In the north the branch in Hanoi remained on paper until August. Early that month Tran Van Tuyen was sent to Hanoi to organize the branch. He gained some support, including that of the imprisoned Nghiem Ke To. In late August they succeeded in staging a demonstration in Hanoi, shouting such slogans as "Support Nguyen Vinh Thuy," "Down with Ho Chi Minh," and "Attain the Unity and Independence of Vietnam."[59] The prestige of Bao Dai grew while the character of anti-French domination was dropped. The reaction of Bao Dai, who was leading a night club life in Hong Kong, was his decision in July to return to Vietnam.[60]

[56] *Ta kung pao* (Shanghai), May 6, 1947.

[57] Department of State, Office of Intelligence and Research, Division of Research for Far East, *Political Alignments of Vietnamese Nationalists* (Washington, D.C., 1949), pp. 107-108.

[58] Hsing Shen-chou, "Report on Vietnamese Situations," August 17, 1947, in "Documents."

[59] Hsieh Chin-hu, "Report on One-Year Work in Vietnam," March 10, 1948, in "Documents."

[60] *Ta kung pao*, July 4, 1947.

The news of Bollaert's willingness to negotiate with Vietnamese political parties for a peace settlement gave the Vietnamese hope for peace during the summer months of 1947. The people were even overly optimistic about Bollaert's scheduled speech in early September. When his long-awaited speech was delivered on September 10 at Ha-Dong, a city near Hanoi, the Vietnamese were disappointed at the French reluctance to grant "independence" to Vietnam.[61] From his jungle headquarters Ho quickly rejected the offer.

Nguyen Hai Than's leadership in the Bao Dai restoration movement reached its height when Bao Dai called for a political conference with the Front and other Bao Dai supporters in Hong Kong for September 9 and 10, 1947. The conference was punctuated by Than's keynote speech attacking the Viet-Minh. On September 11 a statement was issued with the signatures of the 21 participants: "The Communist Viet-Minh is opposed to the unity and independence of our nation; its anti-democratic and anti-unification actions have split the nation and destroyed much of our economic and manpower resources. The Viet-Minh places its ideology above national interests. . . . The people of the whole nation have clearly expressed their faith in the abdicated emperor, Bao Dai. . . . We, therefore, unanimously requested Bao Dai to assume the responsibility for negotiations with France for Vietnam's peace and independence."[62]

Clearly Nguyen Hai Than's Front was only one force in the Bao Dai restoration movement. The political conference was convened by the ex-emperor and the statement was made with his assent. In a formal statement on September 18, Bao Dai criticized the dictatorship of the Viet-Minh and

---

[61] For the text of the speech, see Cole, *Conflict*, pp. 62-66.

[62] *Ta kung pao*, September 14, 1947. The leading participants of the conference were: Nguyen Hai Than (Dong Minh Hoi), Nguyen Tuong Tam (VNQDD), Nguyen Van Sam (Democratic-Socialist Party), Tran Van Ly, Tran Van Lien (Trung-Bo government), Tran Van Tuyen (Bao Dai's representative to Vietnam), Tran Quang Vinh (Cao Dai), Cao Duc Minh (Bao Dai's spokesman), and Nguyen Van Dai (Resistance Front).

"accepted the request of the conferees" to negotiate with France and mediate party disputes.[63] In his report Nguyen Hai Than informed the Chinese of the result of the meeting. Ho Chi Minh's radio reacted immediately by denouncing Bao Dai as a traitor to Vietnam, and asserted that the participants of the conference had no right to represent the Vietnamese people to confer.

The future of the Front was not optimistic. Since it supported Bao Dai, it had to cooperate with the other forces loyal to him. But Nguyen Hai Than's pro-Chinese political line and Nguyen Tuong Tam's association with the Viet-Minh government in early 1946 brought the suspicion of Bao Dai and his supporters of their "sincerity" about cooperating. On the other hand, Than and Tam were annoyed by the increasing influence of pro-French elements. Disappointed, Tam withdrew from the movement on October 29, 1947, and Than criticized the pro-French elements of playing into the hands of the French. Than soon returned to Canton. He again tried to solicit aid from Chang Fa-k'uei who then commanded in Canton. Chang did not come to his assistance.[64] Than's stay in Canton contributed only to his unpopularity as a leader of the Front among the people in Vietnam.

The activity led by Nguyen Van Sam in southern and central Vietnam worried the Viet-Minh. Shortly after his return to Vietnam from the Hong Kong Conference, he was assassinated by Viet-Minh terrorists.[65] Sam's death was a serious blow to the Front. There was no other person to succeed him who could hold the factions together within the Front. The influence of the organization soon declined.

The political maneuvering of various parties and groups presented an ironic but spectacular picture at that time. First, while the French were using Bao Dai against the Viet-Minh, Bao Dai consolidated various political groups to strengthen his bargaining position with the French. Second,

---

[63] *Ta kung pao*, September 19, 1947.
[64] Chang's letter to the author, June 30, 1961.
[65] Hsieh Chin-fu's, "Vietnamese Situations."

as Bao Dai was using various anti–Viet-Minh groups and individuals, the groups and their leaders took advantage of the Viet-Minh resistance war to urge Bao Dai to negotiate with the French for more gains, despite the fact that they were under the protection of the French against the Viet-Minh. The leaders, such as Nguyen Van Xuan and Tran Van An, were of the opinion that only the Viet-Minh war could truly pressure the French. Prolonging the war was therefore necessary, insofar as they could exact more concessions from the French authorities. Third, Nguyen Hai Than and Nguyen Tuong Tam attempted to form a new force against the pro-French group and the Viet-Minh; they temporarily supported Bao Dai, but planned to emerge in due course as the leading power against him.[66] Fourth, in the Bao Dai camp (if we can call it that) Nguyen Van Xuan and Ngo Dinh Diem were working for the same goal of doing away with the Front under Nguyen Hai Than, yet Xuan and Diem were struggling against each other, for Xuan was a strongly pro-French man, whereas Diem insisted on complete independence at all costs. And fifth, within the pro-French group under Bao Dai, a power struggle was going on between two powerful leaders, Nguyen Van Xuan and Le Van Hoach. Nguyen Van Xuan was the president of Cochin-China and Le Van Hoach, as his predecessor, was the leader of the "Nam-Bo Front" influential in southern Vietnam.[67] The political maneuvering within the Indochinese war was between group and individual interests—not unusual in a nation at war. In 1964-1965, when the situation in South Vietnam became extremely unstable, there were at least five similar "wars" within the general fighting against the Communists.[68]

[66] Nguyen Hai Than's reports, November 7, 1947, and January 19, 1948, in "Documents."

[67] Before the founding of the Central Government of Vietnam (South Vietnam) in June 1948, the "Republic of Cochin-China" underwent three weak administrations: Nguyen Van Thinh, June 1945–November 1945; Le Van Hoach, November 1946–October 1947; Nguyen Van Xuan, October 1947–June 1948.

[68] See King C. Chen, "Peking's Strategy in Indochina," *Yale Review* (June 1965), p. 560.

Chinese Influence, 1946-1949

As pro-French influence grew in Vietnam, the pro-Chinese power within the Front declined. The death of Nguyen Van Sam was the turning point. Two months after his assassination Le Van Hoach succeeded in organizing a new league, the Vietnam National Rally, which got the support of the Cao Dai and Hoa Hao away from the Front. Nguyen Hai Than and Nguyen Tuong Tam were surprised. In a statement issued in China on December 7, 1947, they declared that any conference of the nationalists within Indochina could produce no result if the conference was held under the protection of only one government. On December 16 the southern branch of the Front announced its adherence to the National Rally. The Front, in fact, ceased to function in Vietnam. In April 1948 Than announced its dissolution.

The Front was the last Vietnamese nationalist group (in fact, Nguyen Hai Than's) that appealed to Nationalist China for aid prior to Mao's victory. But it suffered from the same incompetent leadership, the same impracticable program, and the same unsolid organization without mass support. Its demise was merely a matter of time.

From early 1948 to June 1949, when Bao Dai proclaimed himself head of the State of Vietnam, the restoration movement was in its second half. Nguyen Van Xuan, Le Van Hoach, Ngo Dinh Diem, and others played the leading roles; Nguyen Hai Than and Nguyen Tuong Tam were not even invited to cooperate with them. In April 1948 Bao Dai sent his spokesman, Cao Duc Minh (Luu Duc Trung), to Nanking for moral support and financial aid. The French were alarmed, and immediately forced the ex-emperor to dismiss Minh. From then on, no significant contacts were made between Bao Dai (or Nguyen Hai Than) and Nanking. Thus the development during the period of the second half had little bearing on Nationalist China.

3. THE INCREASE OF CHINESE COMMUNIST INFLUENCE

Chinese Communist activities in Vietnam during the period 1946-1949 have been a matter of conjecture, but of little evidence. As F. C. Jones observes, "Such contacts as may have existed between the Chinese Communists and the Viet-Minh were not disclosed."[69] In fact, the CCP "smuggled" agents into Hanoi as early as 1945. One of them, Pai Mai-lang, appeared to be active during and after the Chinese occupation period. He probably had served as a reporter for *Chieh fang jih pao* in Yenan and *Hsin hua jih pao* in Chungking. He published a book in 1948 on the Vietnamese war using the pen name "Mai Lang." After the departure of the Chinese Nationalist army the CCP increased its personnel and activity there.

In mid-August 1946 approximately 350 Chinese Communists, mostly in the cultural field, secretly entered Vietnam in groups from Yunnan and Kwangsi. They stayed in Hanoi and Haiphong. The Hanoi group was led by Lin Chin-li, Li P'eng, and Chou Ch'eng. They published *Life of Overseas Chinese* (bi-monthly) and *Overseas Chinese News* (weekly), opened an evening school for adults, and prepared to publish a Sino-Vietnamese daily and open a high school. In the first issue (September 1946) of *Life of Overseas Chinese* they criticized the Nanking government of being corrupt and dictatorial. Vo Nguyen Giap, who was then the actual head of the Viet-Minh, took the initiative to inform the Chinese consulate-general in Hanoi of the matter and promised that he would not allow similar articles to appear in the same periodical again.[70] They used the evening school as an activity center. Meanwhile they criticized both the French and Chinese governments when they paid visits to individual Chinese and Vietnamese merchants.

In Haiphong the Chinese Communists seemed even more active. Their leaders were Cheng K'un-lien and Yen Hsi-

---

[69] Jones, "Indochina," pp. 386-87.
[70] Report of the Chinese Consulate-General in Hanoi, November 12, 1946, in "Documents."

liang, who carried weapons. In addition to cultural activities they sent threatening letters to Chinese merchants for contributions, and attempted to control the Service Team of the Chinese Chamber of Commerce in Haiphong. (The Team was forced to disband on September 20.) They also warned the Chinese consulate in Haiphong not to interfere with their activities. The Viet-Minh, unwilling to offend Nationalist China at the time, occasionally curbed their behavior. Underground, these Chinese Communist elements cooperated with agents of Li Chi-shen from Hong Kong[71] in organizing a "Southern Democratic United Army" in the border areas on the pattern of the "Northeast Democratic United Army" under Lin Piao in Manchuria. By the spring of 1947 the United Army, composed of Communists, youths, deserters, and bandits, had grown to approximately 5,000. The Chinese Communists sent a provincial commissioner, Chin Wei-lin, to the Vietnam border area in late 1946. He visited Ha-Duong and Cao-Bang and helped train Viet-Minh cadres in the border town of Soc-Giang.

Chinese Communist relations with the Viet-Minh gained momentum after 1947. In the spring of that year Liao Ch'eng-chih, then chief of the CCP's South China Bureau, visited Viet-Minh bases in Viet-Bac. In June Fang Fang, a major general in Mao's army, came to Viet-Bac. Liao Ch'eng-chih and Fang Fang had been active in Canton during the KMT-CCP negotiation period from early 1946 to early 1947.[72] After the negotiations failed, they visited Hong Kong, Kwangsi, and Ho Chi Minh's Vietnam. Liao and Fang attended the cadre conference in Soc-Giang on

[71] Li Chi-shen, a former vice-president of the Peking regime, was in Hong Kong at the time. A dissident of the Kuomintang, he turned against Chiang Kai-shek by organizing a revolutionary committee of the Kuomintang in Hong Kong.

[72] Liao Ch'eng-chih, son of Liao Chung-k'ai (Dr. Sun Yat-sen's important aide), was very active in Canton in 1946-1947. In calling Chang Fa-k'uei "Uncle Hua" (Chang's other name is Chang Hsiang-hua), he seemed to be able to use his father's name and influence 20 years earlier in the same city to get along very well with the Kuomintang leaders in Canton. Fang Fang was an able aide to Liao.

August 1, 1947 convened by the Viet-Minh. The Southwest Democratic United Army, now renamed the "Yueh-Kwei Border Democratic United Army," and stationed in the Hundred-Thousand Hills, was temporarily placed under Liao's command to cooperate with the Viet-Minh. At that time, Gen. Hsiang Ying, former deputy-commander of the Communist New Fourth Army, was in Siam (Hsiang went there in the late spring of 1946), responsible for Chinese Communist activities in all of Indochina, and in touch with the Communists in Siam, Malaya, and Indonesia. During his stay in Siam Hsiang was reported to have helped the Viet-Minh arrange the purchase and shipment of arms to Viet-Bac. He was transferred to the China-Vietnam border area in the fall of 1947, where he presumably took over the command of the Democratic United Army from Liao.

It is no longer a secret that the Viet-Minh in 1946-1947 purchased weapons from the West and shipped them from Siam to Viet-Bac.[73] In its two purchases from the Siamese and the British in 1947, the Viet-Minh acquired at least 6,000 rifles, 400 machineguns, 5 anti-aircraft guns, 200 mines (for ships and tanks), and 1,000 grenades.[74] Most of the equipment was American-made. The supply line was closed off in early 1948 when the Bangkok government adopted an anti-Communist policy. But the Viet-Minh had two other sources of war materiel. One was the Chinese Communists, the other home production. In September 1947 the Viet-Minh arranged with the Chinese Communists to purchase 12 million piasters worth of equipment and had it shipped to Viet-Bac before the French fall offensive got underway.[75] Production at home was of extreme importance, especially after the Viet-Minh's connection with the outside world was largely cut off by the French victory in the fall of 1947. Domestic production consisted of three primitive factories and numerous shops. One factory was

[73] George K. Tanham, *Communist Revolutionary Warfare: The Vietminh in Indochina* (New York: Frederick Praeger, 1961), p. 67.
[74] Hsing Shen-chou, "Report on Vietnam," November 22, 1947, in "Documents."
[75] Sixth Section of the Kuomintang, p. 13.

at Phu-Tho in northern Tonkin, another (the largest) at Thap-Muoi in South Vietnam, and a third in central Vietnam. The Thap-Muoi factory employed some Japanese prisoners of war and German expeditionary soldiers who had deserted from the French forces;[76] it employed approximately 500 technicians and workers. Small shops were set up in almost every occupied country to supply local needs. Some Chinese Communists reportedly worked in repair shops near Tra-Linh, a border town, in 1947-1949. They primarily manufactured bazookas, grenades, cartridges, pistols, rifles, and light machineguns.[77] No heavy weapons were produced prior to 1949.

The French offensive in the fall of 1947 compelled the Viet-Minh to abandon all of the main cities in Viet-Bac and spread its forces thin over a large area, including the border with China. The Viet-Minh decided to take three urgent measures:

(1) Those who understand the Chinese language and have previously stayed in China should make use of every means to go to China.

(2) Those who understand tribal languages should seek a way to enter tribal areas and marry tribal girls in order to achieve security and establish new bases.

(3) Those who understand neither the Chinese nor tribal languages should be given one or two ounces of gold; they should disguise themselves as refugees and slip into French-occupied areas for underground activities.[78]

Subsequently there were serious setbacks and difficulties for the Viet-Minh. Ho himself was reported to have moved to the Chinese border area in late October.[79] Vo Nguyen

[76] Hsing Shen-chou, "Report on Vietnam," November 15, 1947, in "Documents."

[77] A Chinese Communist publication carries a similar account. See Hsiao Yang, p. 48.

[78] Hsing Shen-chou, "Report on Vietnam," January 1948, in "Documents."

[79] *Ta kung pao*, October 26, 1947.

Giap reportedly slipped into Kunming in November in an attempt to flee to Hong Kong and then Harbin to establish contact with Lin Piao's forces in Manchuria. The French learned of Giap's plan and asked the Chinese authorities in Kunming to cooperate in searching for him. Giap immediately returned to the border area.[80] Nguyen Duc Thuy, the delegate to Nanking, was imprisoned at Chinghsi. Many Viet-Minh elements in Yunnan, fearing arrest by the Chinese government, attempted to register in December 1947 and January 1948 at the VNQDD office in Kunming as turncoats; the VNQDD registered them.[81] Chinese Communists in the Vietnam border area also found their position difficult, and kept on the move as much as possible. It was at this stage that many French held the view that "There is no military problem any longer in Indochina."

If the French after the fall offensive had instituted an intensive search for the enemy in the jungle and border areas, as the Americans did in the Central Highlands and the Mekong Delta in 1967-1968, the Viet-Minh would have been forced into a still more difficult position. But the French didn't and the Viet-Minh soon came back to life. This does not suggest that if the French had, the Viet-Minh would have been forced to abandon its revolution. It seems that the Viet-Minh struggle was strongly encouraged by Andrei Zhdanov's famous speech on the occasion of the founding of the Cominform in September 1947 at Wiliza Gora in Poland, in which he coined the "two-camp" phrase and urged Communist parties everywhere to "lead the resistance struggle against imperialist expansion and aggression along every line."[82] One fact to support this speculation is the Calcutta Conference of Southeast Asian Youth, February 19-26, 1948. At the meeting the seven-man Viet-Minh delegation, all military officers, presented a report emphasizing armed revolution that was regarded as "the

[80] Hsing Shen-chou, "Report on Vietnam," January 1948, in "Documents."

[81] *Ibid.*

[82] Andrei Zhdanov, "The International Situation," in *For a Lasting Peace, for a People's Democracy*, November 10, 1947, p. 4.

191

keynote message of the conference."[83] As Charles B. McLane observes, "Zhdanovism was actively projected into Asia at Calcutta."[84] Its encouragement to Viet-Minh's revolution was of great significance.

ACCORDING TO Chinese reports from Kwangsi, the cooperation of the Chinese and Viet-Minh Communists in the border area set a pattern of guerrilla warfare.[85] In the fall of 1947, when French forces advanced into northern Tonkin, Chinese Nationalist local forces arrived in Communist-controlled P'ingmeng, a town on the Chinese side, to find that the enemy had disappeared. The French did not reach the border and the Chinese Communists took refuge in Soc-Giang, on the Vietnam side, opposite P'ingmeng. Before leaving P'ingmeng, the Chinese Nationalists cut the transportation link between the two towns. Soon thereafter, the Chinese Reds returned with "traders" from Vietnam. As the French were nearing the border, P'ingmeng was crowded with "refugees" from Vietnam. When the French left, the refugees disappeared. In February 1948 a Communist column of more than 1,000 men, led by two Chinese and one Vietnamese from Pac-Bo, raided the Chinese towns and villages from Chinghsi to Chenpien.[86] Chinese Nationalist forces fought and compelled them to retreat to Pao-Lac, Soc-Giang, and Tra-Linh (Vietnam). Residents of the towns were forced by the Communists to move along with them to the Vietnam side. After the Nationalists had departed, the Communists returned for "armed propa-

[83] Ruth T. McVey, *The Calcutta Conference and the Southeast Asian Uprisings* (Ithaca: Cornell University, 1958), p. 15.

[84] McLane, *Soviet Strategies*, p. 360.

[85] Reports of the Kuomintang office in Kwangsi, January 16, 1948 and July 6, 1948 (the latter was based on Chinghsi office's report of May 1948), in "Documents." The accuracy of the reports is supported by the fact that before the DRV in 1960 made known Ho Chi Minh's original base at Pac-Bo, no Western writer seemed to have had any knowledge of this small village base. The Chinese reports pointed it out in 1948.

[86] The Vietnamese leader was Duong Sam, a strong supporter of Ho since the latter went to Pac-Bo in 1941.

ganda." The Nationalists could not cross the border to pursue the enemy, and the French did not press hard enough toward the border, yet they claimed victory in their operations. The noncooperative and defensive campaigns by the Chinese Nationalists and French were never able to destroy the strength of the Communists who cooperated closely and moved back and forth in the border areas.

Movement by the Communists was speedy and semiconcealed. In "peacetime" small groups of them protected political workers who were engaged in propaganda activities; in "wartime" they easily gathered more than a thousand men with adequate equipment. The people along the Vietnam border were indoctrinated "to support wholeheartedly Mao Tse-tung and Ho Chi Minh." In captured papers which the Communists used in their schools, Ho was described as a world Communist leader and the people were urged to establish a new paradise in Vietnam under him. The Vietnamese Communists also decided to build a highway from Cao-Bang to Pac-Bo, a way of paying homage to Ho's original base in the village. On the bodies of dead Communists (they also discovered some Japanese prisoners of war) the Chinese Nationalists found evidence of membership in "the Chinese Self-Defense Platoon of Viet-Bac." At that moment, Viet-Minh delegate Nguyen Duc Thuy was forced to urge the Viet-Minh to expel the Chinese Communists. As mentioned earlier, Ho might have made the gesture to cut off his ties with the Chinese guerrillas along the border, but never did.

In Yunnan the political situation under Lu Han provided a favorable environment for the Viet-Minh in the border area. First, Lung Shao-wu, a son of former Governor Lung Yun who was then in Nanking, switched to support of the Chinese Communists. He organized a "People's Liberation Army" on the border, to cooperate with the Viet-Minh. Lu Han, who was not hostile toward Ho's regime, made no effort to repress Lung. Second, the local authorities of a few border cities were mostly won over to the Viet-Minh. Officials in Hokow, for instance, in return for a bribe of 50,000

piasters from the Viet-Minh, openly welcomed Ho's delegation to the city in October 1947, and allowed the Viet-Minh
to establish a radio station in an office building. Although
the station was removed after a strong protest from the
Chinese military police in the city (the police were under
the direct command of the central government, not Lu
Han), the Viet-Minh continued to be active with the protection of the local authorities. They engaged in various
activities against the VNQDD and the French, including
cooperating with the bandits in kidnapping Vu Hong
Khanh's wife.[87] Third, some local private armed groups,[88]
of no particular politics and who could turn to either government forces or the bandits, reacted favorably to an offer
of money made by the Chinese Communists and the Viet-
Minh. The Viet-Minh bought arms from the private groups,
and made friends with them. On more than two occasions,
in Yuanchiang (about 150 miles from the border) and
P'ingpien (70 miles from the border), Vu Hong Khanh,
who retreated in February 1948 under the French pressure
with a force of 300 men to Chinp'ing (a Yunnan border
city), sent men to deal with the groups, but encountered
the same answer: "Ho Chi Minh had already sent men to
negotiate with us."[89] Ho's men worked successfully with the
groups, thus offsetting the possibility of their hostility toward the Viet-Minh. In these circumstances, the Viet-Minh
were able not only to seek sanctuary in Yunnan but to gain
strength in the border area.

On the French side the effect of the victory of 1947-1948
was undermined by the notorious behavior and poor disci-

[87] Report of Hsuan Chi-shun and Wang Kang, October 9, 1947,
in "Documents." Hsuan and Wang were Chinese volunteers in Vu
Hong Khanh's unit in 1947. Vu Hong Khanh's letter to the author
confirmed this point.

[88] There were approximately 300,000 men privately armed in
Yunnan in 1946; they were mostly disfavored military men, bandits,
and army deserters. Hsing Shen-chou, "Report on Vietnam," April
11, 1946, in "Documents."

[89] Report of Hsuan Chi-shun and Wang Kang, in "Documents."
In the same manner, Vu Hong Khanh's remnant force of 300 was
able to survive in Chinp'ing until late 1949.

pline of the French expeditionary forces. They tortured, raped, looted, and humiliated religious faiths. Some became "half insane." As some village notables complained to a French reporter, "We know what war always is. We understand your soldiers taking our animals, our jewelry, our Buddhas; it is normal. We are resigned to their raping our wives and our daughters; war has always been like that. But we object to being treated in the same way, not only our sons, but ourselves, old men and dignitaries that we are."[90] These acts of misconduct inflamed hatred of the French among the Vietnamese people and caused French-trained Vietnamese soldiers to defect in groups. On June 20, 1948 a group of about 400 French-trained Vietnamese in Phu-Lu and Bao-Ha suddenly defected to the Viet-Minh with their weapons because French officers had raped their women.[91]

The Viet-Minh's sanctuary in China, cooperation between the Vietnamese and Chinese Communists, the poor discipline among the French troops—all contributed to the survival and growth of the Viet-Minh army in 1947-1948. When Giap's forces attacked Lai-Chau and Lao-Kay in 1948, their strength surprised the French, changing their presumptuousness to fear for the first time. By the end of 1948 three local Chinese Communist units had appeared in the border area: The Chen(pien)-Ching(hsi) People's Liberation Army, the Yunnan-Kwangsi Border People's Salvation Army, and the Yunnan-Vietnam Border People's Liberation Army.[92] This development militarily secured the Viet-Minh's position on the border, although Giap's army was not yet ready to launch a general offensive.

FROM late 1946 to late 1949 the Chinese Communist Party did not issue a policy statement on Vietnam. The only article the present writer has found is "The New-Born

[90] Bodard, *Quicksand War*, p. 60.
[91] Report of the Yunnan Provincial Government, August 4, 1948, in "Documents."
[92] *Chung yang jih pao* (Kweilin), November 5, 1948.

Vietnam," which appeared in late 1946 in the CCP organ at Yenan. It included a short history of Ho Chi Minh's Vietnam, and stated that the "independence of Vietnam was not granted by imperialist countries but [was] achieved by the Vietnamese people under the leadership of the Vietnam Communist Party," of which Ho was the leader.[93] It moderately praised North Vietnam's struggle for independence. In April 1948, however, the CCP radio in North Shensi broadcast that the French army in Indochina "had lost 58,286 men" while the Viet-Minh army had lost only 9,321; it hailed the heroic fighting of the Viet-Minh army, which had increased over 12 times, from 20,000 (1945) to 250,000 (1948), and reported that the French army was in "a desperate situation."[94] The broadcast implied the CCP's support for the Viet-Minh. Yet from April 1948 to late 1949 the CCP radio, in its broadcasts on the civil war, made no more comments about Vietnam. There are several reasons for the silence—the suspension of all publications in Yenan after March 1947, when that Red capital fell into Nationalist hands; the preoccupation with the civil war; and, Ho Chi Minh's cautious policy of not publicizing CCP–Viet-Minh relations, if any. Although Radio Saigon broadcast the existence of links between the Viet-Minh and the CCP in December 1948, the French disclosed no evidence to substantiate the charge.

The Chinese civil war developed drastically in favor of the Communists after the fall of Manchuria in the late autumn of 1948. In Manchuria approximately 470,000 Nationalist troops and their equipment fell into Communist hands. The loss of the battle of Hwai-Hai in the winter of 1948-1949 cost another 550,000 crack Nationalist troops. On November 9, 1948 President Chiang wrote a letter to President Truman, asking for more military aid, and swiftly, and for a high-ranking American military officer to help plan campaigns against the Communists. In his reply to

[93] *Chieh fang jih pao* (Yenan), November 13, 1946.
[94] Radio North Shensi, in Mandarin to China and overseas, April 4, 1948, 5:30 a.m.

Chiang, Truman did not comply with any of these requests.[95] On December 1, Madame Chiang flew to Washington and held a long talk with Secretary of State Marshall, in which she was reported to have asked for aid.[96] On January 8, 1949 Chinese Foreign Minister Wu Tieh-ch'eng probed the attitudes of the United States, the Soviet Union, Great Britain, and France regarding a mission for collective mediation between the Nationalists and the Communists. All of the governments turned down the idea.[97] With no hope for international support, the morale of the Nationalists sagged. On January 14 Mao Tse-tung, in rejecting Nanking's peace terms, set forth a harsh and apparently unacceptable eight-point counterproposal.[98] On January 15 Tientsin fell to the Communists. Two weeks later Peiping surrendered without a fight. Worse still, Nationalist Generals Pai Ch'ung-hsi and Ch'eng Ch'ien demanded Chiang's resignation from the presidency to make way for peace talks.[99] Chiang yielded on January 21 and left for home. Thereupon Vice-President Li Tsung-jen assumed the post

[95] *United States Relations with China* (1949), pp. 888-90.

[96] *Ta kung pao*, December 5, 1948.

[97] *Ta kung pao* (Hong Kong), January 8, 21, 1949; *New York Times*, January 21, 1949.

[98] The conditions (points) were: (1) punishment of the civil war criminals, (2) abolition of the illegitimate constitution, (3) abolition of the illegitimate system, (4) reorganization of all reactionary armies, (5) confiscation of the capital assets of politicians, (6) reform of the land system, (7) abolition of treasonous treaties, and (8) the convening of a political consultation conference free from participation by reactionaries. *Ta kung pao* (Hong Kong), January 15, 1949.

[99] The strong urge for Chiang's resignation by these two generals had never been officially made known, but was not a secret. The real intention behind the demand was for Li Tsung-jen to gain power with the hope for peace negotiations with the Communists. Chiang sent Chang Ch'un, former prime minister and now (1968) secretary-general to Chiang in Taiwan, to persuade the two generals to drop their demands, but failed. See *Ta kung pao* (Hong Kong), March 9, 10, 11, 1949. General Pai, a resourceful strategist of the Kwangsi clique, of which Li Tsung-jen was the head, was then the commander of the Central China Zone in the strategic city of Wuhan. He died in Taiwan in 1967. General Ch'eng was then the Governor of Hunan; he surrendered to Mao in 1949.

of acting president and began to arrange peace negotiations with Mao.

The resignation of Chiang Kai-shek and the fall of Peiping signaled the impending total defeat of the Nationalists. In the later half of March, Mao Tse-tung and his comrades began to set the stage for the new regime. The party machine was first set in motion. A second plenary session of the Seventh Central Committee of the Chinese Communist Party was convened in Shihchiachuang, a city in southern Hopei. At the meeting the Chinese Communists decided to shift party work from the countryside to the city and approved two important proposals submitted by the party politburo: (1) the eight conditions for peace negotiations as the counterproposal of Mao to the Nanking government; and (2) the convention of a new Chinese People's Political Consultative Conference (CPPCC) and the establishment of a Communist government.[100] Following the meeting Mao and his headquarters staff moved to Peiping.

The situation developed rapidly between March and October: the KMT-CCP peace talks were dead; Nanking, Shanghai, and Canton were taken; the CPPCC was convened; and the Communist regime was established. All of this did not lead the CCP to institute a public policy toward Vietnam, yet the impact on the Vietnamese situation was apparent.

Keeping a careful eye on the situation in China, Ho Chi Minh maintained his cautious position toward the northern neighbor, particularly since the Kuomintang still ruled Kwangsi and Yunnan. He issued no statement attacking the Kuomintang government. At a press conference in early March 1949, Ho made his position known: "The population of China forms one fourth of the total population of the world. The victory of democracy in China will certainly have repercussions throughout the whole world, of which

[100] *Ta kung pao* (Hong Kong), March 25, 1949; Hu Ch'iao-mo, *Thirty Years of the Communist Party of China* (Peking: Foreign Languages Press, 1951), pp. 59-60.

Viet-Nam is a part."[101] He dismissed the existence of a Mao Tse-tung–Ho Chi Minh secret agreement as a colonialist rumor, but was "certain" of his victory because of the "favorable international happenings" and the "progress" of the Viet-Minh.

In April Ho still maintained his view on China. In answering a question about how he regarded the recent events in China, he tactfully placed no emphasis on either the Communist victory or future Sino-Vietnamese relations, but said, "Vietnam's independence depends always on her own strength. Like other countries, Vietnam will be more or less affected by the China events."[102] He denounced the charge of "Communist domination" of his government as "pure French imperialist propaganda," and defended his regime as a national coalition government of many parties and nonparty men.[103] Ho was not quite ready to side openly with the Communist camp.

While Ho was playing for time, the French were alarmed with the drastic changes in China. Fearing Chinese Communist intervention, the French government sent Gen. Georges Revers to Vietnam in May 1949 to investigate the situation and make recommendations. After his visit, General Revers recommended the evacuation of the French border garrisons to avoid any possible conflict with the Chinese Communists and to tighten control of the quadrilateral defensive system of Mon-Kay, Lang-Son, Haiphong, and Hanoi.[104] The recommendation was confidential but became known to the Viet-Minh, which broadcast it to propagandize the fear of the French and the impending offensive to be launched by the Viet-Minh.

As of late August 1949, when he was interviewed by an American correspondent, Ho had not altered his views on the subject of China. Although he said that the victories of

[101] Viet-Nam Information, II, No. 2 (March 5, 1949), in Cole, *Conflict*, p. 71.
[102] *Newsweek*, April 25, 1949, p. 44.
[103] Das, *Ho Chi Minh*, p. 5.
[104] *Vietnamese Studies*, No. 7, pp. 98-99; Lancaster, *Emancipation*, pp. 407-10.

the Chinese Communists had shifted the balance of power in Asia and admitted that there were similarities between Mao's "New Democracy" and his views on the future of Vietnam, he tried to make a distinction, saying, "China's New Democracy is Chinese, ours Vietnamese." He denied once again the charges that the Viet-Minh had already made arrangements with the Chinese Communists for military aid, and claimed that the Viet-Minh had always depended on its own resources and that the "Vietnam Republic will be 'of the people, by the people, and for the people.'"[105] What Ho was reluctant to say, however, was revealed by an aide working in South Vietnam. As Pham Ngoc Thach told a French writer in July, "The successes of the Chinese [Communist] Army . . . herald the impending end of [the] dark days" of the Viet-Minh.[106]

On October 1, 1949 Mao Tse-tung announced the establishment of the People's Republic of China. Before long, the Chinese Communist army reached the Sino-Vietnamese border and Lu Han surrendered to Mao. Over a period of a few years, the Chinese Communists had grown from a comparatively small rebel group to an important national power, from an armed unit in remote areas to a powerful army extending to the Vietnam border. Many factors seemed to contribute to Mao's victory: the corruption and incapability of the Kuomintang government; the great opportunity for the CCP to grow during and after the Japanese invasion; the dynamics of Communist social program and mass mobilization; Soviet military aid to the Communist forces in Manchuria; the intellectuals' disappointment with the Kuomintang and illusion of the CCP; and the failure of American policy toward China.

Up to this point, the Viet-Minh radio had not broadcast a direct attack on the Kuomintang. But to Ho Chi Minh, the period of difficult, suffering, dark days was indeed over.

[105] *Ta kung pao* (Hong Kong; pro-Communist since January 22, 1949, one day after Chiang Kai-shek's resignation), August 25, 1949; *The Nation*, September 10, 1949.

[106] Marcel Ner, "Le Viet-nam et la Chine de 1945 à 1954," *Les Temps Modernes* (Paris), 9, No. 93/94 (Août-Septembre, 1953), p. 382.

Mao's swift victory must have taken him and his men by surprise.[107] He issued no more ambiguous statements. A new era of Sino-Vietnamese relations had begun.

4. Chinese Nationalist Troops Retreat to Vietnam

Before we turn to the new relationship between Communist China and North Vietnam, one thing which should not be ignored is the retreat of 30,000 Chinese Nationalist troops to Vietnam at the end of 1949. Toward the end of 1949 the Nationalist government had suffered complete defeat and moved to Taiwan. Acting President Li Tsung-jen did not lead the regime to the island. He flew to the United States during the winter for the treatment of an "illness" and never returned to Nationalist China.[108] On March 1, 1950 Chiang Kai-shek resumed the presidency in Taipei. Geographically, the Nationalist government separated itself completely from North Vietnam, but units of its army entered French Vietnam, causing the Viet-Minh uneasiness and hostility toward its former "ally."

The Nationalist forces moving into Vietnam belonged mostly to the First Army Corps, commanded by Gen. Huang Chieh.[109] The corps was one of five[110] totaling about 300,000

[107] The rapid development of the Chinese civil war in 1948-1949 took many people at home and abroad by surprise, including the Chinese Communists themselves. Chow Ching-wen, former deputy secretary-general of the China Democratic League, which is a minority party in Communist China, reports that when he and other leaders of the league from Hong Kong were given a reception by the Chinese Communist leaders in Peking on April 2, 1949, Marshal Yeh Chien-ying said to him, "The development of the situation was entirely unexpected." See Chow's book, *Ten Years of Storm; the True Story of the Communist Regime in China,* tr. Lai Ming (New York: Holt, Rinehart and Winston, 1960), p. 12.

[108] Li lived comfortably but alone in New Jersey until 1965, when he returned to mainland China. The Peking regime made a fanfare of propaganda over his return.

[109] Gen. Huang Chieh (1903-   ) is a graduate of the Whampoa Military Academy. A professional and "scholarly" soldier, he enjoys a good reputation among the Nationalists. He is one of the best generals and administrators in Nationalist China and is now the Governor of Taiwan (as of 1968).

[110] The other four were: The Third Army Corps, the Tenth Army Corps, the Eleventh Army Corps, and the Seventeenth Army Corps.

under General Pai Ch'ung-hsi, commander of the Central China Zone. Under the pressure from Lin Piao's and Liu Po-ch'eng's armies (550,000) Pai was compelled to retreat from Hupeh, Hunan to Kwangsi during the summer and fall of 1949. On November 5 Pai held a military conference with his commanders at Kweilin to discuss their future course. After deliberation of two plans—to the south with a destination of Hainan Island, or west to Yunnan, General Pai chose the first. As Gen. Huang Chieh recalled, they originally had reached no decision to enter Vietnam.[111]

It was at that time that General Pai was reported to have sent a missionary friend of his, Father Maillot, to Hanoi with a message offering an alliance with the French to fight in Tonkin against any brand of Communists, Chinese or Vietnamese. If the French refused, Pai's soldiers would enter Tonkin by force.[112] And the French did refuse. It was also reported that Pai finally reached a "gentleman's agreement" with Lin Piao, by which Pai "renounced heroism and last-ditch efforts and every kind of hostile act in China and Indochina," while Lin Piao allowed Pai to "carry out an amicable Dunkirk" to Hainan Island.[113] The second item of the report—a "gentleman's agreement"—was certainly not true because no such an agreement had ever been reached. In effect, Lin Piao would never have made any agreement with Pai allowing Pai's army to leave China intact. Between November 5 and December 8 Pai's armies were defeated and retreated from Kweilin, Liuchow, Naning to the Vietnam border with only 40,000. One unit was unexpectedly attacked in early December by local Chinese and Viet-Minh Communists from the north and the south at P'ingmeng and P'ingerhkuan (a Chinese border town about 40 miles from Lungchow), and was wiped out.[114]

[111] Huang Chieh, *Hai wai chi ch'ing* (Memoirs of Indochina) (Taipei, 1958), pp. 38-39, is one of the most useful accounts of the subject.
[112] Bodard, *Quicksand War*, pp. 144-46.
[113] *Ibid.*, p. 150.
[114] Huang Chieh, *Memoirs*, p. 49.

General Pai fled to Hainan. There was no "amicable Dunkirk."

While Pai's forces were retreating south the Peking regime realized the possibility of the Nationalist entry into Vietnam, Laos, or Burma. Chou En-lai, as Minister of Foreign Affairs, issued a warning on November 29 to French Vietnam and other neighboring countries, saying: "The Chiang bandits are pinning their hopes on Vietnam and other territories bordering on China, with an attempt at making those areas into a refuge for the remnant forces, and as a base for their future comeback. . . . The People's Republic of China, thus, formally warns France and . . . other bordering countries: any government which offers refuge to the Kuomintang reactionary armed forces shall bear the responsibility for handling this matter and all its ensuing consequences."[115]

Meanwhile the Chinese Communists intensified their propaganda. They said that T. V. Soong, governor of Kwangtung province, had negotiated with France as early as May 1949 for the establishment of an Asian anti-Communist center in the China-Burma-Vietnam border area, that a Sino-French agreement had been reached in Vietnam in August for the possible entry into Indochina of a defeated Nationalist army, and that the Nationalists in Vietnam would be treated as a Vietnamese army and placed under the command of either Nguyen Van Xuan, minister of defense in Bao Dai's government in Saigon, or Vu Hong Khanh, leader of the VNQDD.[116]

These reports worried Ho. On December 8 his radio denounced and protested "the underhandedness and machinations of the Chinese Kuomintang reactionaries and the French Imperialists." It further charged that the French and the Kuomintang aimed at "violating Vietnam's national sovereignty and establishing bases in North Vietnam for

[115] *Chieh fang jih pao* (Shanghai), November 30, 1949.
[116] *Chieh fang jih pao* (Shanghai), December 1, 1949; *Ta kung pao* (Hong Kong), December 14, 17, 19, 1949.

a last-ditch resistance against the Chinese Liberation Army."[117]

At the same time, the Nationalist forces, mostly under Huang Chieh, were pushed to the final point on the Chinese side of the border across from Lang-Son and Loc-Binh. On December 8 General Huang received a cable from General Pai, vaguely instructing him to avoid a fight with the Communists, and to divide his forces into small units with light equipment for self-preservation and future attacks.[118] For a time, General Huang planned to move his soldiers to the Chinghsi-T'ienpao-Chenpien area where geography would provide him with an advantageous corner from which to resist the Communists. But time did not allow him to do so. The following day Huang received the news of Lu Han's surrender to Mao, which put an end to his hope of entering Yunnan. At this critical juncture came a cable from Gen. Ch'en Ch'eng, then governor of Taiwan and commander of the Southeast China (War) Zone. Ch'en advised Huang to lead his forces into Vietnam and wait for an opportunity to stay in Vietnam or transfer to Taiwan.[119] This suggestion was a new hope in the desperate situation. Huang immediately called for a meeting of his generals, who unanimously agreed to "move into Vietnam and then transfer to Taiwan." Huang made the decision in accordance with the agreement of the generals and informed Ch'en Ch'eng and Pai Ch'ung-hsi. Then he sent Mao Ch'i-keng, chief of his foreign affairs section, and two other officers, to cross the border with a message addressed to French High Commissioner Léon Pignon requesting permission to enter Vietnam. In the letter, Huang wrote: "My Army Corps . . . due to temporary setbacks is gathering at the Sino-Vietnamese border. To respect your national sovereignty and abide by international law, I have instructed my soldiers not to cross the border line. In order

[117] Vietnam News Agency, December 8, 1949.

[118] Huang Chieh, *Memoirs*, p. 48.

[119] *Ibid.*, p. 49. General Ch'en later became vice-president of the Nationalist government in Taiwan. He died in 1965.

to keep our forces for future counterattack, we would like to request passage to your Haiphong port for transfer to Taiwan. I have cabled my government to negotiate with your government on this matter. But in the emergency, I am sending my Foreign Affairs Director to negotiate with you on procedure of the passage. . . . Please grant my request."[120]

The Chinese representatives went to the border town of Aidiem (Aitien) on the morning of December 9. The next day High Commissioner Pignon, who might have been informed of the matter, issued a statement. He announced that the French-Vietnamese authorities had instructed the French army to resist all armed foreign forces who tried to enter the territory of Vietnam, and that those foreign forces that did enter Vietnam would be driven out, disarmed, or detained. He added that the French-Vietnamese government would not allow people who would endanger border security and friendly relations with neighboring countries to use Vietnam as a refuge.[121] It seemed that this statement was a reply to Chou En-lai's warning and Huang Chieh's request. While announcing that the French-Vietnamese authorities would not tolerate the Chinese Nationalists taking refuge in Vietnam, Pignon hinted at the possibility of allowing them to enter Vietnam after having been disarmed. Apparently the French were apprehensive of the result of an entry by the armed Nationalists. As Radio Hue commented, "A Chinese Nationalist invasion will be followed by a Chinese Communist wave. . . . Once the Communists are in Vietnam, nothing will make them retreat."[122]

Whereas the Nationalists resisted fierce Communist attacks in the rear, their representatives negotiated with the French in the front at Chi-Ma, a Vietnam border post. The talks took place on December 11 at a little fort and lasted a whole day. According to the previously cited French report,[123] it was a dramatic negotiation, combining emotion,

[120] *Ibid.*, pp. 50-51.
[121] Radio Hue (French controlled), December 12, 1949.
[122] *Ibid.*
[123] Bodard, *Quicksand War*, pp. 151-52.

anxiety, apprehension with threat, fury, and firmness. Finally the Chinese gave in. On the morning of the 12th their negotiators returned to Aidiem with the accord on which General Huang and his aides had agreed. Mao Ch'i-keng and Ho Chu-pen (chief of staff, who spoke French) were sent back to Chi-Ma to sign the preliminary agreement with Colonel Constans, Commander of the French garrison at Lang-Son. The main items of the accord were:

(1) Both parties are in no position to decide on the problem of a joint action against Ho Chi Minh at the present moment.

(2) The Chinese, in their passage from Haiphong to Taiwan, agree to divide into units (500 men each) and lay down their arms which will be returned through negotiations by both governments.

(3) The French are to supply food until the Chinese leave the port.

(4) General Huang Chieh is in charge of the passage of all of the Kuomintang and local forces.[124]

The accord also provided that Ho Chu-pen and Mao Ch'i-keng were to go to Hanoi or Saigon for further negotiations.

The Chinese Nationalists began to move into Vietnam at 8 a.m. December 13, from Aidiem to Chi-Ma (some 500 feet apart), with the Communists following hard in the rear. As soon as they reached Chi-Ma, the Nationalists surrendered their arms and equipment. The disarmed soldiers marched southward on the highway to Loc-Binh, followed by the disabled, civilians, and dependents—a total of about 30,000. In a few days they moved from Loc-Binh, Tien-Yen to Hon-Gay, near Haiphong. They rested at an abandoned coal pit on the shore of the Bay of Along,[125] suffering from poor shelter, meager food, and even the notorious reputa-

[124] Huang Chieh, *Memoirs*, pp. 51-52.
[125] *Ta kung pao* (Hong Kong), December 19, 21, 31, 1949; *New York Times*, December 15, 1949; VNA, December 28, 1949; *Jen min jih pao* (Peking), January 11, 1950.

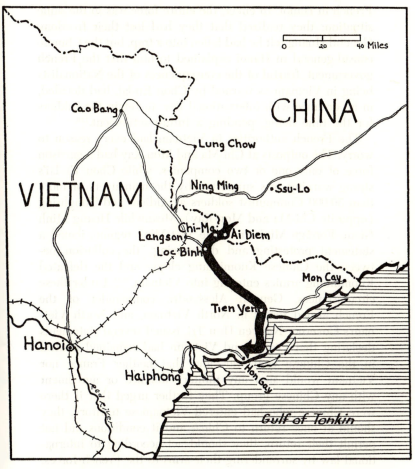

Chinese Nationalist Troops Retreat to Vietnam, December 1949

tion of Lu Han's army during the occupation period. The French were unfriendly and sometimes hostile. General Huang and a few aides were invited and retained by the French in Hanoi. In effect, the entire force was in the same situation; they realized that they had lost their freedom. General Huang felt he had fallen into a trap, but the Chinese consul-general in Hanoi explained to him that the French government, fearful of the consequences of the Nationalists being in Vietnam as warned by Chou En-lai, had decided, in accordance with international law, to retain the soldiers for the time being, pending a future settlement.[126]

The French authorities in Vietnam had every reason to worry. The outposts at Chi-Ma and Mon-Kay had a garrison force of only one or two companies, while Chou En-lai's strong warning was supported by the maneuvers of more than 50,000 Communist soldiers at Aidiem and Tunghsing (opposite Chi-Ma and Mon-Kay). Meanwhile Hoang Minh Giam, Foreign Minister of the Viet-Minh regime, issued a statement protesting and denouncing "the collusion between the Chinese Kuomintang clique and the defeated Kuomintang armies entering into Vietnam."[127] Under these circumstances, General Alessandri, commander of the French armed forces in North Vietnam, and North Vietnam's Governor Nguyen Huu Tri, issued several statements declaring that France and Vietnam had remained neutral in the Chinese civil war, and that neither France nor Vietnam would sign any military alliance or agreement with any Chinese group. They further urged that if there were Chinese who had entered Vietnamese territory, they should at once return to China, and if conditions did not permit their return, they should act according to international law by surrendering their arms to the French forces. Otherwise they would be considered as brigands and be punished accordingly.[128] The Viet-Minh, on the other hand,

[126] Huang Chieh, *Memoirs*, p. 57.
[127] VNA (Ho's), December 18, 1949.
[128] Radio Hanoi (French controlled), in Tonkinese, December 29, 1949.

208

tried to make a Chinese Communist intervention more likely by threatening the French with the possibility of a joint action with Mao Tse-tung's army. On January 3, 1950 the Viet-Minh radio announced that the declaration of "neutrality" and the pledge to "disarm" incoming Kuomintang armies made by the French and the Bao Dai government was to fool the people of China and Vietnam, and warned that "the Vietnam people and army not only would heartily welcome but would also actively support the Chinese Liberation Army, should the latter deem it necessary to pursue the remnant Kuomintang elements into Vietnam."[129] The warning greatly disturbed the French. For a time, they considered a plan for the return of the interned Nationalists to mainland China. One day in January 1950, after High Commissioner Pignon and Commander-in-Chief General Carpentier had visited the Chinese camp, they asked Huang Chieh what would he and his men do should the French accept Mao Tse-tung's request to repatriate them to the mainland. Pointing at the ocean in their front, Huang answered that he and his 30,000 men would resolutely jump into the sea rather than surrender to Mao.[130] Pignon and Carpentier might not have fully understood the moral significance of this self-destructive suggestion in Oriental fashion, but they were greatly surprised by the unexpected, desperate yet firm reply. From then on the repatriation plan was dropped, and the Chinese faced an indefinite period of internment.

The Chinese were transferred to Phu-Quoc Island in the summer of 1950, a small island about 15 miles off the southern coast of the Indochina peninsula. A force of about 5,000 men from Yunnan who had entered Vietnam in January 1950, was shipped in March to Cam Ranh Bay (South Vietnam). Vu Hong Khanh and his few hundred VNQDD men came along with the Yunnan group; but most of them returned to civilian life in South Vietnam.[131] The Chinese,

---

[129] VNA, English, January 3, 1950.
[130] Huang Chieh, *Memoirs*, p. 67.
[131] Vu Hong Khanh served as the Minister of Youth Sports under

except for a few hundred who volunteered to work at the Hon-Gay mine and on Cambodian rubber plantations, began to lead an aboriginal life on the island. They fought against mosquitos, snakes, and tigers; built houses, bridges, auditoriums, and a library; raised pigs, chickens, and vegetables; and stayed away from the Viet-Minh who controlled the jungle on the island. Gradually the French improved the treatment and extended them friendship. In October of the same year, the Taiwan government sent officials to visit them with clothing, medicine, newspapers, magazines, sports equipment, and musical instruments.[132] Their morale was recovering, and they maintained good discipline.

After the summer of 1950 neither the Chinese Communists nor the Viet-Minh made any serious protest or threat against the French and the Nationalists; presumably the Chinese were preoccupied with the Korean war, and the Viet-Minh was mobilizing for an offensive. Negotiations for repatriation to Taiwan started in early 1951. When Gen. de Lattre de Tassigny, the French High Commissioner and commander-in-chief in Indochina, visited Washington in September 1951, Chinese Ambassador Wellington Koo negotiated with the French general and asked the United States government to help persuade de Tassigny to release the Nationalists. But the general strongly refused. The overriding reason was to avoid offending Mao Tse-tung. He told Ambassador Koo that if the repatriation would not provoke war with the Chinese Communists, there was no reason for the French to spend $3 million a year to intern the Nationalists, adding that if the United States would guarantee to support the French army in case of a Chinese

---

Bao Dai in 1952, and joined the presidential race in South Vietnam in 1967 along with 10 other candidates. He received only 148,652 votes (three per cent). *New York Times*, September 5, 1967.

[132] *Chung yang jih pao* (Taipei), July 3, 1953; Huang Chieh, *Memoirs*, pp. 83-87. The Taiwan government sent two missions (1950, 1952) to the island. It began to send subsidies of money in October 1950 to improve living conditions there.

Communist attack, the French would release the Nationalists at any time.[133]

To protest against the endless detainment, the Nationalists fasted on Christmas Day 1951, with no immediate gain.
But the death message of General de Lattre in January
1952 became good news for the interned Chinese. Gen.
Raoul Salan, de Lattre's successor, expressed to the Chinese
his sympathy and friendship; negotiations were soon
stepped up, and a final agreement between Paris and
Taipei was reached in early 1953. The 30,000 interned
Nationalists were shipped to Taiwan in Chinese naval
vessels in May and June. Only 1,500 chose to stay in Vietnam and Cambodia. Neither the Chinese nor the Viet-Minh
Communists seriously protested. Over a period of three and
a half years the French had spent millions of dollars for
nothing!

[133] *Ibid.*, pp. 89, 93.

5. A Chinese Revolutionary Model for Vietnam, 1950-1954

‹‹‹

> "The People's Republic of China has established for the peoples of Asia a model and a goal, on the path of the struggle against aggressive imperialism, the path of building an independent nation and a new life in the political, economic and cultural domains. . . . In their long-term struggle the Vietnamese people, the closest neighbors of China, have followed the example of the Chinese people."
>
> — *Nhan Dan*: "The People's Republic of China, the Vanguard Flag of the Asian Nations." September 22, 1954

WHEN Mao Tse-tung announced the People's Republic of China on October 1, 1949, he declared that the new regime was formed in accordance with the resolution of the Chinese People's Political Consultative Conference (CPPCC) and on the basis of its Common Program passed 10 days earlier. The Peking regime adopted the Common Program as the temporary fundamental law while using the CPPCC as the united front organization which exercised the functions of the future People's Congress.[1] Among the 585 voting delegates of the CPPCC, 142 were from the 14 political parties and groups, which included the Chinese Communist Party with only 16 seats.[2] Under this arrangement the Peking regime was not only founded on the "will

---

[1] Chou En-lai explained the functions of the CPPCC in this manner: "In considering, at the beginning of the reconstruction of the nation, that the people's liberation war has not yet ended, that various political and social reforms have not yet been put into effect, that national economy needs a period of time for recovery, and that people's representative assembly has not yet been convened, the Common Program of the CPPCC is drafted with the provision that before the summoning of the National People's Congress, the Chinese People's Political Consultative Conference exercises the functions of the Congress." *Jen min shou ts'e* (People's Handbook) (Peking: Jen min ch'u pan she, 1953), p. 162.

[2] The other Communist members at this conference were representatives not from the party, but from people's organizations, "liberated" areas, army units, etc.

of the people" as the CPPCC said, but "democratic" in character. In exercising his mandate to build up the regime through the CPPCC, Mao made good use of the united front organization[3]—a technique similar to that of Ho Chi Minh with the Viet-Minh in August 1945.

People all over the world were speculating about the new regime in Peking. What would "the people's democratic dictatorship," which had been announced by Mao three months earlier, be like?[4] Would it be a Western democracy in principle? Or would it be more dictatorial than democratic, on the pattern of the Soviet government? And how could a regime with both "democratic" and "dictatorial" characteristics operate effectively and harmoniously? The world began to learn some of the answers as the names of the government leaders were announced—Mao Tse-tung was chairman; six other Communists and non-Communists were vice-chairmen, Chou En-lai was prime minister; and 38 other Communists and non-Communists were cabinet ministers and commissioners.[5] In reality, the new regime was a coalition government under the dictatorship of the CCP.

Of special interest was the probable policy of the new Peking regime toward Vietnam. Would it entail a new tribute system for Vietnam? Or would Peking build up an

[3] From the beginning in September 1949, the CPPCC was designed and had functioned effectively as a united front organization. After the People's Congress was convened in September 1954 its power as a state organ was taken over by the Congress; but it remained, as *Jen min jih pao* points out, "a people's democratic united-front organization for uniting all nationalities, democratic classes, democratic parties and groups, people's bodies, overseas Chinese and other patriotic democrats . . . under the leadership of the Chinese Communist Party." Editorial in *Jen min jih pao*, December 22, 1954, in *Survey of the China Mainland Press* (SCMP) (Hong Kong: American Consulate-General, December 23, 1964).

[4] Mao Tse-tung, "On the People's Democratic Dictatorship," *Selected Works*, Vol. IV, pp. 411-24.

[5] *Chairman*, Mao Tse-tung; *Vice-Chairmen*, Chu Teh, Liu Shao-ch'i, Kao Kan, Soong Ch'ing-ling (KMT Revolutionary Committee), Li Chi-shen (KMT Revolutionary Committee), Chang Line (China Democratic League); *Cabinet*, Prime Minister Chou En-lai, 21 Communist members, 17 non-Communist members.

equal relationship of socialist fraternity? Above all, what position would Peking take in regard to the Viet-Minh's resistance war?

Publicly the Chinese Communists did not announce an established policy for Vietnam. Yet from various documents and statements, one can see that Peking did have one in mind, that is, a Chinese revolutionary model for Vietnam.

1. A CHINESE MODEL: THE VIEWS OF PEKING AND MOSCOW

In view of the Sino-Soviet dispute today, it is not surprising that Peking, even in the early years of its regime, was of the opinion that it was the Chinese formula, not the Soviet one, that should prevail in the underdeveloped areas. Being a colonial underdeveloped nation, Vietnam was regarded by Peking as a good opportunity in which to apply the Chinese model, a standpoint that originated in the Chinese disagreement with the Soviet view on the Chinese revolution in the early 1920s.

In August 1922, just one year after the organization of the CCP, the Chinese Communists opposed the Soviet (Comintern) policy of a Kuomintang-Communist alliance at the Special Plenum of the Central Committee at Hangchow. The opposition was suppressed by Maring (Sneevliet), the Comintern's representative, who threatened party disciplinary action. Mao Tse-tung's determined opposition to a Comintern-sponsored resolution of the Fifth Congress of the CCP, which called for an immediate, radical land reform, came in 1927 at Hankow on the eve of the Kuomintang-Communist split.[6] Mao argued that foreigners (Comintern representatives) could not understand the Chinese reality, therefore the resolution was unsuited to the

---

[6] M. N. Roy, "Mao Tse-tung: A Reminiscence," *New Republic* (Sept. 3, 1951), pp. 14-15. Chang Kuo-t'ao recently published his important memoirs in Hong Kong. For the Fifth Congress of the CCP he attended in the capacity of a Politburo member, see his *My Memoirs*, Chap. 12, in *Ming pao* (Hong Kong), No. 22 (October 1967), pp. 90-91.

Chinese situation. Other early Communist leaders such as Li Ta-chao, Chang Kuo-t'ao, and Ts'ai Ho-shen expressed a similar view.

But the view that the Chinese revolutionary system should be adopted by the colonial and semi-colonial countries was not made known until 1940, when Mao published "On New Democracy." Mao argued first that the Chinese revolution could not be achieved by either the bourgeois "dictatorship" of the European-American system nor by the Soviet "dictatorship of the proletariat." It could only be achieved by "New Democracy," a democracy with a four-class alliance—the peasantry, proletariat, petty bourgeoisie, and national bourgeoisie—and with a joint dictatorship of various classes under the political system of democratic centralism. Although, Mao argued further, the Soviet-type proletarian dictatorship would be established in all of the capitalist countries, it was "not suitable for the revolutions of all colonial and semi-colonial countries"; instead, New Democracy "must be adopted in the revolutions of all colonial and semi-colonial countries, namely, the new-democratic republic. This form suits a certain historical period and is therefore transitional; nevertheless, it is a form which is necessary and cannot be dispensed with."[7]

Conceivably Mao, when he expressed this view in 1940, did not mean to dispute or challenge the Soviet leadership in the world Communist movement, as he does in the 1960s. He probably meant to place China on the side of the colonial and semi-colonial countries to form a "poor man's club."

Apparently this view of Mao was accepted and taught by other Chinese Communist leaders during the war years. One of the best interpretations is that developed by Liu Shao-ch'i when he, among other Communist theoreticians, talked with Anna Louise Strong in Yenan in early 1946. Liu said that Marx and Lenin were Europeans, and they seldom discussed Asia or China. While the basic principles of

[7] Mao Tse-tung, "On New Democracy," *Selected Works*, II, p. 350.

Marxism were adaptable to all countries, to apply them to a specific revolution in China was difficult. Mao, as a Chinese, had successfully used Marxist-Leninist principles to explain Chinese problems and to lead the Chinese revolution to victory. It was the conviction of the Yenan leaders that Mao's analysis of the way to national independence was people's democracy and people's livelihood, that people's democracy "charts a way not only for the Chinese people but for the billion folk who live in the colonial countries of southeast Asia." Liu went on to explain: "[Mao] has created a Chinese or Asiatic form of Marxism. China is a semi-feudal, semi-colonial country in which vast numbers of people live at the edge of starvation, tilling small bits of soil. Its economy is agricultural, backward, and dispersed. In attempting the transition to a more industrialized economy, China faces the competition and the pressures—economic, political, and military—of advanced industrial lands. This is the basic situation that affects both the relations of social classes and the methods of struggle towards any such goal as national independence and a better, freer life for the Chinese. There are similar conditions in other lands of southeast Asia. The courses chosen by China will influence them all."[8]

"The courses chosen by China" were supported by a revolutionary formula developed by Mao in June 1949, when complete victory over the Kuomintang was in sight. The formula is composed of three elements, namely, a well-disciplined party armed with the theory of Marxism-Leninism, an army under the command of such a party, and a united front of all revolutionary classes and groups under the leadership of such a party.[9] Soon after the establishment of the Peking regime this revolutionary formula was prepared for exporting to colonial and semi-colonial countries. The occasion was the Asian and Australasian Trade Unions conference in Peking in November-December 1949.

[8] Anna Louise Strong, "The Thought of Mao Tse-tung," *Amerasia*, Vol. XI, No. 6 (June 1947), pp. 161-62.
[9] Mao, "People's Democratic Dictatorship," p. 422.

A Chinese Model for Vietnam

The decision on the conference in the new Chinese Communist capital was to recognize, through the World Federation of Trade Unions, the significance of Mao's victory in China and maneuver the Federation into giving a new driving force to the revolution in Asia. The meeting was attended by delegates from the Soviet Union, Mongolia, North Korea, North Vietnam, Siam, Burma, Indonesia, India, Ceylon, the Philippines, Malaya, and Iran. The tasks of the conference were threefold: to hear reports on the activities of the World Federation of Trade Unions, to hear reports on the trade union movement in Asia, and to set up a liaison office of the Federation for Asian and Australasian nations.[10] In effect, an effort to step up Communist activity in Asia through the trade union organization was made clear to the participants.

Liu Shao-ch'i, then vice-president of the Federation and honorary president of the All-China Federation of Labor, delivered the keynote address. He first discussed the struggle against imperialism by the colonial and semi-colonial peoples of Asia and Australasia, and said that this development had "led to a great victory in China." This great victory, he continued, "has set them the best example." He praised the war of national liberation in Vietnam and other Asian nations, saying that the Viet-Minh "has liberated 90 per cent of her territory." Then he pointed out a path of revolution for the participants to follow:

> The path of the Chinese people's victory . . . is the path which should be taken by the people of many colonial and semi-colonial nations who struggle for national independence and people's democracy. The path . . . is . . . (1) The working class must unite all other classes, parties, groups and individuals . . . to be a nation-wide united front. . . . (2) This nation-wide united front must be led by and built around the working class . . . and its party, the Communist Party, with the latter as its center. . . . (3) . . . A Communist party must be established,

[10] *Chieh fang jih pao* (Shanghai), November 17, 1949.

which should be armed with the theory of Marxism and Leninism, knows strategy and tactics, practices self-criticism and strict discipline, and has a close relationship with the masses. (4) It is necessary to set up wherever and whenever possible a national army which is led by the Communist party.[11]

The delegates at the conference were generally in agreement with Liu's speech. The chief delegate of the Viet-Minh, Luu Duc Pho, supported Liu's formula enthusiastically:

In Asia, the decisive victory won by the Chinese people and the Chinese working class is, we shall say, a fatal strike to the imperialists. . . . In the nations in Southeast Asia, the imperialists are still planning to strengthen their military bases, their forces are still strong; the path of the 475 millions of Chinese people is the path to be taken to win a decisive victory over the imperialists.

The essential principles . . . defined by Comrade Liu Shao-ch'i in his opening speech . . . must serve as the compass for all the workers of Southeast Asia.[12]

Pho concluded his speech by suggesting the establishment of a liaison bureau for Asia and Australasia in Peking, stating that the All-China Federation of Labor should play a leading role in this respect. In his second speech the following day, Pho claimed that the liberation movement of the Vietnamese working class had already been combined with the struggle for true independence, unification, and people's democracy. "From 1930 onward," he declared, "with the birth of the Indochinese Communist Party, the

[11] NCNA, Peking, November 23, 1949; also *Chieh fang jih pao* (Shanghai), November 23, 1949.

[12] NCNA, Peking, November 19, 1949; also *Chieh fang jih pao* (November 23, 1949). Luu Duc Pho (real name, Nguyen Duy Tinh) was then a member of the Executive Committee of Vietnam Federation of Workers—the second or third most important figure in the federation. He attended both the Milan and Peking Trade Unions Conferences about that time, and wrote an article for the Cominform journal, *For a Lasting Peace, For a People's Democracy* (October 7, 1949), entitled "Struggle of Vietnam People for Independence."

leadership of the movement for national independence was assumed by the working class."[13] It seems that Pho, in claiming the correct leadership of the Indochinese Communist Party in the Vietnamese revolutionary movement, tried to respond precisely to what Liu had suggested.

An identical theme was equally expressed by some other delegates. S. A. Wickremasinghe from Ceylon spoke loudly, "China today, Ceylon tomorrow!" Shankar Shelwander from India also declared emphatically, "We want to take Mao Tse-tung's path." The Soviet delegate Solovyov, however, avoided supporting the Chinese formula, although he endorsed the Chinese-sponsored proposal for an appeal to the working masses in Holland, France, Great Britain, and the United States, "asking them to urge their governments to stop immediately intervention in Indonesia, Vietnam, Burma, Malaya, and South Korea."[14] A few days later Liu Shao-ch'i took a further step at a Peking rally for the conference to urge the Chinese workers to fulfill their international responsibility "of rendering assistance to the working class and working people of capitalist countries in the world, especially colonial and semi-colonial countries in Asia and Australasia."[15] Before it closed, the conference resolved to establish a liaison bureau in Peking. It also urged the National Trade Union centers in the colonial and semi-colonial countries of Asia to learn from the Chinese experience in order to reach the correct assessment of appropriate methods for revolution, although local conditions and national characteristics should be taken into account.[16] Thus the Peking conference had adopted in principle the Chinese revolutionary path for Asian Communists.

[13] NCNA, November 20, 1949; also *Chieh fang jih pao*, November 26, 1949.

[14] NCNA, November 19, 1949.

[15] NCNA, November 24, 1949; also *Chieh fang jih pao*, November 25, 1949.

[16] "Resolution on the Reports of the National Trade Union Centers of Asian and Australasian Countries," *World Trade Union Movement*, No. 8 (December 1949), p. 40, as cited in John H. Kautsky, *Moscow and the Communist Party of India* (New York: John Wiley & Sons, 1956), p. 99.

A *Chinese Model for Vietnam*

It became apparent that China's attempt, as expressed at the conference, was to encourage and accelerate the revolutionary movement in Asia with a Chinese formula, Chinese assistance, and Chinese leadership.

At this point what really seemed significant was neither a Chinese claim to the impact of the Chinese revolution on Asia in general and Vietnam in particular, nor a Vietnamese acknowledgment of the predominance of China over Vietnam, but an enthusiastic Soviet pronouncement of Chinese influence on the Viet-Minh. In the October 1949 issue of *Voprosy Istorii*, A. Guber, a Soviet writer, published a long article on Vietnam, unequivocally pointing out that the Viet-Minh program of early 1945 was inspired by Mao Tse-tung's New Democracy and that the victory of the Chinese Communists had won them a friendly neighbor. Guber said:

> Several months prior to the defeat of the Japanese and the proclamation of the Republic, Viet Minh published its program. The formulation of this program undoubtedly afforded evidence of Chinese democracy and of the struggle for a new democracy posed by Mao Tse-tung. . . .
>
> The world-wide historic victories of the Chinese people assumed an extremely important significance in the struggle of Vietnam for independence and democracy. They not only inspired the Vietnamese to heroic struggle against the aggressors, but imbued them with confidence that the most difficult period of their resistance to the imperialist invaders is coming to an end, that along with the growth and reinforcement of the internal forces of the republic it will have, in place of the hostile Kuomintang rear, the friendly, neighborly Chinese People's Republic.[17]

Guber's article probably reflected the semi-official views

[17] A. Guber, "The Vietnam People in Their Struggle for Independence and Democracy," *Voprosy Istorii*, No. 10 (October 1949), translated in *Soviet Press Translations*, Vol. v, Nos. 6 and 7 (March 15 and April 1, 1950), pp. 178, 206.

of Moscow. It expressed the Soviet opinion on current Sino-Vietnamese relations, and it claimed that the Soviets were willing to admit the two Communist-oriented nations into the Communist camp. As events turned out, Communist China's influence became predominant in North Vietnam; China and Vietnam became full-fledged members of the Communist bloc, but neither became a Soviet satellite.

Moscow's official response to Liu's speech—an endorsement—came two months later in an editorial in the Cominform journal.[18] While attributing the favorable conditions for a national liberation movement to the defeat of German and Japanese imperialism, the editorial strongly approved of "the Chinese path." It quoted Liu's pronouncement on the proper path to be taken for national independence and people's democracy, and explained that the experience of the Chinese people definitely "teaches" the working class to form a united front, to equip the Communist Party with Marxism-Leninism, and to establish a people's liberation army under the leadership of the Communist Party. It then stressed the significance of armed struggle, using China, Vietnam, and Malaya for examples:

> As the example of China, Viet Nam, Malaya and other countries shows, armed struggle is now becoming the main form of the national-liberation movement in many colonial and dependent countries.
>
> In Viet Nam the armed people have liberated 90 per cent of their country from the French imperialists. The 150,000 French troops in Viet Nam are afraid to leave the occupied towns, are bottled up by the armed forces of the Viet Nam Republic.

Undoubtedly the editorial supported Liu's statement and encouraged the Communists in Vietnam and Malaya to follow the Chinese experience of revolution. The endorsement from the Cominform, which was under Moscow's control,

[18] "Mighty Advance of the National Liberation Movement in the Colonial and Dependent Countries," editorial, *For a Lasting Peace, For a People's Democracy,* January 27, 1950, p. 1.

greatly enhanced the significance of the Chinese viewpoint that was soon to have a far-reaching impact on the Viet-Minh. This suggests that Liu had spoken for Peking *and* Moscow.

In a special article of June 16, 1950, in the form of the editor's reply to a reader, *Jen min jih pao* noted the endorsement of Liu's thesis by the editorial of the Cominform journal (January 27, 1950) and quoted part of the statement issued by Ranadive (secretary-general of the Communist Party of India), to the effect that the lessons of the victorious liberation struggle of the Chinese people "will serve as an infallible compass for the Indian Communist Party and working class." The article reemphasized Liu's view that "armed struggle . . . is the sole path for many colonial and semi-colonial people in their struggle for independence and liberation." "But," it continued, "the time and place for conducting this kind of revolutionary armed struggle must be decided according to concrete conditions." In this respect, it praised the people of Vietnam who had "already scored tremendous success in their struggle."[19]

Up to this point, Peking had established a Chinese path for the colonial and semi-colonial countries of Asia, and had taken Vietnam and Malaya as concrete examples to apply the Chinese formula to. Vietnam, because of its historical, cultural, and geographical ties with China, and because of its strategically important position relative to Laos, Cambodia, and even Thailand, was undoubtedly regarded by Peking as a special showcase of the Chinese revolutionary model for Asia. One specific example was the editorial in *Jen min jih pao* for March 27, 1951, on the organization of the Vietnam Lao Dong Party. In restating the three essential factors (party, united front, army) of the experiences of the Chinese revolution as pronounced by Mao, the editorial stressed the importance of the founding of the Lao Dong Party and implied Peking's hearty

[19] *Jen min jih pao*, June 16, 1950 in *Current Background* (Hong Kong: American Consulate-General), No. 173, pp. 5-6.

congratulations on Vietnam's full acceptance of the Chinese formula, which it had offered for some time.[20]

Communist China's intervention in the Korean War had diverted her major efforts from national reconstruction to the "Anti-American and Aid-Korean" movement; yet the CCP still kept to its principle of "the Chinese path." On the 30th anniversary of the CCP, Lu Ting-yi wrote an article, "The World Significance of the Chinese Revolution," which reemphasized the importance of Mao's three essential factors, claiming the victory of the Chinese revolution to be an "example" of victory in the struggle for national liberation in colonial and semi-colonial countries, and asserting that China's example and experience has "strengthened the fighting will" and "confidence in victory" of the peoples in Vietnam, Burma, Malaya, Indonesia, etc. Mao's theory of the Chinese revolution, Lu continued, "is a new development of Marxism-Leninism" with significance not only for China and Asia but also for the world Communist movement. "It is, indeed, a new contribution to the treasury of Marxism-Leninism." Finally, he divided the "sphere of influence" between the Soviet Union and China by saying that "The classic type of revolution in the imperialist countries is the October Revolution. The classic type of revolution in the colonial and semi-colonial countries is the Chinese revolution. . . ."[21]

Judged by the previously cited article by Anna Louise Strong, which was a result of several interviews with CCP theoreticians, Lu Ting-yi's assertion was nothing but the CCP's official position, and it was actually speaking for Mao. A similar view was expressed by an article in *World Culture*, which said that China had become a good model

[20] See more discussions in the following section.
[21] Lu Ting-yi, "The World Significance of the Chinese Revolution," *Hsueh hsi*, July 1, 1951; also in *For a Lasting Peace, For a People's Democracy*, June 29, 1951, p. 2. On the same occasion Ch'en Po-ta also praised Mao's thought as "the development of Marxism-Leninism in the East." See his article, "Mao Tse-tung's Theory of the Chinese Revolution Is the Combination of Marxism-Leninism with the Chinese Revolution," *Hsueh hsi*, July 1, 1951, p. 20.

for armed rebel movements, and a good example to "all the colonies and semi-colonies, especially those in Asia."[22] In the course of two years (1949-1951), the significance of the Chinese revolutionary experience was promoted by Peking from a regional level in Asia to a worldwide range in "all the colonies and semi-colonies."

The clamorous and persistent voice of Peking for the Chinese model must have annoyed, if not offended, Moscow. A Soviet rebuff finally came from E. M. Zhukov, a leading Soviet theorist, in November 1951 at an Orientalist conference in the U.S.S.R. Academy of Sciences. The Russians openly discussed the subject in a discussion panel entitled, "On the Character and Attributes of People's Democracy in Countries of the Orient." In analyzing the problem, Zhukov agreed that a people's democracy in the Orient was based on a four-class coalition, and that the experience of the Chinese revolution was of "immense significance"; but he warned: ". . . remembering the first tactical principle of Leninism—the principle of obligatory consideration of the particularly and specifically national elements in each individual country—it would be risky to regard the Chinese revolution as some kind of 'stereotype' [sic] for people's revolutions in other countries of Asia."[23]

Apparently Zhukov's views represented the Soviet official position. His intention was to disprove the Chinese assertion of the universal applicability of the Chinese experience to "all the colonies and semi-colonies" in the world. He nevertheless admitted that the "fruitful influence" of the Chinese experience could be found in the Communist Party of India and the Lao Dong Party of Vietnam. This was the clearest Soviet statement, and perhaps the first known disagreement with China, on global strategy in the early 1950s.

Zhukov's views were upheld by an editorial in the Comin-

[22] Hu Wei-te, "New China's International Position," *World Culture*, Vol. 24, No. 11, 1951.

[23] A summary of the meeting was translated in full in *Current Digest of the Soviet Press*, Vol. IV, No. 20, pp. 3-7, 43.

form journal three months later. The editorial was a further deviation from the Chinese position. While acknowledging that a "brilliant example" of the united front was offered by the Chinese people, the editorial argued that "the nature of the liberation movement varies in the different colonial and dependent countries." In some countries it had developed into open armed struggle, such as Vietnam, Malaya, Burma, and the Philippines; in other countries it had developed into a united democratic front (India); and in still others in the Middle East and North Africa, the liberation movement was merely growing.[24] Obviously Moscow meant to limit the Chinese experience to certain countries in Asia where open armed struggle for national liberation movements had already taken place. The "world significance" of the Chinese experience was definitely denied.

On the Soviet side, the argument developed further. Moscow attempted to disprove the Chinese claim to a revolutionary model and replace it with a Soviet one. In January 1953 an editorial in the Cominform journal discussed the issue again. It gave a brief treatment to China and Vietnam, stating that the triumph of the Chinese revolution had dealt "a terrific blow" to the colonial system of imperialism and that the DRV was born in "the fires of fierce battles and gains strength in these battles." But when it turned to the Soviet Union, it said: "The peoples of the colonial and dependent countries look with hope to the great Soviet Union—the true defender of their national independence, the bulwark of peace and security of the peoples. They see in the Union of Soviet Socialist Republics the embodiment of the cherished aspirations of all the oppressed and exploited masses. . . ."[25]

In a period of three years (1950-1953) Moscow's views on the issue of the Chinese experience shifted from enthusi-

[24] "National-Liberation Movement of Peoples in Colonial and Dependent Countries," *For a Lasting Peace, For a People's Democracy*, February 29, 1952, p. 1.
[25] "Growing Upsurge of National-Liberation Movement in Colonial and Dependent Countries," *ibid.*, January 9, 1953.

astic support to complete ignorance. Before the end of the Indochinese war Moscow no longer praised the "Chinese experience" or "Chinese path," no longer believed in the applicability of the Chinese model to Vietnam, Burma, or Malaya, but urged the peoples of the colonial and dependent countries to look to the Soviet Union. The Chinese persisted in their claims. On the 10th anniversary of the establishment of the Peking regime, they asserted that the victory of the Chinese revolution was a "typical example" for "all the oppressed nations" in developing areas striving for liberation.[26] At the Moscow conference in 1960 the Chinese delegation succeeded in including their views in the highly compromised Moscow statement.[27] It said, "by giving a further powerful impetus to the national-liberation movement, it [the Chinese revolution] exerted tremendous influence on the peoples, especially those of Asia, Africa and Latin America." The disagreement between Moscow and Peking, beginning in the early 1950s, became the main current of the Sino-Soviet dispute a decade later.

Against this background North Vietnam's reaction is significant. In an editorial in *Nhan Dan* September 1954, the Vietnamese Communists unequivocally took their stand:

> The People's Republic of China has established for the peoples of Asia a model and a goal, on the path of the struggle against aggressive imperialism, the path of building an independent nation and a new life in the political, economic and cultural domains. . . .
>
> In their long-term struggle the Vietnamese people, the closest neighbors of China, have followed the example of the Chinese people.[28]

[26] Wang Chia-hsiang, "The International Significance of the Chinese People's Victory," in Liu Shao-ch'i et al., *Ten Glorious Years* (Peking: Foreign Languages Press, 1960), pp. 273, 276.

[27] For an excellent analysis of the Moscow Conference, see Donald S. Zagoria, *The Sino-Soviet Conflict, 1956-61* (New York: Atheneum, 1964), pp. 343-69.

[28] "The People's Republic of China: The Vanguard Flag of the Asian Nations," editorial in *Nhan Dan* (The People), September 22, 1954.

A Chinese Model for Vietnam

One decade later, when the Sino-Soviet polemics had reached a climax, North Vietnam commented on the significance of the Soviet and Chinese revolutions. In a speech at the Ninth Plenum of the Third Central Committee of the Vietnam Lao Dong Party in December 1963, Le Duan, secretary-general of the party, praised the Chinese revolution in language almost identical with that of Lu Ting-yi in 1951: "The Chinese revolution marks a new stage of development in the Marxist-Leninist theory of proletarian revolution. . . . If Lenin pointed out that the Russian revolutionary tactics were exemplary tactics for all Communists in the world, then we may say that the Chinese revolutionary tactics are at present exemplary tactics for many Communists in Asia, Africa and Latin America."[29] In view of the consistency of the above two Vietnamese passages over a period of 10 years, there should be little doubt that North Vietnam had accepted the Chinese view. But this acceptance was certainly not tantamount to its complete acceptance of direction from Peking rather than Moscow, or to a challenge to Khrushchev. Rather, North Vietnam merely expressed what she believed and where she stood. But since China rejected the Soviet proposal for united action against American escalation in Vietnam and tried to export to Vietnam Lin Piao's thesis of "people's war," North Vietnam has turned out to be more independent in charting a revolutionary course. As Le Duan said at a military conference in May 1966, "We cannot automatically apply the revolutionary experiences of other countries in our country."[30] Yet so far as the period of "learning from China" (1950-1956) is concerned, the Chinese revolutionary experience prevailed. In the following discussion I will show the Vietnamese acceptance and implementation of the Chinese model.

[29] Le Duan, "Some Questions Concerning the International Tasks of Our Party," *Hoc Tap* (Study), February 1964; also published as a pamphlet by Peking's Foreign Languages Press (1964), pp. 12-13.
[30] Radio Hanoi, July 26, 1966.

2. IDEOLOGICAL, POLITICAL, AND ECONOMIC
   IMITATIONS AND RELATIONS

On the day following the inauguration of the People's
Republic of China, October 1, 1949, the Soviet Union
announced its recognition of the Peking regime and the
withdrawal of its diplomatic mission from the Nationalist
government in Canton. A few days later Bulgaria, Hungary,
Romania, North Korea, Outer Mongolia, and other Communist countries followed suit. By November 22, 1949 all Communist nations had recognized Peking except North Vietnam.

It was almost two months after the establishment of the
Peking regime that Ho Chi Minh sent his first publicized
cable of congratulations to Mao Tse-tung. In moderate and
cautious terms Ho expressed hope for a closer Sino-Vietnamese relationship, "in order to promote the freedom and
happiness of our two nations and defend world democracy
and lasting peace in common." No militant or Communist
words were mentioned. Mao's reply was more aggressive.
He said: "China and Vietnam are on the front line of an
imperialist struggle. With the victorious development of
the struggle for liberation of the two peoples, the friendship between our two peoples will surely become closer
day by day. . . ."[31] Ho's delay in making public the message
can only be explained by his cautious policy. In early
October Kwangtung, Kwangsi, and Yunnan were still in
Nationalist hands. Not until late November did the Chinese
Communist army completely defeat the Nationalists. Moreover, there were rumors in early 1949 that a military
agreement between Ho and Mao had been concluded.[32] A
delayed and moderate message to Mao, Ho might have
hoped, would help kill the rumors and would not for sure
provoke an attack against him by the remaining Nationalist
troops in the three provinces. The complete victory of the

[31] *Chieh fang jih pao* (Shanghai), November 26, 1949.
[32] *Ta kung pao* (Hong Kong), August 25, 1949; also in Cole, *Conflict*, p. 71.

CCP, nevertheless, encouraged Ho and his associates immensely. As Ho put it, "We are fully confident in our final victory, because we are growing stronger day by day and because the democratic movement of the world is gaining more and more. The complete victory of the Chinese People's Republic proves this point."[33]

The first significant Viet-Minh move toward the Communist camp in general and toward Communist China in particular was the first National Conference of Vietnam Trade Unions, held one month after the Peking conference of Asian Trade Unions. Judging from the timing of the former, the Vietnam conference must have been stimulated by the meeting in Peking. As Ho's radio broadcast stated, one of the purposes of the convention was ". . . to work out plans for carrying through the decisions taken by the . . . Asian Conference of Trade Unions in Peking."[34]

The conference was held in northern Vietnam from late December 1949 to mid-January 1950, but the Viet-Minh broadcasting of it lasted continuously from late December to late March, apparently as an indication of the importance of the convention. The meeting was attended by 800 trade union delegates and group leaders, "representing a million Vietnamese workers."[35] High-ranking government officials and organization leaders such as Truong Chinh, Hoang Quoc Viet, Pham Van Dong, Vo Nguyen Giap, and Nguyen Van Tao were present. A Chinese delegate from the Chinese Trade Unions attended the meeting.[36] Huge portraits of Stalin, Mao Tse-tung, Ho Chi Minh, Truong Chinh, and Hoang Quoc Viet hung over the rostrum. Ho sent greetings to the conference and urged the delegates especially to organize "all workers—laborers and intellectuals," and "to establish close and brotherly relations . . . in particular with the working people of China and France."[37] The main report was given by Truong Chinh, secretary-general of the Marxist Study Group, who stressed the unity of all the

---

[33] *Chieh fang jih pao* (Shanghai), December 25, 1949.
[34] VNA, December 27, 1949.   [35] VNA, January 21, 1950.
[36] VNA, March 2, 1950.   [37] VNA, January 21, 1950.

Vietnamese people as the urgent task of the conference. In the speeches there were three outstanding points. First, the "national liberation movement" had replaced the "independence movement" or "resistance war" of 1945-1948;[38] obviously this was a follow-up pronouncement after Peking and Moscow. Second, the officials, especially Hoang Quoc Viet, stressed the combination of the working class with the people's army and the peasantry, for six per cent of the Vietnamese workers could not significantly establish "the driving force" of the revolutionary movement without the participation of the peasantry and the army. Third, the Vietnamese workers were clearly labeled as "Marxist workers," and the delegates pledged themselves to follow the heroic example of Soviet workers and promised to cooperate closely with the Asian trade unions.[39] These three features indicated that a political and ideological alignment with the Communist camp was clarified.

After 30 meetings the conference passed resolutions and closed by electing Hoang Quoc Viet president of the Standing Committee of the Vietnam Labor Federation.[40] The resolutions expressed the conference's agreement with the pronouncements of the Trade Union conference in Peking and praised the victory of the Chinese people which had had "a great effect upon the liberation movement throughout the world" and had "bent the balance of power on the side of the democratic camp."[41] They also set forth several tasks for Vietnamese workers—to increase industrial and agricultural production, coordinate with the working people of France, China, and the colonial countries, to cooperate with all other classes in Vietnam under the National United Front, and to support the liberation struggle of the people of Laos and Cambodia.[42]

The importance of the conference was multifold. It sided itself firmly with Moscow and Peking, echoed what the Peking conference had stated, pledged itself to promote the

<hr>

[38] VNA, March 2, 1950.   [39] VNA, February 7, 10, 1950.
[40] Voice of South Vietnam (Ho's), January 29, 1950.
[41] VNA, March 8, 1950.   [42] *Ibid.*

war effort, and urged the consolidation of the Vietnamese people for national liberation. Above all, it laid the foundation for a workers' party in early 1951.

After Zhdanov's famous "two-camp" speech in 1947 the Chinese Communists followed his line by siding with the "anti-imperialist, democratic camp" headed by the Soviet Union. This was demonstrated by Mao's "lean-to-one-side" policy toward Moscow in June 1949. Mao said that the "forty years' experience of the Communist Party have taught us to lean to one side, and we are firmly convinced that in order to win victory and consolidate it we must lean to one side. . . . All Chinese without exception must lean either to the side of imperialism or to the side of socialism. . . . Internationally, we belong to the side of the anti-imperialist front headed by the Soviet Union."[43] Peking's leaning to Moscow led automatically to Mao's deference to Stalin. Numerous literature in 1949-1953 praised Stalin and the Soviet Union unreservedly. Kuo Mo-jo hailed Stalin as "the sun that shines forever," and Ch'en Po-ta extolled Stalin as the "teacher of genius . . . great scientist of dialectical materialism . . . greatest figure in the world."[44] There is no doubt that the amicable and "unbreakable" Sino-Soviet relationship reached its peak, in public at least, just before the death of Stalin.

North Vietnam's siding with the "anti-imperialist" camp was demonstrated at the First Vietnam Trade Union conference. But the Stalin-Mao-Ho alliance was made possible only after the Viet-Minh regime was recognized by Stalin and Mao.

It was reported that prior to the recognition of the Viet-Minh government Ho had sent secret missions to China. A French source disclosed that Giap visited Nanning in early January 1950. There he met several important Chinese persons. A few days after their meeting Ho asked for the establishment of diplomatic relations.[45] A Chinese source indi-

[43] Mao, "People's Democratic Dictatorship," pp. 415, 417.
[44] Ch'en Po-ta, "Stalin and the Chinese Revolution," NCNA, December 19, 1949.
[45] Philippe Devillers informed me on this point.

cated that in late December 1949 a Vietnamese military mission was sent to Peking for negotiations on military equipment and supplies. A trade agreement on military materials was signed in Peking on January 18, 1950[46]—the same day Peking granted diplomatic recognition to North Vietnam. Judging from the character of Ho's cautious policy and the prompt recognition by Peking after his request, arrangements for diplomatic relations may have been made ahead of time.

The Viet-Minh government requested the establishment of diplomatic relations with the governments of the world on January 14, 1950. Peking granted its recognition on January 18. The following day *Jen min jih pao* carried a portrait of Ho Chi Minh on its front page for the first time, together with a headline about recognition. On the same day Ho's radio broadcast an enthusiastic welcome of the recognition, and tried to ally Vietnam with China as the two "first shock peoples" and "shock nations in the struggle for real independence and for real democracy in Asia."[47] Undoubtedly Chinese recognition had greatly encouraged the Viet-Minh. As Foreign Minister Hoang Minh Giam said: "This was Vietnam's greatest diplomatic victory since the war of resistance began. The more important new China's position in the world becomes, the greater will be the significance of this victory. . . ."[48]

The Soviet government recognized the Viet-Minh regime on January 31, 1950. A few days later Communist nations in eastern Europe and North Korea followed suit. This marked a significant change in Soviet policy toward Vietnam, for prior to this point Moscow had "abandoned" the Vietnamese Communists—which was well known in international Communist circles.[49] The delay of Soviet recognition (in comparison to China's) is explained by the conten-

[46] Sixth Section of the KMT, p. 14. For more discussions on Chinese military aid see the following section.

[47] Voice of South Vietnam (Ho's), in Annamese, January 19, 1950.

[48] VNA, January 27, 1950.

[49] Ruth Fischer, "Ho Chi Minh: Disciplined Communist, *Foreign Affairs* (October 1954), p. 94.

tion that the change in policy took some time to deliberate and that the Soviet government intended to belittle the importance of this diplomatic move so as not to cause any alarm in the West, although an editorial in *New Times* defended Soviet recognition as only "natural."[50]

The significance of the Chinese and Soviet recognition, though highly understandable, is best shown by reactions from North Vietnam. On February 11, 1950 a group of 13 officials and leaders sponsored a Sino-Vietnam Friendship Association because "there were many similarities between the struggles for national liberation of China and Vietnam" and because the Chinese and Vietnamese peoples "have become the two closest allies on the eastern front of the anti-imperialist struggle."[51] The Association was later headed by Ho Tung Mau, a founder of the Thanh Nien and a veteran of the CCP. Cadre training classes in the Viet-Minh area studied a new lesson, "New circumstances, new tasks," under the Soviet-China-Vietnam alliance.[52] On the occasion of May Day, 1950 the Lien Viet and the Viet-Minh jointly publicized for the first time that North Vietnam belonged to "the democratic front headed by the powerful Soviet Union."[53] On his birthday, May 19, Ho thanked the nation, saying that after the Viet-Minh regime was recognized by China, the Soviet Union and other nations, North Vietnam's position in "the international field has never been as glorious as at present. . . ."[54] In late May a special daily entitled *China-Vietnam* was published to make "the new democratic China better known to the Vietnam people, acquaint them with the constructive work in the friendly country [China], and promote ever closer friendship between the people of China and Vietnam."[55] In early June a group of leaders proposed the organization of a Vietnam-Soviet Friendship Association. The impressive list of the

[50] *New Times*, February 6, 1950, p. 1.
[51] VNA, North Vietnam, February 11, 1950.
[52] Hoang Van Chi, *Colonialism to Communism*, p. 141.
[53] VNA, North Vietnam, April 30, 1950.
[54] VNA, May 22, 1950.
[55] VNA, North Vietnam, May 26, 1950.

37 members for the preparatory committee included almost all important officials and leaders except Ho Chi Minh and Pham Van Dong. On the occasion of the fifth anniversary of the August Revolution and of Vietnam Independence Day, Ho regarded the recognition of North Vietnam by the Soviet Union and China as "the greatest victory" in the history of Vietnam, which would be an "incentive" for future military victories.[56] To top things off, the Viet-Minh government decided to make January 18 a commemoration day of the Chinese recognition, a day of "joy throughout Vietnam" and a way to show North Vietnam's gratitude to China.[57]

The recognition of the Viet-Minh regime changed the balance of power between the two governments in Vietnam and caused great concern to the West. Prior to the recognition the Viet-Minh was isolated without any foreign aid, whereas the Bao Dai government in Saigon was politically and militarily supported by France. After recognition, however, the prestige of Ho's regime rapidly increased and Chinese aid became "legitimate."

The concern caused by the Soviet and Chinese recognition prompted the French National Assembly to ratify, on February 2, 1950, the Elysée Agreement with Bao Dai which had been concluded 11 months earlier (March 8, 1949) and which granted for the first time a status of "independence" to Vietnam, Cambodia, and Laos. The United States and Great Britain moved quickly, and on February 1 recognized the governments of South Vietnam, Cambodia, and Laos. The Department of State declared the recognition "consistent" with the fundamental policy of the United States.[58] In March two ships of the U.S. Navy visited Saigon to show American support for the Bao Dai government. These developments foreshadowed American military and economic aid to Indochina. Underground elements of the

[56] Voice of South Vietnam (Ho's), in Cochin-Chinese, August 24, 1950.

[57] Hoang Minh Giam's message to Chou En-lai, January 15, 1951, NCNA, Peking, January 18, 1951.

[58] Department of State, *Bulletin*, February 20, 1950, p. 291.

Viet-Minh immediately launched protest demonstrations in Hanoi and Saigon.

The French government made a formal request for American aid to Indochina in late February, which was granted on May 8 for "the development of genuine nationalism."[59] The Korean war prompted President Truman to accelerate the flow of military aid and to send a military mission to Vietnam.[60] In mid-July Ho criticized the United States, saying that the American imperialists had openly interfered in the Indochinese war for several years, that the Americans intended to "kick out" the French colonialists and "occupy" Indochina themselves, and that they would be defeated in Vietnam as they had been in China.[61] In a period of six months the United States had moved from a position of nonrecognition (nonintervention) to military and economic "intervention." Apparently this was a result of the containment policy against Asian Communism. As Louis J. Halle, a former member of the State Department's policy-planning staff, points out: "In 1950 the United States had embarked on a policy of active containment in Asia as in Europe, in the Pacific as in the Atlantic."[62] As time went on this containment measure developed into a situation of confrontation between the United States and China in that area.

AFTER THE establishment of diplomatic relations with most of the foreign nations, the most important of the Viet-Minh's "new tasks" was to launch a "general mobilization" campaign in preparation for military attacks. Toward this end, the Viet-Minh government decreed "general mobilization" on February 21, 1950, then convened a series of conferences to mobilize and consolidate its forces, which had been scattering around in various parts of the country since the outbreak of the war. The spring of 1950 was a "conference

[59] *Ibid.*, June 12, 1950, p. 977.
[60] *Ibid.*, July 3, 1950, p. 5.
[61] Ho Chi Minh's interview with Voice of Vietnam, VNA, in English, July 16, 1950.
[62] Halle, *The Cold War as History* (London: Chatto & Windus, 1967), p. 299.

season," in which more than 12 conferences (apart from the First All-Vietnam Trade Union Conference discussed above) were held. They were:[63]

The Education Congress
The National Military Congress
The National Resistance and Administration Conference
The First Nation-Wide Youth Congress
The Arts and Letters Conference
The Students League Conference
The Salvation Farmers' Conference
The Labor Conference of the Fifth Interzone
The Nationwide Security Service Congress
The First National Women's Conference
The National Information (information and propaganda) Congress
The Study (of warfare) Congress

In a period of three months (February to April) the 12 conferences were held in North Vietnam or South-Central Vietnam, and were attended by 100 to 700 delegates at a time. A strong drive for the "general mobilization of manpower" and the reorientation of ideology, strategy, and tactics was launched throughout Viet-Minh–controlled areas. Workers, educators, soldiers, administrators, youths, intellectuals, farmers, security police, and women were involved. Although the convention of the All-Vietnam Trade Union Conference and the National Women's Conference was stimulated by the Asian Trade Unions Conference and the Asian Women Conference in Peking,[64] the other conferences

[63] NCNA, Peking, March 4, 1950; VNA (North Vietnam), March 5, 11, April 9, 19, May 23, 1950; Voice of South Vietnam, in Annamese, March 14, 20, April 10, 13, 17, 1950.

[64] The Asian Women Conference was held in Peking in mid-December 1949, which was attended by 198 delegates from 19 countries and republics in Asia and the Middle East, including the Viet-Minh.

were held on their own for mobilization.[65] They well demonstrated Ho's ability to organize for mobilization.

To carry out the general mobilization order effectively the Viet-Minh radio repeatedly explained the order and urged each citizen to contribute his or her share. The mobilization, the broadcasts said, was an extremely "great and important work," and was to push the resistance "with might to the general counteroffensive." All the forces of "the whole people, manpower, natural and financial resources, must be mobilized, must be called upon and put into use. . . . Everything for the front lines. Everything for the people's war; everything for victory." The broadcasts warned that those who did not carry out the order would be brought before "the Military Tribunal."[66] Thus mobilization was to be carried out through persuasion and coercion.

It was during the preparations for mobilization that Ho reportedly made a secret visit to Peking. The French-controlled Radio Saigon announced that Chinese assistance treaties with Ho were signed in Peking in March.[67] Hoang Van Chi reported that Ho was criticized by Chinese leaders in Peking for being "rightist" in devoting too much attention to the patriotic war and too little to the establishment of Communism in Vietnam.[68] At any rate, after Ho was rumored to have returned to Vietnam, events developed decisively toward a more militant Communist line. Anti-American propaganda was intensified, the "two-camp" theory was followed closely and loudly by the Viet-Minh radio, Chinese aid in various forms materialized, a campaign for studying the Chinese revolutionary experience

---

[65] In 1949 there were other conferences in Peking: The All-China Women Congress in late March, the All-China Youth Congress in early May, North China Education Conference in mid-May, the North China Finance Conference in late May, and the All-China Federation of Labor Conference in late May. Though inferred, the Viet-Minh might have learned from the Chinese to hold its own conferences.

[66] Voice of South Vietnam, in Annamese, March 2, 1950, and Vietnam Station, in Vietnamese, March 26, 1950.

[67] Radio Saigon, in Mandarin, April 1, 1950.

[68] Hoang Van Chi, *Colonialism to Communism*, p. 71.

was led by Ho, and a Communist party—the Lao Dong Party—was established.

Ho's statement on the fifth anniversary of the August Revolution was a determined and vigorous attack on American "imperialism"; and Ho allied North Vietnam with the Communist camp. In railing at the United States, he predicted that both the French colonialists and American imperialists were doomed to failure in Vietnam; in announcing North Vietnam's alignment with the Communists, he dropped his pre-1949 notion of a "coalition" and "independent" Viet-Minh government, and declared that the DRV was "definitely on the democratic side" and belonged to the "anti-imperialist bloc of eight hundred million people."[69] With Chinese supplies flowing in, the drive for general mobilization was set in high gear. In the publicized regular cabinet meetings after May 1950, the Viet-Minh regime decided to order all citizens between 16 and 55 years of age to take part in the war, and demanded that every woman join the militia. Their slogan was "all for a speedy passage to the general counter-offensive."[70] The campaign was truly impressive.

Giap kicked off his autumn military campaign by assaulting Dong-Kne in mid-September. While he was making surprising progress in the border areas, the Viet-Minh news media propagandized to tighten Sino-Vietnamese relations. On the occasion of the first anniversary of the establishment of the Peking government, Ton Duc Thang, vice-president of the Lien Viet, and Hoang Quoc Viet, secretary-general of the Viet-Minh (Front), sent a joint greeting to Peking hailing the "gigantic Chinese victory" which had "greatly inspired the peoples of Southeast Asia," particularly the Vietnamese, and said that "the Vietnamese people . . . pledge themselves to learn the experience of the Chinese people."[71] More precisely, an article in *Su That* compared

[69] Voice of South Vietnam, August 16, 1950.

[70] VNA, in English, June 4, 1950; Voice of South Vietnam, in Cochin-Chinese; and VNA, in English, July 15, 1950.

[71] VNA, in English, October 3, 1950.

the Vietnamese anti-imperialist struggle with that of China, claimed the revolutionary phases and methods of both peoples to be "comparatively the same," and said that "the fighting example of the Chinese people is a great lesson" to the Vietnamese. "The Chinese Government has declared that the People's Democratic Republic of China stands with the world peace front . . . and thus has allied itself with all peace-loving nations, especially with the Soviet Union, the new democratic countries and the small countries under oppression. The above policy of the Chinese government is the policy of the Vietnamese government."[72]

That "the policy of the Chinese government is the policy of the Vietnamese government" was the official Viet-Minh view expressed for the second time. While one could argue that the first expression in 1946 was made by Ho Chi Minh under the irresistable pressure of the Chinese Nationalists, the second one must have been made by the free will of the Viet-Minh. Both occasions, nevertheless, indicate Chinese influence.

As Chinese influence grew stronger in North Vietnam, one function expected of the Viet-Minh government was the good treatment of Chinese residents in the Viet-Minh areas and an accusation of French persecution of the same group. From June to December 1950, for instance, the Viet-Minh radio repeatedly denounced ill treatment by the French of Chinese students in Saigon, Cholon, Quang-Nam, and other areas, while praising the good policy of the Viet-Minh toward Chinese residents in its own regions. The Chinese, the Viet-Minh said, had organized professors' leagues, youths' associations, women's unions and liberation alliances to support the Viet-Minh.[73]

Giap's autumn offensive was an unprecedented victory over the French, of "great international significance," as Ho

[72] "Relationship between Vietnam and China," in *Su That*, as carried by Voice of South Vietnam, in Cochin-Chinese, September 30, 1950.

[73] VNA, North Vietnam, in English, June 16, September 1, December 4, 1950; Voice of South Vietnam, in Cochin-Chinese, June 29, August 30, November 1, 27, and December 28, 1950.

put it. "Now we have a vast rear area in North Vietnam connected with the democratic world."[74] While the victory was still fresh, Ho began a study of the Chinese experience that lasted for several years. The study campaign, begun in late 1950, was carried to almost every Viet-Minh unit, civilian and military. Cadres were urged, sometimes even demanded, to read, discuss, and draw lessons from Chinese writings. Some 30 to 40 documents by Mao Tse-tung, Chu Teh, and Liu Shao-Ch'i were translated into Vietnamese. By late 1953, 47 writings had been published in Vietnamese and 193,880 copies distributed; of these, 57,305 were copies of 17 different works by Mao. Ho himself translated Mao's *On Practice* and *On Contradiction*. The most popular were Mao's *On Protracted War*, *The Chinese Revolution and the Chinese Communist Party*, *On New Democracy*, and *On People's Democratic Dictatorship*. Liu Shao-ch'i's *On the Party* and *How to Be A Good Communist* were also highly valued. In the preparatory stages of the Viet-Minh land reform movement in 1953-1954, Jen Pi-shih's *Questions in the Land Reform* was found to be most useful.[75]

The most significant single result of the campaign was North Vietnam's learning and completion of the three weapons of Mao's revolutionary formula. She added a newly organized Communist party (the Lao Dong Party) to the existing united front and the army.

THE ORGANIZATION of the Lao Dong Party in February 1951 and the merger of the Viet-Minh Front into the Lien Viet the following month was the most important political move since the beginning of the war. Its far-reaching significance in the Vietnamese revolution may well be as great as the establishment of the ICP or the Viet-Minh. In the documents issued during and immediately after the conference, the party was treated as an entirely new organization estab-

[74] Ho's interview with *Jen min jih pao*'s correspondent NCNA, Peking, in English, January 12, 1951.

[75] NCNA, Peking, January 12, 1951; Tran Haoi Nam, *Struggle of Vietnamese People*, p. 62; Hsiao Yang, pp. 70-71; NCNA, North Vietnam, January 12, 1954.

lished by the special congress. Related publications made available several years later indicate that the party was merely the continuation of the ICP under a new name, and that the congress in which the party was born was the Second Congress of the ICP. The congress (the Viet-Minh named it the "National Congress of Unification") was held February 11-19 in North Vietnam and was attended by more than 200 delegates, including some old members of the Canton Commune in 1927 and the Nghe-An Soviet in 1930. Truong Chinh, then secretary-general of the Marxist Study Group, delivered the principal speech, "Complete the National Liberation, Develop People's Democracy, Advance Toward Socialism."[76] During the meeting the congress heard reports on administrative, military, economic, and financial affairs, on the activities of the Viet-Minh Front, and the patriotic emulation campaign. It passed a series of resolutions, political program, and manifesto, and elected a central executive committee. Ho was elected president and Truong Chinh secretary-general.

The congress was convened at a time when the Vietminh's struggle was moving uphill. Delegates were cheerful, confident, and enthusiastic in support of the leadership of Ho and the party. Ho regarded the congress not only as a party conference, but a conference of the resistance war and unification. In explaining the nature and significance of the Lao Dong (Workers') Party, Ho showed a borrowing from Chinese thinking by quoting a passage from the teachings of *Mencius* (originally for the quality of "the great man"). He said that the party was a party of the working class and of the working people. By the "working class" Ho meant those who were most determined and ardent workers, peasants and thinkers. By the "working people" he meant those "who cannot be tempted by wealth and honor, worried by poverty, or subdued by force and power."[77]

[76] VNA, North Vietnam, in English, March 17, 1951.

[77] VNA, North Vietnam, April 11, 1951. To support my judgment that Ho used the passage from *Mencius*, two translations of this passage from the Chinese text of *Mencius* are cited below: "Wealth and honours cannot make him arrogant; poverty and neglect cannot

A Chinese Model for Vietnam

The congress of the merger of the Viet-Minh with the Lien Viet was attended by representatives from Vietnam, Laos, and Cambodia. Among them was Prince Souphanouvong, president of the Laos-Issarak Front.[78] Ho was particularly delighted with the presence of the "two brother peoples," and declared his desire "to realize soon the great union of Viet Nam, Laos and Cambodia." Before it closed, the congress passed resolutions, adopted a political program, declaration, and elected a national committee. It urged the formation of an alliance among the Vietnamese, Laotian, and Cambodian peoples on the basis of "mutual equality and reciprocal aid in the struggle against the common enemy.[79] Its political program emphasized bringing together all of the people's organizations into a solid national bloc for national liberation. Ho was elected honorary president of the Front, Ton Duc Thang, president.

That the Viet-Minh's learning of the three elements of Mao's formula was complete was reflected in its released documents and related publications. Soon after the party and the Front were established, Ho's radio commented: "The Vietnam Labor Party will bind the Vietnam people closely to the Laotian and Cambodian people, and is determined to liberate Indochina and to defend world democratic peace. On the revolution path we already have the Vietnam Labor Party, the Lien Viet Front, the armed

---

pervert him; power and force of arms cannot bind him—such a man is called truly great and courageous." By the Rev. E. Faber, tr. the Rev. Arthur B. Hutchinson, *The Mind of Mencius* (Boston: Houghton Mifflin, 1882), p. 123. "To be above the power of riches and honours to make dissipated, of poverty and mean condition to make swerve from principle, and of power and force to make bend— these characteristics constitute the great man." By James Legge, *The Chinese Classics*, Vol. II, *The Works of Mencius* (Hong Kong University Press, 1960), p. 265.

[78] Voice of Vietnam, March 19, 1950. Prince Souphanouvong, born in 1912, is a half-brother of Prince Souvanna Phouma, the Premier of Laos (1968). Educated in France and leader of the Pathet Lao, he is a good friend of Ho, Giap, and many other leaders of North Vietnam. His wife is a Vietnamese.

[79] *Ibid.*

struggle movement, and with these three elements . . . we will certainly overcome every difficulty and smash every obstacle."[80]

Congratulations were showered on North Vietnam by China. For a time, Peking's news media carried detailed news of the Viet-Minh conference. In an editorial on March 27, *Jen min jih pao* linked Mao's theory with the significance of the founding of the party:

> Of these three factors in the experience of the Chinese people, the first one—the establishment of a Marxist-Leninist political party of the working class—is the most important.
>
> Only under the leadership of such a revolutionary political party can an invincible people's army and an invincible revolutionary united front be established, and malignant imperialism and its lackey—domestic reactionary clique—defeated.
>
> From this it can be seen how important the Vietnam Lao Dong Party is to the Vietnam people's difficult struggle against French and American imperialist aggression.[81]

The Viet-Minh's learning of the propaganda on this point was carried on until the end of the Indochinese war. In an appeal to Viet-Minh armed units in various parts of that country, Nguyen Chi Thanh, chief of the central political bureau of the army, urged the army to be "determined to remain faithful to the people, to the National United Front, and to the Party."[82] In Nambo, Nguyen Binh (the commander) and Le Duan (the political commissioner) issued a vigorous appeal to their troops: "We must never lose sight of the fact that the Labor Party, the Unified National Front, and the people's troops are the three essential conditions of our success against the enemy. If one of these conditions

---

[80] "The Birth of the Viet Nam Labor Party Is a Great Political Victory," Voice of South Vietnam, March 13, 1951. The same theme was repeated in a March 14 broadcast.

[81] *Jen min jih pao*, March 27, 1951, in *SCMP*, No. 88 (March 25-27, 1951), pp. 1-2.

[82] Voice of South Vietnam, in Cochin-Chinese, April 9, 1951.

is lacking, the others will run the risk of failure."[83] Ho repeated the theme on several occasions. On the first anniversary of the founding of the Lao Dong Party, he said that the Vietnamese would certainly win their revolution because they *had* the three elements, party, united front, and the army.[84] This note was repeated by almost every government official and party leader, including Giap[85] and Truong Chinh.[86]

Yet Ton Duc Thang, then president of the Lien Viet, now vice-president of the DRV, came down the most squarely on the Viet-Minh's learning of Mao's theory. It was on January 18, 1954, the occasion of the inauguration of Vietnam-Soviet-Chinese Friendship Month. At this unprecedented international celebration, thousands of propaganda pamphlets, photographs, films, papers, and songs were showered on the people. In the capacity as president of the Vietnamese-Soviet Friendship Association and of the Organization Committee of Friendship Month, Ton Duc Thang presided over the meeting and delivered a speech that should be regarded as the most significant of all the messages on the occasion. After praising Soviet friendship, Thang expressed North Vietnam's gratitude to Communist China for Mao's thoughts:

> With the brotherly neighboring people of China the Viet Nam people also have very old bonds of friendship.
> Thanks to this friendship, the Viet Nam people learn precious lessons from the Chinese revolution and people. These are the thoughts of Mao Tse-tung. . . . These are the three lessons on national united front, armed struggle and the building of the vanguard party which have led the Chinese revolution to success and which President

[83] "Appeal to the Troops of Nambo in Favor of the Labor Party and the Unified National Front," April 10, 1951, by Nguyen Binh, Le Duan and Quoc Chinh; Voice of Nambo, in Cochin-Chinese, May 3, 1951.

[84] "The Great Victory of the Vietnamese People," *World Culture*, No. 11 (March 22, 1952), p. 9.

[85] Giap, in Ho Chi Minh et al. *Achievements*, p. 21.

[86] Truong Chinh, *President Ho*, p. 38.

A Chinese Model for Vietnam

Ho Chi Minh and the Viet Nam Lao Dong Party have ingeniously applied to the concrete conditions of Viet Nam.[87]

From the perspective of ideology several other features could be drawn from the establishment of the Lao Dong Party and the Front. First, the characteristics of the party. In the earlier documents of the Viet-Minh, the feature of anti-imperialism for national independence and freedom was apparent, but the character of anti-feudalism was obscure. In the early manifestoes and programs of the CCP, anti-imperialism and anti-feudalism were declared the goals of the party's struggle. But in its political program, which was obviously along the lines of the documents of the CCP, the Lao Dong Party noted the collapse of the old feudal society in Vietnam, and maintained that "Vietnam society is partly people's democratic society and partly colonial and semi-feudal society." The basic tasks of the Vietnamese revolution were to expel the imperialist aggressor, achieve complete independence and unity, eliminate the colonial regime in the enemy occupied areas, "uproot the slightest traces of feudalism and semi-feudalism" in order to give land to the peasants, develop the people's democratic regime, and lay down a foundation for socialism. Consequently the policy of the Lao Dong Party was to "complete the national liberation, to liberate the people from feudalism and colonialism, to regain independence and unity for the country in order to lead it to socialism."[88]

The change from "anti-imperialism for national independence and freedom" to liberation of the people "from colonialism and feudalism" is significant. It indicated not only a party that was tending strongly toward Communism, but a party that was drawing closer to the CCP. This is evident in Truong Chinh's writings nine years after the founding of the party. The aims of the Vietnamese revolu-

[87] NCNA, January 21, 1954, in *SCMP*, No. 734, January 23-25, 1954.
[88] *Hsin hua yueh pao* (*New China Monthly*, Peking), April 1951, p. 1,287; and Voice of Vietnam, in Tonkinese, March 11, 1951.

tion were to wipe out imperialism and feudalism, to complete national independence, to carry out the policy of land-to-the-tiller, and to develop people's democracy and socialism.[89] The feature of anti-feudalism was viewed during the second half of the Indochinese war, as important as anti-imperialism. Toward the end of the war the Chinese land reform program was used as a model for eliminating the last trace of feudalism; the program was initiated by the Lao Dong Party. And the single, responsible person was the powerful Truong Chinh, leader of the pro-Chinese faction in North Vietnam.

The second feature of the Lao Dong Party was its emphasis on "four-class alliance" revolution. As discussed earlier, Mao defined the social basis of the Chinese revolution as an alliance of peasants, workers, petty bourgeoisie, and national bourgeoisie, all led by the Communist Party. After the founding of the Lao Dong Party, the previous "coalition" nature of the Viet-Minh revolution was dropped, and the four-class thesis appeared in party documents. The political program of the party stated that the revolutionary forces were workers, peasants, petty bourgeoisie and national bourgeoisie, together with patriotic and progressive persons and landlords. The most important class was the workers.[90] Truong Chinh said: "According to the viewpoint of our Party and President Ho, the Vietnam revolution is a new form of bourgeois democratic revolution in a colonial country. Our Party often calls it 'national people's democratic revolution.' It is a people's revolution fought by the workers, peasantry, petty bourgeoisie and national bourgeoisie with the leadership of the workers."[91]

In view of the fact that the workers are less than 10 per cent of the Vietnamese population, and that about 90 per cent are peasants, the Lao Dong theoreticians emphasized the importance of a "worker-peasant alliance." They stressed the peasants' contribution to the war and insisted

[89] Truong Chinh, *President Ho*, p. 37.
[90] *Hsin hua yueh pao*, p. 1,287; VNA, March 13, 1951.
[91] Truong Chinh, *President Ho*, p. 34.

on accomplishing realistic land reform in order to improve the peasants' living conditions. Twelve years later (1963), when Khrushchev and Mao were in serious dispute, Le Duan, secretary-general of the party, moved a step further toward Mao's theory on the peasantry:

> In this country the peasantry is not only seen as the greatest ally of the proletariat and the greatest reserve in the proletarian revolution, but the main force of the revolution. Here exists not only the question of revolutionary forces but a series of questions concerning the revolutionary line and methods. . . . Some genuine Marxists, both past and contemporary, doubted the truth of these theories. . . . Nevertheless, these theories have become tried and tested truths, thanks to the victory of the Chinese revolution.[92]

With a different emphasis Vietnamese party leaders tried to theorize their revolutionary forces from the "four-class" alliance to the "main force" of the peasantry. But however they argued, their views were still confined within the framework of Chinese theory. Le Duan in 1963 seems to have defended the Chinese position on this point in order to safeguard Vietnam's revolutionary path.

The third feature was the people's democratic dictatorship. It is interesting that the nature of the North Vietnamese regime was defined in precisely the same way as that of Communist China. In June 1949 Mao defended his regime as a democratic dictatorship: " 'You are dictatorial.' My dear sirs, you are right, that is just what we are. All the experience the Chinese people have accumulated through several decades teaches us to enforce the people's democratic dictatorship. . . . The combination of these two aspects, democracy for the people and dictatorship over the reactionaries, is the people's democratic dictatorship."[93]

In the political program of the Lao Dong Party, the Viet-Minh regime was defined as "a people's democratic regime.

[92] Le Duan, *Some Questions*, pp. 12-13.
[93] Mao, *Selected Works*, IV, pp. 417-18.

. . . The form of this regime is the People's Democratic Republic. Its essence is the people's democratic dictatorship—democratic toward the people, dictatorial toward the imperialist aggressors and the reactionaries."[94]

The complete identity of the Lao Dong Party's view with that of Mao is not accidental. It must have come about after a long period of deliberation, for a few years later Truong Chinh was still of the same opinion that the Viet-Minh regime should carry out people's democratic dictatorship—democratic toward the people, dictatorial toward the enemy of the people.[95]

Fourth, a closer alliance with the CCP. The Lao Dong Party showed a different attitude in its messages of greeting to the Communist parties of the Soviet Union, China, North Korea, and France.[96] A comparison of these messages will show the degree of difference:

To the Communist Party of the U.S.S.R.:

The Vietnam Lao Dong Party . . . begs to send its respectful greetings to the Bolshevik Party of the USSR and to express its confidence in the Bolshevik Party and Comrade Stalin—great leader of the workers and peoples of the world.

To the Chinese Communist Party:

The Vietnam Lao Dong Party . . . pledges itself to follow the heroic example of the Communist Party of China to learn the Mao Tse-tung concept which has been leading the peoples of China and Asia on the road to independence and democracy.

To the No Dong Dang (Labor Party) of North Korea:

The Vietnamese people, who are now fighting for liberation, are profoundly elated by the victories of the Korean people. . . .

To the Communist Party of France:

The Lao Dong Party . . . sends you its friendly greet-

[94] VNA, March 13, 1950; *Hsin hua yueh pao*, April 1951, p. 1,288.
[95] Truong Chinh, *President Ho*, p. 36.
[96] VNA, March 21, 1951.

ings and expresses its confidence in the love for peace, freedom, and justice of the working class and people of France.

The language in the messages was weighed carefully. In pledging to learn Mao's thoughts and follow China's example, the Lao Dong Party had placed itself in a closer position to the CCP than to the Soviet Communist Party, to which it merely paid its respects.

IF 1951 WAS a year of military stalemate, if not setback, for the Viet-Minh, it was also a year of political and ideological achievement for Ho, an achievement which generally paralleled the betterment of Sino-Vietnamese relations, which rose sharply after 1950. North Vietnam drew closer diplomatically to Communist China by sending an ambassador to Peking. He was Hoang Van Hoan, a member of the Thanh-Nien, a graduate of the Whampoa Military Academy, and a veteran of the ICP. Before and during the Second Sino-Japanese war, he was active in Canton, Nanking, Kunming, Kweilin, Liuchow, and Chinghsi, where he was a major in the Nationalist army, a self-employed tailor, and a Viet-Minh revolutionist.[97] He understood Chinese affairs well and was regarded as pro-Chinese. Hoan went to Peking to present his credentials in late April 1951.

In the flush of good Sino-Vietnamese relations, another already eminent pro-Chinese leader, Truong Chinh, grew still more powerful. In March 1951 *Nhan Dan* published his biography.[98] It described Truong Chinh's prison life in 1931-1936 and his Democratic Front activities in 1936-1939, praising him as the "soul" of the newspapers *Le Travail,* *Thoi The, En Avant, Tin Tuc, Notre Voix,* and *Doi Nay.* Truong Chinh was not a graduate of Whampoa, but a mem-

[97] Hoang Van Hoan went to China in 1926, in 1935 organized the Association for Viet Nam Independence League (forerunner of Viet-Minh) with Ho Ngoc Lum in Nanking, and was a founder of the Viet-Minh in 1941. He is (1969) a Politburo member of the Lao Dong Party and vice-president of the Standing Committee of the National Assembly in Hanoi.

[98] *Nhan Dan,* March 25, 1951, in VNA, April 20, 1951.

ber of Ho's Thanh-Nien in Vietnam. He met Ho for the first time in May 1941. Yet he had a firm grip on the party until 1956, when he was removed from the position of secretary-general because of the failure of the land reform, for which he was held responsible. He became the leading party theoretician on almost every important occasion, such as "The Party's New Policy" after the Viet-Minh was established in 1941, "The Pacific War and Our Party's Stand" in early 1942, "Prepare for a General Uprising" in August 1945, and "The Resistance Will Win." The biography concluded that during the five years of resistance, Truong Chinh had been Ho's closest collaborator. "While President Ho Chi Minh is the soul of the Vietnam revolution and Vietnam's resistance, Comrade Truong Chinh is their builder and commander. . . ." The purpose behind the release of the biography was clear: to establish Truong Chinh as second in command to Ho.

The pro-Chinese sentiment (as shown by Ho Tung Mau, Truong Chinh, Hoang Quoc Viet, and Ton Duc Thang) continued to rise and took various forms. In early June *Cuu Quoc*, in commenting on the United Nations embargo on shipments to Communist China and on the French-British-American military conference in Singapore for a Pacific pact, carried an editorial calling on the Vietnamese people to be vigilant against all plots and intrigues of French and American imperialism. It denounced the separate peace treaty with Japan, condemned the United Nations embargo resolution against China, and protested against the proposed Pacific pact. It urged the Vietnamese people to unite with other Asian peoples "under the leadership of President Mao Tse-tung" in order to raise the resistance for the complete liberation of the country, defeat all the imperialist plots, and contribute to the preservation of peace in Asia.[99] This was the first article of such nature from North Vietnam, implying that the only Asian force that could check Western "imperialism" in Asia was an organized "Asian

[99] VNA, North Vietnam, in English Morse to Southeast Asia, June 2, 1951.

bloc" under the leadership of China. Accordingly a confrontation between the United States and Communist China was an inevitable conclusion.

On July 23 a Vietnam people's delegation headed by Hoang Quoc Viet arrived in Peking. The 14-member delegation was the first publicized formal mission to China. It was a well-selected group, and included a Catholic priest, professor, newsmen, a medical doctor, a worker, a farmer, resistance heroes, and party men. Le Tung Son, a long-time member of the ICP–Viet-Minh in Yunnan and Kwangsi, was secretary of the delegation.[100] Peking welcomed the group on a fully equal basis. Li Chi-shen, vice-president of the CPPCC and vice-president of the Chinese regime, led the Chinese delegation that received the Vietnamese. *Jen min jih pao*'s editorial of July 24 expressed a warm welcome. The Vietnam delegation visited various parts of China, receiving an enthusiastic welcome wherever they went. Hoang Quoc Viet published an article in *Jen min jih pao* on the sixth anniversary of the August Revolution to introduce the history of the Vietnamese struggle to the Chinese people.[101] He concluded a "Sino-Vietnamese Friendship Agreement" with Chou En-lai. The agreement provided that Chinese technicians and medicine would be sent to North Vietnam in exchange for Vietnamese agricultural and mineral products, and that Vietnamese students would go to China for training.[102] It was also during this visit that Hoang Quoc Viet said, "The rich experience of the Chinese people's revolution in the past thirty years is . . . the only path that the oppressed people should take in order to overthrow the imperialist rule and obtain independence and freedom."[103]

Ton Duc Thang, too, headed a delegation to Peking in late September for the celebration of the second anniver-

---

[100] NCNA, Peking, in English Morse to North America, July 24, 1951.

[101] Radio Peking, in English Morse to North America, August 26, 1951.

[102] Sixth Section of the KMT, pp. 15-16.

[103] *Ibid.*, p. 12.

sary of the Peking regime. (He later visited Korea.) He was so impressed by the events in China that he said on Radio Peking:

> What has excited us most in China are the wonderful things the Chinese people have accomplished under the leadership of Chairman Mao Tse-tung and the Chinese Communist Party. . . . Everywhere we saw evidence that the slogan 'resist American aggression and aid Korea' and patriotic pacts are put into practice. . . . All this is due to the brilliant leadership of Chairman Mao Tse-tung and the Chinese Communist Party, to the warm love of the Chinese people for their motherland and for peace. . . .[104]

While the "pro-Chinese" sentiment was strong, Ho Chi Minh tried to check the "pro-Chinese" group in party front organizations with a moderate group in the governmental machinery. This group was led by Pham Van Dong, Ho's protege since 1926. There is evidence that at every cabinet meeting after June 1950, Ho, Pham Van Dong, and Vo Nguyen Giap were the only three cabinet members mentioned by the Viet-Minh radio. Ho Tung Mau was mentioned once before he died in August 1951—this is significant. Ho's trust in the moderate group and his plans for Dong as his successor, became apparent when he named Dong to be his vice-president in early 1952. The shift in Dong's position since then, from vice-president, vice-premier, and foreign minister to premier, and the decline of Truong Chinh's influence since 1956 indicate that Ho has so far succeeded in his plan.

It must not be thought, however, that North Vietnam's efforts to learn from the Chinese experience were ever reduced during the war. It was not until 1956, after the failure of the land reform and the "hundred-flower" movement, that North Vietnam curtailed its adherence to China's Communizing policies.

[104] Ton Duc Thang, "Inspired by Victory of Chinese People, Vietnam People are Confident," NCNA, Peking, October 22, 1951, in *SCMP*, No. 200, pp. 6-7.

A Chinese Model for Vietnam

In 1950-1952 the Viet-Minh accepted another bit of Chinese advice in totaling reforming its finances and taxation system.[105] Beginning in early 1951 the government abolished all people's contributions on agriculture to the national budget and local funds, such as land tax contributions in grain, contributions to the entertainment of crop-protection squads, grain contributions for mass education, grain contributions to local people's forces and to village funds, grain contributions for road construction, etc.[106] It also abolished the wine, salt, and opium taxes which had been imposed by the French.[107] In their place were five taxes: agriculture, trade, forestry, slaughtering, and import-export taxes. The National Bank of Vietnam was also established, and Nguyen Luong Bang was appointed the first director. A new currency was issued; the new bank notes were printed in Shanghai.[108] The Viet-Minh radio urged the people to support the new notes as the Chinese people did their new national currency.[109]

Of the five taxes the most important was the agricultural one promulgated in May 1951. It was to be paid by landlords and peasants alike, and was determined by income and family expenditures.[110] The taxation percentage was to be decided by the cadres and the people. Apart from the major part of the tax to be paid to the national government, a one-percent tax would go to the local budget. Since this

[105] The strongest evidence for this point was Pham Van Dong's speech in Peking in August 1954. On his way back to North Vietnam after the Geneva Conference, Dong was warmly welcomed by Peking leaders. In one of his speeches he said: "We have learned from China's experience in . . . financial and economic work during the war of resistance. By combining China's valuable experience with the practical conditions of . . . Vietnam, we have . . . achieved outstanding results in . . . financial and economic work." *Jen min jih pao*, August 4, 1954.

[106] VNA, in English Morse to Southeast Asia, May 9, 1951.

[107] Hsiao Yang, *op.cit.*, p. 51.

[108] Taipei Radio, in Mandarin, November 14, 1950.

[109] VNA, in Vietnamese, June 5, 1951.

[110] An official scale of the agricultural tax was given by *Cuu Quoc*, July 6, 1952, as quoted in Hoang Van Chi, *Colonialism to Communism*, pp. 76-77.

was a Chinese system, foreign to the Vietnamese cadres and people, the government established a special agricultural tax bureau to study the system, opened training classes to train the tax collectors, and attempted to explain the new system to the people. It said the old system was "too complicated" and the peasant had to pay numerous taxes; but the new tax was "very simple," with equitable and democratic characteristics (percentages to be established by the people and cadres). It therefore was convenient to both the government (tax collectors) and the people (taxpayers).[111] Whenever minor mistakes were made by the collectors, Pham Van Dong immediately promised correction. In addition, the Viet-Minh urged the army, trade union members, and students to study the tax system and take part in assisting tax collection.[112] The campaign was impressive. According to a Vietnamese report in 1952, the tax system was a success in 1951,[113] although other sources claimed that because of excessively large assessments, the landlords and richer peasants suffered from overtaxation and exploitation.[114]

THROUGHOUT the Indochinese war, North Vietnam continued to imitate and learn from Communist China in non-military affairs. With Chinese cooperation and aid, particularly in communication and transportation, North Vietnam broadened her activities on the international level, including sending Ambassador Nguyen Luong Bang to Moscow (April 1952) and delegations to Europe, with a resulting increase in international prestige.

On the second anniversary of Chinese recognition, the

[111] Voice of Vietnam, in Tonkinese to Indochina, August 23, 24, 25, 1951.

[112] Voice of Vietnam, in Tonkinese, September 20, 22, 29, October 4, 1951.

[113] Hong Ha, "The Vietnam People Progress Steadily on the Line of Economic Struggle," *World Culture*, No. 32 (August 16, 1952), p. 8.

[114] Hoang Van Chi, *Colonialism to Communism*, pp. 80-84; Radio Saigon (French controlled), in Cochin-Chinese, July 24, 1953.

Viet-Minh revealed "unconditional aid" from China. To establish a closer relationship with China and show gratitude for Chinese aid, the Viet-Minh stressed that China and Vietnam had suffered from the same fate—"feudal domination and foreign invasion." The Viet-Minh radio also said that Chinese recognition and friendship were accompanied by "unconditional aid" from the Chinese people. The diplomatic victory had brought North Vietnam "continual military victories," and "changed completely the situation in Indochina" in its favor.[115] Though the aid was unspecified, the Viet-Minh had already indicated that it was essential and even vital to North Vietnamese military victory.

The first nonmilitary delegation from Peking to North Vietnam was one of 38 members led by Liao Ch'eng-chih for the celebration of the seventh anniversary (1952) of the founding of the DRV. On this occasion Pham Van Dong published an article in *Shih chieh chih shih* (*World Culture*),[116] Hoang Van Hoan and Truong Chinh wrote respectively for *Jen min ih pao*,[117] hailing the achievements of the DRV and close Sino-Vietnamese relations. At a reception at the Vietnamese embassy on the same occasion, Liu Shao-ch'i spoke of the "unbreakable friendship" between the two nations and of his conviction of a Vietnamese victory.[118]

As a symbol of the "unbreakable friendship" Peking took the initiative in early 1953 by changing the name of Chennan-kuan (Pass of the Repressing South), an important pass between Kwangsi and Vietnam, to Mu-nan-kuan (Pass of the Friendly South). The friendship was further expressed by a Vietnamese article commemorating the third anniversary of the Chinese recognition of the DRV (1953).

[115] "The People's Friendship, Essential Factor of Our Victories," Voice of Nambo, in French to South Vietnam, January 18, 1952.

[116] Pham Van Dong, "The Seven Years of the Resistance War of the Democratic Republic of Vietnam," *World Culture*, No. 34 (August 30, 1952), pp. 8-10.

[117] NCNA, Peking, September 2, 3, 1952.

[118] NCNA, Peking, September 2, 1952 in *SCMP*, No. 410, p. 7.

A Chinese Model for Vietnam

Apart from the propaganda cliche of praising China and Vietnam, it touched on some specific points about the achievements of Chinese national reconstruction, particularly land reform and the patriotic emulation movement. The article said the Vietnamese were determined to learn from the Chinese in all fields.[119] Apparently this was an indication of Vietnam's further imitation of the Chinese emulation movement—land reform and the "three-anti" campaign (anti-bureaucratism, anti-corruption, and anti-waste), which had already been launched or was beginning to go into effect on the Chinese mainland.

The signing of "The Sino-Vietnamese Postal Agreement," November 6, 1952, for the exchange of postal service between the two nations, was significant. It was the first time since the Indochinese war that the Viet-Minh had established postal service to another country. Obviously the new service was made possible with Chinese help, and the "exchange" was more Chinese service to North Vietnam than Vietnam to China. On March 3, 1953 Chinese post offices began accepting ordinary mail for and from North Vietnam, which facilitated communication between North Vietnam and the outside world. It was also evidence of the Viet-Minh's actual control of various parts of the country where postal service was introduced.[120]

While the Viet-Minh's activities in China and Europe were increased, the effect of the armistice of the Korean war in July 1953 was significant. Along with its growing military aid to the Viet-Minh, Peking increased its propaganda for Ho's regime; news media carried more and more items on Vietnam. On September 2 *Jen min jih pao* carried on its

[119] "Long Live Unbreakable Friendship Between Vietnam and Chinese Peoples," in *Jeh min jih pao*, January 19, 1953.
[120] Sixth Section of the KMT, p. 17; NCNA, Peking, March 2, 1953, in *SCMP*, No. 522, p. 4. The postal service which opened in North Vietnam in March 1953 included the following areas: (1) North Vietnam United District: Lao-Kay, Ha-Giang, Cao-Bang, Lang-Son, Bac-Giang, Yen-Bay, Phu-Tho, Tuyen-Quang, Tien-Yen, Bac-Kan; (2) Third United District: Hao-Binh, Ha-Nam, Ninh-Binh; (3) Fourth United District: Thanh-Hoa, Nghe-An, Ha-Tinh; (4) Fifth United District: Quang-Yen, Quang-Tri, Binh-Dinh.

front page the full text of Ho's National Day message to his army and people. The issue included an editorial entitled "Great Success of the Vietnam People's Fight for Independence and Peace," and an article by Phan Van Dong commemorating the founding of the DRV. Other major newspapers in Peking such as *Kwang ming Daily, Peking Daily,* and *Daily Worker* featured Ho's message prominently. Despite the propagandistic effect and the Communist jargon, there was something new: the urge for negotiations to settle the Vietnam war.[121]

INTERNAL policies in North Vietnam in 1952-1953 were directed to increase the country's ability to resist the French and to Communize the country. Much of China's policy was followed.

Although a new drive for increasing production was launched by Ho's regime in April 1951,[122] the Chinese example of "patriotic emulation" was urged. In early October 1951, when the Viet-Minh drive (to emulate China) was still in effect, *Nhan Dan* in strong language urged that the Vietnamese people "follow" the rich experiences of the Chinese in patriotic emulation.[123] The Viet-Minh intensified its "patriotic emulation" in the military, industry, and agriculture. At the end of the first year of the drive a "Congress of Emulation Combatants and Model Cadres" was held on May Day 1952. Progress was reported in all fields, with agriculture the greatest. A Vietnamese report indicated that in 1952-1953 agricultural production in the Third United District of northern Vietnam had increased from 20 to 50 per cent.[124] Small industrial products were improved in quality and quantity; the price was being grad-

---

[121] *Jen min jih pao,* September 2, 1953, in *SCMP,* No. 643, p. 7. For the peace settlement see the next chapter.

[122] VNA, North Vietnam, in English Morse, April 18, 1951.

[123] Voice of Nambo, Saigon-Cholon, in Cochin-Chinese, October 8, 1951.

[124] Jen Hsiao, "Great Achievements of the Democratic Republic of Vietnam in the Financial-Economic and Political Fields," *World Culture,* No. 16 (August 20, 1954), p. 14.

ually stabilized; and the financial situation had improved.[125] Domestic (in Indochina) and foreign trade had also increased. The main trading country with North Vietnam was China, beginning in 1951. As of 1954 the total amount of Chinese trade was four times as much as that for 1952. The basic items were timber and agricultural products, in exchange for Chinese machines and daily supplies.[126]

The "rectification" campaign launched in 1952-1953 was another follow-up policy of the Chinese "cheng feng" (rectification) movement. Within a year, more than 15,800 cadres underwent "thought reform." Its pattern was strikingly similar to that of the Chinese program in 1942-1944. This movement was reported to have raised thought levels, political consciousness, discipline, and effectiveness in work.[127]

The Chinese three-anti campaign of 1951 was followed by the Viet-Minh in 1953.[128] It was intended for the Viet-Minh cadres, to cleanse the party and government agencies. But Ho did not follow the Chinese "five-anti" campaign of 1951-1952 (against bribery, tax evasion, fraud, theft of government property, and theft of state economic secrets). Presumably these "five poisons," as the Chinese called them, did not exist in North Vietnam.

As was known to the West, the Viet-Minh land reform campaign of 1953-1956 followed the Chinese pattern. It was divided into two periods—reduction of land rent (1953-1954) and land reform proper (1954-1956). On December 9, 1952 Ho appealed to the nation, stating that the peasants had contributed the "largest part" to the resistance and to the reconstruction of Vietnam, but that they were the

[125] *Ibid.*, p. 15.

[126] Phan An, "The Achievements of Vietnam's Industry and Commerce in the Past Nine Years of Resistance War and One Year of Peace," in Ho Chi Minh et al., *Achievements*, p. 65; Tran Hoai Nam, *Struggle of Vietnamese People*, p. 44.

[127] Jen Hsiao, "Great Achievements," No. 16 (August 20, 1954), p. 16; Minh Nghe, "The Glorious Victory of the Vietnam Anti-Aggression War," *World Culture*, No. 5 (March 5, 1954), p. 10.

[128] Voice of Nambo, in Cochin-Chinese, May 11, 1953; Jen Hsiao, "Great Achievements," p. 16; Truong Chinh, *President Ho*, p. 36.

"most miserable" because of the lack of land for cultivation.[129] In January 1953 the Fourth Plenary Session of the Lao Dong Party unanimously passed a resolution which provided for the mobilization of the masses for the fulfillment of land rent reduction. The Viet-Minh regime put it into effect in 1953-1954.[130] To promote the campaign the Viet-Minh invited Chinese advisers, sent cadres to China for training, and used Chinese methods, including visiting the poor and miserable and the "three together system" ("san tung" in Chinese).[131] The three together system (trained cadres lived, ate, and worked with and for the peasants without any compensation) was the most intimate and effective way to learn about peasants' miseries and complaints against the landlords. Having learned their hosts' complaints, the cadres encouraged them to struggle against their landlords. After two or three months of quiet preparation, the campaign began vigorously in "experimental" 22 villages in the North Vietnam United District and in the Third United District. The campaign was a success. It resulted in broader support for the regime, voluntary military and resistance service on a broad basis, rent reduction by 65 per cent, and confiscation of 1,800 Viet *mau* (one *mau* equals 3,650 square feet).[132]

With the initial success of the land rent reduction campaign, the Viet-Minh pressed on with its land reform. At the First National Congress of the Lao Dong Party, November 14-23, 1953, Truong Chinh submitted a draft of the agrarian reform law, which was passed unanimously. The law was approved by the Third Congress of the National Assembly on December 4, and Ho signed it into law and promulgated it on December 19, the seventh anniversary of the beginning of the war. It provided that the government would confiscate the land and property of the French, of the traitors

[129] Voice of Vietnam, in Tonkinese, May 30, 1953.
[130] Tran Hoai Nam, *Struggle of Vietnamese People*; Jen Hsiao, "The Great Success of the Land Policy of the Democratic Republic of Vietnam," *World Culture*, No. 3 (February 5, 1954), p. 10.
[131] *Ibid.*, p. 11; Hoang Van Chi, *Colonialism to Communism*, p. 169.
[132] Jen Hsiao, "Great Success," pp. 10-11.

and of reactionary and evil landlords. The government would purchase the land and property of religious groups and of the landlords who assisted in the war. It would redistribute confiscated and purchased land and property to the peasants, based on population.[133] The government planned to carry out the campaign in 1954, but it was interrupted in 1954 and 1955 by Dien-Bien-Phu and the ensuing mass exodus of approximately one million refugees to the south. The reform effort failed in 1956, culminating in a peasant revolt in Nghe-An, Ho's home province, and the removal of Truong Chinh as secretary-general. Yet throughout 1954 Chinese influence in North Vietnam reached new heights, due to their aid to the Dien-Bien-Phu battle, the Geneva Conference, and the continuation of the land reform campaign.

3. CHINESE MILITARY AID

Peking's military assistance to North Vietnam during 1950-1954 was a constant concern to the French-Vietnamese authorities. Apart from the Viet-Minh's following Mao's strategy and tactics, the issue of Chinese aid raised several questions: Was there any assistance agreement (not necessarily a military pact) between Communist China and North Vietnam? How much aid did Peking offer to the Viet-Minh? How did it operate? In probing these questions of "military secrecy" (as the Chinese called them), one encounters insurmountable difficulties. Unless either the Chinese or Vietnamese Communists make known their diplomatic and military documents, which is highly unlikely in the foreseeable future, no study by outside observers can claim to be complete and accurate. Therefore the discussion here is an observation and an inference from various sources, in the hope that a rational and logical approach has been pursued.

As discussed earlier, Ho prior to September 1949 repeatedly denied the existence of a Ho-Mao agreement,

[133] *Ibid.*; Tran Hoai Nam, *Struggle of Vietnamese People*, p. 41.

claiming that it was a French colonialist rumor. But in mid-December, 20 days after he had sent his first publicized greetings to Mao, Ho changed his mind. He told a Western newsman that there was no Chinese aid to his regime under any pact, but that if China was willing to make arrangements for aid, the offer would be considered.[134] The shift in Ho's position hinted at the possibility of Chinese aid.

The arrival of the Chinese Communists at the Vietnamese border, and Peking's accusation of a French "violation" of Chinese territory in Kwangsi and Yunnan, placed the conclusion of an agreement on aid within the realm of possibility. A Taiwan source reported a "Vietnam military delegation" under Nguyen Dai Chi visiting Peking in late December 1949,[135] and the French in Saigon announced Ho's departure to Peking on March 15, 1950.[136] Whereas the French announcement offered no details about a Ho-Mao pact, the Chinese source reported more specifically. It said that the Vietnamese delegation had concluded with China on January 18, 1950, a "Sino-Vietnamese Trade Agreement on Military Supplies," which provided that China would sell to the Viet-Minh 150,000 Japanese rifles, 10,000 American carbines, and ammunition. On February 10, an office was set up in Nanning to direct the transportation of Chinese military supplies. In March two "Vietnam Cadres Training Classes" opened in Nanning and Wenshan (Yunnan); the periods of instruction were to be three to six months. Meanwhile a Chinese group of "cultural workers" under Nguyen Dai Chi was sent to Vietnam. Judging by the fact that the Viet-Minh broadcast Ho's name at the monthly cabinet meeting, which started in April 1950, and that the flow of Chinese advisers and aid began in the late

[134] Voice of South Vietnam, December 15, 1949.

[135] Sixth Section of the KMT, pp. 14-15.

[136] Radio Indochina, in English, March 13, 1950. The announcement was made by High Commissioner Léon Pignon in Saigon: "Ho Chi Minh . . . is to go to Peking on March the 15th . . . where he will sign a treaty with . . . Mao Tse-tung and . . . Chou En-lai; he will sign similar treaties with . . . Stalin."

spring, Ho or other Viet-Minh leaders may have visited Peking seeking aid.

I mentioned earlier that the spring of 1950 was a "conference season" during which the Viet-Minh launched a general mobilization campaign in preparation for future counterattacks. As Chinese aid and advisers flowed in, Peking, according to Hoang Van Chi, sent Lo Kuei-po to serve as the chief military adviser to General Giap.[137] Also, the Chinese were reported to be using Yulin port on recently taken Hainan Island to ship arms and other supplies to the Viet-Minh.[138] Throughout the summer at least 20,000 Viet-Minh troops were trained and equipped by the Chinese in Yunnan and Kwangsi and returned to Vietnam. Thousands of unarmed Vietnamese crossed the border to China by truck at night.[139] Lungchow was reported to be an important assistance center. In Nanning in August, Generals Chang Yun-i (governor of Kwangsi) and Ch'en Keng (governor of Yunnan) conferred with Viet-Minh generals on intensifying preparations for attack.[140] The Chinese Second Field Army in Yunnan and Kwangsi helped train five Viet-Minh divisions in 1950—the 304th, 308th, 312th, 316th, and 320th. Later in 1951 a heavy division (the 351st) took shape and was completed in 1952. Working toward the goal of "self-reliance," the Viet-Minh developed its military factories. By October 1950 it had an arsenal in every Viet-Minh province and a workshop in every district, which could produce various types of mortars.[141] The southwest arsenal of China, in Kunming, was organized to aid the Viet-Minh. From January to September 1950 the Viet-Minh received from China about 40,000 rifles, 125 machineguns, 75 mor-

[137] Hoang Van Chi, *Colonialism to Communism*, p. 63. Chi's account on Lo Kuei-po remains to be confirmed.

[138] *New York Times*, May 9, 1950.

[139] *Ibid.*, August 13, 1950; Sixth Section of the KMT, p. 15.

[140] *Kung Sheung Daily News* (*Industrial and Commercial Daily*, Hong Kong), May 9, 1950; also *New York Times*, May 10, 1950; Sixth Section of the KMT, p. 15.

[141] Chang Ch'u-kun, "The New Military Victory of the Vietnamese People," *World Culture*, Vol. 22, No. 17 (October 28, 1950), p. 12.

tars, 3,000 boxes of ammunition, and 870 tons of other military equipment. During the period of reorganization of the army in 1950, Giap succeeded, with Chinese assistance, in reorganizing his forces, establishing a sound political commissar system, and opening more military schools. The Chinese Communists also began in mid-October the construction of a railway extension from Liuchow to Chennan-kuan via Nanning. The completion of the extension would provide a direct rail link between Manchuria and Indochina.[142] Prior to the fall offensive the Viet-Minh army was reported to have 250,000 regular and guerrilla fighters, with 30 artillery pieces, 140 mortars, 230 machineguns, and 100,000 rifles.[143] Morale was high. As the Viet-Minh radio put it, "The general counteroffensive atmosphere is full of emotion."[144] A French communique in Saigon announced in mid-August that in a matter of months a well-trained Viet-Minh army would be able to launch powerful large-scale attacks against the French.[145] Eight days later Radio Peking broadcast that after five years of hit-and-run jungle raids, Viet-Minh forces were ready to launch a general offensive against the French army.[146] The Peking announcement was significant; it not only revealed China's full knowledge of Viet-Minh military activity, but indicated that Peking was serving virtually as the military spokesman for the Viet-Minh.

American military aid to the French was stepped up. After American warships called on Saigon in June the United States Military Assistance Advisory Group (MAAG) appeared in Indochina in August to supervise the distribution of aid. While the Americans favored direct aid to the Vietnamese army under Bao Dai, the French were absolutely opposed to it. General Carpentier, commander-in-chief of the French forces, was so adamant in his opposition to the American proposal for direct aid that he threatened

[142] Taipei Radio, in English Morse, October 20, 1950.
[143] Sixth Section of the KMT, p. 25.
[144] Voice of South Vietnam, July 12, 1950.
[145] *New York Times*, August 13, 1950.
[146] NCNA, August 20, 1950.

to resign within 24 hours if the proposal was put into effect.[147] The French won the argument and, accordingly, the aid. Yet the Vietnamese forces under the French were an army without effective and responsible leadership, good training, strict discipline, inspiration, high morale, and the people's support. The French expeditionary forces, too, lacked enthusiasm, good discipline, and the people's support. In comparing the quality of the French-Vietnamese army with that of the Viet-Minh, it was obvious that the French were not going to win the war even with superior American equipment.

Less than one month after Peking announced the forthcoming counteroffensive, Giap's army launched powerful, fierce, well-planned, and astonishing attacks on the French in Dong-Khe, That-Khe, Cao-Bang, Lang-Son, and Lao-Kay. From September 16 to November 2, it scored great victories and took all the areas.[148] "In the Cao-Bang Lang-Son area alone," Giap claimed at the cabinet meeting in November, "the Vietnam People's Army has wiped out over 10,000 enemy troops, including over 8,000 crack troops, captured a considerable quantity of war equipment, liberated five provincial capitals . . . smashed open the French east-west corridor, threatening thereby the enemy position in the Red River Basin."[149] As observed by Bernard Fall, the French had suffered their greatest colonial defeat since Montcalm at Quebec. "They had lost 6,000 troops, 13 artillery pieces and 125 mortars, 450 trucks and three armored platoons, 940 machineguns, 1,200 submachineguns and more

[147] *New York Times*, March 9, 1950.

[148] The Vietnam people's full support to this campaign could clearly be seen from Ho's statement before the operation was over. He thanked the people of Cao-Bang, Bac-Kan, and Lang-Son for their help and paid "particular tribute to the tremendous efforts made by the women of Cao-Bac-Lang. Tens of thousands of women of the Vietnamese, Tho, Thai, Nung, Man, and other nationalities have helped in repairing roads, carrying munitions, and doing other work to help the People's Army." VNA, October 14, 1950.

[149] VNA, North Vietnam, in English Morse to Southeast Asia, November 27.

than 8,000 rifles."[150] At the same November cabinet meeting, which was also attended by the members of the standing committee of the Vietnam National Assembly, Giap was honored by Ho with the Third Class Ho Chi Minh Medal. Soon after, Giap spoke at a meeting of his cadres on the experience of the battles: "From this battle, we understand more the greatness of the thought of Mao Tse-tung. I hope that all of you will double your efforts to study his thought, especially his military theory."[151]

What worried the French most was the possibility of massive Chinese intervention, apprehension that was first expressed in early 1950 over a report that there were about 30,000 Chinese troops of the Second Field Army on the Vietnam border. After the Chinese "volunteers" for the Korean war moved into North Korea on October 25, French concern increased. In late November the Chinese lodged a "stern protest" against the French for their "violation" of Chinese territory. Peking accused French ground and air forces of numerous "provocative invasions" of Yunnan, Kwangsi, and Kwangtung, and listed 91 border incidents between December 1949 and October 1950, with "more intensified" cases in the most recent two months. The violations, Peking charged, had caused "heavy losses to Chinese lives and property."[152] General Carpentier immediately denied Peking's charges. "We have," he replied, "no idea where or how French troops could have crossed the border. On the other hand, there are numerous examples of border violations by the Chinese Communists."[153] In the next few months Peking's charges were repeated periodically, often accompanied by strong warnings of retaliatory military action against the French.[154] If the Chinese intervened it would be all over in a few days in the Tonkin area. As

[150] Bernard B. Fall. *Street Without Joy: Indochina at War, 1946-54* (Harrisburg: Stackpole, 1961), p. 28.
[151] Hsiao Yang, *op.cit.*, p. 71.
[152] *Jen min jeh pao*, November 24, 1950.
[153] *New York Times*, November 25, 1950.
[154] NCNA, December 8, 1950, April 11, 1951.

observed by a French reporter in the field, "There would be nothing but death, massacre, captivity. . . . Mao's Chinese could win a total victory in Indochina."[155]

While the possibility of Chinese intervention was strong, the Viet-Minh employed every possible means to make good use of the situation for its cause. Four months after Lt.Col. Charton was captured during the fall offensive of 1950, the Viet-Minh army forced him to sign a propaganda article stating that there was no hope for the French to win the war because China supported the Viet-Minh. He said: "I am a captive. . . . For the first time in my life I have time to ponder. . . . Can France continue this war with some hope of winning it? No, for Asia wants her freedom and China, with her 475 million people, borders on Vietnam. . . . Since order reigns in China, no matter what political ideology prevails there, the part of foreigners is reduced to mere exchanges between independent nations. Vietnam, aided by China, can carry on an endless war against our Expeditionary Forces. Therefore, unlike in Greece, the Vietnam people's uprising cannot be put down."[156]

The severe setback in the fall of 1950 brought the appointment of Gen. de Lattre de Tassigny as commander-in-chief and high commissioner in Indochina.[157] Fresh from his recent victory, Giap was overconfident of his ability to defeat the famous French general, saying "We will defeat him on his [home] ground."[158] The Viet-Minh propagandized that Ho would return to Hanoi for the 1951 Tet (New Year, which falls in late January or early February). Convinced by his own intuition that the time for a counter-offensive was ripe and encouraged by the Chinese-Korean Communist victory in the "liberation" of Seoul in Korea in early January 1951, Giap in January attacked Vinh-Yen, 37

[155] Bodard, *Quicksand War*, p. 343.

[156] VNA, North Vietnam, in English Morse, March 29, 1951.

[157] The shifts in command of the French forces from 1949 to June 1954 were: 1949-Dec. 1950, Gen. Marcel Carpentier; Dec. 1950-Jan. 1952, Gen. de Lattre de Tassigny; Apr. 1952-May 1953, Gen. Raoul Salan; May 1953-June 1954, Gen. Henri-Eugene Navarre.

[158] *Le Monde*, December 5, 1950.

miles northwest of Hanoi.[159] The offensive (Operation Hoang Hoa Tham I) was repulsed by the French-Vietnamese forces, and at least 6,000 Viet-Minh were killed. Unconvinced that his calculations and strategy were wrong, Giap dismissed the Chinese advice to be cautious.[160] In March he attacked again (Operation Hoang Hoa Tham II), which resulted in another heavy defeat. The Viet-Minh radio emphasized the necessity of imitating Mao Tse-tung's strategy and tactics, saying that the Vietnamese resistance war was similar in many ways to the Chinese resistance war against Japan and the Communists against the Nationalists. "We must, therefore, imitate the strategy used by Mao Tse-tung." It urged the avoidance of any battle that the Viet-Minh was unsure of winning, and reasserted that the essential purpose was the progressive extermination of the enemy's vital forces and not the conquest and occupation of towns and regions. Guerrilla warfare must be developed intensively. "It is our duty," it continued, "to digest the principles of the great Mao Tse-tung's strategy and to make good use of them by adapting them to the circumstances of the moment and place, and taking into account our own situation in the interior of the country."[161] This probably was a warning to Giap from the "pro-Chinese" group. But Giap, anxious to be independent of the Chinese, launched a third offensive against the French in late May in Ninh-Binh province. It ended in June in another bloody defeat; Giap retreated to Viet-Bac for "a period of rest, ideological re-

[159] From September 1950 to May 1954 the Viet-Minh fought the following battles:

Dong-Khe (Sept. 1950)	Hoa-Binh (Nov. 1951-Feb. 1952)
Cao-Bang (Oct. 1950)	Nghia-Lo (Oct. 1952)
Lang-Son (Oct. 1950)	Na-San (Dec. 1952)
Lao-Kay (Nov. 1950)	Sam-Neua (Apr. 1953)
Vinh-Yen (Jan. 1951)	Lai-Chau (Dec. 1953)
Mao-Khe (Mar. 1951)	Dien-Bien-Phu (Mar.-May 1954)
Ninh-Binh (June 1951)	

[160] Edgar O'Ballance, *The Indo-China War, 1945-1954; A Study in Guerrilla Warfare* (London: Faber and Faber, 1964), pp. 141-42.

[161] "One Must Know Strategy," Voice of Vietnam, in Tonkinese to Indochina, May 5, 1951.

moulding, reorganization and military training."[162] The three defeats had cost him more than 9,000 men and forced him back to reevaluate and observe Chinese strategy and advice.

Giap's reevaluation of Mao Tse-tung's military theory ("ideological remoulding") was completed about three months after his third defeat. In an article commemorating the sixth anniversary of North Vietnam's independence (September 2, 1951), he expressed his preference for the Chinese military system (over that of the Soviet Red army): "From the Soviet Red Army, it [the Viet-Minh People's Army] has learned the lesson of proletariat internationalism and tenacious and unshakable loyalty to the people and the people's interest. From the Chinese People's Liberation Army, it has gained a complete system of military thought and a strategy and tactics suitable for colonial and semi-colonial countries. . . . This victory [in defeating the enemy] . . . has important international significance, for it has proved that it is possible in this postwar period . . . to win the armed struggle in the colonial and semi-colonial countries. It has become possible not only in such a vast and populous country as China, but also in such small countries as Korea and Vietnam."[163]

It is significant that after his defeats in the first half of 1951, Giap committed no more strategic mistakes, and boasted no more of a "general counteroffensive."[164] He gradually turned the military tide of the remaining years of the war in his favor.

North Vietnam continued to seek aid from China. In

[162] *Vietnamese Studies*, No. 7, p. 111.

[163] Vo Nguyen Giap (Wu Yuan-chia in Chinese), "The Viet-Minh People's Army Fights for Freedom, Independence and Democracy," *Ta kung pao*, December 22, 23, 24, 1951, tr. *Soviet Press Translations*, Vol. 7, No. 6 (March 15, 1952), p. 170.

[164] It should be noted that it was Nguyen Duy Trinh, then chairman of the Resistance-Administrative Committee of South Central Vietnam and Foreign Minister of Hanoi today (1969), who first pointed out that the fall 1950 offensive was not a general counteroffensive and that the time for such an offensive was not ripe. Voice of South Vietnam, in Cochin-Chinese, November 29, 1950.

November 1950 Ho reportedly was in Nanning for a conference with the Chinese (presumably Generals Ch'en Keng and Chang Yun-i) and Soviet leaders.[165] He brought back the draft of a Chinese—Viet-Minh agreement whereby the Chinese would supply munitions, machine tools, and medicine in exchange for timber and Indochinese rice. A similar agreement was reportedly signed in November 1951.[166] A Viet-Minh defector, Pham Le Bong, who had served with the regime from 1946 to 1952, made known in 1953 that a Viet-Minh–Chinese–Soviet tripartite pact had been concluded in 1951, which provided that China and the Soviet Union would offer the Viet-Minh munitions, technical assistance, and industrial equipment, but would not intervene in the war unless the Viet-Minh was confronted with a situation of grave danger. The former Viet-Minh official also reported that he had seen many high-ranking Chinese and Soviet advisers in Viet-Minh areas.[167] Whether or not the reports were true, none of the agreements, strictly speaking, was a military pact.

Probably the strongest evidence of Chinese aid was the completion of the rail line from Liuchow to Chen-nan-kuan via Nanning in October 1951.[168] Work had begun in September 1950, when an office for the construction of this line was established at Liuchow with approximately 200 engineers and 30,000 workers participating in the project. When completed, the line was the busiest supply route from China to North Vietnam. Nanning became the key city for the forwarding of supplies. Under the direction of the

[165] Saigon Radio, France-Asie, in Cochin-Chinese, November 15, 1950.

[166] *Kung Sheung Daily News*, May 13, 1952.

[167] *Sing Tao jih pao* (*Star Island Daily*, Hong Kong), January 28, 1953; *Le Monde*, January 28, 1953.

[168] According to a leading Chinese transportation official during the war, this rail line, which links with the Hunan-Kwangsi Railroad, was under construction during the Sino-Japanese war. By the autumn of 1939 about 60 per cent of it had been completed. The work, however, was interrupted by the Japanese invasion of Kwangsi. See Kung Hsueh-sui, *Chung-kuo chan shih chiao t'ung shih* (A History of the War-Time Transportation of China) (Shanghai: Commercial Press, 1947), p. 154.

liaison office in Lungchow (later moved to Nanning) centers were established and operated from 1950 to 1954 at Nanning, Chinghsi, Lungchow (in Kwangsi), Tunghsing (Kwangtung), Yulin and Haikow (Hainan Island), Wenshan, Malipo, Hokow, and Kwangnan (Yunnan). In 1950 there were about 20,000 Viet-Minh troops who were trained in these centers. In 1951 and 1952 about 20,000 more were reported. Besides these, there were about 10,000 trained officers, engineers, technicians, political workers, and paratroops.[169] The training surely resulted in fresh and powerful reinforcements for the Viet-Minh army. As the original guerrilla and regional forces advanced to become the regular army, after retraining and reequipping, Giap found new recruits to replace them. By early 1951 the Viet-Minh claimed it already had a regular army of more than 300,000 men and a militia of more than 2,000,000.[170]

The increase in Viet-Minh manpower posed a mounting threat to the French-Vietnamese army, which was forced to recruit more troops for the battlefield. Since "France had lacked the will to draft its own young men for service in Indochina" as Gen. Matthew Ridgway commented,[171] reinforcements became a serious problem, which Giap fully realized. He boasted to an American visitor: "We have captured prisoners of no less than 24 nationalities."[172]

General de Lattre was the ablest general France sent to Indochina. By defeating the Viet-Minh army at Vinh-Yen he saved Hanoi. By winning the battles of Mao-Khe, Ninh-Binh, and Hoa-Binh he took over the offensive from Giap. Even a North Vietnamese account had to admit that he

---

[169] For the training bases and the amount of the trained men, see the *New York Times*, August 3, 13, 1950, June 29, 1951; *Times* (London), March 8, 1951; *Kung Sheung Daily News*, November 21, 23, 1951; March 12, 1952; *Hong Kong shih pao* (*Hong Kong Times*), November 3, 1952; *Wah kiu yat pao* (*Overseas Chinese Daily*), November 23, 1951; *Sing Tao jih pao*, June 14, 1954.

[170] Hsiao Yang, p. 32.

[171] Matthew B. Ridgway, *Soldier: The Memoirs of Matthew B. Ridgway* (New York: Harper, 1956), p. 275.

[172] Joseph R. Starobin, *Eyewitness in Indo-China* (New York: Cameron & Kahn, 1954), p. 70.

was able to restore the east-west corridor, which had been cut off after the 1950 campaign, and gain control of important highways between Viet-Bac and Interzones III and IV. He was "an obstinate and skillful colonial general. In one year he was able to do all that could be done."[173] He was so confident that he said he could defeat the Viet-Minh army in 18 to 24 months if there were no Chinese Communist intervention.[174] But he died in France on January 11, 1952. Six weeks after his death, Giap took Hoa-Binh, although his "human wave" of some 160,000 men was exposed to French air strikes. Not until then was Giap able to say that de Lattre's attempt to regain the initiative in the war had failed.

As pointed out before, Chinese "unconditional aid" to North Vietnam was first admitted by the Viet-Minh radio on January 18, 1952. Though unspecified, it said that the unconditional aid had brought the Viet-Minh continual military victories that changed completely the military situation in its favor. On January 23 the French authorities in Saigon reported that during the preceding four months Communist China had sent to the Viet-Minh 4,000 tons of weapons, including 100,000 hand grenades, 10,000 75mm. shells, 10 million cartridge cases, a large quantity of Russian-made explosives, many 75mm. cannons of Russian and Chinese make, many modern Skoda rifles, and several German-made guns.[175] Robert Guillain also reported in February that after the opening of armistice negotiations in Korea, Peking increased its aid, presumably with light arms, machineguns, mortars, anti-aircraft guns, and ammunition.[176] When the 351st heavy division was fully equipped in 1952, other units of the main force also obtained modern weapons. It was estimated, though without citing sources, that in 1952 the Viet-Minh army received from China: 40,000 rifles, 4,000 submachineguns, 450 mortars, 120 recoilless rifles, 45-50

---

[173] *Vietnamese Studies*, No. 7, pp. 110, 119.
[174] *New York Times*, October 10, 1951.
[175] Radio Saigon, France-Asie, in Cochin-Chinese, January 23, 1952.
[176] *Manchester Guardian*, February 11, 1952.

anti-aircraft guns, and 30-35 field guns.[177] It became apparent in 1952 that Chinese aid now included considerable quantities of European-made weapons. The Viet-Minh made no distinction in receiving aid from helping nations; it had no preference between China and the Soviet Union, but pledged to "follow the example of the Chinese and Soviet peoples" to win its war.[178]

One of the significant activities of the Viet-Minh in requesting Chinese aid was the signing of a "Sino-Vietnamese Goods Exchange Agreement" by Hoang Minh Giam and Chou En-lai in Peking in July 1952. According to this accord China would supply North Vietnam with military and medical equipment, machine tools and daily supplies in exchange for Vietnamese timber and agricultural products. A "Sino-Vietnamese Control Committee for Goods Exchange" was to be established, with Teng Tzu-hui (Chinese) as chairman and Hoang Quoc Viet and Vo Van Giam as vice-chairmen, to supervise the shipment of goods. Twelve transportation teams were to be organized for the shipment under the direction of the control committee.[179] In March 1953 the Viet-Minh ambassador, Hoang Van Hoan, negotiated with Peking for a supplement to the agreement, signed in May, which provided for two important items— more Chinese aid to support the Viet-Minh's autumn offensive in 1953, and permission to send wounded Viet-Minh soldiers to China for treatment.[180] This goods exchange agreement was renewed in 1954 with an increase in quantities. Judging from the fact that North Vietnam's trade with China began in 1951 and increased four times by 1954, and that goods exchange agreements have been signed with China and the Soviet Union almost every year,[181] *this* agreement and its predecessors, reportedly signed by Hoang Quoc Viet in 1950 and by Ho Chi Minh

[177] O'Ballance, *Indo-China War*, p. 171.

[178] Voice of South Vietnam, in Cochin-Chinese, February 14, 1952.

[179] Sixth Section of the KMT, pp. 16-17.

[180] *Ibid.*, p. 18.

[181] For instance, similar agreements with the Soviet Union and Communist China were signed in December 1964, 1965, and 1966.

in 1951, were nothing but trade accords, which could well be the "Sino-Vietnamese military pact" reported by the French and by Hong Kong in 1950 and 1951. If there were any Sino-Vietnamese pact or treaty during the Indochinese war, it must have been this goods exchange agreement, "economic-cultural" protocol, or other accords of a similar nature, but not a military alliance pact. It should be pointed out, however, that trade from 1951 to 1954 based on goods exchange agreements was in return for more Chinese military equipment, while those after 1954 were for more common goods and commodities.

The Chinese Communist army did not plunge into Indochina as it had in Korea, but it did send advisers, technicians, and medical service men. In June 1951 the Chinese contingent was estimated at 4,000 to 6,000,[182] and in 1952 at 7,000 to 8,000.[183] In addition, 1,000 medical service men were sent to Vietnam in September 1952, and more were recruited in 1953 and 1954, although the exact number is not known.[184] Secretary of State Dean Acheson reported on March 20, 1952 that there were "Chinese nationals" with the Viet-Minh in the war, but gave no details. A report from *Le Monde*, November 10, 1952, said Chinese officers in the Viet-Minh army were estimated at 3,000 to 4,000, including three or four generals. At the end of 1952 a document was found which indicated that the Chinese Communists were sending "troops" and political workers to North Vietnam;[185] no figure was given. If this captured document is correct, the "troops" sent by China must have been in the category of medical service men, truck drivers, radio operators, and "Kung ping" (construction-work soldiers). At the battle of Dien-Bien-Phu Chinese officers, technicians,

---

[182] *New York Times*, June 29, 1951.

[183] Hanson W. Baldwin, in *New York Times*, March 27, 1952. Richard P. Stebbins, in his *The United States in World Affairs, 1954* (New York: Harper, 1956), p. 217, estimates about 2,000.

[184] *Sing tao jih pao*, September 13, 1952; *Kung Sheung Daily News*, June 10, October 30, 1953; February 10, 1954.

[185] "Handbook for Political Workers Going to Vietnam, December 1952," in Cole, *Conflict*, pp. 125-30.

artillerymen, and gun men (anti-aircraft guns) were believed to be with the Viet-Minh army.

From the fall of 1952 to the spring of 1953 the Viet-Minh won battles in Nghia-Lo, Na-San, and Sam-Neua. The Viet-Minh victory in Sam-Neua province of Laos was solid evidence of its invasion of Laos. The Viet-Minh radio repeatedly broadcast that "the Lao-Vietnamese troops attacked and liberated Sam Neua," that "Sam Neua is the first province to be liberated in Laos," and that "this victory is due to the patriotism of the Vietnamese forces" and the Laotian people.[186] The invasion was denied by Pham Van Dong at the Geneva Conference, who, nevertheless, was finally persuaded to give in by Chou En-lai (see next chapter).

When the truce in Korea became a reality in the spring of 1953, not only the French but the new Eisenhower administration were worried that the armistice might release Chinese forces for service in Indochina.[187] To reinforce the speculation Wellington Koo, the Chinese Nationalist ambassador at the United Nations, reported in early May the conclusion of a Soviet–Chinese–Viet-Minh agreement providing that Communist China would send 300,000 troops to North Vietnam, and Russia would supply weapons for five divisions.[188] *Pravda* immediately denied the report;[189] Peking denounced it as a KMT–American fabrication. Chinese troops were not used in Vietnam, but Chinese aid greatly increased.

It was reported that in the summer of 1953 the rail shipment from North China to Chen-nan-kuan was active, that river transportation from Canton to Wuchow and then to Vietnam was intensified, and that the newly constructed airports in Nanning, Lungchow, and Lang-Son were opened for traffic, with 20 to 30 Soviet-made transport planes operating out of them.[190] The flow of war materiel alarmed

[186] Voice of Nambo, in Cochin-Chinese, April 20, 1953; Voice of Nambo, in Cambodian, April 21, 1953.

[187] Halle, *Cold War*, p. 289.

[188] *New York Herald Tribune*, May 7, 1953.

[189] See McLane, *Soviet Strategies*, p. 440.

[190] Radio Taipei, June 11, 1953; Radio Saigon, France-Asie, in

the French military authorities, who ordered large-scale air strikes on the Vietnamese border. General Hsiao Ke was reported to have been sent to Cao-Bang to head a 228-member Chinese military group in charge of assisting the training and organization of the Viet-Minh army. A "Sino-Vietnamese Economic-Cultural Agreement" was signed by Hsiao Ke, which provided that Peking would help the Viet-Minh develop economic and cultural affairs. Moreover, Peking's military council sent Gen. Li Tien-yu, then chief-of-staff of the Kwangsi Military Zone, to confer with Vo Nguyen Giap at Nanning from October 17 to 20, 1953; they reached an agreement on the shipment of war supplies and protecting the Lang-Son airfield.[191] Gen. Li Tien-yu was put in charge of Vietnamese military affairs by the military council in 1954, and visited North Vietnam in 1962 with Marshal Yeh Chien-ying.

The routes for shipping war materiel were overland and by sea. The land route had three lines—a highway from Tunghsing to Mon-Kay (Mon-Cay); a rail line from Nanning to Chen-nan-kuan, then by truck to Dong-Dang, from there to Lang-Son (south), and to Cao-Bang (north); and a rail line from Kunming, Hokow to Lao-Ky. In late 1953 and early 1954 a special road was built from Mengtse (Yunnan) via Lai-Chau to the Dien-Bien-Phu area. The sea route included a line from Yulin and Haikow ports (Hainan Island), a line from Ch'in-chow-wan (Yian-chow-wan), and a line from Wei-chow-tao. Shipments by sea went to the Viet-Minh areas near Haiphong, Nghe-An, Quang-Tri, Quang-Ngai and Da-Nang.[192] The most important route was the railroad from Chen-nan-kuan to North Vietnam, which operated on a 24-hour basis.

Estimates of the precise quantity of Chinese aid have

English Morse, June 14, 1953; Radio Taipei, June 30, 1953; Radio Saigon, in Tonkinese, July 2, 1953; Voice of Free China, Taipei, in Mandarin, July 31, 1953.

[191] Sixth Section of the KMT, pp. 19-20.

[192] *Ibid.*, pp. 18-19.

varied.[193] In 1951 it was unofficially estimated to have averaged 300 to 500 tons per month. In 1952, after the Nanning-Chennankuan rail line was opened, it was increased to about 1,500 tons.[194] In 1953 it was estimated by the French authorities to have increased to about 3,000 tons; and in early 1954, it mounted to about 4,000 tons per month.[195] The supplies were mainly Chinese-made,[196] but also included Soviet, Czechoslovak, and Hungarian products. American-made arms were found as well. Soviet trucks and weapons, presumably from China, were first found in late November 1952 at Phu-Tho, a Viet-Minh supply center.

While Chinese aid to the Viet-Minh was essential, American aid to French Indochina became indispensable. It was estimated and reported that American military and economic aid to Indochina reached about $119 million in 1951, $300 million in 1952, $500 million in 1953 (including a special grant of $385 million), and $1 billion in 1954. Up to July 1954 the total was approximately $2.2 billion, of which $1.1 billion had been delivered.[197] Interestingly, the amount of

[193] The sources used here are carefully selected. An estimate given by a RAND Corporation researcher (George K. Tanham, *Communist Revolutionary Warfare*, pp. 68-69) seems conservative. His estimate is: 1951, about 10 to 20 tons per month; 1952, about 250 tons; 1953, 400 to 600 tons; 1954, 1,500 to 4,000 tons.

[194] *Manchester Guardian*, February 11, 1952; *New York Times*, November 25, 1952, *Kung sheung Daily News*, March 29, 1952.

[195] Robert Guillain, *La Fin des Illusions* (Paris: Centre d'Etudes de Politique Etrangere, 1954), p. 41. General Salan estimated over 3,000 tons per month in 1953. See also *Sing tao jih pao*, July 15, 1953, February 26, 1954; Sixth Section of the KMT, p. 19; Lancaster, *Emancipation of French Indochina*, p. 255.

[196] Apart from the Southwest Arsenal in Kunming, two arsenals in Canton were also set in operation in 1951, producing mainly grenades, rifles, machine guns and other light arms for the Viet-Minh.

[197] U.S. Congress, Senate, Committee on Foreign Relations, *Indochina: Report of Senator Mike Mansfield on a Study Mission to the Associated States of Indochina*, 83d Congress, 1st Session, October 27, 1953, pp. 4-5; *New York Times*, February 16, May 23, July 5, August 2, 1954; William Adams Brown, Jr. and Redvers Opie, *American Foreign Assistance* (Brookings Institution, 1953), pp. 495-96.

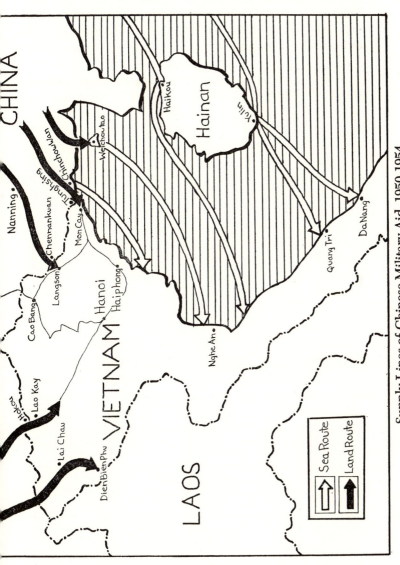

Supply Lines of Chinese Military Aid, 1950-1954

American aid during the period August 1950 to January 1952 exceeded the total amount of Chinese aid to the Viet-Minh in 3½ years (January 1951-June 1954). American aid was reported to total 100,000 tons;[198] Chinese aid was estimated at only 82,000.[199]

[198] *New York Times*, January 29, 1952.
[199] My estimate of the figure is based on the above-mentioned tonnage of Chinese aid.

6. The Geneva Settlement, 1954

‹‹

> "The Geneva Conference has demonstrated to the whole world that the use of force to settle international disputes is fruitless and that the age of settling international disputes by negotiation is definitely here to stay."
> — *Jen min jih pao*, July 22, 1954

> "We wish the brilliant leader of the Chinese people, the glorious sun of the Asian people, Chairman Mao Tse-tung, a long life!"
> — Pham Van Dong, at the Vietnamese embassy's reception in Peking, August 3, 1954

WAR IS the continuation of politics in a different form, and all wars end by negotiations. The Indochinese war was no exception. In view of the peace talks in Paris concerning a settlement for Vietnam, a study of the Geneva accord of 1954 should be more meaningful if it is directed to probe why the Viet-Minh came to the negotiation table and how the settlement was reached, rather than merely to restate the facts of the conference at Geneva. Such an examination involves a few questions: Did the Viet-Minh come to negotiations originally on its own initiative, or under international pressure? Was there a policy debate on peace talks within the Viet-Minh? What was its strategy for negotiation? An investigation of these questions will enable us to understand the international implications of the 1954 Geneva settlement. And an understanding of the past will help us to evaluate the present Vietnam situation, because in Vietnam, as two students of Vietnam suggest, "past is present."[1]

1. NORTH VIETNAM COMES TO THE CONFERENCE TABLE

Despite the fact that Ho Chi Minh repeatedly urged the French to discuss peace in 1946-1947, and that the leftist

[1] George McT. Kahin and John W. Lewis, *The United States in Vietnam* (New York: Delta, 1967), p. 325.

deputies in the French National Assembly demanded peace with Vietnam in January 1950, there were no peace moves. From 1950 to early 1953 Giap's army won several battles. North Vietnam, with Chinese aid, intensified its campaigns for progress in various aspects, aiming at a "final victory" over the French, while the French girded themselves with American equipment for further military action. No peace talks were even suggested.

An analysis of Communist periodicals and broadcasts of 1953-1954 in Bucharest, Moscow, Peking, and North Vietnam suggests that during March 6 to 28, 1953 Moscow must have made a decision or agreement with some world Communist leaders on relaxing international tension. It was this decision/agreement that developed into the armistice in Korea and the Geneva settlement for Indochina—the "thaw" of the post-Stalin period. In support of this contention I have included a selected chronology of the peace campaign below to highlight the developments from March 1953 to April 1954 that led the Viet-Minh to the Geneva Conference:

1953

MARCH 5   Stalin dies.

MARCH 29   The World Peace Council makes an appeal to the governments of five powers (the United States, the Soviet Union, Britain, France, and Communist China), suggesting that a peace pact be reached (no such appeal before March).

MARCH 30   Chou En-lai proposes to resume immediately the negotiations for a cease-fire in Korea.

APRIL 1   Kim Il Sung and Molotov agree and support Chou En-lai's proposal.

APRIL 6   Negotiations at Panmunjom resumed.

MAY-DEC.   Almost every issue of *For a Lasting Peace, For a People's Democracy* carry news items (sometimes editorials) on "peace pact" or "peaceful settlement of international problems." A strong peace negotiations campaign is under way.

The Geneva Settlement, 1954

MAY-JULY Almost every issue of *Jen min jih pao* carries news and editorials about Korean armistice negotiations or a peaceful settlement of international problems. *Pravda* sometimes runs editorials on a peaceful settlement of international issues.

MAY 7 World Peace Council issues a communiqué strongly urging negotiations to settle international problems.

MAY 22 *For a Lasting Peace, For a People's Democracy* carries an editorial supporting the appeal of the World Peace Council.

MAY 24 *Pravda* prints an editorial supporting the appeal of the World Peace Council.

MAY 31 *Jen min jih pao* runs an editorial supporting *Pravda's* editorial of May 24.

JUNE 20 The World Peace Council, meeting in Budapest, issues a declaration and appeal again urging a peaceful settlement of international differences and disputes.

JULY 27 Armistice in Korea signed.

JULY 28 *Jen min jih pao* carries an editorial on the armistice in Korea, advocating that it is possible to settle other international disputes by peaceful means. *Pravda* publishes a similar editorial.

JULY 31 Editorial in *For a Lasting Peace, For a People's Democracy* on the armistice in Korea urges further peace negotiations to settle international disputes.

SEPT. 2 Dulles speaks in St. Louis: "We want peace in Indochina also . . . if Red China wants it. . . . The United States would welcome such a development."

SEPT. 19 Malenkov speaks in the Kremlin urging the peace-loving people to transform the armistice in Korea into a starting point for further lessening of international tension in the world, including the East.

SEPT. 28 The Soviet government suggests the convening of a five-power conference to examine measures for lessening international tension and a four-power conference on the German issue.

OCT. 8 Chou En-lai issues a statement endorsing the Soviet proposal for a five-power conference.

Oct. 23　The leftists in the French National Assembly urge their government to negotiate with Ho Chi Minh.

Oct. 27　French Premier Laniel speaks in the National Assembly, and says that Ho Chi Minh does not seem to agree to the reestablishment of peace in Indochina, but the French government is ready to make peace.

Nov. 23　Le Dinh Tham, North Vietnam's chief delegate to the meeting of the World Peace Council at Vienna, says the Vietnamese have advocated peace negotiations to end the Indochinese war.

Nov. 26　Ho replies to the Swedish newspaper *Expressen*, that he is willing to negotiate with the French on the Indochinese war.

Dec. 7　At the Bermuda conference President Eisenhower, Prime Minister Churchill, and Premier Joseph Laniel decide to discuss the issues of Germany, Australia, and Indochina with the Soviet Union at the foreign-minister level.

Dec. 17　Ho reiterates his willingness to negotiate with the French for a peaceful settlement of the Vietnam problem.

Dec. 18 and 19　Peking holds a rally to mark "International Day of Solidarity with the People of Vietnam." The Peking press the following day urges peace talks on Vietnam. The Moscow press carries a similar theme.

Dec. 25　*For a Lasting Peace, For a People's Democracy* says: "World Public Opinion Demands End to War in Vietnam."

1954:

Jan. 25　The Berlin conference opens.

Feb. 19　The Berlin conference ends and issues a communiqué suggesting the convening of a five-power conference in Geneva with the participation of nations concerned about the peaceful settlement of the Korean problem and the restoration of peace in Indochina.

Feb. 26 and March 4　Editorials in *Nhan Dan* support the proposal for convening the Geneva Conference.

APRIL 30 Ho appoints Pham Van Dong to lead the Viet-
Minh delegation to the Geneva Conference.

MAY 7 Dien-Bien-Phu is taken by the Viet-Minh army.

MAY 8 Geneva Conference on Indochina opens.

The chronology suggests that prior to Stalin's death there
was no significant move for peace negotiations from the
Communist camp, although armistice talks in Korea had
begun in July 1951. After Stalin's death, the peace movement gained momentum. Apparently it was Stalin's uncom-
municative position on Korea that prevented a Korean
cease-fire from materializing.[2] It was probably in mid-
March, when a plenary session of the central committee of
the Soviet Communist Party was held in Moscow, that
Soviet leaders decided to start a new peace campaign. On
March 30, four days after his return from Stalin's funeral,
Chou En-lai proposed resuming armistice negotiations in
Korea immediately. Then the Panmunjom talks promptly
resumed, and reached the first agreement (on the exchange
of sick and wounded prisoners) on April 11.

Speculation that the initiative in the peace movement
came from the new Kremlin leaders was supported by other
evidence. A few days after Chou En-lai's proposal for peace
talks on Korea, almost every Communist country endorsed
the proposal; North Vietnam did not. Malenkov's speech
before the Supreme Soviet in April, which suggested that
controversial international problems be settled by peaceful
means, encouraged *Pravda* (April 25) and *Jen min jih pao*
(April 29) to push the new campaign for peaceful settlement of international disputes and the Korean war. The
appeal of the World Peace Council for peace negotiations
was supported by the Cominform journal (May 22), *Pravda*
(May 24), and *Jen min jih pao* (May 31). Peking even went
so far as to say that peace negotiations were the "only way"

[2] Harold C. Hinton suggests that there was a strong possibility
that Stalin in February 1953 was planning for a general war and was
killed by his aides who were opposed to his war plan. *Communist
China in World Politics* (Boston: Houghton Mifflin, 1966), p. 227.

to settle international problems and the Korean war.[3] A worldwide campaign for peace negotiations was well underway. Communist nations publicly endorsed the campaign except Yugoslavia, which was at odds with Russia, and North Vietnam which was, presumably, not ready to respond.

The drive for peace negotiations initiated by the Communist camp in early 1953 was announced by the World Peace Council after its meeting in Budapest, June 15-20, 1953:

> The events of *recent months* have convinced the people that settlement of all international differences by peaceful means is possible of attainment. . . . .
>
> It is on these grounds that the World Peace Council *has decided to launch* a world-wide campaign for negotiations.[4]

In more succinct but strong language the council, on the same occasion, published an appeal asking international help in advancing the peace drive:

> A great hope has been born. Everybody now sees that agreement is possible. The slaughter can be ended. The cold war can be stopped.
>
> In this hour we solemnly call upon the peoples to demand of their governments that they negotiate and agree.
>
> It is for us all to support every move—from whatsoever government it may come—to solve disputes by peaceful means. It is for us all to frustrate the efforts of those who prevent or delay agreement. . . .[5]

Among the various Communist editorials about the council's peace drive, the most significant was that of the Comin-

[3] "The Only Way to Settle the Present International Problems," editorial, *Jen min jih pao*, May 31, 1953.

[4] Emphasis added. Declaration of the World Peace Council, June 20, 1953, in *For a Lasting Peace, For a People's Democracy*, June 26, 1953.

[5] Appeal of the WPC, June 20, 1953, in *ibid*.

form journal, which instructed the Communist and Workers' Parties to carry out the appeal: "The duty of the Communist and Workers' Parties is to act as initiators in building this unity in town and countryside, in factory and office, in houses and city blocks. The duty of the Party propagandist and agitators of the Communist and democratic press is to give the maximum support to the international campaign for negotiations."[6]

It became apparent that the Cominform intended to transform the peace movement from a drive of an international front organization (WPC) to a "duty" of the world Communist and Workers' Parties. The Cominform's call was undoubtedly also for the Vietnam Lao Dong Party, although the party was not a member of the Cominform. But North Vietnam did not respond immediately.

The signing of the armistice in Korea was welcomed by the Soviet Union, China, North Korea, Outer Mongolia, and the European Communist countries. Editorials in *Pravda* and *Jen min jih pao* on July 28 reiterated the thesis that "there is no international dispute that cannot be settled through negotiations." But no similar editorial or broadcast came from North Vietnam. Even in his greetings to Mao Tse-tung on the armistice, Ho Chi Minh merely stated that "the Vietnamese people are boundlessly delighted" over the news of the ending of the Korean war, that "this is a great victory of the Korean people, the Chinese Volunteer Army, and the world peace-democratic camp."[7] No mention was made of a possible peaceful settlement for the Indochinese war. In both articles by Din (probably Ho Chi Minh) and by Pham Van Dong, which appeared in the Cominform journal in August and September, Vietnamese leaders were concerned only about their growing military might and their greater determination "to drive the French" out of

[6] "Negotiations—Way to Peaceful Settlement of International Problems," Editorial, *For a Lasting Peace, For a People's Democracy,* July 10, 1953.

[7] *Jen min jih pao,* August 4, 1953.

Indochina.[8] In a message on September 2, Ho urged his army and people to fight for a "final victory."

No matter how remote, however, rumors and hopes for a peaceful settlement in Indochina came first from Paris. Immediately after the signing of the Korean armistice French leftists asked why their government could not negotiate with Ho for peace as the United States had with Kim Il Sung.[9] The Laniel government hoped armistice negotiations with North Vietnam could be arranged.[10]

The warning given by Secretary of State Dulles on September 2, against Communist China's intervention in the Indochinese war was not a factor in attempting to prevent the Chinese Communists from entering the war, since Peking had already decided to adopt a soft-line policy in international affairs. But Dulles' statement about a peaceful settlement in Indochina encouraged Laniel's search for peace with Ho.[11] There were encouraging developments in Moscow. On September 19 Malenkov spoke at a dinner honoring Kim Il Sung's delegation. Malenkov stressed that the peace-loving people of the world "can and must transform the armistice in Korea into a starting point for fresh efforts for the further lessening of the international tension throughout the world, including the East." The Cominform journal immediately echoed the statement.[12] Vyshinsky, the Soviet's delegate to the United Nations, introduced in the General Assembly on September 21 a resolution designed to avert a new world war. He emphasized that the cessation of hostilities in Korea was an important contribution to the reduction of international tension, and that armaments and

[8] Din, "We Are Sure of Final Victory," *For a Lasting Peace, For a People's Democracy*, August 21, 1953; and Pham Van Dong, "People of Vietnam Will Win Final Victory in Struggle for Freedom and National Independence," *ibid.*, September 11, 1953.

[9] *Chronicle*, p. 59.

[10] Joseph Laniel, *Le Drame Indochinois: De Dien-Bien-Phu au Pari de Genève* (Paris: Plon, 1957), p. 17.

[11] *New York Times*, September 3, 1953. Laniel on October 27 referred to Dulles' speech on a peace settlement in Indochina.

[12] "For Final Peaceful Settlement of Korean Question," editorial, *For a Lasting Peace, For a People's Democracy*, September 25, 1953.

propaganda among the major powers must be reduced or ended in order to avert the threat of a new war.[13] More significantly, the Soviet proposal on September 28 for a five-power conference to examine measures for lessening international tension was favorably received in the Communist camp and in the West. In a statement issued on October 8, Chou En-lai fully endorsed the Soviet proposal and raised the issues of a Communist Chinese seat in the U.N. and easing international tension in the Far East: ". . . without the participation of the People's Republic of China, it is impossible to settle many major international questions, above all the questions of Asia. Therefore, the United Nations . . . must first restore the legitimate rights of the People's Republic of China [in the United Nations]. The . . . government of the People's Republic of China . . . is constantly striving for the over-all easing of international tension so as to consolidate peace in the Far East and throughout the world."[14]

The following day *Jen min jih pao's* editorial hailed Chou's statement and supported the convening of a five-power conference; so did an editorial in *World Culture*.[15] In view of the fact that there was a 10-day interval between the Soviet proposal and Chou's statement, the Peking leaders must have held a policy meeting to decide on an endorsement of the Soviet suggestion. Undoubtedly, about this time Peking decided to further moderate its already soft line to a conciliatory policy toward the West, with admission to the U.N., settlement of Taiwan, and a possible peaceful settlement for Indochina in mind. The policy lasted until 1959, when Peking provoked the border dispute with India.

The Cominform journal continued to press the campaign for peace negotiations. It must have whipped up many

[13] United Nations, *General Assembly, Eighth Session, Official Records, 438th Plenary Meeting*, September 21, 1953, pp. 51-61.

[14] NCNA, Peking, October 8, 1953.

[15] "Support the Convention of a Five-Power Conference of Foreign Ministers," *World Culture*, October 18, 1953, No. 20, p. 3.

Communists and leftists in non-Communist countries to participate in the drive. In late October the French National Assembly debated the Indochinese war again, and the leftist delegates demanded that their government negotiate with Ho, a demand that bore fruit. On October 27, in his reply to the Assembly, Premier Laniel discussed the views of various world leaders on easing tension in the Far East, and declared his willingness to negotiate for peace in Indochina: "Is it necessary for me to say what France thinks? Who among us would object to the idea of negotiations, in an international framework, in order to reestablish peace in Indochina? Unhappily, there is someone who does not seem to be in agreement, it is Ho Chi Minh, it is the general staff of the Viet Minh. . . . My government is ready to seize all occasions to make peace, whether in Indochina or on the international level. . . ."[16]

After an all night session the National Assembly adopted a resolution, 315-251, upholding Laniel's policy of searching for "peace in Asia by negotiation," but insisting on the independence of the Associated States in Indochina, "within the structure of the French Union." It must be noted that in 1948 there were only five non-Communists in the Assembly who voted against the war in Indochina; in October 1953, 151 non-Communist members voted against it[17] (a pattern that seems to have been followed by American Congressmen from 1964 to 1968 on the Vietnam war).

Laniel repeated his views to the Assembly on November 12. "I must repeat in the clearest and most categorical fashion," he said, "that the French Government does not consider the Indochinese problem as necessarily requiring a military solution." "If an honorable solution were in view," he added, "France, I repeat, like the United States in Korea,

[16] *Journal Office*, Assemblée Nationale, October 27, 1953, p. 4,606, in Hammer, *Struggle for Indochina*, p. 312; a similar translation is in Cole, *Conflict*, pp. 137-38.

[17] *Chronicle*, pp. 63-64; a similar report was made by *New York Times*, November 28, 1953.

would be happy to welcome a diplomatic solution to the conflict."[18]

It was probably about this time that the Soviet Union decided to place the Indochinese war and the Korean problem, rather than general international issues, on the agenda of the proposed five-power conference. At a press conference November 13, Molotov reiterated the necessity of Communist China's participation in such a meeting, and said that no one could seriously talk about the settlement of pressing international problems without involving the United States and Communist China.[19] On November 18 an editorial in *Jen min jih pao* supported Molotov's views and reiterated Chou En-lai's statement of October 8: "It is impossible to solve pressing international questions without the participation of China with her population of several hundred millions. The Chinese people have proved themselves a mighty force in the preservation of world peace. They have every justification to demand the restoration of their legitimate rights in international affairs."[20]

While Moscow and Peking were in agreement on a high-level conference, their emphasis was different. To Moscow, China's participation in the meeting was necessary for the *settlement* of international problems; whether or not China was a big power, was secondary. To Peking, it was necessary because China's "mighty force" as a *big* power deserved such participation; whether international issues could be settled, was not primary. This difference in approach was displayed at the Geneva Conference in 1954, and has grown much greater since.

North Vietnam's response to the campaign for peace negotiations finally came from its chief delegate, Le Dinh Tham, to the World Peace Council, which was meeting in Vienna from November 23-28, 1953. In his speech at the

[18] As cited in Hammer, *Struggle for Indochina*; also see *Chronicle*, p. 64.

[19] *Jen min jih pao*, November 15, 1953.

[20] "Support the Statement of Foreign Minister Molotov," editorial, *Jen min jih pao*, November 18, 1953.

opening session, Tham declared: ". . . The Korean War had already ended on the basis of peaceful negotiations. To stop the Vietnam war through peaceful negotiations is completely necessary and also possible. We Vietnam people long for peace, and we stand for an end to the Vietnam war and peaceful settlement of the Vietnam question by means of peaceful negotiations. . . . this is the common wish of the peoples all over the world, and also in the interest of both the Vietnamese and French peoples."[21]

The Peking delegation to the conference, led by Kuo Mo-jo, endorsed Tham's statement. But as Tham stated, the Vietnamese people's support for a peaceful settlement of the Vietnam war was primarily due to the "common wish of the peoples all over the world," and not because of Vietnam's initiative in search of peace. Thus the influence of the WPC's peace campaign on the Viet-Minh proposal became apparent. In a general resolution of November 28, the WPC made this point clear: "The Budapest Appeal for negotiations, launched by the World Peace Council, has had profound repercussions and has won the widest support. . . . The idea of ending hostilities and reaching a peaceful solution in Indochina is making progress both in France and in Vietnam. . . . The World Peace Council welcomes the proposal made in this direction by the delegation of the Democratic Republic of Vietnam and supported by the delegation of the Chinese People's Republic. This proposal . . . could serve as a basis for a settlement."[22]

Immediately after the Vienna conference of the WPC, Peking began an open campaign for peace negotiations in Vietnam. On November 29 Radio Peking accused the United States of being openly opposed to a peaceful settlement in Vietnam while the Vietnamese people, the French people, and peace-loving people in the rest of the world, "are demanding an end to the war by peaceful negotia-

[21] NCNA, Peking (from Vienna, November 23, 1953), English Morse, November 26, 1953; also *Jen min jih pao*, November 27, 1953.
[22] "General Resolution of World Peace Council," in *For a Lasting Peace, For a People's Democracy*, December 4, 1953.

tions."[23] This peace campaign gained momentum when Ho publicized the following day his willingness to negotiate with the French.

In view of the background to peace negotiations discussed thus far, it seems logical that Ho's reply to the newspaper *Expressen* on November 26, 1953, on his willingness to negotiate, was not coincidental or an isolated case, but a new development in the peace campaign. In its questions, the Swedish newspaper referred to the debate in the French National Assembly on a settlement in Vietnam through peace negotiations. In his reply, Ho asked for a genuine French "respect" for the independence of Vietnam as the basis for peaceful settlement.[24] On December 1 *Jen min jih pao* published the full text of Ho's reply and carried an editorial endorsing Ho's proposal. On December 12 the Vietnam News Agency (DRV) interpreted Ho's statement and reaffirmed Vietnam's readiness to negotiate if the French government would respect the independence of Vietnam and wished to put an end to the war.[25] In his message to the Vietnamese people and army on the seventh anniversary of the resistance war (December 19, 1953), Ho repeated his proposal and conveyed his "cordial greetings to the French people"[26]—the same way he did so to the American people in his New Year statement of 1968. On the evening of December 18 Peking held a rally to mark "International Day of Solidarity" with the Vietnamese people, at which the Chinese speaker Liu Ning-i (vice-president of the All-China Federation of Trade Unions) and Vietnamese Le Dinh Tham (chairman of the Vietnam Peace Committee), stressed that the peace-loving people of the world "demanded" a peaceful settlement for Vietnam. Tham said further that Ho's reply to *Expressen* was "in perfect conformity with the demand of the world peace

[23] Radio Peking, in English Morse, November 29, 1953.
[24] Radio Peking, in English Morse to Southeast Asia, Europe, and North America, November 30, 1953.
[25] *Ibid.*, December 14, 1953.
[26] NCNA, Peking (from VNA), December 17, 1953.

movement for the easing of international tension."[27] The next day all of Peking's newspapers carried either news items or editorials or both, praising the Vietnamese heroic struggle and supporting Ho's proposal. The day of solidarity with the Vietnamese people was observed throughout China.[28]

While the Cominform journal in December-January of 1953-1954 intensified its campaign for an "end to war in Vietnam" and a "peaceful settlement of international problems," *Pravda* joined in the call for peace.[29] It appears that at the end of 1953 and in early 1954, the peace movement for Vietnam reached its peak. Although the campaign was originally sponsored by the Cominform, Peking seemed to express a stronger interest in ending the Vietnam war than Moscow did. On January 18, 1954, at a reception at the North Vietnam embassy in Peking, to celebrate the fourth anniversary of the establishment of Sino-Vietnamese diplomatic relations, Soviet ambassador Yudin praised "the struggle of the Vietnamese people for independence and freedom," while Chou En-lai stressed "the desire of all peace-loving people" in the world for "the prompt ending of the war of aggression in Vietnam."[30]

The Berlin Four-Power conference opened January 25, 1954. Just before the conference, the Soviet Foreign Minister Molotov offered French Foreign Minister Georges Bidault the good offices of his government in arranging an armistice in Indochina in exchange for French withdrawal from the European Defense Community (EDC). Bidault, though firm in his stand on EDC, wanted the Soviet assistance in arranging a peace talk with the Viet-Minh, with the understanding that Secretary of State Dulles would not be cast aside.[31] On the second day of the conference Bidault

[27] NCNA, Peking, December 19, 1953.
[28] *Ibid.*, December 20, 1953.
[29] See *New York Times*, December 14, 1953, January 6, 1954.
[30] *Daily News Release* (Peking), January 19, 1954, as cited in Shen-yu Dai, "Peking and Indochina's Destiny," *Western Political Quarterly* (September 1954), pp. 363-64.
[31] *New York Times*, February 6, 1954.

met privately with Molotov, who made the same offer for Indochina.[32] The conference ended on February 18 without any results on either the reunification of Germany or an Austrian treaty. But, the four foreign ministers agreed on Molotov's proposal for a five-power conference to be held in Geneva in April. Dulles, however, insisted that Communist China not be included among the "inviting" nations; it was understood that "neither the invitation to, nor the holding of, the above-mentioned conference shall be deemed to imply diplomatic recognition in any case where it has not already been accorded."[33] Dulles clarified the United States' position when he returned home. He said that the Chinese Communist regime would not come to Geneva, "to be honored by us, but rather to account before the bar of world opinion" for her intervention in the Korean and Indochinese wars.

The Berlin conference issued a communiqué on February 19 formally suggesting convening a five-power conference in Geneva on Korea and Indochina, with the participation of the nations concerned. *Pravda* praised the success of the Berlin conference; *Jen min jih pao* commented that the holding of the future Geneva conference would ease international tensions, and believed that the Indochinese war could truly be settled by peaceful negotiations. The Cominform journal said on February 26 that the five-power conference would "undoubtedly contribute" to the "establishment of peace in Indochina." And *Nhan Dan*, on February 26, praised the holding of the Geneva Conference as a victory for world peace and democracy. From then to the opening of the conference, the press and radio of North Vietnam frequently carried editorials, commentaries, and news items on peace and the scheduled Geneva conference.[34] On April

[32] *Ibid.*, February 12, 1954.

[33] *Documents on American Foreign Relations, 1954* ed. Peter V. Curl (New York: Harper, 1955), p. 219.

[34] For instance, *Nhan Dan*, March 4, 1954; Voice of Vietnam, March 12, 1954; Vietnam News Agency, March 21, 1954; Voice of Vietnam, April 5, 1954; VNA, April 15, 1954; *Quan Doi Nhan Dan*

30 Ho appointed Pham Van Dong as acting foreign minister, replacing Hoang Minh Giam, to lead the Viet-Minh delegation to Geneva. On May 8 the Geneva Conference on Indochina opened. As the situation developed, North Vietnam appeared to be a strong supporter of peace talks, while the United States was accused of being the "saboteur" of the conference.[35]

The discussion thus far is intended to make one point: North Vietnam's coming to the Geneva conference table and the peaceful settlement of the Indochinese war were not initiated by North Vietnam, but by the Cominform and by Moscow. Although the peace campaign for Vietnam after Stalin's death was so remote and slow in coming, once it gained momentum it became a powerful movement which neither North Vietnam nor the United States could resist. The significance of the development lies in the indication of the dependency of North Vietnam's foreign policy on Moscow and Peking and in the influence of the campaign of the Communist camp on the Western Allies. Moreover, as the Geneva conference demonstrated, once peace negotiations started there was a good chance of reaching a settlement. This was further proven by the Geneva conference on Laos in 1961-1962.

IN NORTH VIETNAM there may have been debates on negotiations before or after Ho's reply to the Swedish newspaper, yet no evidence of such has been found. Two factors must have been dominant in North Vietnam's decision on peace negotiations: world pressure for a peace movement; and Ho's leadership. After 1950, as the Vietnamese resistance war went well, Ho's position as chief of the party and the state was strengthened. If there were hawkish Viet-Minh members in favor of all-out war for "final" and "total" victory, Ho's prestige and persuasion must have convinced

as broadcast by Voice of Vietnam, April 20, 1954; Voice of Vietnam, April 21, 1954; VNA, April 22, 1954; *Nhan Dan*, April 23, 1954.
[35] *Nhan Dan*'s editorial: "Expose the Saboteur of the Geneva Conference," in NCNA (North Vietnam), April 23, 1954.

them that a peaceful settlement was the desire of the "world" and would serve the interests of Vietnam. This, in turn, mirrored the stability of Ho's leadership at the time. One observation can be made, however. Militant Viet-Minh leaders such as Vo Nguyen Giap must have prevailed in contending that a military victory was necessary for a strong Viet-Minh position in future negotiations. Consequently *Quan Doi Nhan Dan*, the organ of the Viet-Minh People's Army, did not issue its endorsement of the Geneva Conference until late April, when the seizure of Dien-Bien-Phu was inevitable.[36]

2. THE CRISIS OF DIEN-BIEN-PHU

To understand the impact of the battle of Dien-Bien-Phu on the quest for peace, an examination of the decisive Chinese aid and lack of intervention by the United States and Communist China is necessary, although I have not attempted a military history of Dien-Bien-Phu in this section.[37]

The purpose of the French defense of Dien-Bien-Phu was to safeguard northern Laos, which the Viet-Minh army had invaded in the spring of 1953. After a "mutual" defense treaty between France and Laos in October 1953, the French government instructed General Navarre, then the French commander-in-chief in Indochina, to defend the landlocked kingdom. In Navarre's judgment, "Laos could not be defended by a war of movement," because the nature of its terrain was not adapted to the French army. The only possible way, he thought, was to establish "fortified camps" which would prevent a massive invasion, although light enemy activities could not be prevented.[38] Dien-Bien-Phu,

---

[36] *Quan Doi Nhan Dan*, "With Regard to the Geneva Conference: A New Success of Our Camp," as broadcast by Voice of Vietnam, in Tonkinese, April 20, 1954.

[37] Among other works on Dien-Bien-Phu, an excellent account is given by Bernard B. Fall, *Hell in a Very Small Place: The Siege of Dien-Bien-Phu* (New York: Lippincott, 1967).

[38] Henri-Eugène Navarre, *Agonie de l'Indochine (1953-1954)* (Paris: Plon, 1956), p. 191.

a Vietnamese village near the border of northern Laos, was selected for the "fortified camps"; it was designed as a ground-air base. Surrounded by high hills, the village would be difficult for the Viet-Minh to assault. It was, in the estimate of French artillerymen, out of range of Viet-Minh artillery beyond the hills. The Viet-Minh army would have to occupy the surrounding high hills before it could bring its guns to bear, which would be impossible because they would soon be discovered by French observation posts in the village and immediately silenced by French counter-fire.[39] The French also believed that Vo Nguyen Giap would not risk a siege and decisive battle. After these estimates were approved, the French army occupied Dien-Bien-Phu in November 1953.

However, they had miscalculated the strategy, tactics, and strength of the Viet-Minh army. After four years of Chinese military aid, Viet-Minh artillery had grown far beyond the strength estimated by the French military authorities. The tactics and methods of the Viet-Minh were too primitive and too astonishing for the French to have anticipated.

As soon as the French had placed their forces in Dien-Bien-Phu in late November 1953, the Viet-Minh decided to "liberate" it.[40] This Viet-Minh determination was put into effect by an amazing mobilization of the people for cooperation with its armed forces. Everyone moved under cover of darkness. They dismantled most of the guns and carried them to hilltop positions, where they fired directly and effectively down on French artillery. As General Navarre said, the Viet-Minh's camouflage was so good and their mobilization of the people so effective that the attack took the French completely by surprise.[41]

The battle began in mid-March. The Viet-Minh was under the direction of Chinese advisers. One Chinese general stayed at the headquarters of Giap and many officers were

[39] *Ibid.*, pp. 195-96.
[40] Vo Nguyen Giap, *Dien Bien Phu* (Hanoi: Foreign Languages Publishing House, 1959), pp. 17-39.
[41] Navarre, *Agonie*, pp. 218-19.

assigned to various levels of the Viet-Minh army. In addition to this and to the construction of the special road from Mengtze to the Dien-Bien-Phu area, the Chinese reinforced the Viet-Minh in early March with one anti-aircraft regiment, providing Giap with 64 37mm. anti-aircraft guns. Chinese soldiers operated the guns and drove the approximately 1,000 Molotova trucks that brought supplies in.[42] With about 80 anti-aircraft guns and 100 105mm. guns the Viet-Minh army was able to establish effective firepower from the hilltops east to the French positions. They shot down or damaged at least a dozen French aircraft in the first three days of the attack (March 13-15), and effectively cut off French supplies by air to the besieged camp in daytime. The French air force tried to make daily strikes against Viet-Minh gun emplacements, but either hit the wrong targets or were driven off. Meanwhile, Viet-Minh artillery bombarded the French outposts. On March 15 two important outposts, Béatrice and Gabrielle, fell to the Viet-Minh. On the evening of March 17 Anne-Marie, another outpost, was abandoned. Had Giap's forces launched a general attack on the base at that time, it might have fallen in late March or early April. But the final attack was postponed until May 6.

While the battle was going on, the French tried time and again to get American military action to save them at Dien-Bien-Phu. On March 20 Gen. Paul Ely, French chief-of-staff, flew from the Far East to Washington. His urgent appeal gave the United States cause for serious concern. He was reported to have convinced some American civilian and military officials of the danger at Dien-Bien-Phu. On March 29 Dulles suggested "united action" by the West against Communist expansion in Asia. He admitted that this action might involve serious risks, but argued: "these

[42] Report of Secretary of State Dulles to the Foreign Affairs Committee of the House, Department of State *Bulletin*, April 19, 1954, pp. 579-83; Navarre, *Agonie*, pp. 210f., 218, 243f.; Hoang Van Chi reported that the Chinese general who directed the battle was Lo Kuei-po (*Colonialism to Communism*, p. 65). No name was given in Chinese sources.

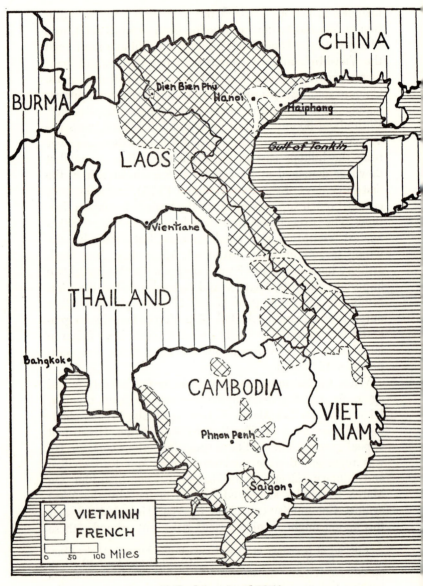

Indochina, April 1954

risks are far less than those that will face us a few years from now if we dare not be resolute today."[43] The next day President Eisenhower announced his support of Dulles' suggestion.[44]

The Dulles proposal brought an unfavorable response from Britain, however. After Roger Makins, British ambassador in Washington, reported the matter to London, Foreign Secretary Eden instructed Makins on April 1 to inform Dulles that failure to realize the unfavorable conditions in Indochina would "increase the difficulty of reaching tripartite agreement" at Geneva.[45] Makins also told Dulles and Under-Secretary Bedell Smith of the British feeling that partition of Indochina was the least damaging solution. In reply, Smith said the United States, after careful studies, had rejected the partition plan because it would only be a temporary palliative.[46] Dulles also disagreed with Eden's viewpoint.[47]

Peking's reply to Dulles' speech was a series of vicious attacks. In an editorial, *Jen min jih pao* commented: "What Dulles means by 'united action' is that the countries following the American lines should renounce their own interests and their independent foreign policy to pull the chestnuts out of the fire for the United States. What will the so-called united action lead to? . . . The answer has already been given in the Korean War."[48] This was clearly a warning and a threat. If the United States intervened militarily in the Indochinese war in any form of united action by the West, there would be another Korean war, a new military confrontation between the United States and Communist China.

---

[43] Department of State, *Bulletin*, April 12, 1954, p. 540.

[44] *New York Times*, April 1, 1954.

[45] Anthony Eden, *Full Circle; The Memoirs of Anthony Eden* (Boston: Houghton Mifflin, 1960), p. 102.

[46] In opposing the partition plan, the U.S. government was reported to have tried persuading the French to keep on fighting in Indochina for one or two years, at which time an American-trained Vietnamese army would be able to take over. *New York Times*, March 28, 1954.

[47] Eden, *Full Circle*, p. 103.

[48] NCNA, April 3, 1954, *SCMP*, 781, April 3-5, 1954.

Despite London's unfavorable reaction and Peking's warning, Dulles worked on a unilateral intervention plan. On April 3 he called a secret meeting at the Department of State with five senators and three congressmen,[49] ostensibly at the request of the President. Others who attended the meeting were Adm. Arthur W. Radford, chairman of the Joint Chiefs of Staff, Under-Secretary of Defense Roger Kyes, Navy Secretary Robert B. Anderson, and Thruston B. Morton, Dulles' assistant for congressional relations. The legislators were briefed about the dangers of the Indochinese situation. Then Admiral Radford presented a proposal for air and navy intervention. He told the meeting that 200 planes from U.S. Navy carriers in the South China Sea and some Air Force planes in the Philippines could be used for a single strike at Dien-Bien-Phu. If this was not successful, further steps would follow, which would not include the use of ground forces. The proposal was presented for a joint congressional resolution to authorize the administration to use the forces suggested. After learning that Dulles had not yet consulted the United States' allies about the plan, the legislators unanimously agreed that he should first seek their support.

On April 5 Dulles spoke before the House Foreign Affairs Committee, giving another warning to Communist China that her actions in Indochina could provoke United States retaliation.[50] Meanwhile a new proposal was sent to Britain, France, Australia, New Zealand, the Philippines, and Thailand, to the effect that the allies should issue, before the Geneva Conference, a solemn warning about Chinese continued intervention in the Indochinese war. The proposed

---

[49] A good report on this subject was made by Chalmers M. Roberts, "The Day We Didn't Go to War," *Reporter* (September 14, 1954), pp. 31-35. The eight legislators were: Senate Majority Leader William F. Knowland, Senate Minority Leader Lyndon B. Johnson, Sen. Earle C. Clements, Sen. Eugene D. Millikin, Sen. Richard B. Russell, House Speaker Joseph P. Martin, House Minority Leader John W. McCormack, and Rep. J. Percy Priest. Also see Victor Bator, *Vietnam: A Diplomatic Tragedy* (New York: Oceana, 1965), pp. 51-66.

[50] Department of State, *Bulletin*, April 19, 1954, pp. 579-83.

warning would contain the threat of naval and air action in Indochina and against the Chinese coast. Furthermore, an ad hoc coalition, including the above-mentioned nations and three "Associated States" in Indochina, would organize a collective defense system for southeast Asia.[51] On the same day President Eisenhower cabled Prime Minister Churchill, urging him to agree with the American proposal and suggesting that Dulles go to London for further discussions. Apparently American intervention in Indochina was much on Dulles' mind.

Eden welcomed the American proposal for the organization of a collective defense in southeast Asia, but was disturbed by the proposal for a unified military warning to China. He thought no threat would be strong enough to force Communist China to "swallow so humiliating a rebuff as the abandonment of the Vietminh without any face-saving concession in return," and that any blockade or bombing of China's transportation lines would only give China "every excuse for invoking the Sino-Soviet Treaty, and might lead to a world war."[52]

Dulles arrived in London on April 11, and held discussions with Eden for two days. He told Eden that the American government did not think the French alone could hold Indochina. If they collapsed, Thailand, Burma, Malaya, and Indonesia would be exposed to the danger of Communism. He stated further that the United States had considered, but now had declined, acting alone in Indochina if France granted real independence to the Associated States and if the allies supported the proposed American action. However, Dulles still wanted to see the formation of an ad hoc coalition leading to a southeast Asia defense organization.

Eden held a different viewpoint. He distinguished the issue of defense organization in southeast Asia from the proposed "united action." On the first issue, he welcomed the idea, but said it would require careful study, particularly the problem of membership. To Eden, under no con-

---

[51] Eden, *Full Circle*, p. 103.   [52] *Ibid.*, pp. 104-105.

ditions should India be excluded from the organization. On the second issue Eden stated that any allied intervention before Geneva, military or otherwise, would require extremely careful consideration. Furthermore, the allies should wait and see what proposals the Communists made at Geneva. Consequently Eden made clear to Dulles that before the Geneva Conference, Great Britain would not support the "united action" nor the formation of a defensive system in southeast Asia.[53]

A joint communiqué was issued after the talks, declaring that the two governments agreed to take part, together with other countries concerned, "in an examination of the possibility of establishing a collective defense" to assure peace, security, and freedom in southeast Asia and the western Pacific.[54] The Indochina issue was not mentioned. Dulles went on to Paris. On April 15 a Franco-American communiqué in the same vein was made, except for an emphasized point that peace in Indochina was the basic objective of the two powers at Geneva.[55]

Peking's policy at this moment was to kill any possibility of American military intervention in Indochina and let the Geneva Conference proceed. If the United States would not intervene at Dien-Bien-Phu, the Communists could count on a military victory there, which might result in a major diplomatic success at Geneva. Peking, therefore, interpreted Dulles' trip to Europe as having two purposes: "to force Britain and France to join in 'united action' in order to extend the Indochina war," and "to sabotage the Geneva Conference." It also denounced the Dulles-Eden communiqué as being produced under Dulles' pressure for the purpose of obstructing a peaceful settlement at Geneva.

[53] *Ibid.*, pp. 106-108. During their discussions Eden urged Dulles to include India as a member of the proposed Southeast Asia organization. Dulles declined, and suggested that both controversial India and Formosa be excluded from membership. Eden did not like this balance of India against Formosa, but no final decision was reached. *Ibid.*, pp. 107-109.

[54] Department of State, *Bulletin*, April 26, 1954, p. 622.

[55] *Ibid.*, p. 623.

In regard to the Franco-American joint pronouncement, Peking repeated the same attacks, adding that Dulles had dragged France into a military alliance in southeast Asia.[56] Ho Chi Minh's radio assailed the United States for attempting to "sabotage" the Geneva Conference, and denounced the American "imperialists" as "the main obstacle" to a peaceful settlement of Indochina.[57] The central theme of the propaganda from Peking and North Vietnam was almost identical.

In Washington there was a debate in the Pentagon over intervention in Indochina. The proposed intervention would not be limited to air strikes at Dien-Bien-Phu; it would involve the use of ground forces in North Vietnam. As Gen. James M. Gavin, serving as Army Chief of Plans at the time, disclosed in February 1968,[58] Admiral Radford "strongly favored" air strikes and "landing a force in the Haiphong-Hanoi area, even at the risk of war with Red China." Gen. Nathan F. Twining and Adm. Robert B. Carney supported Radford's stand, but General Ridgway was strongly opposed.[59] It was Eisenhower who finally decided not to commit United States forces to Vietnam. As he wrote later, such military action should not be undertaken without the support of Congress and the allies.[60]

The hawkish view of Admiral Radford, nevertheless, was shared by Vice-President Nixon. On April 16 Nixon spoke to a meeting of newspaper editors in Washington, "off the record." Nixon asserted that it was vital to hold Indochina and that if it was necessary to send American troops, the United States "must face up to the situation and dispatch

[56] NCNA, April 15, 1954, in *SCMP*, 790, April 16, 1954.

[57] *Ibid.*; NCNA, April 21, 1954, *SCMP*, 793, April 23, 1954.

[58] James M. Gavin, "We Can Get Out of Vietnam," *Saturday Evening Post*, February 24, 1968, p. 24.

[59] General Ridgway also expressed his opposition to American military intervention in Indochina. See his *Soldier*, pp. 96-97, 275-76.

[60] Dwight D. Eisenhower, *Mandate for Change: The White House Years, 1953-1956* (New York: Doubleday, 1963), p. 347.

forces.[61] Peking denounced the address as a "warmongering speech" and "war cry."[62]

The Pentagon's tendency toward intervention did not die out immediately after Eisenhower took his stand. It revived at the end of April when the Dien-Bien-Phu situation had become extremely critical. On April 23, one day after Dulles went to Paris for a NATO council meeting which both Eden and Bidault attended, General Navarre sent a telegram to the French government, requesting a powerful air strike by the United States in the next 72 hours to save Dien-Bien-Phu. Dulles informed Eden of the request and sought British support to do so. Eden realized the seriousness of the situation and immediately reported to Prime Minister Churchill. The following day Radford arrived in Paris and Eden discussed the situation with him and Dulles. At the meeting Radford offered a plan of "military effort to assist the French without delay," and suggested that British R.A.F. units be transferred to Tonkin from Malaya. Eden questioned Radford on whether he had considered how the Chinese Communists would react. Radford replied that he did not think they would intervene. That same afternoon Eden and Dulles conferred with Bidault, and Dulles again proposed American military action if France and the other allies so desired. The French minister expressed his government's request for the action. An uneasy Eden rushed back to London for consultation. The British government finally decided to "reject" the American proposal, declaring that Great Britain was "not prepared to support any undertaking now, in advance of the Geneva Conference, concerning United Kingdom military action in Indo-China."[63] As Eden

[61] A summary of Nixon's speech is in *New York Times*, April 18, 1954. In his book Eisenhower said about Nixon's speech: "He said . . . that '. . . if to avoid further Communist expansion in Asia and Indo-china, we must take the risk now by putting our boys in, I think the Executive has to take the politically unpopular decision and do it.'" Eisenhower, *Mandate*, pp. 353f.

[62] NCNA, April 19, 20, 1954, in *SCMP*, 791, 792, April 20, 21-22, 1954.

[63] Eden, *Full Circle*, p. 119; also see Eisenhower, *Mandate*, pp. 349-51.

explained to the House of Commons later: "[This was] for three reasons. . . . First, we were advised that air action alone could not have been effective. Secondly, any such military intervention could have destroyed the chances of a settlement at Geneva. And thirdly, it might well have led to a general war in Asia."[64]

The proposal for allied military action in Indochina was finally dropped in the face of strong opposition from the British. But noncommitment policy resulted in America's refusal to endorse the Geneva Agreements. Moreover, it was carried out by a compromise between the Hawks and Doves in the Eisenhower administration, a compromise that led to American support for South Vietnam under Ngo Dinh Diem.[65]

With no expectation of help from the allies, the fall of Dien-Bien-Phu was inevitable. The Viet-Minh army launched a final attack on May 6, and captured it the following day. On May 8 the Geneva Conference on Indochina opened. General Navarre observed that the timing of the attacks was decided on the advice of the Chinese (or a Sino-Soviet) military mission,[66] in order to strengthen the Viet-Minh position at Geneva. In the battle the French lost approximately 16,000 men, and North Vietnam about 25,000 to 30,000.[67] No sooner had Ho received the news of the victory than he cabled Giap: "The victory is big, but it is only the beginning." Apparently the message meant Ho and his men were expecting total victory over the French by taking the whole of Vietnam through armed struggle or peaceful means in a forseseeable future.

While the United States did not intervene in the war, the Chinese army stayed out of Vietnam for several outstanding reasons. First, North Vietnam did not face a really dangerous situation, as did North Korea in 1950, and the security of Communist China was not "threatened" by the French

[64] Great Britain, *Parliamentary Debates* (Commons), Vol. 529, Cols. 434-35.
[65] Gavin, "We Can Get Out."   [66] Navarre, *Agonie*, pp. 210f.
[67] *Ibid.*, pp. 228-29; *Jen min jih pao*, May 11, 1954.

forces. Chinese military intervention was not needed. As Pham Le Bong, a defected Viet-Minh official, disclosed in 1953, North Vietnam had reached an understanding with China that Chinese troops would not intervene in the war unless North Vietnam was in grave danger.[68] Everett F. Drumright, assistant secretary for Far Eastern affairs, observed in May 1954: "the Viet-Minh have been doing well without Chinese troops. It is doubtful that Chinese would send their troops in when they are not needed."[69] Under these circumstances, Ho, who well remembered the lesson of the Chinese military occupation in 1945-1946, must have firmly declined to invite Chinese troops into his country, although he was enthusiastic about learning from China and soliciting Chinese aid. Ho was opposed to Chinese Communist entry because he feared Chinese control of Vietnam's political, military, and economic affairs. Second, the Chinese Communists were preoccupied with the Korean war prior to mid-1953, and were interested in a peaceful settlement of the Indochinese war after that time. As General Marshall said in mid-1951, the Korean war had deterred a Chinese Communist plunge into Vietnam.[70] After the Korean armistice negotiations got under way in 1953, conciliation with the outside world seems to have served as the guiding principle of Peking's foreign policy. Military intervention in Indochina might have provoked a second Korean war, which would have encountered this principle. Third, the economic situation in China did not allow Peking to engage in another war. In March 1950 Mao urged the nation to retrench "military and administrative expenditures" in order to "bring about a fundamental turn for the better" in the financial condition of China.[71] On May Day of the same year Liu Shao-ch'i expressed the hope that after Taiwan was "liberated . . . the country's military

[68] See p. 269.

[69] As cited in Melvin Gurtov, *The First Vietnam Crisis* (New York: Columbia University Press, 1967), p. 148.

[70] *New York Times*, May 13, 1951.

[71] As quoted in an editorial in *People's China*, May 16, 1950, p. 4.

expenditures can be greatly reduced, a great increase in investment in economic construction can then be made, and our country can move ahead on the road to transitional economic reconstruction."[72] It was therefore obvious that prior to the Korean war Peking planned to direct its national resources to reconstruction rather than the military. But its intervention in Korea shattered the plan. Another war in Vietnam with a formidable enemy would certainly prove costly for China. As events developed, the three aforesaid reasons were borne out by Peking's peaceful policy toward the outside world and by its economic plans for reconstruction in the post-Geneva years.

While Chinese and American nonintervention at Dien-Bien-Phu hastened peace negotiations, Britain made a maximum effort to protect the movement from any disturbance. North Vietnam's desire for peace talks grew stronger as the seizure of Dien-Bien-Phu became more certain. And the French sought a face-saving withdrawal from Indochina. In late April it became clear that most of the participants at the Geneva Conference wanted to negotiate. The peace campaign initiated by the Communist camp took a new turn toward a settlement in Vietnam.

3. THE ROLE OF CHINA AND VIETNAM IN
    THE GENEVA CONFERENCE

The Geneva Conference opened on April 26, 1954, with two issues on the agenda: Korea and Indochina. After the Korean issue reached a deadlock, the Western nations suggested discontinuing the discussion on the issue on June 15. Discussion of the Indochina issue began on May 8 between nine participants—France, the Soviet Union, Communist China, Great Britain, the United States, North Vietnam, South Vietnam, Laos, and Cambodia. The Soviet Union and Britain were co-chairmen. It ended on July 20 with the well-known Geneva Agreements. Since the conference has been covered by many studies, it is unnecessary to repeat

[72] *Hsin hua yueh pao*, May 1950, pp. 5-10.

the factual development of the meeting here. It seems meaningful, however, to examine the roles of both Communist China and Vietnam in this conference that have not yet been fully explored.

As mentioned before, both Moscow and Peking asserted that it was impossible to settle any serious international problems without the participation of Communist China. North Vietnam echoed this view. Immediately after the opening of the Geneva Conference, North Vietnam's news media propagandized that China was a "great power" and that "without China, the Asian problem cannot be solved; without China, there can be no solutions of questions of international relations."[73] As the conference proceeded, Chou En-lai tried hard to portray Communist China as a nonaggressive country. He said, "The government of the People's Republic of China and the Chinese people consistently work for peace and against war," and China "has never committed and will never commit aggression against other countries."[74] At home, the Chinese news media arrogantly asserted that Chou En-lai spoke not only for the "500 million Chinese people," but for "the whole of the peace-loving people in Asia."[75] This view was again supported by the North Vietnamese. Throughout the conference, the Viet-Minh delegation led by Pham Van Dong[76] seems to have followed more closely Chou En-lai than Molotov. The North Vietnamese were intransigent, while the Chinese were adamant and the Soviets not uncompromising. Their different attitudes, however, were understand-

[73] Voice of Vietnam, "The People's Republic of China," in Tonkinese, April 26, 1954; *Nhan Dan*, "Important Voice of the People's Republic of China at the Geneva Conference," in VNA, English, April 29, 1954; *Cuu Quoc*, "The Vietnamese People Support the Geneva Conference," in VNA, May 1, 1954.

[74] NCNA, April 28, 1954.

[75] "Asian Peoples' Wishes Absolutely Cannot be Ignored," editorial, *World Culture*, No. 11 (June 5), 1954, p. 3.

[76] The other delegates were Phan Anh, Minister of Industry and Commerce; Tran Cong Tuong, Vice-Minister of Justice; Ta Quang Buu, Vice-Minister of National Defense; and Hoang Van Hoan, Ambassador to China.

able, for the Soviets were arranging a deal with the French to reject the European Defense Community, in exchange for Soviet help in obtaining a Vietnam settlement; the Chinese had undertaken a peaceful coexistence policy; and the North Vietnamese were expecting to attain complete independence and control of the entirety of Vietnam.

At Geneva Chou spoke up much more on Indochina than on Korea. Some delegates of the West observed that there was greater firmness in the Chinese than in the Soviet declarations. As Molotov told Anthony Eden, "China was very much her own master in these [Indochinese] matters."[77] The Chinese attitude gave some observers the impression that China was more intent on working for her "big power" position than on a peace settlement.[78] This may be true. But the Chinese delegation did make significant contributions to the settlement of various issues.

FOR THE convenience of discussion here, the conference is arbitrarily divided into three phases. The first was from May 8 to June 20, during which various proposals were made by delegations for seeking solutions to problems. The second phase lasted from June 21 to July 9, with chief delegates of major powers returning home for consultation while lower-level committees continued their meetings at Geneva. The third phase was from July 10 to 21, in which the delegates engaged in intensive activities and reached agreement. Throughout the three phases, Chou En-lai played a significant role in (1) persuading North Vietnam to withdraw its forces from Laos and Cambodia; (2) obtaining Ho Chi Minh's agreement to go along with the general peace plan at Geneva, and (3) settling the tangled issue of the composition of the international commission for supervision and control.

On the first issue the non-Communists and Communists held opposite views. The delegations of Laos and Cambodia accused the Viet-Minh of invading their countries, refused

[77] Eden, *Full Circle*, p. 136.
[78] Thomas J. Hamilton, in *New York Times*, June 13, 1954.

to recognize the "resistance governments" of Khmer and Pathet Lao, and requested the withdrawal of Viet-Minh troops from Laos and Cambodia. On the other hand, the Viet-Minh repeatedly denied its invasion and the presence of its troops in Laos and Cambodia, argued for the "resistance" movement in these two kingdoms as a "self-development" from the people, and requested the participation in the conference of the "resistance governments" of Khmer and Pathet Lao.[79] In fact, the Viet-Minh forces did invade Laos and established together with the Pathet Lao a local Communist regime in Sam-Neua province; in Cambodia Viet-Minh "volunteers" under Nguyen Thanh Son invaded Cambodia and stayed there until the armistice in Cambodia was signed by Son on July 24, 1954.[80]

As the arguments went on, little progress was made. Many conferees became impatient. Frustrated by this issue and other disagreements among the delegations, Eden saw danger in the negotiations.[81] At the plenary session of June 10 he urged reaching an agreement on the issues of Viet-Minh troops in Laos and Cambodia and on the composition of the proposed international commission in a short period of time; otherwise he might call for adjournment of the conference.[82] When the discussion on Korea was suspended five days later (June 15), the participants sensed the seriousness of Eden's warning and the danger of a breakdown in the meeting if no progress was made in a few days.

The danger was avoided by Chou En-lai. On the morning of June 16 he visited Eden,[83] and told the foreign secretary that he could persuade the Viet-Minh to withdraw its troops from Laos and Cambodia and that China could recognize the two royal governments provided that there were no

[79] *Jen min jih pao*, May 27, June 11, 12, 13, 1954; *New York Times*, May 15, 18, 24, June 5, 1954.

[80] VNA, in English, July 26, 1954. Wilfred Burchett, an Australian Communist writer, also reported the presence of Viet-Minh "volunteers" in the two kingdoms. See Fall, *Two Viet-Nams*, pp. 458-59n.

[81] *New York Times*, June 9, 10, 1954.

[82] *Ibid.*, June 11, 1954.

[83] *Jen min jih pao*, June 17, 1954.

American bases in these kingdoms. Eden had the "strong impression that Chou wanted a settlement." He immediately urged Bidault, France's chief delegate, to seek an interview with Chou and "begged" the French foreign minister to discuss this new offer with the Chinese Premier with the "utmost seriousness."[84] At the restricted session in the afternoon, Chou made a formal proposal for the withdrawal of Viet-Minh troops from Laos and Cambodia and Chinese recognition of the two kingdoms.[85] His proposal was supported by the other conferees. Even Bedell Smith (the U.S. chief delegate) said the Chinese proposal was worthy of study. Western newspapers reported favorably on Chou's suggestion and regarded it as progress in the conference,[86] a stride toward the path of agreement,[87] and a proposal which could give new life to the Indochinese negotiations.[88] It was indeed the most encouraging and constructive proposal yet made.

After Chou had presented his proposal, Pham Van Dong for the first time mentioned the royal governments of Laos and Cambodia and their rights to unity and independence.[89] His earlier request for the participation of the two "resistance governments" was dropped. At the restricted session the following day, Dong admitted that "the Viet-Minh volunteers army" had fought in Laos and Cambodia, but claimed that it had already been evacuated. He conceded, however, that "If there are still some troops staying there, they should also be withdrawn[90]—a reverse apparently made under pressure from Chou En-lai. Following his proposal, Chou held a series of conversations with Eden, Bidault, Pham Van Dong, Tep Phan (chief delegate from Cambodia), and Phouy Sananikone (chief delegate from Laos), to facilitate an agreement on Laos and Cambodia.

[84] Eden, *Full Circle*, p. 145.
[85] *Jen min jih pao*, June 18, 1954.
[86] *Times* (London), June 17, 1954.
[87] *Le Monde*, June 17, 1954.
[88] *Manchester Guardian*, June 17, 1954.
[89] *New York Times*, June 17, 1954.
[90] *Jen min jih pao*, June 20, 1954.

Chou also took Tep Phan and Phouy Sananikone to meet their formerly uncompromising opponent, Pham Van Dong. On June 19, a first cease-fire accord for Cambodia and Laos was reached, a salutary success during the first phase.

DURING THE second phase the chief delegates returned home for consultations, and there were some important events outside the conference. On June 23 Mendès-France, the new French premier, who had announced on assuming the premiership that he would resign if peace in Indochina could not be attained by July 20,[91] met Chou En-lai at Bern, Switzerland. The meeting was urged by Eden, but was reported to have hit Geneva like a bombshell. There were three main items on which Mendès-France and Chou agreed. First, the Geneva Conference should agree on a political settlement as well as an armistice for Vietnam, Laos, and Cambodia. Second, a unified government of Vietnam should eventually be formed through national elections. Third, the French-sponsored governments in Laos and Cambodia would be recognized [by Peking], with the condition that they remain neutral.[92] The terms were reported to have been given in mid-June by Chou to Eden, who relayed them to Smith. If this was true, then they were initiated by Chou En-lai.

After his meeting with Mendès-France, Chou visited India. It should be noted that India's concern over peace in Indochina was no less serious than any of the nine participants. Two days before the Geneva Conference opened, Nehru spoke to the House of People of India, suggesting a cease-fire, complete independence, direct negotiations between parties, and nonintervention in Indochina by foreign powers.[93] After the conference began, he sent Krishna Menon to Geneva to serve as an intermediary. Menon's

[91] Mendès-France later announced that the reason for his setting such a peace deadline was that he did not think the French could hold the Red River delta longer than a month. The delta was under bitter Viet-Minh attack in June. *New York Times*, July 23, 1954.

[92] *Ibid.*, June 24, 1954.

[93] NCNA, April 26, 1954.

active role in Geneva must have placed constructive pressure on many participants, including Chou En-lai. It was apparently at Nehru's invitation through Menon that Chou visited India. Having received a warm welcome from the Indian people, Chou held a cordial talk with Nehru. They issued a joint communiqué urging a political settlement for Indochina and a neutral status for the three Associated States. They proclaimed five principles of peaceful coexistence intended to guide Sino-Indian relations for several years. The principles were (1) mutual respect for each other's territorial integrity and sovereignty; (2) nonaggression; (3) nonintervention in each other's internal affairs; (4) equality and mutual benefit, and (5) peaceful coexistence.[94] Chou then visited Burma, where he and Prime Minister U Nu repeated the five principles. It seemed that Chou and Nehru were paving the way to peaceful coexistence, which must have influenced North Vietnam's decision to reach a settlement.

A more significant but less publicized meeting was held by Chou En-lai and Ho Chi Minh at an unnamed place on the Sino-Vietnamese border from July 3 to 5. The official communiqué of the meeting merely stated that they "had a full exchange of views on the Geneva Conference with respect to the question of the restoration of peace in Indochina and related questions."[95] What Chou actually persuaded Ho to agree on was never disclosed. But one day after their meeting, Ho issued a conciliatory statement of his views on the armistice in Indochina. *Ta kung pao* praised it as a "sincere desire" for peace and "helpful to the progress of the Geneva Conference."[96] And five days later an editorial in *Nhan Dan* commented that the meeting had "brought about important results. If the Mendès-France government is determined to get rid of its dependence" on the United States, it was "certainly" possible to bring about

---

[94] Text in *New York Times*, June 29, 1954.

[95] NCNA, Peking, July 7, 1954.

[96] Radio Peking, in English Morse to Southeast Asia, and North America, July 11, 1954.

an armistice in Indochina.[97] Judging by these two statements, and the reports on Chou's meetings with Mendès-France and Nehru, the "important results" of Chou's pressure on Ho must have centered on three main issues: an armistice in Indochina and a temporary demarcation line, a political settlement (unity) of Vietnam through national elections, and the neutrality of Laos and Cambodia.

On the non-Communist side, some important events transpired during the second phase. In late June Churchill and Eden went to Washington for talks. In a joint statement of June 28, they said, among other things, that they would continue to fulfill the plan for a collective defense in Southeast Asia, to meet either the success or failure of the Geneva Conference.[98] This determination for a Southeast Asia Treaty Organization cast a shadow over the fulfillment of the eventual Geneva Agreements.

In South Vietnam and Paris two treaties were initialed. According to these documents, France would recognize Vietnam as a fully independent state and Vietnam would accept membership in the French Union. The newly promised status of full independence for Vietnam encouraged Ngo Dinh Diem to assume the premiership on June 16; he was enthusiastically welcomed by the South Vietnamese people. The forming of his cabinet on July 7 became a "new hope" for American assistance to South Vietnam.

The third phase of the conference began with the arrival of Mendès-France and Molotov in Geneva on July 10. Eden and Chou En-lai returned on July 12, but informal contacts among chief delegates had already begun. They engaged in frequent interviews, conversations, and a few meetings on the issues of the demarcation line, the date for general elections, the composition of the international commission, etc.

The United States was unenthusiastic. Fearing that Mendès-France would make concessions on important principles to the Communists, Dulles informed the French

[97] NCNA, Peking (from VNA, July 10), July 10, 1954.
[98] Department of State, *Bulletin*, July 12, 1954, p. 49.

premier that the United States would not return to the Geneva talks at the ministerial level. Eden and Mendès-France immediately asked for a meeting with Dulles in Paris, which was held on July 13 and 14. Impressed by the meeting, Dulles finally agreed to send Bedell Smith back to Geneva—which delighted Eden and Mendès-France, but irked Chou En-lai. On July 17 Chou held a "crucial meeting" with Eden and accused the West of planning to split southeast Asia in two with an anti-Chinese alliance. He insisted on the status of independence, sovereignty, and neutrality for the Associated States.[99] Chou's stormy meeting with Eden may have been motivated by two considerations. The first was a reaction to the Western tripartite talks in Paris held three days earlier, which Chou regarded as a new device for undermining the Geneva Conference and opposing China. The second was pressure on Eden so as to force the West to go along with whatever direction the Communists (particularly the Chinese) moved toward.

A significant contribution made by Chou En-lai during the third phase was his proposal for the composition of the international commission for supervision. The issue had become a thorny problem since Molotov raised it on May 14. The Soviet delegation proposed four "neutral" nations as members—Poland, Czechoslovakia, India, and Pakistan—but the non-Communists were opposed to it. Eden proposed five Colombo Plan nations, which Molotov rejected. South Vietnam suggested the United Nations, with which Communist China disagreed. Both sides eloquently and stubbornly disagreed with each other. Until July 17 no agreement was reached, and a solution seemed unlikely. On the afternoon of July 18, however, Chou En-lai proposed India, Poland, and Canada as the members. The proposal was accepted unanimously. "From that moment," as Eden recalled, "the tangled ends of the negotiations began to sort themselves out."[100] In making the proposal, the Chinese delegation again acted in the sense of compromise. This was obviously Chou En-lai's stand in Geneva, a position

[99] Eden, *Full Circle*, p. 158.   [100] *Ibid.*, p. 159.

which the Chinese strongly urged other participants to share.[101]

At the meeting the importance of the Viet-Minh position gradually increased, while South Vietnam's decreased. The situation was inevitable, since the conferees were negotiating for an armistice between the French and the Viet-Minh. Moreover, since the South Vietnamese government did not achieve full independence until after the Geneva settlement (January 1, 1955), it could only act in a supporting role to France. This was why Mendès-France and other chief delegates of the major powers directly negotiated with Phan Van Dong and ignored Bao Dai's delegates. South Vietnam felt "sold out" by its "friends" and enemies.

At the outset South Vietnam appeared to have an equal voice against the North. When North Vietnam presented its eight-point proposal, the South Vietnamese delegation made a seven-point counterproposal. In his suggestion, Nguyen Quoc Dinh (chief delegate of South Vietnam) eloquently set forth South Vietnam's conditions for negotiations. He claimed the Bao Dai government as the only legal government in Vietnam, and argued for the merger of the Viet-Minh army into the Vietnam national army (South Vietnam's); he declared that his government would reject any "division, direct or indirect, definitive or provisional, de facto or de jure" and argued that general elections should be placed under the supervision of the United Nations. His position was strengthened by Smith's statement, that the United States' policy was one of no recognition of the Viet-Minh regime, and agreed with South Vietnam's proposal for elections under United Nations auspices.[102] As the confer-

[101] "Chinese Delegation Urges Conciliatory Spirit in Indochina Talks," Radio Peking, in English to Southeast Asia, Europe, and North America, July 7, 1954. "Indochina Peace Depends Upon Spirit of Compromise," *Jen min jih pao*, July 19, 1954, as broadcast by Radio Peking, in English to Asia, Europe, and North America, July 19, 1954.

[102] Great Britain, Foreign Office, *Documents Relating to the Discussion of Korea and Indo-China at the Geneva Conference, April 27-June 15, 1954* (Cmd. 9186) (London: 1954), pp. 124-25.

ence dragged on, Nguyen Quoc Dinh's position gradually lost support. On June 1, when the French and Viet-Minh military representatives began to negotiate at Geneva, the Saigon delegation did not have position in the parley. On June 10 Molotov suggested direct French–Viet-Minh discussions on the political problem of Vietnam without the participation of the south. On June 20 Eden urged Mendès-France to meet the Chinese and Viet-Minh delegates. This made the Viet-Minh position even more important.

South Vietnam was treated coolly during the final phase of the meeting. In informal contacts France dealt with the Viet-Minh, the Soviet Union, Communist China, and Great Britain, often without the participation of South Vietnam. Under these arrangements, the North Vietnamese became active in meeting with other delegations, while the South Vietnamese could hardly find an opportunity to confer with the major powers.[103] Table 3 shows the situation:

TABLE 3

INFORMAL CONTACTS OUTSIDE THE CONFERENCE, JULY 10-20, 1954

Delegation	Number of Contacts with others
France (Mendès-France)	17
U.S.S.R. (Molotov)	15
China (Chou En-lai)	14
Britain (Eden)	13
Viet-Minh (Pham Van Dong)	13
Cambodia (Tep Phan)	6
U.S.A. (Johnson, Smith)	5
South Vietnam (Tran Van Do)	4
Laos (Phouy Sananikone)	3

Sources: *Jen min jih pao*, the *New York Times*, and Radio Peking, July 10-21, 1954.

[103] See *Jen min jih pao* and *New York Times*, both July 10-21, 1954.

Mendès-France had the busiest schedule, and apparently held the decisive position in the negotiations of the last 11 days. The U.S. delegates remained inactive. Pham Van Dong was surprisingly active; Tran Van Do was almost completely ignored, which only embittered the already bitter delegation of South Vietnam. Do, therefore, declared that his government reserved the right to decide whether it would go along with any French–Viet-Minh agreement.[104] Two days after the Western tripartite talks ended in Paris in mid-July, Tran Van Do handed a note to Mendès-France, expressing "surprise" that the French delegation had failed to inform South Vietnam of the details of the talks. The note reiterated South Vietnam's stand against partition of Vietnam.[105] Do even sought a meeting with Pham Van Dong in an attempt to persuade him to join Do in an effort to block the partition plan. Dong, under pressure from Chou and Molotov, declined. The complaints and resentments of the South Vietnamese were well understood by the French, who, however, paid no heed to them. On July 18 Tran Van Do seriously declared at a restricted session that his government would refuse to sign any cease-fire agreement that divided his country.[106]

The complaints and protests of Tran Van Do at the final meeting were the most impressive. The first speaker, he complained of the rejection of South Vietnam's original proposal "without examination" and protested against the hasty conclusion of the armistice agreement by the French and Viet-Minh high commands, which abandoned territories controlled by South Vietnam to the Viet-Minh. He also denounced the French for their unilateral decision on the date for general elections in Vietnam. He declared that his government would reserve full freedom of action, "in order to safeguard the sacred right of the Vietnamese people to territorial unity, national independence and freedom."[107]

[104] *New York Times*, July 17, 1954.
[105] *Ibid.*, July 18, 1954.
[106] *New York Herald Tribune*, July 19, 1954.
[107] NCNA, July 23, 1954, in *SCMP*, 855, July 25-26, 1954.

Mendès-France replied that the French undertook responsibility for their decision, and expressed the hope that Ho Chi Minh would observe the promise of protection of people's freedom in the areas turned over to North Vietnam. In his second and final speech Do proposed that his government's reservations and objections be added to the final declaration of the agreement, which was overruled by the chairman, Eden.

No one had mentioned South Vietnam's position, except Tep Phan. His sympathy, nevertheless, only made Do feel more resentful of the result of the conference. Immediately after the meeting Do cabled Premier Ngo Dinh Diem to report the result and to submit his resignation: "We fought desperately against partition and for a neutral zone in the Catholic area of North Vietnam. Absolutely impossible to surmount the hostility of our enemies and the perfidy of false friends. Unusual procedures paralyzed the action of our delegation. . . . All arrangements were signed in privacy. We express our deepest sorrows in this total failure of our mission. We respectfully submit our resignation." On July 22 he refused Chou En-lai's invitation to a dinner reception for all the delegates from Indochina.[108]

Tran Van Do repeatedly protested, while Pham Van Dong was silent. This did not mean that Dong had nothing to say, but that Dong, under pressure from the Soviets and the Chinese, could not express his views freely. It was not a secret that the Viet-Minh delegates were unhappy about the peace settlement. As reported by the *New York Times*, some Viet-Minh delegates "declared openly that pressure from Chinese Communist Premier Chou En-lai and Soviet Foreign Minister Vyacheslav M. Molotov forced their regime to accept less than it rightfully should have obtained" at Geneva. They also thought the settlement was made in the interests of Soviet and Chinese Communist international relations; they saw victory over the French in Vietnam within a year, but the victory had been cut short and the revolution "slowed down, if not halted, right on the verge

[108] *Jen min jih pao*, July 24, 1954.

of complete success."[109] Other reports were similar.[110] Apparently the outstanding Soviet international "interest" at the moment was the French withdrawal from the EDC, and the Chinese interest was the peaceful coexistence policy announced by Chou and Nehru. Under these circumstances, all Pham Van Dong could do was go along with the Soviets and Chinese while pinning his hope for reunification on the scheduled national elections. In his statement at the final session on July 21, Dong hailed the settlement as a great victory for the people of North Vietnam, of Indochina, as well as for France and Asia. He said, the "happy conclusion" of the conference had added to the proof that it was possible "to settle all international disputes, even the most serious conflicts, through negotiation," and promised to carry out the agreements "faithfully and strictly," but he insisted on the unification of South and North Vietnam:

> A big step has been taken. More steps remain to be taken. We have to build up a stable and lasting peace in Indochina by settling the political questions, of which the most important is the achievement of the national unification of our people by means of elections, that is to say, by peaceful and democratic means. . . .
>
> The conference has fixed a date for our unification. This unity we shall make and win as we have won peace.
>
> No force in the world, internal or external, will turn us aside from our road to unity by peace and democracy. This will be the crowning achievement of our national independence.[111]

It became evident that North Vietnam's acceptance of the Geneva settlement was a result of the peace campaign in 1953-1954 by the Communist camp. When he was "forced" or persuaded to discontinue his military struggle, Ho Chi Minh twisted his policy toward peace. A peaceful

[109] Report by Tillman Durdin, *New York Times*, July 25, 1954.

[110] See Fischer, "Ho," p. 95; also Jean Lacouture and Philippe Devillers, *La Fin d'une Guerre, Indochine 1954* (Paris: Editions du Seuil, 1960), pp. 282-85.

[111] NCNA, Geneva, July 21, 1954, in *SCMP*, 854, pp. 6-7.

solution to the Vietnam problem was not entirely counter to the interests of the Viet-Minh. For by this settlement, Ho, first of all, gained complete control over the territory north of the 17th parallel, although he would have to withdraw his forces from a large occupied area in the south. Second, the withdrawal of Viet-Minh forces from Laos and Cambodia would be in exchange for the neutrality of the two. Third, there were no provisions in the agreements prohibiting "resistance" elements in Laos and Cambodia from continuing their revolutionary activities. Fourth, to win a complete military victory over the French would be very costly, if not impossible, while unification through general elections two years hence could be achieved without bloodshed. But so far as the final goal of unification was concerned, Ho and his men did not give an inch in principle. It is therefore conceivable, though not necessarily justifiable, that in their struggle for unification the North Vietnamese have since 1960 shifted from political (peaceful) to military (violent) means whenever they and their southern comrades deemed it the only suitable strategy.

4. The Settlement and Its Aftermath

The Geneva settlement was based on two basic documents concluded at Geneva: the Agreement on the Cessation of Hostilities in Vietnam, and the Final Declaration.[112] The second document was unsigned, but the participants accepted it. This presents a new form of international documents. As Jean Lacouture and Philippe Devillers rightly observe: "The Geneva Conference will thus have invented a new form of peaceful coexistence—that which results from the tacit consent of the negotiators—as well as a new form of legal obligation between states: the unsigned treaty."[113]

[112] For the text see Appendix IV.
[113] Lacouture and Devillers, *La Fin d'une Guerre,* as cited in Bernard B. Fall, *Viet-Nam Witness: 1953-1966* (New York: Frederick Praeger, 1966), p. 75.

The outstanding features of the two documents are summarized as follows:

(1) A cease-fire and military demarcation line. The documents provided that the cease-fire would become effective on July 27 in northern Vietnam, August 1 in central Vietnam, and August 11 in the south (in Cambodia it was August 7, and in Laos, August 8). Viet-Minh forces were to leave Laos and Cambodia, while French troops were to withdraw from all three.

A provisional military demarcation line was drawn along a river beneath the 17th parallel, for regrouping of the forces of both sides after their withdrawal. The Viet-Minh were to regroup to the north of the line and the French to the south. The maximum period for regrouping was 300 days from the date the armistice went into effect. The demarcation line was interpreted as neither a political nor a territorial boundary. It was to be eliminated after the general elections in July 1956.

(2) A ban on military assistance and alliance. The Vietnam armistice agreement did not allow the introducing into Vietnam of "any troop reinforcements and additional military personnel." It prohibited the introduction of any reinforcements "in the form of all types of arms, munitions and other war material, such as combat aircraft, naval craft, pieces of ordnance, jet engines and jet weapons and armoured vehicles." It also banned the establishment of new military bases under foreign control and military alliance for the resumption of hostilities.

(3) The establishment of an International Commission for Supervision and Control (ICC). The ICC was to be composed of representatives of India, Canada, and Poland, with the Indian representative serving as chairman. Its main function was to be "responsible for supervising the proper execution by the parties of the provisions of the agreement." It was to control the movement of the armed forces of the two parties, supervise the demarcation lines, control the operations of releasing prisoners of war and civilian internees, and supervise, at ports and airfields as

well as along all the frontiers of Vietnam, the execution of the provisions of the agreement.

(4) Independence, general elections, and reunification. The Final Declaration again assured the principles of full independence, unity, and territorial integrity for Vietnam, Laos, and Cambodia. It provided that general elections were to be held in July 1956 under the supervision of an international commission composed of representatives of the member states of the ICC, with the understanding that Vietnam would be reunified as a result of this free expression of the national will (this provision, apparently, was the final political settlement for Vietnam as conceived and agreed upon by Chou En-lai and Mendès-France in late June).

South Vietnam and the United States did not subscribe to the agreements. Whether or not this was done under the collaboration between the two delegations, it subsequently gave them a pretext to act otherwise, although the United States said it would "refrain from the threat or the use of force to disturb" the agreements.

Reactions from the three Communist countries—North Vietnam, Communist China, and the Soviet Union—were favorable and enthusiastic. On July 22 Ho issued an appeal to his people and army, emphasizing peace, independence, and unification:

> The French government has recognized the independence, sovereignty, unity and territorial integrity of our country; it has agreed to withdraw French troops from our country. . . .
>
> The regroupment in two regions is a temporary measure. . . . Regroupment in regions is in no way a partition of our country. . . .
>
> North, Central and South Vietnam are territories of ours. . . . We must endeavor to struggle for the holding of free general elections throughout the country to reunify our territory.[114]

[114] Ho Chi Minh, *Selected Works*, IV, 17-20.

The Geneva Settlement, 1954

Nhan Dan's editorial on July 25 expressed an "enthusiastic welcome" of the Geneva Settlement. It pointed out that the Viet-Minh victory at Dien-Bien-Phu constituted an especially "strong prop" for the success in Geneva. It hailed the settlement as a great diplomatic victory of North Vietnam and a "bitter defeat" of the American "imperialists." It pledged to fight for the "consolidation of peace and strictly implement the agreements on the cessation of hostilities," and for the materialization of "unity, independence and democracy."[115]

Peking's reaction, as expressed by *Jen min jih pao,* differed from Hanoi's on only two points. While upholding Vietnam's peace, independence, and unity through national elections and condemning the United States for its building of a new "colonial empire" in southeast Asia, Peking emphasized the victory of peaceful negotiations and the "big power" status of China:

> The Geneva Conference has demonstrated to the whole world that the use of force to settle international disputes is fruitless and that the age of settling international disputes by negotiation is definitely here to stay. . . .
>
> For the first time, the People's Republic of China, in the role of one of the big Powers, joined the other major Powers in negotiation on vital international problems, and made its contribution that won the acclaim of wide sections of world public opinion. The international position of the People's Republic of China as one of the big world Powers has been recognized universally. Its international prestige has been greatly enhanced.[116]

Pravda's editorial expressed a similar view to that of *Jen min jih pao* on peace and independence in Indochina, the "defeat" of the United States, and the success of peaceful negotiations, but differed on China's "big power" status:

[115] "We Enthusiastically Welcome the Restoration of Peace in Indo-China," editorial, *Nhan Dan* in VNA, July 25, 1954.

[116] "Another Great Victory of Peaceful Negotiation," editorial, *Jen min jih pao,* July 22, 1954, in *SCMP,* 854, pp. 14-17.

The restoration of peace in Indochina . . . is in close and inseparable connection with the effort launched earlier by the peace-loving camp. . . .

The achievement of an agreement on Indochina now clears the road to a settlement of other international problems not settled so far.

. . . The prestige of the USSR is at present at an unprecedented height in the eyes of the world and is considered the banner bearer of peace by the peoples. The political importance of the participation of the Chinese People's Republic in the solving of urgent international problems has become clear at present as never before.[117]

In comparing the reactions from these three Communist countries, one thing, apart from others that have already been discussed, should be pointed out, that is, North Vietnam's silence on "the settlement of international disputes by means of peaceful negotiations." While Moscow was moderate in upholding the principle of "peaceful negotiations," Peking, in much stronger language, stressed that "the use of force to settle international disputes is fruitless" and that "the age of settling international disputes by negotiation is definitely here to stay"—an opposite view to its militant policy toward Vietnam in the late 1960s. All this, on the one hand, indicates that North Vietnam was primarily interested in the issues of its own independence and reunification rather than general international problems. On the other hand, it proves further that a peaceful settlement for Indochina was initiated and brought about mainly through the efforts of Moscow and Peking, not those of the Viet-Minh.

A study of the broadcasts from the three Communist countries during the third phase of the conference indicates a few significant points of their respective propaganda efforts. To show them, a table is given:

[117] "Serious Victory of the Forces of Peace," *Pravda* editorial, in Radio Moscow, Soviet Home Service, July 22, 1954.

TABLE 4

COMPARISON OF VIETNAMESE, CHINESE, AND SOVIET
BROADCASTS ON THE GENEVA CONFERENCE,
JULY 10-22, 1954

Date	Viet-Minh broadcasts				Chinese broadcasts				Soviet broadcasts			
	short	long	D	F	short	long	D	F	short	long	D	F
10					2	1	3					
11					2	1	3			1	1	
12					4	1	5		1		1	
13					7		7		4	3	3	4
14					8	2	10		1	2		3
15												
16					1	1	2					
17					9	2	11					
18					4	3	7					
19		1		1	2	3	5					
20					5	1	6					
21					6	3	9		4	4	5	3
22	2	2		4	1	5	6		2	4	2	4
Totals	2	3		5	51	23	74		12	14	12	14
	5		5		74		74		26		26	

Note: "long" includes documents, commentaries, longer and detailed reports. "Short" includes only brief news items and reports. "D" indicates domestic consumption; "F" indicates foreign consumption.

Sources: Broadcasts from Communist China, the Soviet Union, and the Viet-Minh, as monitored in Washington, D.C., July 10-22, 1954.

The table warrants the following analysis: (1) Communist China made the greatest effort (74 Chinese broadcasts, 26 Soviet, 5 Viet-Minh) in reporting the development of the meeting (including the Western tripartite talks in Paris in mid-July) during the third phase. It shows, therefore, her greatest concern over the conference. (2) While China broadcast on almost a daily basis, showing an interest in both important and unimportant events of the entire conference, the Soviet radio broadcast for five days out of 11, showing its interest only in important events at the beginning and at the end of the meeting. The Viet-Minh radio broadcast for only two days at the end of the conference. The different patterns indicate that China was the most enthusiastic about making known her performance at this the first international conference she had had a part in the outcome of. (3) The broadcasts of China and the Viet-Minh were in English and for foreign consumption (southeast Asia, Europe, and North America); the Soviet ones were directed partly for foreign (mostly Europe) and partly for domestic consumption. This shows China's keen interest in international propaganda. (4) Soviet efforts indicate a moderate position on Indochina, while the Chinese efforts show her greater interest and more aggressive attitude toward the area. These different attitudes, therefore, support the observation that Indochina has never been a vital area of Soviet national interests, but a key region of China's national security.

PHAM VAN DONG's delegation returned to Vietnam from Geneva via China. During his two-day sojourn in Peking, Dong received an enthusiastic welcome from the Chinese government and people. On his arrival at the Peking airport on August 2, he saluted "affectionately" the Chinese people and "the brilliant sun of the Asian people, Chairman Mao Tse-tung."[118] At the Vietnamese embassy's reception on August 3 in honor of Pham Van Dong, Chou En-lai spoke of the significance of settling international issues through peace negotiations, and Dong repeatedly hailed Chinese aid and friendship, saying: "During the eight years of the war of resistance, the Vietnamese people had the warm sympathy and support of the Chinese people, the Chinese Communist Party and the Government of the Chinese People's Republic. . . . We have learned from China's experience in armed struggle, people's war, democratic and land reforms, and in financial and economic work during the war of resistance. By combining China's valuable experience with the practical conditions of the war of resistance in Vietnam, we have won tremendous military victories and achieved outstanding results in land reforms, financial and economic work and in other fields."[119]

[118] NCNA, Peking, August 2, 1954, in *SCMP*, 861, p. 3; also *Jen min jih pao*, August 3, 1954.
[119] NCNA, Peking, August 3, 1954, in *SCMP*, 861, pp. 12-13.

Significantly the slogan, "Mao Tse-tung—the brilliant sun of the Asian people," was new in Vietnamese Communist jargon. First used by Pham Van Dong, it was repeated by Hoang Minh Giam, minister of propaganda, and other Viet-Minh leaders who went to Peking in late September for the celebration of the fifth anniversary of the establishment of the Peking regime.[120] After four years of close relationship, the Viet-Minh now began to follow the Chinese personality cult of Mao, which had been established gradually since the Second Sino-Japanese war.

Sino-Vietnamese relations after the Geneva Conference were further strengthened by the appointment of Lo Kuei-po as the first Chinese Communist ambassador to North Vietnam. The Soviet Union appointed Alexander Lavri-shchev as its envoy to the DRV, but the Viet-Minh welcomed and received Lo Kuei-po with much greater fanfare than it did the Soviet envoy. Clinging to the concept of the traditional tributary system, Ho was polite to the Chinese envoy, sending five high-ranking officials to welcome and escort Lo at the border.[121] The courtesy was offered by Vietnam in the past, particularly at the beginning of a new Chinese or Vietnamese dynasty. When, for instance, the Minh dynasty was established in 1368, the Chinese court sent Chang Yi-ning as its envoy in the following year to Annam with the mission of granting the title of king to the Tran dynasty. The king of Annam sent his high-ranking official, Nguyen Nu Luong, to welcome the Chinese envoy.[122] When Chinese President Liu Shao-ch'i visited Hanoi in May 1963 Ho Chi Minh sent Minister of Culture Hoang Minh Giam and the Vietnamese ambassador to China,

[120] NCNA, Peking, September 26, 1954, in *SCMP*, 892, September 25-27, 1954.

[121] The five officials were: Tran Cong Tuong (Vice-Minister of Justice); Maj.Gen. Chu Van Tan; Nguyen Huu Ang (member of the Administrative Committee of the North Vietnam Interzone); Hoang Van Cheo (Chairman of the Administrative Committee of Lang-Son Province); and Le Thanh Nghi (Central Committee member of the Lao Dong Party).

[122] "Annan," in *Ming shih* (History of the Ming Dynasty), (Shanghai, reprinted 1934), p. 819/7905.

Tran Tu Binh, to Kunming to welcome and escort Liu from China to Hanoi.[123]

In response to Ho's wish, made on August 2, 1954, for greater Chinese support and encouragement, Chou En-lai promised to provide the support. He reported to the first session of the Chinese People's Congress in Peking on September 23: "In its struggle for the complete fulfillment of the [Geneva] agreements and for the restoration of national economy, the Democratic Republic of Vietnam will obtain full support from China."[124] Yet before the Geneva Agreements were implemented, SEATO was organized and American assistance to South Vietnam was accelerated. On December 8, 1954 Pham Van Dong, North Vietnam's foreign minister, delivered his first post-Geneva letter to Molotov and Eden, which complained about American intervention in Vietnam:

> The government of the United States has recently sent to Saigon General Lawton Collins as U.S. Ambassador to the Ngo Dinh Diem government. In General Collins' own words, the special mission with which he has been entrusted in this capacity, aims at "giving U. S. unconditional support to the Ngo Dinh Diem government" and at "aiding it by every possible means." This aid essentially consists of the "training by the American mission of the forces of the Viet-Nam army" whose equipment "will be 90 per cent American."
>
> Thus, the aggressive aim of the Manila treaty begins to be materialized [sic] in Southern Viet-Nam with the coming of the mission of General Collins. . . .
>
> The Viet-Namese people and the Government of the Democratic Republic of Viet-Nam strongly oppose these extremely serious breaches of the Geneva agreements, of which General Collins' activities and declarations have brought incontrovertible proof."[125]

[123] Radio Hanoi, in English, to Europe and Asia, May 10, 1963.
[124] *Jen min jih pao*, September 24, 1954, p. 3.
[125] VNA, Hanoi, December 8, 1954.

The Geneva Settlement, 1954

The era of French colonialism was over, but a new one of American involvement had just begun. Ironically, 14 years later, the agony of the American fighting in Vietnam caused Lyndon B. Johnson to decline seeking a second term of presidency for the unity of his party and for a peace settlement with North Vietnam.

7. Epilogue: Peking, Hanoi and a New Peace for Vietnam

<<<<<<<<<<<<<<<<<<<<<<<<<<<<<<<<<<<<<<<<<<<<<<<<<

"This is a new big fraud by the Johnson Administration. . . .
"The Vietnam question can be solved only by completely
defeating the U.S. aggressor on the battlefield and driving it
out of South Vietnam."
— *Peking Review* (April 12, 1968) on President
Johnson's call for a peace talk with North
Vietnam on March 31, 1968

AN EXAMINATION of Sino-Vietnamese relations from 1938
to 1954 makes it evident that several fundamental factors
played a significant role. While Chinese Nationalist policies
differed remarkably from those of the Communists, the
pattern of the relationship showed no major change from
that of the past. My intention in this chapter is to highlight
the basic factors that helped shape Sino-Vietnamese relations, to indicate the significance of the different policies
of these two nations, to establish a pattern of the development of the relationship, and to compare the peace movement of 1954 with the new peace campaign in the late
1960s.

Four factors have served as outstanding elements in the
development of Sino-Vietnamese relations in the past. First,
geographical contiguity is a reasonably permanent factor
drawing the two nations together. When this geographical
situation is complicated by a resurgent, powerful Chinese
regime, China does often influence Vietnam's destiny, regardless of the character of the Chinese government—
imperial, nationalist, or Communist. If Vietnam is at war
and its sea route is closed or restricted by hostile power(s),
it would willingly or not have to depend on China as an
avenue to the outside world and as a main source of foreign
aid. Otherwise it would be engaged in a hopelessly isolated
war. On the other hand, the Chinese occasionally use Vietnam as their revolutionary base and take refuge there.

Epilogue: Peking, Hanoi

Modern technology has not yet been able to completely overcome the territorial barrier. The Indochinese war, the Nationalists' retreat to Vietnam, and the present American fighting in Vietnam have demonstrated the importance of this factor of geopolitics. It is therefore valid to assert that if the Viet-Minh forces had been in a geographical situation like the Huks in the Philippines or the Communists in Malaya, without continued and essential foreign aid, they would have in all likelihood suffered the same desperate situation from their enemy as the Huks and the Malayan Communists did.

Second, the long historic and cultural background has developed a sentiment of looking to China among the Vietnamese whenever China is engaged in a significant political development, cultural movement, or social change. From the self-imposed status of "small dragon" and "southern kingdom" in ancient times to the civil service examinations and anti-foreign campaign in the modern age, Vietnam has learned much from China, not only in principle but in technique. French political and cultural influence, of course, should not be ignored. But the colonial status of Vietnam somewhat offset French influence and served to increase longing for sympathy and support from China, which suffered a similar fate from Western powers. It should be pointed out, however, that determined Vietnamese resistance to China in the past indicates that Vietnam has never automatically or indistinctively imitated China.

Third, racial affinity and the similarity of socio-economic conditions have developed into considerable natural ties between the two peoples. The Vietnamese have a Chinese origin. Their physical appearance is not as distinguishable as that of Indonesians or Thais from the people of southern China. Vietnamese social rites, customs, religious practices, rice planting, and agriculture are either originally imported from China or similar to those of China. Against this background, it is not surprising to read Ho Chi Minh's description of the Sino-Vietnamese relationship as "particularly intimate" and as "one hundred favors, a thousand loyal

332

affections, [and] ten thousand loves."[1] Accordingly, it is only natural that the Vietnamese frequently imitate successful and applicable Chinese social innovations and economic developments. The Chinese way of life in various social and economic aspects is to a certain extent even more applicable to Vietnam than to the Chinese province of Sinkiang.

Fourth, a similar revolutionary cause and ideology have helped cement the relationship, particularly during the Communist period. Although the goal of the Vietnamese revolution is not entirely identical with that of China, its revolutionary process, from the organization of the VNQDD and the ICP, the resistance war to the land reform campaign, has generally followed that of China within two to 10 years. When the revolutionary interests of one nation coincide with those of the other, their relationship grows particularly intimate; otherwise, it declines. The Vietnamese nationalist revolution was modeled after and benefitted from that of China; the ICP and the Viet-Minh received no significant assistance from the KMT. But Communist China's aid to North Vietnam from 1950 to 1954 was decisive in her victory over the French. Their relations were good throughout.

In addition to these factors, Ho's charismatic leadership was crucial. The training he received, the hardship he experienced, and the knowledge of world affairs he learned all enriched his perspicacity in dealing with difficult problems under various circumstances. He is a man with nationalist sentiment, Communist faith, Vietnamese will, Oriental mentality, and a special trait of patience and flexibility none of his contemporaries could match. He will never allow himself to get in a situation from which he cannot retreat when events run against him. After he returned to Asia in 1938, the Vietnamese revolution reached a new stage. Apparently under the influence of Mao Tsetung's theory and strategy, Ho rebuilt his revolution on a

[1] Vietnam Information *Bulletin* (DRV, Rangoon), August 9, 1961.

comparatively solid ground by establishing the close-knit organization of the Viet-Minh and the secure revolutionary base of Pac-Bo under the command of the ICP. He was so skillful in masking his Communist cause with nationalism that even Chang Fa-k'uei, a powerful Nationalist general in southern China during World War II, selected him as the most promising Vietnamese leader for the war against Japan in Vietnam, as well as for Vietnam's independence movement. In the eyes of Chang Fa-k'uei, Ho was the only man among the wartime Vietnamese leaders in China with the necessary qualities to lead the Vietnamese revolution. Chang's choice enhanced Ho's prestige. But Ho's declaration of independence convinced the Vietnamese people that he was the first man able to declare Vietnam's independence, for which they had fought for 80 years. He was praised as the successor to Vietnamese resistance heroes, Phan Dinh Phung, Hoang Hoa Tham, Phan Boi Chau, and Nguyen Thai Hoc. Although he was denounced for being a Communist, his resistance war was not criticized by anti-Communist Vietnamese. On the contrary, many anti–Viet-Minh leaders in Saigon took advantage of the war against the French to exact personal gains from the French. Aroused by patriotism and disgusted with those who allied themselves with the French colonialists, thousands of Vietnamese, intellectuals and peasants alike, turned to Ho. By 1950 Vietnamese nationalism had fused with Communism and helped Ho through the most difficult and isolated stage of the war.

The Vietnam policies of the Chinese Nationalist government were a series of reactions to events as they unfolded. Sometimes the Nationalists had no policy; sometimes it arrived at a policy without sufficient deliberation. One excuse China maintained was that Chungking was too preoccupied with the war with Japan. When Vietnamese events attracted China's attention, it was Chang Fa-k'uei, not the foreign ministry in Chungking, who projected an ambitious plan for allying Vietnamese interests with those of China against their common enemy, Japan. After Japan was defeated, Chang hoped Vietnam would obtain independence under the aegis of China. The significance of this policy lies in the manifestation of China's interest in Vietnam as nourished by her historic tradition and revolutionary interests. With a strong nationalistic sentiment, Chang did not take the French position into consideration. As the Second World War approached its end, a French return to Indochina became more apparent, and Chungking put aside Chang's suggestion; it worked out a policy for dealing with the French instead.

Yet China's neutral position during the occupation period and immediately afterward was actually in favor of a French return—against the will of the Vietnamese, nationalist or Communist. Apparently it was in deference to French colonial policy in Indochina and a reversal of China's long-cherished principle of assisting oppressed Asian peoples to achieve independence. At that time the United States had already shown her deference to the former colonial power in Indochina, Burma, and India; it is equally true that China had obtained good concessions from France regarding Indochina. But the neutral "deference," coupled with the notorious behavior of Lu Han's occupation forces, damaged China's reputation in Vietnam. China's good revolution-inspired image was destroyed. Some Vietnamese, unaware of the increasing difficulties of the Chinese government with its Communist rivals, even cast doubt on China's willingness and ability to help Vietnam achieve independence. They complained that China had used and exploited Vietnam for her own purposes, while giving no needed assistance in return. When Vietnamese revolutionary interests conflicted with those of China, China did not extend sympathy to Vietnam, to say nothing of material aid. Naturally Sino-Vietnamese relations declined.

To Ho Chi Minh, Chinese Nationalist policies toward Vietnam could probably best be described by an Oriental term, "sweet and sour." During the war Ho saw China as a necessary ally of his revolutionary cause. In staying in China, he well understood China's Vietnam policies. His plans for the future of his country made him dependent on Chinese support. But he was fully aware of the fact that that support would be limited. Mao was too far away to help. Most of the leaders in the Kuomintang government disapproved of Ho's activities. All he could depend on were a few leaders who were sympathetic with his cause. In Vietnam there were problems everywhere. The French, the Japanese, the Bao Dai puppet regime, and various opportunistic political groups had to be eliminated from Vietnamese soil. It was therefore only natural that Ho turned to China. He first received favorable, semi-secret treatment, and later spent a year and a half in Chinese prisons, which almost ruined his health. The "plan" he submitted to Chang Fa-k'uei was actually a blueprint for his future revolutionary program for training, organizing, and other activities in northern Tonkin. When Ho realized that Chang planned to use him, he used Chang first. Ho did not receive much assistance from Chang. He did, however, receive much encouragement and some aid from the OSS teams.

U.S. deference to France after the war cost the United States a golden opportunity to save thousands of American lives in Vietnam in the 1960s. Had Washington insisted on granting independence to Vietnam, as Britain did to India, the American involvement in Vietnam in the 1960s might well have been avoided. But the United States did not come to Ho's assistance when he was in dire need of it. Nationalist China was no longer a supporter. Disappointed by China and America, Ho turned to his former colonial master. The conflict between the returned French colonialism and resurgent Vietnamese nationalism led to the Indochinese war. Ho's realization of the difficulties of the war prevented him from adopting a drastic policy toward hostile Nationalist China in the rear. He held on and waited for a change on the China mainland and in France, without an expectation of help from Mao.

The significance of the Chinese revolutionary model for Vietnam lies in Peking's offer of material aid, which helped to implement the model, and in Vietnam's learning from the

Chinese experience. Chinese Communist leaders believed early in the Second World War that China's experience was applicable throughout southeast Asia. They arranged to export it in late 1949 while their victory over the Kuomintang was still fresh. In doing so, Peking employed party apparatus and front organizations rather than formal diplomacy. Prior to Vietnam's open acceptance of the Chinese experience in late 1950, Peking had already begun to extend unconditional material aid to the Viet-Minh. Throughout the remaining years of the Indochinese war, the increasing Chinese assistance in the fields of the military and the economy, as well as in the party policy, was intended to show the applicability of the Chinese revolutionary model. On the Viet-Minh side the soft party line, the bandit-type guerrilla forces, and the inadequate financial and economic system were in great need of reorientation, reorganization, and reform. Since China could throw out foreign powers, defeat the Nationalist government, and establish a Communist regime, why could not the Viet-Minh do the same? Thus inspired, North Vietnam moved swiftly toward China in almost every aspect, from learning of Mao's thought to the agricultural tax. The Viet-Minh victory in the fall of 1950 was the first manifestation of the new, successful relationship. As the resistance war progressed, the friendship was crowned by the battle of Dien-Bien-Phu. During 1950-1954 North Vietnam's learning from China was characterized by a strong pro-Chinese sentiment. Pro-Chinese leaders such as Ho Tung Mau (who died in 1951), Truong Chinh, Hoang Quoc Viet, Hoang Van Hoan, and Tran Huy Lieu formed a powerful unit in North Vietnam. Chinese influence was raised far above the level enjoyed by Vietnam's imperial and nationalist predecessors.

The Soviet Union took an increasing interest in Vietnam after 1950, but remained behind China. There are at least two major reasons for the Soviet Union remaining second to China. First, there are fundamental differences between Russia and Vietnam, geographically, historically, culturally, and in socio-economic conditions. Vietnam has never been of vital national and revolutionary interest to the Soviet Union. Consequently Soviet policy toward the area prior to 1950 was characterized by indifference and indecision. Second, from 1950 to 1954 the world was at the height of the cold war period. Communist nations remained solidly behind the Soviet Union. China was a new Communist country, leaning to one side, and making no challenge to Soviet leadership of world Communism. Since China had acknowledged its deference to Russia, its influence in Vietnam did not run counter to Soviet interests there; there was no need to compete with China in Vietnam. Thus the Soviet Union gave only propaganda and moral support to the Viet-Minh, leaving material aid and the leading role to Peking.

While the peace campaign of 1953-1954 was initiated by the Communist camp, the Communist initiative, it must be emphasized, was taken only after the Communists had met stiff resistance from the allies in Korea. The peace movement resulted in the armistice in Korea, raising high hopes for a peace settlement in Indochina. In accepting Soviet and Chinese persuasion to reach a settlement at Geneva, Ho depended on Russia and China for the realization of reunification through elections to be held in 1956. Although it was beyond imagination in 1954 that the Soviet Union and Communist China would soon be in serious dispute (which has undermined united Communist action against the United States in Vietnam in the late 1960s), North Vietnam must have by now realized the adverse consequences of the Soviet and Chinese role in dividing Vietnam. Hanoi might well have complained that both China and Russia should bear responsibility for her disaster and hardship under the destructive American bombing.

The Chinese role at Geneva is a good indication that her action or inaction could affect the destiny of the "small dragon." Historically, Chinese influence on Vietnam's destiny is even more apparent, because China was for Vietnam a military protector as well as aggressor, an economic promoter and an exploiter, a cultural teacher and an indoctrinator. In the development of their relationship, a pattern was established: when China was powerful and magnanimous, Vietnam paid tribute to and imitated China; when China was weak or disorganized, Vietnam was more independent. When China was aggressive, Vietnam resisted. Under French rule the pattern was complicated by new international factors; China and Vietnam extended sympathy to each other after the intrusion from the West. Sometimes China provided Vietnam with revolutionary inspiration, training bases, and refuge; sometimes Vietnam was the helping country. From 1938 to 1954 China was weak, helpful, aggressive (but did not invade), chaotic, powerful, and magnanimous. Accordingly, Vietnam enjoyed more independence, quietly resisted, paid gratitude to, and imitated China.

In the Communist activities during the Kuomintang period, the Sino-Vietnamese border proved to be a vital region. When the enemy attacked, one side (the Viet-Minh or the Chinese Communists) retreated from their original position to the other side of the border. Then when the enemy retreated, they regrouped and returned to their original base. With this flexibility the Viet-Minh and Chinese Communists survived and grew stronger. During 1950-1954 the border area was used for training, organization, and storage of equipment and supplies. Under the impact of American air raids in the late 1960s, North Vietnam again depended heavily on Chinese assistance in the border area for war material shipments, railroad repairing, and stationing airplanes.

After the coming of the French, Vietnam's internal power patterns shifted; they shifted more as more foreign powers were involved. Despite the number of political groups in the struggle, one group would certainly be looking to China for help, while the other(s) sought aid from another foreign power(s). So often has it been the case that the internal struggle turned out to be a microcosmic image of international conflict. The internal struggle invited international conflict; the conflict sharpened the struggle. As the record shows, there have been several conflicts with China, on one hand, and with France, Japan, or the United States, on the other. The rise of Communist China signaled the comeback of Chinese influence in Vietnam, replacing French colonialism. After France was gone, the United States stepped in. In the internal struggle since 1954, the level has been broadened, with China, the Soviet Union, and other Communist nations on one side, and the United States and its allies on the other. Vietnam became the focus of international conflict between the Communists and the United States, a conflict between East and the West.

IT WOULD NOT be straying from the subject of this book to compare briefly the 1968-1969 peace movement for Vietnam with that of 1954. Although the origins of the Paris peace talks between the United States and North Vietnam can be traced back to 1962, when the United States began to sharply increase her manpower in Vietnam, genuine movement began in 1965. Hoping to stop North Vietnam's infiltration in the south, the United States escalated the war in February 1965 by initiating air attacks on the north. The escalation invited more Soviet aid to North Vietnam. As the war increased in scope and tempo both sides shipped in more advanced weapons. The United States virtually placed itself in an endless arms race with the entire Communist bloc, accompanied by rapidly increasing manpower. The assumption that North Vietnam can be subdued with air raids is to underestimate the will of the Vietnamese people and a misunderstanding of the whole issue. To many intellectuals, the United States commitment to Vietnam has little to do with American national interests. Starting with the Washington "teach-in" on May 15, 1965, the Vietnam issue has been debated and redebated. Anti-war sentiment has grown from peaceful discussions to massive demonstrations. The failure of persuasions for peace talks by various world leaders was regarded as a reason for further escalation. And further escalation accelerated the development of the anti-war movement. As the war has been escalated, so has the anti-war campaign. Before long, the campaign developed into an almost worldwide peace movement. The problem inevitably became a 1968 presidential campaign issue. When Senators Eugene J. McCarthy and Robert F. Kennedy took up the issue against President Johnson's war policy, the turmoil of political disunity in the Democratic Party and in the nation prompted Johnson to call for a new peace talk and to announce his decision not to run for a second term.

There are some outstanding comparisons between the 1954 and 1968 peace movements. First, the 1954 campaign was initiated by the World Peace Council of the Communist camp; the 1968 peace move started with the intellectuals in the United States. The former spread from the Soviet Union to all Communist countries (including North Vietnam) and France; the latter spread from the United States to almost all its major allies. While the former took the form of mass organization and support under the auspices of governments, the latter was among intellectuals and students against the Johnson administration. This comparison suggests that when a peace movement gains momentum with international implications, it can influence the government (Communist or non-Communist) to change its policy. Yet insofar as Communist control of its subject peoples remains unchanged, such a movement can only spread out from, rather than penetrate into, the Communist world.

Second, China's attitude in 1968 was vastly different from that of 1954. In 1954 China was one of the major champions of peace in Indochina. Sometimes she appeared even more anxious to see peace there than did Russia. In 1968 Peking insisted on rejecting any peace talks on Vietnam. As Maj. Gen. Nguyen Van Vinh, chairman of the reunification department of the Lao Dong Party and deputy chief of the general staff of North Vietnam's army, said in April 1966, "China holds the view that conditions for negotiations are not yet ripe." The Chinese position in 1966 was virtually unchanged in 1968. In April 1968 Peking denounced Johnson's March 31, 1968 proposal for a peace talk as a "new fraud," and urged the Vietnamese people to "fight on to the end." When the Paris talks began May 10, 1968, Peking again expressed disapproval. (The news of the Paris talks was not released in China until mid-October 1968). Compared with its compromising attitude and strongly conciliatory views in 1954 that "the age of settling international disputes by negotiation is *definitely* here to stay," its hardened position in 1968 had come nearly full circle. Undoubtedly Peking is continuing to fight for its policy, which has three major goals: to exclude all Western powers from Asia, for Asians to settle Asian affairs, and to lead all Asian nations. China's policy toward Vietnam has been directed toward keeping the United States bogged down as long as possible in an attempt to drain U.S. financial and manpower resources in order to compel her to capitulate—unconditional withdrawal from Vietnam. However, it is doubtful whether Peking's present militant attitude toward the new peace moves, which Hanoi apparently welcomes, would help Peking achieve any of these goals. Will Peking intervene in the new Vietnam peace talks? China can do nothing to undermine the four-party (U.S., South Vietnam, North Vietnam, and Viet Cong) talks in Paris[2] except to register opposition to them. But she will sabotage any

[2] Xuan Thuy (original name, Nguyen Xuan Thuy, from Ha-Dong province, b. 1912), the chief delegate of North Vietnam to the 1968 Paris preliminary talks (December 1968), was improperly labeled as pro-Moscow by the American press (for instance, *New York Times,* May 4, 1968). Before he became Hanoi's Foreign Minister in 1963, the important positions he held were chief editor and director of *Cuu Quoc,* chairman of the Journalist Association, secretary-general of the Vietnam Peace Committee, vice-president of the Vietnam-Chinese Friendship Association, member of the North Vietnam delegation to the 1961-1962 Geneva Conference on Laos, and secretary-general of the Standing Committee of the National Assembly (of which Truong Chinh was and is the chairman). From August 1964 to April 1965 his correspondence with Chinese Foreign Minister Ch'en Yi protesting American air raids in the North appeared together several times in Peking's *Jen min jih pao.* His views on this issue were surprisingly attuned to those of Ch'en Yi. His removal from the post of Foreign Minister in April 1965 was due to the shift of Hanoi's policy from pro-Peking to neutral after Kosygin's visit to North Vietnam. If Thuy is not pro-Peking, he is, as of December 1968, a neutral figure in Hanoi, and not pro-Moscow.

future international settlement by refusing to attend such a settlement conference unless the United States offers a handsome concession to China, Hanoi reaches an understanding with Peking, or Peking changes its leadership to be conciliatory. If, however, there is to be no new international settlement for Vietnam, it is very unlikely that Peking will have a chance to intervene seriously.

Third, while Hanoi's diplomacy today is much more sophisticated and independent than in 1954, its strategy of war-and-negotiation remains unchanged. In 1954 North Vietnam followed the lead of the Soviet Union and Communist China in coming out for peace talks. Her dependency on Russia and China at Geneva was conspicuous. In 1968 North Vietnam agreed to preliminary peace talks with the United States against the Chinese will and without previous consultation with Russia. The sophistication and independence of Hanoi's diplomacy can be attributed to at least four causes: (1) Failure to fulfill the 1954 Geneva Agreements on the reunification of Vietnam has taught Hanoi to be more independent of Russia and China. (2) The Sino-Soviet conflict since 1960 has altered the world Communist movement from monolith to polycentrism, which gives an opportunity to smaller Communist countries (such as North Korea, Rumania, and Cuba) to hold a more independent position from Peking and Moscow; Hanoi follows this small group. (3) China's refusal to the Soviet proposal for united Communist action against the United States in Vietnam, originally suggested by Pham Van Dong, greatly disappointed Hanoi. By implication, Hanoi felt it should be more independent in its own policies from any foreign influence, particularly Chinese. (4) The convulsion and chaos in China, especially in Yunnan, Kwangsi, and Kwangtung, created by the Chinese "cultural revolution" has cost Vietnam's respect for and fear of China. Peking's influence on Hanoi has greatly declined. One of the most solid evidences is the trend of the Sino-Vietnamese delegation exchanges from 1964 to 1968. In 1964, when Hanoi took a slightly pro-Peking stand in the Sino-Soviet dispute,[3] North Vietnam sent 34 delegations to China (17 to Russia), and China sent 17 in return (Russia sent eight to North Vietnam); in 1968 North Vietnam sent only five to China (18 to Russia), while China did not send a delegation to Hanoi (Russia sent six to Hanoi). The table and figure on the next page illustrate the pattern.

The pattern indicates the drastic decline in Sino-Vietnamese delegation exchanges and the comparatively stable situation in Soviet-Vietnamese contacts. Apart from the above four major factors that caused such a change, other reasons are Russia's great efforts to send military aid to Hanoi and her attitude toward peace negotiations, which was more acceptable to Hanoi than Peking's intransigent, militant policy. The present cool relationship between Peking and Hanoi falls into the second pattern of the Sino-Vietnamese relations pointed out earlier: when China is weak, Vietnam enjoys more independence.

In 1954 North Vietnam's war-and-negotiation strategy was to fight for a military victory at Dien-Bien-Phu, to enable its delegation at Geneva to negotiate from strength. The victory resulted in the end of French colonialism in Indochina. Prior to the 1968 peace talks, Hanoi had already decided to adopt a similar strategy in dealing with future peace moves. "While negotiating," said Maj. Gen. Nguyen Van Vinh in April 1966, "we will continue fighting the enemy more vigorously . . . because the decisive factor lies in the battle field." Le Duan, first secretary of the Lao Dong Party, also disclosed Hanoi's adoption of the same strategy. Both Vinh and Duan emphasized the successful application of the strategy by the Viet-Minh to its fighting against the French and by the Chinese Communists against Chiang Kai-shek and the United States. In early April 1968, after Hanoi had agreed to peace talks, *Quan Doi Nhan Dan* called the attention of its armed forces to the "new situation," which was a "most decisive and combat [sic] situa-

[3] For Hanoi's position see King C. Chen, "North Vietnam in the Sino-Soviet Dispute," *Asian Survey*, Vol. IV, No. 9 (September 1964), pp. 1,023-36.

TABLE 5

NORTH VIETNAM'S DELEGATION EXCHANGES
WITH CHINA AND RUSSIA, 1964-1968

	1964	1965	1966	1967	1968
N. Vietnam to China	34	17	26	13	5
N. Vietnam to Russia	17	11	13	17	18
China to N. Vietnam	17	17	8	2	0
Russia to N. Vietnam	8	8	6	10	6

FIGURE 1

TREND OF THE DELEGATION EXCHANGES, 1964-68

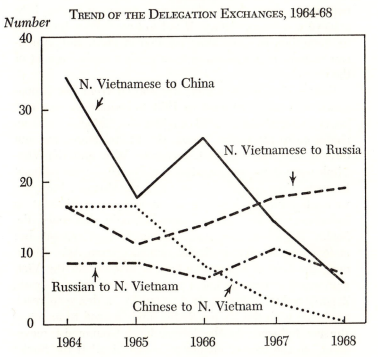

Source: Broadcasts from North Vietnam, Communist China and the Soviet Union as monitored in Washington, D.C., 1964-1968.

tion" and which would "decide the fate" of Vietnam. It also urged them to "make outstanding progress in all fields, to overcome all difficulties and defeat all enemies." The newspaper left no doubt that they should take advantage of the bombing halt by shipping more arms and men to the south, so as to prepare for decisive attacks on the enemy at an opportune time. In view of the fact that the infiltration of North Vietnamese troops south in April-May 1968 increased by "at least two or three times," and that their troop and supply movements quadrupled in the southern part of North Vietnam in November-December of the same year, Hanoi seems to have made maximum use of the new situation (of the bombing halt), and faithfully put its war-and-negotiation strategy into effect. Its purpose, of course, is to achieve a military victory, if not a second Dien-Bien-Phu, to strengthen its bargaining position in Paris. But, American military might seems able to prevent such a repeat of the feat.

Fourth, the Soviet Union has shifted from her propaganda and moral support in 1954 to serious concern and heavy material aid in 1968. In 1954 the Chinese made no challenge to the Soviet Union, the United States was not directly involved in the Indochinese War, and the Viet-Minh were doing well against the French. Soviet national interests were not at stake in Vietnam. Moscow, however, was interested in bringing about a peace settlement in Indochina. In 1968 the Chinese not only challenged the Soviet Union in the world Communist movement but endeavored to exclude Soviet influence from Asia. Moreover, the United States was heavily involved in the Vietnam war. The present Soviet policy in Indochina, as Donald Zagoria rightly observes, is directed by "a desire to reach a détente with the United States" and "a need to maintain Russian influence in the international Communist movement," in the face of challenge from China.[4] If the Soviet Union had taken no active role in aiding Vietnam, her

[4] Donald S. Zagoria, *Vietnam Triangle* (New York: Pegasus, 1967), p. 42.

influence in Vietnam would have been excluded by China, and North Vietnam would have faced an extremely difficult situation under the American military pressure. If, on the other hand, the Soviet Union had made too much effort in assisting North Vietnam, it would have jeopardized Soviet-American relations. Under these circumstances, the Soviet Union was compelled by China and the United States to extend substantial military aid to North Vietnam, but was restrained from going too far by the fear of a Soviet-American military confrontation. To avoid such a military danger, the Soviet Union was, and still is, in favor of deescalation and a settlement through negotiations. Her present desire for peace is the same as that of 1954, yet her concern over the Vietnam situation is much more serious than it was 15 years ago.

Fifth, both French and American internal politics were an important factor in the peace movements of 1954 and 1968. In 1953-1954 French dissent grew in influence in the National Assembly. The dissidents demanded that the government enter into peace negotiations with the Viet-Minh. Its outcome was generally predicted by the Viet-Minh leaders in 1947. In the case of the United States, Ho believes the longer he fights the more divided the United States will become. Although conditions in North Vietnam during the persistent American air raids from 1965 to 1968 were very difficult, Ho's unshakable will and long-range strategy have led him to believe that the American commitment to Vietnam will eventually cease under the pressure of prolonged fighting, American internal politics, and the international situation. In 1966-1967 the Vietnam problem became an American political issue; it developed to become a presidential campaign issue in 1968. The success of the Viet Cong Tet offensive of 1968 questioned the optimistic views on the war held by the Johnson administration and the "hawks." The feeling among the public grew, that further escalation of the war would eventually lead the United States to a hopeless and dangerous situation. Hanoi's favorable response to Johnson's call for peace talks in April 1968 was not due entirely to the reduction of the bombing in the north, but instead to the more dramatic and important announcement by President Johnson not to seek a second term. And the agreement to the enlarged Paris talks by Hanoi and the Viet Cong was conditioned by the total bombing halt in the north. This gave them a psychologically face-saving opportunity to come out in favor of talks. Hanoi and the Viet Cong had already realized the influence of American internal politics on the war, and saw no need to wait for the outcome of the presidential elections. American internal politics had become a significant factor, similar to that of French internal politics on Indochina in 1953-1954.

In the foregoing discussion the question of Ho Chi Minh's successor often arises. To answer this question, let us turn to a few promising contenders and their factions:

TRUONG CHINH: chairman of the National Assembly standing committee; formerly secretary-general of the Indochinese Communist Party and the Lao Dong Party; leader of the pro-Chinese faction.

LE DUAN: first secretary of the Lao Dong Party; formerly political commissar of the Viet-Minh resistance forces in South Vietnam; recently shifted from pro-Chinese to neutral.

VO NGUYEN GIAP: minister of defense and commander-in-chief of the Vietnamese People's Army; leader of the pro-Soviet faction.

PHAM VAN DONG: premier; formerly vice-premier, vice-president and foreign minister; leader of the moderate group.

At this writing, events indicate that Truong Chinh has lost his opportunity to succeed Ho. Although he is trying hard to stage a comeback, his success will depend very much on the restoration of a truly cordial Sino-Vietnamese relationship, a relationship similar to that of 1950-1955, which is difficult to restore. Le Duan will probably grow more powerful in the party, but not in the government. Vo Nguyen Giap is popular and has a firm control over the armed forces, but Ho's policy that "the party commands the army," rather than "the army commands the party," precludes the chances of Giap's becoming an immediate heir of Ho. The only promising figure is Pham Van Dong.

First, Dong and Giap are Ho's two most trusted lieutenants. Dong is a protégé of Ho dating to 1926; Giap first met Ho in Kunming in 1940. On several extremely important and critical occasions since the Ho-Dong reunion in China in 1940, Ho has entrusted Dong and Giap with serious responsibilities. In 1942, when he left Vietnam for China, Ho designated Dong (until 1944) to assume the leadership of the Viet-Minh administration, Giap, military affairs. In July 1945, when Ho was seriously ill, he called in the two men to give his final words. Since 1950 Dong has served as vice-premier (premier, Ho Chi Minh), vice-president, foreign minister, and premier. In the military council, of which Ho is chairman, Dong and Giap are the only two vice-chairmen. Foreign visitors to North Vietnam in the past few years have reported Ho's poor health, and Dong's assumption of a greater political burden in running the country. These arrangements indicate that Ho has been building up Dong's position and prestige. In Oriental countries, particularly an Oriental Communist country like Vietnam (as well as China), a father-image leader like "Uncle Ho" has a considerably strong power to designate his heir. If, therefore, the situation remains unchanged when Ho passes away from the political scene, Pham Van Dong would likely be the first choice to succeed him. Vice-President Ton Duc Thang might become a figurehead president, but the real power would be in Dong's hands.

Second, Giap strongly supports Dong. A rival of Truong Chinh, General Giap is no supporter of Le Duan. He has associated with Dong closely since 1936, and is probably the most dependable friend and powerful comrade of Dong. Since military power is always a decisive factor in Communist politics (for example, the military power in the Chinese Cultural Revolution and the military role in the decision on the Soviet invasion of Czechoslovakia), and since Giap is a powerful and popular military leader, his support would definitely increase the strength and prestige of Dong when the succession issue arises.

Third, Dong does not identify himself as either pro-Peking or pro-Moscow, but maintains good relations with both factions. As moderate and neutral, he remains aloof from the factions' power struggle and is respected by both. Generally, a neutral leader will be supported by rivaling groups when their struggle ends in a draw, but will not be truly trusted by either. Dong's position, however, is somewhat different, because he enjoys strong support from the pro-Soviet military leader, Giap. This factor makes Dong even more indispensable, because the pro-Chinese faction, whose influence now declines, needs Dong to hold in check the overexpansion of the power of the pro-Soviet group.

Nevertheless, Le Duan's position should not be underestimated. Well known for his Communist theory since the 1930s, and reportedly a graduate of the Whampoa Military Academy, Duan is building up his strength in the party. In his shift from a formerly slightly pro-Chinese position to a neutral one, he is probably imitating Ho or Dong to rid himself of any factional identity. If Ho recommends Dong to head the party, Duan would be able to keep his present post against Truong Chinh.

An era in Vietnam will end when Ho Chi Minh dies. His influence will undoubtedly linger, but eventually there will be changes. Much will depend on Hanoi's new leadership, conditions in the south, the situation in China and the Soviet Union, and the American commitment in southeast Asia. In any event, North Vietnam will always face problems with China.

As I completed my final check of the galleys on September 3, 1969, Hanoi announced Ho's death. I don't expect an immediate, drastic change in Hanoi's policies and the succession issue, and maintain the above observations.

APPENDICES AND
BIBLIOGRAPHY

Appendix I
Poems From *Prison Diary**
by Ho Chi Minh

<<<<<<<<<<<<<<<<<<<<<<<<<<<<<<<<<<<<<<<<<<<<<<

Hard is the Road of Life

I
Having climbed over steep mountains and high peaks,
How should I expect on the plains to meet greater danger?
In the mountains, I met the tiger and came out unscathed;
On the plains, I encountered men, and was thrown into
  prison.

II
I was a representative of Vietnam
On my way to China to meet an important personage.
On the quiet road a sudden storm broke loose
And I was thrust into jail as an honoured guest.

III
I am a straightforward man with no crime on my
  conscience.
But I was accused of being a spy for China.
So life, you see, is never a very smooth business.
And now the present bristles with difficulties.

Alert in Vietnam

[news from the Xichdao Agency
published in the Nanning press]

Better death than slavery! Everywhere in my country
The red flags are fluttering again.
Oh, what it is to be a prisoner at such a time!
When shall I be set free, to take my part in the battle?

* Source: Ho Chi Minh, *Prison Diary* (Hanoi: Foreign Languages
Publishing House, 1966).

Appendix I

At the End of Four Months

"One day in jail is equal to a thousand years outside it. . . ."
How right were the ancients, expressing it in those words!
Four months leading a life in which there is nothing human
Have aged me more than ten years.
Yes: in a whole four months I have never eaten my fill,
In four months I have never had a comfortable night's
    sleep,
In four months I have never changed my clothes, and in
    four months
I have never taken a bath.
So: I have lost a tooth, my hair has grown grey,
And, lean and black as a demon gnawed by hunger,
I am covered with scabies.

                       Fortunately
Being stubborn and patient, never yielding an inch,
Though physically I suffer, my spirit is unshaken.

Seriously Ill

My body has been battered under the changing weather
    of China,
My heart is sorely troubled by the misfortunes befallen
    Vietnam.
Oh, what a bitter thing it is to fall ill in prison!
But, instead of weeping, I prefer to keep singing.

At the Political Bureau [Department] of the Fourth (War) Zone of Resistance [in Liuchow]

I have travelled the thirteen districts of Kwangsi Province,
And tasted the pleasures of eighteen different prisons.
What crime have I committed, I keep on asking?
The crime of being devoted to my people.

Autumn Night

In front of the gate, the guard stands with his rifle.
Above, untidy clouds are carrying away the moon.

354

The bed-bugs are swarming round like army-tanks on
    manoeuvres,
While the mosquitoes form squadrons, attacking like
    fighter-planes.
My heart travels a thousand li towards my native land.
My dream intertwines with sadness like a skein of a
    thousand threads.
Innocent, I have now endured a whole year in prison.
Using my tears for ink, I turn my thoughts into verses.

After Prison a Walk in the Mountains

The clouds embrace the peaks, the peaks embrace the
    clouds,
The river below shines like a mirror, spotless and clean.
On the crest of the Western Mountains, my heart stirs as I
    wander
Looking towards the southern sky and dreaming of old
    friends.

Appendix II
Declaration of Independence of the
Democratic Republic of Viet-Nam*

<<<<<<<<<<<<<<<<<<<<<<<<<<<<<<<<<<<<<<<<<<<<<<<

(September 2, 1945)

All men are created equal; they are endowed by their Creator with certain unalienable Rights; among these are Life, Liberty, and the pursuit of Happiness.

This immortal statement was made in the Declaration of Independence of the United States of America in 1776. In a broader sense, this means: All the peoples on the earth are equal from birth, all the peoples have a right to live, to be happy and free.

The Declaration of the French Revolution made in 1791 on the Rights of Man and the Citizen also states: "All men are born free and with equal rights, and must always remain free and have equal rights."

Those are undeniable truths.

Nevertheless, for more than eighty years, the French imperialists, abusing the standard of Liberty, Equality, and Fraternity, have violated our Fatherland and oppressed our fellow citizens. They have acted contrary to the ideals of humanity and justice.

In the field of politics, they have deprived our people of every democratic liberty.

They have enforced inhuman laws; they have set up three distinct political regimes in the North, the Center, and the South of Viet-Nam in order to wreck our national unity and prevent our people from being united.

They have built more prisons than schools. They have mercilessly slain our patriots; they have drowned our uprisings in rivers of blood.

* Source: Ho Chi Minh, *Selected Works* (Hanoi: Foreign Languages Publishing House, 1961), Vol. III.

They have fettered public opinion; they have practiced obscurantism against our people.

To weaken our race they have forced us to use opium and alcohol.

In the field of economics, they have fleeced us to the backbone, impoverished our people and devastated our land.

They have robbed us of our rice fields, our mines, our forests, and our raw materials. They have monopolized the issuing of bank notes and the export trade.

They have invented numerous unjustifiable taxes and reduced our people, especially our peasantry, to a state of extreme poverty.

They have hampered the prospering of our national bourgeoisie; they have mercilessly exploited our workers.

In the autumn of 1940, when the Japanese fascists violated Indochina's territory to establish new bases in their fight against the Allies, the French imperialists went down on their bended knees and handed over our country to them.

Thus, from that date, our people were subjected to the double yoke of the French and the Japanese. Their sufferings and miseries increased. The result was that, from the end of last year to the beginning of this year, from Quang Tri Province to the North of Viet-Nam, more than two million of our fellow citizens died from starvation. On March 9 (1945), the French troops were disarmed by the Japanese. The French colonialists either fled or surrendered, showing that not only were they incapable of "protecting" us, but that, in the span of five years, they had twice sold our country to the Japanese.

On several occasions before March 9, the Viet-Minh League urged the French to ally themselves with it against the Japanese. Instead of agreeing to this proposal, the French colonialists so intensified their terrorist activities against the Viet-Minh members that before fleeing they massacred a great number of our political prisoners detained at Yen Bay and Cao Bang.

Appendix II

Notwithstanding all this, our fellow citizens have always manifested toward the French a tolerant and humane attitude. Even after the Japanese "Putsch" of March, 1945, the Viet-Minh League helped many Frenchmen to cross the frontier, rescued some of them from Japanese jails, and protected French lives and property.

From the autumn of 1940, our country had in fact ceased to be a French colony and had become a Japanese possession.

After the Japanese had surrendered to the Allies, our whole people rose to regain our national sovereignty and to found the Democratic Republic of Viet-Nam.

The truth is that we have wrested our independence from the Japanese and not from the French.

The French have fled, the Japanese have capitulated, Emperor Bao Dai has abdicated. Our people have broken the chains which for nearly a century have fettered them and have won independence for the Fatherland. Our people at the same time have overthrown the monarchic regime that has reigned supreme for dozens of centuries. In its place has been established the present Democratic Republic.

For these reasons, we, members of the Provisional Government, representing the whole Viet-Namese people, declare that from now on we break off all relations of a colonial character with France; we repeal all the international obligation that France has so far subscribed to on behalf of Viet-Nam, and we abolish all the special rights the French have unlawfully acquired in our Fatherland.

The whole Viet-Namese people, animated by a common purpose, are determined to fight to the bitter end against any attempt by the French colonialists to reconquer their country.

We are convinced that the Allied nations, which at Teheran and San Francisco have acknowledged the principles of self-determination and equality of nations, will not refuse to acknowledge the independence of Viet-Nam.

A people who have courageously opposed French domination for more than eighty years, a people who have fought side by side with the Allies against the fascists during these last years, such a people must be free and independent.

For these reasons, we, members of the Provisional Government of the Democratic Republic of Viet-Nam, solemnly declare to the world that Viet-Nam has the right to be a free and independent country—and in fact it is so already. The entire Viet-Namese people are determined to mobilize all their physical and mental strength, to sacrifice their lives and property in order to safeguard their independence and liberty.

Appendix III
Treaty, Agreement and Exchange of Notes Between the Republic of China and France, 1946*

◄◄◄

Exchange of notes between Republic of China and France relating to the relief of Chinese troops by French troops in North Indochina (translation)

No. 1. His Excellency Mr. Jacques Meyrier, French Ambassador, to His Excellency Dr. Wang Shih-chieh, Minister for Foreign Affairs.

Chungking, 28 February 1946

Sir:

I have the honor to confirm to Your Excellency that the French Command is prepared to assume entire responsibility for guarding the Japanese prisoners, the maintenance of order and security, and the protection of Chinese nationals in the territories of the Indochinese Union to the north of the 16th degree of latitude and to propose for this purpose that the relief of Chinese troops by French troops be carried out upon the following bases:

The relief of Chinese troops stationed in Indochina to the north of the 16th degree of latitude shall begin between 1 and 15 March and should be completed at the latest on 31 March. The Chinese and French Military Staffs shall come to an agreement within the scope of the conversations now taking place at Chungking, with respect to the procedure for carrying out this operation.

Any units of the Chinese Army which are to be moved by sea but may not be able to embark after the relief will

* Source: Yin-ching Chen (Com. and ed.), *Treaties and Agreements Between the Republic of China and Other Powers, 1929-1954* (Washington: Sino-American Publishing Service, 1957), pp. 258-70.

be regrouped in the stationing areas adjacent to the ports of embarkation, it being agreed that their evacuation shall be carried out as rapidly as physical conditions may permit. These areas shall be defined by local agreement between the Chinese and French Commands. With regard to the Chinese units which are to be withdrawn by other routes, their movements shall be governed by local agreement between the Chinese and French Commands.

I should be grateful if you would be good enough to inform me whether the Chinese Government agrees to the arrangements referred to above.

I avail, &c.

(Signed) Jacques Meyrier

No. 2. His Excellency Dr. Wang Shih-Chieh, Minister for Foreign Affairs, to His Excellency Mr. Jacques Meyrier, French Ambassador.

Chungking, 28 February 1946

Sir:

In your note of today's date you were good enough to inform me of the following:

[As in No. 1.]

I have the honour to inform you that the Chinese Government agrees to the arrangements referred to above.

I avail, &c.

(Signed) Wang Shih-Chieh

Treaty Between Republic of China and France for the Relinquishment by France of Extra-territorial and Related Rights in China (translation)

Signed at Chungking, February 28, 1946. Came into force, June 8, 1946.

The National Government of the Republic of China, and the Provisional Government of the French Republic, equally desirous of strengthening the ties of friendship which have long prevailed between the two countries and recognizing the need, as equal and sovereign States, for the adjustment of certain matters relating to jurisdiction in China, have resolved to conclude a treaty for this purpose and have appointed as their Plenipotentiaries:

The National Government of the Republic of China:
His Excellency Dr. Wang Shih-Chieh, Minister for Foreign Affairs of the Republic of China, and
The Government of the French Republic:
His Excellency Mr. Jacques Meyrier, Ambassador Extraordinary and Plenipotentiary of the French Republic to China,
Who, having communicated to each other their full powers found to be in good and due form, have agreed upon the following articles:

Article 1. (1) The territories of the High Contracting Parties to which the present Treaty applies are, on the part of the National Government of the Republic of China, all the territories of the Republic of China; and, on the part of the Government of the French Republic, metropolitan France, Algeria, all French colonies and protectorates overseas, and all territories placed under the mandate of France. Any reference in subsequent articles of the present Treaty to the territories of one or the other High Contracting Party shall be deemed to relate to all the territories of that High Contracting Party [to] which the present Treaty applies.

(2) In the present Treaty, the term "nationals of the one or of the other High Contracting Party" shall, in relation to the Republic of China, mean all nationals of the Republic of China; and, in relation to the Government of the French Republic, all French citizens and subjects and all French administered and protected persons belonging to the territories to which the present Treaty applies.

(3) The expression "companies of the one or of the other High Contracting Party" shall in the application of the present Treaty be interpreted as meaning companies or associations constituted under the laws of the territories of

the High Contracting Party to which the present Treaty applies.

Article 2. All those provisions of treaties or agreements in force between China and France which authorize the French Government or its representatives to exercise jurisdiction over French companies or French nationals in the territories of the Republic of China are hereby abrogated. French companies and nationals shall be subject in China to the jurisdiction of the National Government of the Republic of China in accordance with the principles of international law.

Article 3. (1) The Government of the French Republic considers that the Final Protocol concluded at Peking on 7 September 1901 between the Chinese Government and other Governments, including the Government of the French Republic, has lapsed in so far as it concerns the French Government.

The Government of the French Republic relinquishes all the rights accorded to it under that Protocol and the agreements supplementary thereto.

(2) The Government of the French Republic will cooperate with the Government of the Republic of China for the reaching of any necessary agreements with the other Governments concerned for the transfer to the National Government of the Republic of China of the administration and control of the diplomatic quarter at Peiping, including the official assets and obligations of the diplomatic quarter, it being mutually agreed that the National Government of the Republic of China, in taking over administration and control of the diplomatic quarter, will assume the official obligations and liabilities of the diplomatic quarter and will protect all legitimate rights therein.

(3) The National Government of the Republic of China shall accord to the Government of the French Republic a continued right to use for official purposes the plots of land which have been allocated to the Government of the French Republic in the diplomatic quarter in Peiping.

Article 4. (1) The Government of the French Republic considers that the International Settlements at Shanghai and Amoy should, in so far as they concern the French Government, revert to the administration and control of the Government of the Republic of China, and hereby relinquishes the rights accorded to it in relation to those International Settlements.

(2) The Government of the French Republic shall cooperate with the Government of the Republic of China for the reaching of any necessary agreement of the Republic of China of the administration and control of the International Settlements, at Shanghai and Amoy, including the official assets and the official obligations of those Settlements, it being mutually understood that the National Government of the Republic of China, in taking over administration and control of those Settlements, will assume the official obligations and liabilities of those Settlements and will protect all legitimate rights therein.

(3) The Government of the French Republic relinquishes the rights over the French Concessions at Shanghai (including the two extensions), at Tientsin (including the district of Laosikai), at Hankow and at Canton, and agrees that those Concessions shall be placed under the exclusive authority of the National Government of the Republic of China, it being agreed that the National Government of the Republic of China will assume the official obligations and liabilities of those Concessions and will protect all legitimate rights therein.

Article 5. (1) To obviate any questions as to the existing rights and titles to real property in the territories of the Republic of China possessed by French companies or nationals or by the Government of the French Republic, and in particular questions which might arise from the abrogation of the provisions of treaties and agreements provided for in article 2 of the present Treaty, the High Contracting Parties agree that such existing rights or titles shall be indefeasible and shall not be questioned upon any ground except upon proof, established through due process of law, of fraud or of fraudulent or dishonest practices in the acquisition of such rights or titles, it being agreed that no right or title shall be rendered invalid by virtue of any subsequent change in the original procedure through which it was acquired. It is also agreed that the exercise of these rights or titles shall be subject to the laws and regulations of the Republic of China concerning taxation, national defense and the right of eminent domain, and that such rights or titles shall not be alienated to the Government or nationals or companies of any third country without the express consent of the National Government of the Republic of China.

(2) The High Contracting Parties also agree that, if it should be the desire of the National Government of the Republic of China to replace by new deeds of ownership existing leases in perpetuity or other documentary evidence relating to real property held by French companies or nationals or by the Government of the French Republic, the replacement shall be made by the Chinese authorities without charges of any sort and the new deeds of ownership shall fully protect the holders of such leases or documentary evidence, and their legal heirs and assigns without diminution of their prior rights and interests, including the right of alienation.

(3) The High Contracting Parties agree further that French companies or nationals or the Government of the French Republic shall not be required or asked by the Chinese authorities to make any payments of fees in connection with land transfers for or in relation to any period prior to the effective date of this Treaty.

Article 6. (1) The Government of the French Republic, having long accorded rights to nationals of the Republic of China to travel, reside and carry on commerce within all the territories of the French Republic, the National Government of the Republic of China agrees to accord similar rights to French nationals within all the territories of the Republic of China.

(2) Each High Contracting Party will endeavor to accord in his territories to nationals and companies of the other High Contracting Party in regard to all legal proceedings and in matters relating to the administration of justice and the levying of taxes and dues in connection therewith treatment not less favorable than that accorded to his own nationals and companies.

Article 7. The consular officers of one High Contracting Party, duly provided with exequaturs, shall be permitted to reside in such ports, places and cities of the territories of the other High Contracting Party as may be agreed upon. The consular officers of either High Contracting Party shall have the right within their consular districts to communicate with, interview and to advise their nationals, and the nationals of the two countries shall have the right at all times to communicate with their consular officers. The consular offices of one and the other High Contracting Parties shall be informed immediately by the appropriate local authorities when any of their nationals are arrested or detained in their consular districts by the local authorities. They shall have the right to visit within the limits of their districts any of their nationals who are under arrest, in prison or awaiting trial. Communications from the nationals of one High Contracting Party in prison in the territories of the other High Contracting Party addressed to their consular officers shall be forwarded to such officers by the local authorities. Consular officers of one High Contracting Party shall be accorded in the territories of the other High Contracting Party all the privileges and immunities enjoyed by consular officers under modern international usage.

Article 8. (1) The High Contracting Parties shall enter into negotiations for the conclusion of a comprehensive modern treaty or treaties of friendship, commerce and navigation and a consular convention and convention of establishment upon the request of either of the High Contracting Parties. The treaty or treaties to be thus negotiated will be based upon the principles of modern international law, international usages and the modern treaties which each of the High Contracting Parties has respectively concluded with other Powers in recent years.

(2) Pending the conclusion of the comprehensive treaty or treaties referred to in the preceding paragraph, if any questions affecting the rights in the territories of the Republic of China of French companies or nationals, or of the Government of the French Republic, should arise in the future and if these questions are not covered by the present Treaty or by the provisions of existing treaties, conventions and agreements between the High Contracting Parties which are not abrogated by or inconsistent with the present Treaty, such questions shall be discussed by the representative of the High Contracting Parties and shall be decided upon in accordance with generally accepted principles of international law and with modern international practice.

Article 9. With respect to article 2 and article 8, paragraph 2, of the present Treaty, it is agreed that:

(1) The Government of the French Republic relinquishes all the rights held under former treaties relating to the system of Treaty Ports in China. The National Government of the Republic of China and the Government of the French Republic agree that merchant vessels of the one High Contracting Party shall be permitted freely to come to ports, roadsteads and waters in territories of the High Contracting Party which are or may be opened to overseas merchant shipping and that the treatment accorded to such vessels in such ports, places and water shall be no less favorable than that accorded to national vessels and shall be as favorable as that accorded to vessels of any third country. The term "vessels" of a High Contracting Party means all vessels registered under the law of any of the territories of that High Contracting Party to which the present Treaty applies.

(2) The Government of the French Republic relinquishes all the rights held under former treaties relating to the

Appendix III

special courts in the International Settlements at Shanghai and Amoy and in the French Concession at Shanghai.

(3) The Government of the French Republic relinquishes all rights held under former treaties with regard to the employment of foreign pilots in the parts of the territories of the Republic of China.

(4) The Government of the French Republic relinquishes all rights held under former treaties relating to the entry of its naval vessels into the territorial waters of the Republic of China; and the National Government of the Republic of China and the Government of the French Republic shall extend to each other in connection with the visits of the warships of the one High Contracting Party to the ports of the other High Contracting Party mutual courtesy in accordance with ordinary international usage.

(5) The Government of the French Republic relinquishes the right to claim the appointment of French citizens in the Chinese Postal Service.

(6) All the courts of the Government of the French Republic which have hitherto been sitting in the territories of the Republic of China shall be closed in accordance with article 2 of the present Treaty, and the orders, writs, judgments and other acts of all the French courts in China shall be considered as *res judicata* and shall, when necessary, be enforced by the Chinese authorities; further, any cases pending before any of the courts of the Government of the French Republic at the time of the coming into effect of the present Treaty shall, if the plaintiff or petitioner so desires, be transferred to the appropriate Chinese courts which shall proceed to dispose of them as expeditiously as possible and in so doing shall apply the law which the French courts would have applied.

(7) The Government of the French Republic relinquishes the special rights which its vessels have been accorded with regard to coasting trade and inland navigation in the waters of the Republic of China, and the National Government of the Republic of China is prepared to take over any properties of French companies or nationals which have

been used for the purposes of those trades and which the owners may wish to dispose of and to pay adequate compensation therefor. Should one High Contracting Party accord in any of its territories the right of coasting trade or inland navigation to the vessels of any third country, such rights would similarly be accorded to the vessels of the other High Contracting Party, provided that the latter High Contracting Party permits the vessels of the former High Contracting Party to engage in the coasting trade or inland navigation of its territories. Coasting trade and inland navigation are excepted from the requirement of national treatment and are to be regulated according to the laws of each High Contracting Party in relation thereto. It is agreed, however, that the vessels of either High Contracting Party shall enjoy within the territories of the other High Contracting Party with regard to coasting trade and inland navigation treatment as favorable as that accorded to the vessels of any third country subject to the abovementioned proviso.

Article 10. With regard to the last sentence of article 5, paragraph 1, of the present Treaty, the National Government of the Republic of China declares that the restriction of the right of alienation of existing rights and titles to real property referred to in that article will be applied by the Chinese authorities in an equitable manner and that, if the Chinese Government declines to assent to a proposed transfer, the Chinese Government will, in a spirit of justice and with a view to precluding loss on the part of the French nationals or French companies whose interests are affected, undertake, if so requested by such nationals or companies, to take over the rights and titles in question and pay adequate compensation therefor.

Article 11. It is agreed that the abolition of the system of Treaty Ports will not affect existing property rights and that the nationals of each High Contracting Party will enjoy the right to acquire and hold real property throughout the territories of the other High Contracting Party in accordance with the conditions and requirements prescribed in the laws and regulations of the High Contracting Party.

Article 12. It is agreed that questions which may affect the sovereignty of the Republic of China and which are not covered by the present Treaty shall be discussed by the representatives of the National Government of the Republic of China and of the Government of the French Republic and decided in accordance with the generally accepted principles of international law and modern international practice.

Article 13. The present Treaty, of which the Chinese and French texts are equally authentic, shall be ratified and the instruments of ratification shall be exchanged at Chungking or at Nanking as soon as possible. The Treaty shall come into force on the date of the exchange of ratifications.

In faith whereof, the above-mentioned Plenipotentiaries have signed the present Treaty and affixed thereto their seals.

Done at Chungking in duplicate this twenty-eighth day of the second month of the thirty-fifth year of the Republic of China, corresponding to 28 February 1946.

(Signed) Wang Shih-Chieh
(Signed) Jacques Meyrier

Agreement Between Chinese Government and French Government Respecting Sino-Indochinese Relations (translation)

Signed at Chungking, February 28, 1946

The Chinese Government and the French Government, equally desirous of strengthening their traditional bonds of friendship, and in accordance with the terms of the exchange of notes between China and France of 13 March 1945, of restoring and developing the economic relations between China and Indo-China, have resolved to conclude an agreement for this purpose and have appointed as the plenipotentiaries:

The National Government of the Republic of China:

His Excellency Dr. Wang Shih-chieh, Minister of Foreign Affairs of the Republic of China, and

The Provisional Government of the French Republic:

His Excellency Mr. Jacques Meyrier, Ambassador extraordinary and Plenipotentiary of the French Republic to China,

Who having communicated to each other their full powers found to be in good and due form, have agreed upon the following articles:

Title I. Conditions of Establishment

Article 1. Chinese nationals shall continue to enjoy the rights, privileges and exemptions which they have traditionally held in Indochina, particularly in relation to entry and exit, taxation, the acquisition and possession of rural and urban real property, commercial bookkeeping, establishment of primary and secondary schools, and occupation in agriculture, fishing, inland and coastal navigation, and any other free occupations.

Article 2. With regards to the right to travel, reside, engage in commercial, industrial and mining undertakings, and acquire and hold real property, the treatment to be enjoyed by Chinese nationals in Indochina shall be no less favourable than that enjoyed by the nationals of any third most-favored nation.

Article 3. Taxes levied in accordance with article 1 on Chinese nationals residing in Indochina, and in particular to capitation tax, may not be heavier than those imposed on Indochinese nationals.

Article 4. Chinese nationals in Indochina shall enjoy in regard to legal proceedings and the administration of justice the same treatment as that enjoyed by French nationals.

Title II. International Transit

Article 1. The French Government shall reserve in the port of Haiphong a special zone, including the warehouses,

371

berths and, if possible, the wharves necessary for the free transit of merchandise on the way from or to China. The Chinese customs authorities shall be responsible for customs supervision in that zone and the French authorities shall be responsible for all other matters, in particular public safety and health.

Article 2. Merchandise on the way from or to China's territory, and transported over the railways of Tonkin, shall pass free of duty between the Sino-Indochinese frontier and the zone reserved for Chinese international transit in the port of Haiphong. Such merchandise shall be transported in wagons which shall be sealed at the time of their departure by the Chinese customs authorities.

Article 3. Merchandise on the way from or to China, and transported by railway in Indochina, shall be exempt from all transit dues or taxes.

Title III. Sino-Indochinese Commerce

Commerce between China and Indochina shall be regulated by a commercial agreement on the basis of the treatment of the most-favoured nation.

Title IV. The Indochina-Yunnan Railway

Article 1. The agreement between China and France concerning the Indochina-Yunnan Railway, concluded on 29 October 1903, shall be terminated on the date of the signing of the present agreement.

Article 2. The property, material and equipment of the section of the Indochina-Yunnan Railway situated in Chinese territory between Kunming and Hokow shall be transferred in their present condition to the Chinese Government by advanced repurchase.

Article 3. The French Government shall advance to the Chinese Government the amount of the compensation due for the advanced repurchase, which shall be determined by a joint Chinese-French Commission. No portion of this amount shall be refunded to the French Government except in so far as it may be chargeable to the reparations imposed on the Japanese Government in respect of the claims made by the Chinese Government for compensation for material loss sustained by the Chinese Government and Chinese merchants as a result of the stoppage of the operation of the Indochina-Yunnan Railway and the closing of the port of Haiphong in June 1940 due to Japanese intervention.

The present agreement, drawn up in duplicate in Chinese and French, both texts being equally authentic, shall enter into force provisionally on the date of its signature, pending its ratification which shall be made as soon as possible. The instruments of ratification shall be exchanged at Chungking or at Nanking.*

In faith whereof the above-mentioned plenipotentiaries have signed the present agreement and affixed thereto their seals.

Done at Chungking this twenty-eighth day of the second month of the thirty-fifth year of the Chinese Republic, corresponding to 28 February 1946.

(Signed) Wang Shih-Chieh
(Signed) Jacques Meyrier

Exchange of Notes

No. 1. French Ambassador to Chinese Minister for Foreign Affairs

Chungking, 28 February 1946

Sir:

With reference to title IV of the agreement between China and France respecting Sino-Indochinese relations signed today, I have the honour, on behalf of the French Government, to make to Your Excellency the following declaration.

The French Government intends to submit at an early date to the Chinese Government a plan for the improvement of the railway communications between China and Indo-

---

* Came into force provisionally on 28 February 1946, as from the date of signature, in accordance with article 3, title IV. The instruments of ratification have been exchanged on 8 June 1946.

china. The French Government desires to state in particular that should the Chinese Government, which is the owner of the section of the Indochina-Yunnan Railway situated in Chinese territory between Kunming and Hokow, decide to grant to the French interests a participation in the Chinese company responsible for operating that section, the French Government would, on its part, reserve for the Chinese interests a proportionate participation in the French company responsible for operating the section situated in Indochinese territory between Laokay and Haiphong.

I avail, &c.

(Signed) Jacques Meyrier

No. 2. Chinese Minister for Foreign Affairs to French Ambassador

Chungking, 28 February 1946

Sir:

I have the honour to acknowledge the receipt of your note of today's date reading as follows:

[As in Note 1.]

I have the honour, on behalf of the Chinese Government, to take note of this declaration.

I avail, &c.

(Signed) Wang Shih-Chieh

Appendix IV
Geneva Agreements*

◄◄

A. Agreement on the Cessation of Hostilities in Viet Nam
(July 20, 1954)

CHAPTER I

Provisional Military Demarcation Line and Demilitarized Zone

Article 1

A provisional military demarcation line shall be fixed, on either side of which the forces of the two parties shall be regrouped after their withdrawal, the forces of the People's Army of Viet Nam to the north of the line and the forces of the French Union to the south.

The provisional military demarcation line is fixed as shown on the map attached, see Map No. 1.

It is also agreed that a demilitarised zone shall be established on either side of the demarcation line, to a width of not more than 5 kms. from it, to act as a buffer zone and avoid any incidents which might result in the resumption of hostilities.

Article 2

The period within which the movement of all forces of either party into its regrouping zone on either side of the provisional military demarcation line shall be completed shall not exceed three hundred (300) days from the date of the present Agreement's entry into force.

Article 3

When the provisional military demarcation line coincides with a waterway, the waters of such waterway shall be open to civil navigation by both parties wherever one bank is

* Source: *Further Documents Relating to the Discussion of Indo-China at the Geneva Conference, June 16-July 21, 1954.* Miscellaneous No. 20 (1954), Command Paper 9239 (London: Her Majesty's Stationery Office, 1954).

controlled by one party and the other bank by the other party. The Joint Commission shall establish rules of navigation for the stretch of waterway in question. The merchant shipping and other civilian craft of each party shall have unrestricted access to the land under its military control.

Article 4

The provisional military demarcation line between the two final regrouping zones is extended into the territorial waters by a line perpendicular to the general line of the coast.

All coastal islands north of this boundary shall be evacuated by the armed forces of the French Union, and all islands south of it shall be evacuated by the forces of the People's Army of Viet Nam.

Article 5

To avoid any incidents which might result in the resumption of hostilities, all military forces, supplies and equipment shall be withdrawn from the demilitarised zone within twenty-five (25) days of the present Agreement's entry into force.

Article 6

No person, military or civilian, shall be permitted to cross the provisional military demarcation line unless specifically authorised to do so by the Joint Commission.

Article 7

No person, military of civilian, shall be permitted to enter the demilitarised zone except persons concerned with the conduct of civil administration and relief and persons specifically authorised to enter by the Joint Commission.

Article 8

Civil administration and relief in the demilitarised zone on either side of the provisional military demarcation line shall be the responsibility of the Commanders-in-Chief of the two parties in their respective zones. The number of persons, military or civilian, from each side who are permitted to enter the demilitarised zone for the conduct of civil administration and relief shall be determined by the respective Commanders, but in no case shall the total number authorised by either side exceed at any one time a figure to be determined by the Trung Gia Military Commission or by the Joint Commission. The number of civil police and the arms to be carried by them shall be determined by the Joint Commission. No one else shall carry arms unless specifically authorised to do so by the Joint Commission.

Article 9

Nothing contained in this chapter shall be construed as limiting the complete freedom of movement, into, out of or within the demilitarised zone, of the Joint Commission, its joint groups, the International Commission to be set up as indicated below, its inspection teams and any other persons, supplies or equipment specifically authorised to enter the demilitarised zone by the Joint Commission. Freedom of movement shall be permitted across the territory under the military control of either side over any road or waterway which has to be taken between points within the demilitarised zone when such points are not connected by roads or waterways lying completely within the demilitarised zone.

CHAPTER II

Principles and Procedure Governing Implementation of the Present Agreement

Article 10

The Commanders of the Forces on each side, on the one side the Commander-in-Chief of the French Union forces in Indo-China and on the other side the Commander-in-Chief of the People's Army of Viet Nam, shall order and enforce the complete cessation of all hostilities in Viet Nam by all armed forces under their control, including all units and personnel of the ground, naval and air forces.

Article 11

In accordance with the principle of a simultaneous cease-fire throughout Indo-China, the cessation of hostilities shall be simultaneous throughout all parts of Viet Nam, in all areas of hostilities and for all the forces of the two parties.

Taking into account the time effectively required to transmit the cease-fire order down to the lowest echelons of the combatant forces on both sides, the two parties are agreed that the cease-fire shall take effect completely and simultaneously for the different sectors of the country as follows:—

Northern Viet Nam at 8:00 a.m. (local time) on July 27, 1954.

Central Viet Nam at 8:00 a.m. (local time) on August 1, 1954.

Southern Viet Nam at 8:00 a.m. (local time) on August 11, 1954.

It is agreed that Peking mean time shall be taken as local time.

From such time as the cease-fire becomes effective in Northern Viet Nam, both parties undertake not to engage in any large-scale offensive action in any part of the Indo-Chinese theatre of operations and not to commit the air forces based on Northern Viet Nam outside that sector. The two parties also undertake to inform each other of their plans for movement from one regrouping zone to another within twenty-five (25) days of the present Agreement's entry into force.

Article 12

All the operations and movements entailed in the cessation of hostilities and regrouping must proceed in a safe and orderly fashion:—

(a) Within a certain number of days after the cease-fire Agreement shall have become effective, the number to be determined on the spot by the Trung Gia Military Commission, each party shall be responsible for removing and neutralising mines (including river- and sea-mines), booby traps, explosives and any other dangerous substances placed by it. In the event of its being impossible to complete the work of removal and neutralisation in time, the party concerned shall mark the spot by placing visible signs there. All demolitions, mine fields, wire entanglements and other hazards to the free movement of the personnel of the Joint Commission and its joint groups, known to be present after the withdrawal of the military forces, shall be reported to the Joint Commission by the Commanders of the opposing forces;

(b) From the time of the cease-fire until regrouping is completed on either side of the demarcation line:—

(1) The forces of either party shall be provisionally withdrawn from the provisional assembly areas assigned to the other party.

(2) When one party's forces withdraw by a route (road, rail, waterway, sea route) which passes through the territory of the other party (see Article 24), the latter party's forces must provisionally withdraw three kilometres on each side of such route, but in such a manner as to avoid interfering with the movements of the civil population.

Article 13

From the time of the cease-fire until the completion of the movements from one regrouping zone into the other, civil and military transport aircraft shall follow air corridors between the provisional assembly areas assigned to the French Union forces north of the demarcation line on the one hand and the Laotian frontier and the regrouping zone assigned to the French Union forces on the other hand.

The position of the air corridors, their width, the safety route for single-engined military aircraft transferred to the south and the search and rescue procedure for aircraft in distress shall be determined on the spot by the Trung Gia Military Commission.

Article 14

Political and administrative measures in the two regrouping zones, on either side of the provisional military demarcation line:—

Appendix IV

(a) Pending the general elections which will bring about the unification of Viet Nam, the conduct of civil administration in each regrouping zone shall be in the hands of the party whose forces are to be regrouped there in virtue of the present Agreement.

(b) Any territory controlled by one party which is transferred to the other party by the regrouping plan shall continue to be administered by the former party until such date as all the troops who are to be transferred have completely left that territory so as to free the zone assigned to the party in question. From then on, such territory shall be regarded as transferred to the other party, who shall assume responsibility for it.

Steps shall be taken to ensure that there is no break in the transfer of responsibilities. For this purpose, adequate notice shall be given by the withdrawing party to the other party, which shall make the necessary arrangements, in particular by sending administrative and police detachments to prepare for the assumption of administrative responsibility. The length of such notice shall be determined by the Trung Gia Military Commission. The transfer shall be effected in successive stages for the various territorial sectors.

The transfer of the civil administration of Hanoi and Haiphong to the authorities of the Democratic Republic of Viet Nam shall be completed within the respective time-limits laid down in Article 15 for military movements.

(c) Each party undertakes to refrain from any reprisals or discrimination against persons or organisations on account of their activities during the hostilities and to guarantee their democratic liberties.

(d) From the date of entry into force of the present Agreement until the movement of troops is completed, any civilians residing in a district controlled by one party who wish to go and live in the zone assigned to the other party shall be permitted and helped to do so by the authorities in that district.

Article 15

The disengagement of the combatants, and the withdrawals and transfers of military forces, equipment and supplies shall take place in accordance with the following principles:—

(a) The withdrawals and transfers of the military forces, equipment and supplies of the two parties shall be completed within three hundred (300) days, as laid down in Article 2 of the present Agreement;

(b) Within either territory successive withdrawals shall be made by sectors, portions of sectors or provinces. Transfers from one regrouping zone to another shall be made in successive monthly installments proportionate to the number of troops to be transferred;

(c) The two parties shall undertake to carry out all troop withdrawals and transfers in accordance with the aims of the present Agreement, shall permit no hostile act and shall take no step whatsoever which might hamper such withdrawals and transfers. They shall assist one another as far as this is possible;

(d) The two parties shall permit no destruction or sabotage of any public property and no injury to the life and property of the civil population. They shall permit no interference in local civil administration;

(e) The Joint Commission and the International Commission shall ensure that steps are taken to safeguard the forces in the course of withdrawal and transfer;

(f) The Trung Gia Military Commission, and later the Joint Commission, shall determine by common agreement the exact procedure for the disengagement of the combatants and for troop withdrawals and transfers, on the basis of the principles mentioned above and within the framework laid down below:—

1. The disengagement of the combatants, including the concentration of the armed forces of all kinds

and also each party's movements into the provisional assembly areas assigned to it and the other party's provisional withdrawal from it, shall be completed within a period not exceeding fifteen (15) days after the date when the cease-fire becomes effective.

The general delineation of the provisional assembly areas is set out in the maps (2) annexed to the present Agreement.

In order to avoid any incidents, no troops shall be stationed less than 1,500 metres from the lines delimiting the provisional assembly areas.

During the period until the transfers are concluded, all the coastal islands west of the following lines shall be included in the Haiphong perimeter: meridian of the southern point of Kebao Island, northern coast of Ile Rousse (excluding the island), extended as far as the meridian of Campha-Mines,

2. The withdrawals and transfers shall be effected in the following order and within the following periods (from the date of the entry into force of the present Agreement):—

Forces of the French Union

Hanoi perimeter	80 days
Haiduong perimeter	100 days
Haiphong perimeter	300 days

Forces of the People's Army of Viet Nam

Ham Tan and Xuyenmoc provisional assembly area	80 days
Central Viet Nam provisional assembly area—first installment	80 days
Plaine des Joncs provisional assembly area	100 days
Central Viet Nam provisional assembly area—second installment	100 days
Pointe Camau provisional assembly area	200 days

Central Viet Nam provisional
assembly area—last installment ....300 days

CHAPTER III

Ban on the Introduction of Fresh Troops, Military
Personnel, Arms and Munitions, Military Bases

Article 16

With effect from the date of entry into force of the present
Agreement, the introduction into Viet Nam of any troop
reinforcements and additional military personnel is prohibited.

It is understood, however, that the rotation of units and
groups of personnel, the arrival in Viet Nam of individual
personnel on a temporary duty basis and the return to Viet
Nam of the individual personnel after short periods of leave
or temporary duty outside Viet Nam shall be permitted
under the conditions laid down below:—

(a) Rotation of units (defined in paragraph (c) of this
Article) and groups of personnel shall not be permitted for French Union troops stationed north of
the provisional military demarcation line laid down
in Article 1 of the present Agreement during the
withdrawal period provided for in Article 2.

However, under the heading of individual personnel not more than fifty (50) men, including
officers, shall during any one month be permitted to
enter that part of the country north of the provisional
military demarcation line on a temporary duty basis
or to return there after short periods of leave or
temporary duty outside Viet Nam.

(b) "Rotation" is defined as the replacement of units or
groups of personnel by other units of the same
echelon or by personnel who are arriving in Viet
Nam territory to do their overseas service there.

(c) The units rotated shall never be larger than a battalion—or the corresponding echelon for air and
naval forces.

(d) Rotation shall be conducted on a man-for-man basis, provided, however, that in any one quarter neither party shall introduce more than fifteen thousand five hundred (15,000) members of its armed forces into Viet Nam under the rotation policy.

(e) Rotation units (defined in paragraph (c) of this Article) and groups of personnel, and the individual personnel mentioned in this Article, shall enter and leave Viet Nam only through the entry points enumerated in Article 20 below.

(f) Each party shall notify the Joint Commission and the International Commission at least two days in advance of any arrivals or departures of units, groups of personnel and individual personnel in or from Viet Nam. Reports on the arrivals or departures of units, groups of personnel and individual personnel in or from Viet Nam shall be submitted daily to the Joint Commission and the International Commission.

All the above-mentioned notifications and reports shall indicate the places and dates of arrival or departure and the numbers of persons arriving or departing.

(g) The International Commission, through its Inspection Teams, shall supervise and inspect the rotation of units and groups of personnel and the arrival and departure of individual personnel as authorised above, at the points of entry enumerated in Article 20 below.

Article 17

(a) With effect from the date of entry into force of the present Agreement, the introduction into Viet Nam of any reinforcements in the form of all types of arms, munitions and other war material, such as combat aircraft, naval craft, pieces of ordnance, jet engines and jet weapons and armored vehicles, is prohibited.

(b) It is understood, however, that war material, arms and munitions which have been destroyed, damaged, worn out or used up after the cessation of hostilities may be replaced on the basis of piece-for-piece of the same type and with similar characteristics. Such replacements of war material, arms and ammunitions shall not be permitted for French Union troops stationed north of the provisional military demarcation line laid down in Article 1 of the present Agreement, during the withdrawal period provided for in Article 2.

Naval craft may perform transport operations between the regrouping zones.

(c) The war material, arms and munitions for replacement purposes provided for in paragraph (b) of this Article, shall be introduced into Viet Nam only through the points of entry enumerated in Article 20 below. War material, arms and munitions to be replaced shall be shipped from Viet Nam only through the points of entry enumerated in Article 20 below.

(d) Apart from the replacements permitted within the limits laid down in paragraph (b) of this Article, the introduction of war material, arms and munitions of all types in the form of unassembled parts for subsequent assembly is prohibited.

(e) Each party shall notify the Joint Commission and the International Commission at least two days in advance of any arrivals or departures which may take place of war material, arms and munitions of all types.

In order to justify the requests for the introduction into Viet Nam of arms, munitions and other war material (as defined in paragraph (a) of this Article) for replacement purposes, a report concerning each incoming shipment shall be submitted to the Joint Commission and the International Commission. Such reports shall indicate the use made of the items so replaced.

(f) The International Commission, through its Inspection Teams, shall supervise and inspect the replacements permitted in the circumstances laid down in this Article, at the points of entry enumerated in Article 20 below.

Article 18

With effect from the date of entry into force of the present Agreement, the establishment of new military bases is prohibited throughout Viet Nam territory.

Article 19

With effect from the date of entry into force of the present Agreement, no military base under the control of a foreign State may be established in the re-grouping zone of either party; the two parties shall ensure that the zones assigned to them do not adhere to any military alliance and are not used for the resumption of hostilities or to further an aggressive policy.

Article 20

The points of entry into Viet Nam for rotation personnel and replacements of material are fixed as follows:
—Zones to the north of the provisional military demarcation line: Laokay, Langson, Tien-Yen, Haiphong, Vinh, Dong-Hoi, Muong-Sen;
—Zone to the south of the provisional military demarcation line: Tourane, Quinhon, Nhatrang, Bangoi, Saigon, Cap St. Jacques, Tanchau.

Chapter IV

Prisoners of War and Civilian Internees

Article 21

The liberation and repatriation of all prisoners of war and civilian internees detained by each of the two parties at the coming into force of the present Agreement shall be carried out under the following conditions:—
(a) All prisoners of war and civilian internees of Viet Nam, French and other nationalities captured since the beginning of hostilities in Viet Nam during military operations or in any other circumstances of war

and in any part of the territory of Viet Nam shall be liberated within a period of thirty (30) days after the date when the cease-fire becomes effective in each theatre.

(b) The term "civilian internees" is understood to mean all persons who, having in any way contributed to the political and armed struggle between the two parties, have been arrested for that reason and have been kept in detention by either party during the period of hostilities.

(c) All prisoners of war and civilian internees held by either party shall be surrendered to the appropriate authorities of the other party, who shall give them all possible assistance in proceeding to their country of origin, place of habitual residence or the zone of their choice.

CHAPTER V

Miscellaneous

Article 22

The Commanders of the Forces of the two parties shall ensure that persons under their respective commands who violate any of the provisions of the present Agreement are suitably punished.

Article 23

In cases in which the place of burial is known and the existence of graves has been established, the Commander of the Forces of either party shall, within a specific period after the entry into force of the Armistice Agreement, permit the graves service personnel of the other party to enter the part of Viet Nam territory under their military control for the purpose of finding and removing the bodies of deceased military personnel of that party, including the bodies of deceased prisoners of war. The Joint Commission shall determine the procedures and the time limit for the performance of this task. The Commanders of the Forces of the two parties shall communicate to each other all information in their possession as to the place of burial of military personnel of the other party.

Article 24

The present Agreement shall apply to all the armed forces of either party. The armed forces of each party shall respect the demilitarized zone and the territory under the military control of the other party, and shall commit no act and undertake no operation against the other party and shall not engage in blockade of any kind in Viet Nam.

For the purposes of the present Article, the word "territory" includes territorial waters and air space.

Article 25

The Commanders of the Forces of the two parties shall afford full protection and all possible assistance and cooperation to the Joint Commission and its joint groups and to the International Commission and its inspection teams in the performance of the functions and tasks assigned to them by the present Agreement.

Article 26

The costs involved in the operations of the Joint Commission and joint groups and of the International Commission and its Inspection Teams shall be shared equally between the two parties.

Article 27

The signatories of the present Agreement and their successors in their functions shall be responsible for ensuring the observance and enforcement of the terms and provisions thereof. The Commanders of the Forces of the two parties shall, within their respective commands, take all steps and make all arrangements necessary to ensure full compliance with all the provisions of the present Agreement by all elements and military personnel under their command.

The procedures laid down in the present Agreement shall, whenever necessary, be studied by the Commanders of the two parties and, if necessary, defined more specifically by the Joint Commission.

CHAPTER VI

Joint Commission and International Commission for Supervision and Control in Viet Nam

Article 28

Responsibility for the execution of the agreement on the cessation of hostilities shall rest with the parties.

Article 29

An International Commission shall ensure the control and supervision of this execution.

Article 30

In order to facilitate, under the conditions shown below, the execution of provisions concerning joint actions by the two parties, a Joint Commission shall be set up in Viet Nam.

Article 31

The Joint Commission shall be composed of an equal number of representatives of the Commanders of the two parties.

Article 32

The Presidents of the delegations to the Joint Commission shall hold the rank of General.

The Joint Commission shall set up joint groups, the number of which shall be determined by mutual agreement between the parties. The joint groups shall be composed of an equal number of officers from both parties. Their location on the demarcation line between the re-grouping zones shall be determined by the parties whilst taking into account the powers of the Joint Commission.

Article 33

The Joint Commission shall ensure the execution of the following provision of the Agreement on the cessation of hostilities:—

(a) A simultaneous and general cease-fire in Viet Nam for all regular and irregular armed forces of the two parties.

(b) A re-groupment of the armed forces of the two parties.

389

(c) Observance of the demarcation lines between the re-grouping zones and of the demilitarised sectors.

Within the limits of its competence it shall help the parties to execute the said provisions, shall ensure liaison between them for the purpose of preparing and carrying out plans for the application of these provisions, and shall endeavour to solve such disputed questions as may arise between the parties in the course of executing these provisions.

Article 34

An International Commission shall be set up for the control and supervision over the application of the provisions of the agreement on the cessation of hostilities in Viet Nam. It shall be composed of representatives of the following States: Canada, India, and Poland.

It shall be presided over by the Representative of India.

Article 35

The International Commission shall set up fixed and mobile inspection teams, composed of an equal number of officers appointed by each of the above-mentioned States. The mixed teams shall be located at the following points: Laokay, Langson, Tien-Yen, Haiphong, Vinh, Dong-Hoi, Muong-Sen, Tourane, Quinhon, Nhatrang, Bangoi, Saigon, Cap St. Jacques, Tranchau. These points of location may, at a later date, be altered at the request of the Joint Commission, or of one of the parties, or of the International Commission itself, by agreement between the International Commission and the command of the party concerned. The zones of action of the mobile teams shall be the regions bordering the land and sea frontiers of Viet Nam, the demarcation lines between the re-grouping zones and the demilitarised zones. Within the limits of these zones they shall have the right to move freely and shall receive from the local civil and military authorities all facilities they may require for the fulfillment of their tasks (provision of personnel, placing at their disposal documents needed for supervision, summoning witnesses necessary for holding enquiries, ensuring the security and freedom of movement of the inspection teams, &c . . . . .). They shall have at their disposal such modern means of transport, observation and communication as they may require. Beyond the zones of action as defined above, the mobile teams may, by agreement with the command of the party concerned, carry out other movements within the limits of the tasks given them by the present agreement.

Article 36

The International Commission shall be responsible for supervising the proper execution by the parties of the provisions of the agreement. For this purpose it shall fulfill the tasks of control, observation, inspection and investigation connected with the application of the provisions of the agreement on the cessation of hostilities, and it shall in particular:—

(a) Control the movement of the armed forces of the two parties, effected within the framework of the regroupment plan.

(b) Supervise the demarcation lines between the regrouping areas, and also the demilitarised zones.

(c) Control the operations of releasing prisoners of war and civilian internees.

(d) Supervise at ports and airfields as well as along all frontiers of Viet Nam the execution of the provisions of the agreement on the cessation of hostilities, regulating the introduction into the country of armed forces, military personnel and of all kinds of arms, munitions and war material.

Article 37

The International Commission shall, through the medium of the inspection teams mentioned above, and as soon as possible either on its own initiative, or at the request of the Joint Commission, or of one of the parties, undertake the necessary investigations both documentary and on the ground.

Appendix IV

Article 38

The inspection teams shall submit to the International Commission the results of their supervision, their investigation and their observations, furthermore they shall draw up such special reports as they may consider necessary or as may be requested from them by the Commission. In the case of a disagreement within the teams, the conclusions of each member shall be submitted to the Commission.

Article 39

If any one inspection team is unable to settle an incident or considers that there is a violation or a threat of a serious violation, the International Commission shall be informed; the latter shall study the reports and the conclusions of the inspection teams and shall inform the parties of the measures which should be taken for the settlement of the incident, ending of the violation or removal of the threat of violation.

Article 40

When the Joint Commission is unable to reach an agreement on the interpretation to be given to some provision or on the appraisal of a fact, the International Commission shall be informed of the disputed question. Its recommendations shall be sent directly to the parties and shall be notified to the Joint Commission.

Article 41

The recommendations of the International Commission shall be adopted by majority vote, subject to the provisions contained in Article 42. If the votes are divided, the chairman's vote shall be decisive.

The International Commission may formulate recommendations concerning amendments and additions which should be made to the provisions of the agreement on the cessation of hostilities in Viet Nam, in order to ensure a more effective execution of that agreement. These recommendations shall be adopted unanimously.

Appendix IV

Article 42

When dealing with questions concerning violations, or threats of violations, which might lead to a resumption of hostilities, namely:—

(a) Refusal by the armed forces of one party to effect the movements provided for in the regroupment plan;

(b) Violation by the armed forces of one of the parties of the regrouping zones, territorial waters, or air space of the other party;

the decisions of the International Commission must be unanimous.

Article 43

If one of the parties refuses to put into effect a recommendation of the International Commission, the parties concerned or the Commission itself shall inform the members of the Geneva Conference.

If the International Commission does not reach unanimity in the cases provided for in Article 42, it shall submit a majority report and one or more minority reports to the members of the Conference.

The International Commission shall inform the members of the Conference in all cases where its activity is being hindered.

Article 44

The International Commission shall be set up at the time of the cessation of hostilities in Indo-China in order that it should be able to fulfill the tasks provided for in Article 36.

Article 45

The International Commission for Supervision and Control in Viet Nam shall act in close co-operation with the International Commissions for Supervision and Control in Cambodia and Laos.

The Secretaries-General of these three Commissions shall be responsible for co-ordinating their work and for relations between them.

Appendix IV

Article 46

The International Commission for Supervision and Control in Viet Nam may, after consultation with the International Commissions for Supervision and Control in Cambodia and Laos, and having regard to the development of the situation in Cambodia and Laos, progressively reduce its activities. Such a decision must be adopted unanimously.

Article 47

All the provisions of the present Agreement, save the second subparagraph of Article 11, shall enter into force at 2400 hours (Geneva time) on July 22, 1954.

Done in Geneva at 2400 hours on the 20th of July, 1954, in French and in Vietnamese, both texts being equally authentic.

> For the Commander-in-Chief of the French Union Forces in Indo-China:
> Deltiel,
> Brigadier-General

> For the Commander-in-Chief of the People's Army of Viet Nam:
> Ta-Quang-Buu, Vice-Minister of National Defence of the Democratic Republic of Viet Nam

B. Final Declaration of the Geneva Conference on the Problem of Restoring Peace in Indo-China, in Which the Representatives of Cambodia, the Democratic Republic of Viet Nam, France, Laos, the People's Republic of China, the State of Viet Nam, the Union of Soviet Socialist Republics, the United Kingdom and the United States of America Took Part

(July 21, 1954)

1. The Conference takes note of the agreements ending hostilities in Cambodia, Laos and Viet Nam and organising international control and the supervision of the execution of the provisions of these agreements.

2. The Conference expresses satisfaction at the ending of hostilities in Cambodia, Laos and Viet Nam; the Conference expresses its conviction that the execution of the provisions set out in the present declaration and in the agreements on the cessation of hostilities will permit Cambodia, Laos and Viet Nam henceforth to play their part, in full independence and sovereignty, in the peaceful community of nations.

3. The Conference takes note of the declarations made by the Governments of Cambodia and of Laos of their intention to adopt measures permitting all citizens to take their place in the national community, in particular by participating in the next general elections, which, in conformity with the constitution of each of these countries shall take place in the course of the year 1955, by secret ballot and in conditions of respect for fundamental freedoms.

4. The Conference takes note of the clauses in the agreement on the cessation of hostilities in Viet Nam prohibiting the introduction into Viet Nam of foreign troops and military personnel as well as of all kinds of arms and munitions. The Conference also takes note of the declarations made by the Governments of Cambodia and Laos of their resolution not to request foreign aid, whether in war material, in personnel or in instructors except for the purpose of the effective defence of their territory and, in the case of Laos, to the extent defined by the agreements on the cessation of hostilities in Laos.

5. The Conference takes note of the clauses in the agreement on the cessation of hostilities in Viet Nam to the effect that no military base under the control of a foreign State may be established in the regrouping zones of the two parties, the latter having the obligation to see that the zones allotted to them shall not constitute part of any military alliance and shall not be utilised for the resumption of hostilities or in the service of an aggressive policy. The Conference also takes note of the declarations of the Governments of Cambodia and Laos to the effect that they will not join in any agreement with other States if this agreement includes the obligation to participate in a military

alliance not in conformity with the principles of the Charter of the United Nations or, in the case of Laos, with the principles of the agreement on the cessation of hostilities in Laos or, so long as their security is not threatened, the obligation to establish bases on Cambodian or Laotian territory for the military forces of foreign Powers.

6. The Conference recognises that the essential purpose of the agreement relating to Viet Nam is to settle military questions with a view to ending hostilities and that the military demarcation line is provisional and should not in any way be interpreted as constituting a political or territorial boundary. The Conference expresses its conviction that the execution of the provisions set out in the present declaration and in the agreement on the cessation of hostilities creates the necessary basis for the achievement in the near future of a political settlement in Viet Nam.

7. The Conference declares that, so far as Viet Nam is concerned, the settlement of political problems, effected on the basis of respect for the principles of independence, unity and territorial integrity, shall permit the Vietnamese people to enjoy the fundamental freedoms, guaranteed by democratic institutions established as a result of free general elections by secret ballot. In order to ensure that sufficient progress in the restoration of peace has been made, and that all the necessary conditions obtain for free expression of the national will, general elections shall be held in July 1956, under the supervision of an international commission composed of representatives of the Member States of the International Supervisory Commission, referred to in the agreement on the cessation of hostilities. Consultations will be held on this subject between the competent representative authorities of the two zones from July 20, 1955, onwards.

8. The provisions of the agreements on the cessation of hostilities intended to ensure the protection of individuals and of property must be most strictly applied and must, in

particular, allow everyone in Viet Nam to decide freely in which zone he wishes to live.

9. The competent representative authorities of the Northern and Southern zones of Viet Nam, as well as the authorities of Laos and Cambodia, must not permit any individual or collective reprisals against persons who have collaborated in any way with one of the parties during the war, or against members of such persons' families.

10. The Conference takes note of the declaration of the Government of the French Republic to the effect that it is ready to withdraw its troops from the territory of Cambodia, Laos and Viet Nam, at the request of the Governments concerned and within periods which shall be fixed by agreement between the parties except in the cases where, by agreement between the two parties, a certain number of French troops shall remain at specified points and for a specified time.

11. The Conference takes note of the declaration of the French Government to the effect that for the settlement of all the problems connected with the re-establishment and consolidation of peace in Cambodia, Laos and Viet Nam, the French Government will proceed from the principle of respect for the independence and sovereignty, unity and territorial integrity of Cambodia, Laos and Viet Nam.

12. In their relations with Cambodia, Laos and Viet Nam, each member of the Geneva Conference undertakes to respect the sovereignty, the independence, the unity and the territorial integrity of the above-mentioned States, and to refrain from any interference in their internal affairs.

13. The members of the Conference agree to consult one another on any question which may be referred to them by the International Supervisory Commission, in order to study such measures as may prove necessary to ensure that the agreements on the cessation of hostilities in Cambodia, Laos and Viet Nam are respected.

Appendix IV

C. Extracts from Verbatim Record of
Eighth Plenary Session
(July 21 1954)

The Chairman (Mr. Eden): As I think my colleagues are aware, agreement has now been reached on certain documents. It is proposed that this Conference should take note of these agreements. I accordingly propose to begin by reading out a list of the subjects covered by the documents, which I understand every delegation has in front of them.

First, agreement on the cessation of hostilities in Viet Nam; second, agreement on the cessation of hostilities in Laos; third, agreement on the cessation of hostilities in Cambodia. I would draw particular attention to the fact that these three agreements now incorporate the texts which were negotiated separately concerning the supervision of the Armistice in the three countries by the International Commission and the joint committees.

I should also like to draw the attention of all delegations to a point of some importance in connexion with the Armistice Agreements and the related maps and documents on supervision. It has been agreed among the parties to each of these Agreements that none of them shall be made public for the present, pending further agreement among the parties. The reason for this, I must explain to my colleagues, is that these Armistice terms come into force at different dates. And it is desired that they should not be made public until they have come into force.

The further documents to which I must draw attention, which are in your possession, are: fourth, declaration by the Government of Laos on elections; fifth, declaration by the Government of Cambodia on elections and integration of all citizens into the national community; sixth, declaration by the Government of Laos on the military status of the country; seventh, declaration by the Government of Cambodia on the military status of the country; eighth, declaration by the Government of the French Republic on the withdrawal of troops from the three countries of Indochina.

Finally, gentlemen, there is the Draft (final) Declaration by the Conference, which takes note of all these documents. I think all my colleagues have copies of this Draft Declaration (3) before them. I will ask my colleagues in turn to express themselves upon this Declaration.

The Representative of France.

M. Mendès-France (France): Mr. Chairman, the French Delegation approves the terms of this Declaration.

The Chairman: The Representative of Laos.

Mr. Phoui Sananikone (Laos): The Delegation of Laos has no observations to make on this text.

The Chairman: The Representative of the People's Republic of China.

Mr. Chou En-lai (People's Republic of China): We agree.

The Chairman: On behalf of Her Majesty's Government in the United Kingdom, I associate myself with the final Declaration of this Conference.

The Union of Soviet Socialist Republics.

M. Molotov (U.S.S.R.): The Soviet Delegation agrees.

The Chairman: The Representative of Cambodia.

Mr. Tep Phan (Cambodia): The Delegation of Cambodia wishes to state that, among the documents just listed, one is missing. This is a Cambodian Declaration which we have already circulated to all delegations. Its purport is as follows: Paragraphs 7, 11, and 12 of the final Declaration stipulate respect for the territorial integrity of Viet Nam. The Cambodian Delegation asks the Conference to consider that this provision does not imply the abandonment of such legitimate rights and interests as Cambodia might assert with regard to certain regions of South Viet Nam, about which Cambodia has made express reservations, in particular at the time of the signature of the Franco-Khmer Treaty of November 8, 1949, on relations between Cambodia and France and at the time the French law which linked Cochin-china to Viet Nam was passed. Faithful to the ideal of peace, and to the international principle of non-interference, Cambodia has no intention of interfering in the internal affairs of the State of Viet Nam and associates herself fully with the principle of respect for its integrity, provided certain adjustments and regularisations be arrived at with regard to the borders between this State and Cambodia, borders which so far have been fixed by a mere unilateral act of France.

In support of this Declaration, the Cambodian Delegation communicates to all members of this Conference a note on Cambodian lands in South Viet Nam.

The Chairman: If this Declaration was not inscribed on the agenda on the list of documents I have read out, it is because it has only at this instant reached me. I do not think it is any part of the task of this Conference to deal with any past controversies in respect of the frontiers between Cambodia and Viet Nam.

The Representative of the Democratic Republic of Viet Nam.

Mr. Pham Van Dong (Democratic Republic of Viet Nam): Mr. Chairman, I agree completely with the words pronounced by you. In the name of the Government of the Democratic Republic of Viet Nam we make the most express reservations regarding the statement made by the Delegation of Cambodia just now. I do this in the interests of good relations and understanding between our two countries.

The Chairman: I think the Conference can take note of the statements of the Delegation of Cambodia just circulated and of the statement of the Representative of the Democratic Republic of Viet Nam.

I will continue calling upon countries to speak on the subject of the Declaration. I call upon the United States of America.

Mr. Bedell Smith (United States): Mr. Chairman, Fellow Delegates, as I stated to my colleagues during our meeting on July 18, my Government is not prepared to join in a

Declaration by the Conference such as is submitted. However, the United States makes this unilateral declaration of its position in these matters:—

DECLARATION

The Government of the United States being resolved to devote its efforts to the strengthening of peace in accordance with the principles and purposes of the United Nations
Takes Note
of the Agreements concluded at Geneva on July 20 and 21, 1954, between (a) the Franco-Laotian Command and the Command of the People's Army of Viet Nam; (b) the Royal Khmer Army Command and the Command of the People's Army of Viet Nam; (c) Franco-Vietnamese Command and the Command of the People's Army of Viet Nam, and of paragraphs 1 to 12 of the Declaration presented to the Geneva Conference on July 21, 1954.

The Government of the United States of America
Declares
with regard to the aforesaid Agreements and paragraphs that

(i) it will refrain from the threat or the use of force to disturb them, in accordance with Article 2 (Section 4) of the Charter of the United Nations (4) dealing with the obligation of Members to refrain in their international relations from the threat or use of force; and (ii) it would view any renewal of the aggression in violation of the aforesaid Agreements with grave concern and as seriously threatening international peace and security.

In connexion with the statement in the Declaration concerning free elections in Viet Nam, my Government wishes to make clear its position which it has expressed in a Declaration made in Washington on June 29, 1954, as follows:—

In the case of nations now divided against their will, we shall continue to seek to achieve unity through free elections, supervised by the United Nations to ensure that they are conducted fairly.

Appendix IV

With respect to the statement made by the Representative of the State of Viet Nam, the United States reiterates its traditional position that peoples are entitled to determine their own future and that it will not join in an arrangement which would hinder this. Nothing in its declaration just made is intended to or does indicate any departure from this traditional position.

We share the hope that the agreement will permit Cambodia, Laos and Viet Nam to play their part in full independence and sovereignty, in the peaceful community of nations, and will enable the peoples of that area to determine their own future.

Thank you, Mr. Chairman.

The Chairman: The Conference will, I think, wish to take note of the statement of the Representative of the United States of America.

I call on the Representative of the State of Viet Nam.

Mr. Tran Van Do (State of Viet Nam): Mr. Chairman, as regards the final Declaration of the Conference, the Vietnamese Delegation requests the Conference to incorporate in this Declaration after Article 10, the following text:—

The Conference takes note of the Declaration of the Government of the State of Viet Nam undertaking:

to make and support every effort to re-establish a real and lasting peace in Viet Nam;

not to use force to resist the procedures for carrying the cease-fire into effect, in spite of the objections and reservations that the State of Viet Nam has expressed, especially in its final statement.

The Chairman: I shall be glad to hear any views that my colleagues may wish to express. But, as I understand the position, the final Declaration has already been drafted and this additional paragraph has only just now been received; indeed, it has been amended since I received the text a few minutes ago. In all the circumstances, I suggest that the best course we can take is that the Conference should take note of the Declaration of the State of Viet Nam in this respect. If any of my colleagues has a contrary view, perhaps they would be good enough to say so. (*None.*) If none of my colleagues wishes to make any other observations, may I pass to certain other points which have to be settled before this Conference can conclude its labours?

The first is that, if it is agreeable to our colleagues, it is suggested that the two Chairmen should at the conclusion of this meeting address telegrams to the Governments of India, Poland and Canada to ask them if they will undertake the duties of supervision which the Conference has invited them to discharge. Is that agreeable? (*Agreed.*) Thank you.

The last is perhaps the least agreeable chapter of all our work. Certain costs arise from the decisions which the Conference has taken. It is suggested that it should be left here to your Chairmen as their parting gift to try to put before you some proposal in respect of those costs. I only wish to add in that connexion that, as this Conference is peculiar in not having any Secretariat in the usual sense of the term, the two Chairmen with considerable reluctance are prepared to undertake this highly invidious task. The costs to which I refer are not our own but those of the International Commission.

Does any delegate wish to make any further observation? (*None.*)

Gentlemen, perhaps I may say a final word as your Chairman for this day. We have now come to the end of our work. For a number of reasons it has been prolonged and intricate. The co-operation which all delegates have given to your two Chairmen has enabled us to overcome many procedural difficulties. Without that co-operation, we could not have succeeded in our task. The Agreements concluded to-day could not, in the nature of things, give complete satisfaction to everyone. But they have made it possible to stop a war which has lasted for eight years and brought suffering and hardship to millions of people. They have also, we hope, reduced international tension at a point of instant danger to world peace. These results are surely worth our many weeks of toil. In order to bring about a cease-fire, we have drawn up a series of agreements. They are the best that our hands could devise. All will now depend upon the spirit in which those agreements are observed and carried out.

Gentlemen, before we leave this hospitable town of Geneva, I'm sure you would wish your Chairmen to give a message of gratitude to the United Nations and its able staff who have housed and helped us in our work.

And lastly let me express our cordial thanks to the Swiss Government and to the people and authorities of Geneva who have done so much to make our stay here pleasant as well as of service to the cause of peace.

The Representative of the United States of America.

Mr. Bedell Smith (United States): If I presume to speak for my fellow delegates, it is because I know that they all feel as I do. I hope that they join me in expressing our thanks to the two Chairmen of this Conference. Their patience, their tireless efforts, and their goodwill have done a great deal to make this settlement possible. We owe them our sincere thanks.

The Chairman: The Representative of the Union of Soviet Socialist Republics.

M. Molotov (U.S.S.R.): Mr. Chairman, as one of the Chairmen at the Geneva Conference, I would like to reply to the remarks just made by Mr. Bedell Smith, who spoke highly of the work done by the Chairmen. Naturally I must stress the outstanding services and the outstanding role played by our Chairman of to-day, Mr. Eden, whose role in the Geneva Conference cannot be exaggerated. And I would also like to reply and thank Mr. Bedell Smith for his warm words of to-day.

The Chairman: Has any other delegate anything else they want to say?

The Representative of Viet Nam.

Mr. Tran Van Do (State of Viet Nam): Mr. Chairman, I expressed the view of the Delegation of the State of Viet

Nam in my statement and I would have this Conference take note of it in its final act.

The Chairman: As I think I explained, we cannot now amend our final act, which is the statement of the Conference as a whole, but the Declaration of the Representative of the State of Viet Nam will be taken note of.

Any other observations? (*None.*)

I would like to be allowed to add my thanks for what General Bedell Smith has said and also to thank M. Molotov for his words. Both were undeserved, but even if things are not true, if they are nice things it's pleasant to hear them said.

But I do want to close this Conference with this one sentence: I'm quite sure that each one of us here hopes that the work which we have done will help to strengthen the forces working for peace.

Bibliography

<<<<<<<<<<<<<<<<<<<<<<<<<<<<<<<<<<<<<<<<<<<<<<<<<

CHINESE DOCUMENTS AND REPORTS

Chiang, Yung-ching, comp. *Yueh-nan wen chien hui pien, 1941-1948* (unpub. collection of documents on Vietnam, 1941-1948). Taiwan, 1966.

Chinese International Information Bureau. *China Handbook, 1937-1945*, rev. ed. Nanking: International Information Bureau, 1947.

Chinese Ministry of Foreign Affairs (Taiwan). *Treaties between the Republic of China and Foreign States* (1927-1957). Taipei: China Engraving & Printing Works, 1958.

Chung-hua jen min kung ho kuo wai chiao pu pien. *Chung-hua jen min kung ho kuo tiao yueh chi, 1949-1951* (Collection of Treaties of the People's Republic of China, 1949-1951), Vol. I. Peking: Fa lu chu pan she, 1957.

Chung yang yen chiu yuan, chin tai shih yen chiu so. *Chung Fa Yueh-nan chiao she tang, 1875-1911* (Archives of Sino-French Negotiations on Vietnam, 1875-1911), 7 vols. Taipei, 1962.

Hai-fang hua ch'iao shan hou wei yuan hui. *Yueh-nan Hai-fang hua ch'iao sun shih pao kao shu* (Report on the Loss of the Chinese Residents in Haiphong, Vietnam). Haiphong, 1947.

Shih chieh chih shih she. *Jih-nei-wa hui i wen chien hui pien* (Collection of Documents of the Geneva Conference). Peking, 1954.

VIETNAMESE OFFICIAL PUBLICATIONS

Democratic Republic of Vietnam, Foreign Languages Publishing House. *Statements by President Ho Chi Minh After the Geneva Conference.* Hanoi, 1955.

———. *XVth Anniversary of the Democratic Republic of Vietnam, 1945-1960.* Hanoi, 1960.

————. News Service. *Viet-Nam Information Bulletin*. Rangoon, 1959-1968.

————. Vietnam Fatherland Front. *For Peace and Reunification of Vietnam*. Hanoi, 1958.

————. Central Statistical Department. *Three Years of Economic Rehabilitation and Cultural Development, 1955-1957*. Hanoi, 1958.

————. Vietnam Peace Committee. *Six Years of the Implementation of the Geneva Agreements in Vietnam*. Hanoi, 1960.

————. Service d'Information. *Discours de M. Pham-Van-Dong*. Paris, 1946.

————. *Le Président Ho-Chi-Minh*. Paris, 1947.

Republic of Vietnam, Embassy in Washington. *News from Viet-Nam*, and *Vietnam Bulletin* (1958-1968). Washington, D.C.

————. Press Office. *Major Policy Speeches of President Ngo Dinh Diem*. Saigon, November 1960.

————. Secretary of State for Foreign Affairs. *Vietnam in World Affairs*, Vol. I, Nos. 3-4. Saigon, December 1956.

————. *Violations of the Geneva Agreements by the Viet-Minh Communists*. Saigon, 1959, 1960.

United States Official Sources

The American Consulate General in Hong Kong. *Survey of the China Mainland Press* (1950-1961).

————. *Current Background* (1950-1955).

————. *Extracts from China Mainland Magazines* (1950-1955).

The Department of State. *A Threat to the Peace: North Viet-Nam's Effort to Conquer South Viet-Nam*, Parts I and II. Washington, D.C., 1961.

————. *Bulletin* (1945-1955).

————. *Communist Propaganda Activities in the Far East*. Washington, D.C., 1957.

————. *Foreign Relations of the United States*. Washington, D.C., 1939.

Bibliography

The Department of State. *Foreign Relations of the United States, Diplomatic Papers, 1943, China.* Washington, D.C., 1957.

——. *Papers Relating to the Foreign Relations of the United States: Japan, 1931-1941.* Washington, D.C., 1943.

——. *United States Relations with China, 1944-1949.* Washington, D.C., 1949.

——. Bureau of Intelligence and Research. *Chinese Communist World Outlook; A Handbook of Chinese Communist Statements: The Public Record of a Militant Ideology.* Washington, D.C., 1962.

——. Office of Intelligence and Research, Division of Research for Far East. *Political Alignments of Viet-Namese Nationalists.* Washington, D.C., 1949.

Foreign Broadcast Information Service. *Daily Report.* Washington, D.C., 1948-1968.

U.S. House of Representatives. *The Communist Conspiracy: Strategy and Tactics of World Communism.* House Reports 2241, 2242. Washington, D.C., 1956.

——. *The Strategy and Tactics of World Communism.* House Document 154. Washington, D.C., 1956.

——. *Vietnam.* Report by Walter H. Judd. House Report No. 2147. 84th Cong., 2d Sess., 1955.

U.S. Senate, Committee on Foreign Relations. *Indochina: Report of Senator Mike Mansfield on a Study Mission to the Associated States of Indochina; Vietnam, Cambodia, Laos.* 83d Cong., 1st Sess. Washington, D.C., October 27, 1953.

——. *Report on Indochina: Report of Senator Mike Mansfield on a Study Mission to Vietnam, Cambodia, Laos.* 83d Cong., 2d Sess. Washington, D.C., October 15, 1954.

——. *The Southeast Asia Collective Defense Treaty.* 84th Cong., 2d Sess. Washington, D.C., 1955.

——. *Vietnam, Cambodia and Laos.* Report by Senator Mike Mansfield, October 6, 1955. 84th Cong., 1st Sess. Washington, D.C., 1955.

Bibliography

BRITISH GOVERNMENT PUBLICATIONS

Great Britain, Foreign Office. *Documents Relating to the Discussion of Korea and Indochina at the Geneva Conference, April 27-June 15, 1954* (Cmd. 9186). London, 1954.

——. *Further Documents Relating to the Discussion of Indochina at the Geneva Conference, June 16-July 21, 1954* (Cmd. 9239). London, 1954.

——. Parliament, House of Commons. *Parliamentary Debates* (Session 1953-1954), Vol. 529. London, 1954.

UNITED NATIONS PUBLICATIONS

United Nations. *General Assembly, Eighth Session, Official Records, 438th Plenary Meeting*, September 21, 1953.

BOOKS AND MEMOIRS

Ball, W. MacMahon. *Nationalism and Communism in East Asia*. Victoria, Australia: Melbourne University Press, 1956.

Barnett, A. Doak. *Communist China and Asia: Challenge to American Policy*. New York: Harper, 1960.

——. *Communist Economic Strategy: The Rise of Mainland China*. Washington, D.C.: National Planning Association, 1959.

——, ed. *Communist Strategies in Asia: A Comparative Analysis of Governments and Parties*. New York: Frederick Praeger, 1963.

Bator, Victor. *Vietnam: A Diplomatic Tragedy*. New York: Oceana, 1965.

Beloff, Max. *Soviet Policy in the Far East, 1944-51*. London: Oxford University Press, 1953.

Bodard, Lucien. *The Quicksand War: Prelude to Vietnam*. Tr. and with a introduction by Patrick O'Brian. Boston: Little, Brown, 1967.

Brandt, Conrad. *Stalin's Failure in China, 1924-1927*. Cambridge: Harvard University Press, 1958.

Bibliography

Brandt, Conrad, Benjamin Schwartz, and John K. Fairbank. *A Documentary History of Chinese Communism.* Cambridge: Harvard University Press, 1952.

Brimmell, J. H. *Communism in South East Asia, A Political Analysis.* London: Oxford University Press, 1959.

Brown, William Adams, Jr. and Redvers Opie. *American Foreign Assistance.* Washington, D.C.: Brookings Institution, 1953.

Buttinger, Joseph. *The Smaller Dragon: A Political History of Vietnam.* New York: Frederick Praeger, 1958.

————. *Vietnam: A Dragon Embattled.* 2 vols. New York: Frederick Praeger, 1967.

Butwell, Richard. *Southeast Asia Today and Tomorrow.* New York: Frederick Praeger, 1961.

Cady, John F. *The Roots of French Imperialism in Eastern Asia.* Ithaca: Cornell University Press, 1954.

————. *Southeast Asia: Its Historical Development.* New York: McGraw-Hill, 1964.

Calvocoressi, Peter, ed. *Survey of International Affairs, 1947-1948.* London: Oxford University Press, 1949.

Chang, Fa-k'uei. *K'ang chan hui i lu* (Memoirs of the Resistance War), in *United Review* (weekly). Hong Kong, 1962.

Chang, Kuang-piao. *Ts'ung chih min ti tao tu li ti Yueh-nan* (Vietnam: From Colonialism to Independence). Peking: *World Culture*, 1951.

Chang, Kuo-t'ao. *My Memoirs*, in *Ming pao* (monthly). Hong Kong, 1966- .

Ch'en, Chung-shin. *Chung-kuo jen tao Tung-nan-ya* (The Chinese Immigration to Southeast Asia). Hong Kong: Freedom Press, 1956.

————. *Tung-nan-ya lieh kuo chih* (The Southeast Asian Countries), 2 vols. Hong Kong: Freedom Press, 1958.

Ch'en, Hsiu-ho. *Yueh-nan ku shih chi ch'i min tsu wen hua chih yen chiu* (Study of Vietnam's Ancient History, People and Culture). Kunming: Yunnan University, 1943.

————. *Chung Yueh liang kuo jen min ti yu hao kuan hsi ho wen hua chiao liu* (Friendship and Cultural Intercourse of Sino-Vietnamese Peoples). Peking: Chung-kuo ch'ing nien ch'u pan she, 1957.

Ch'en, Yin-ching, ed. *Treaties and Agreements between the Republic of China and Other Powers, 1929-1954.* Washington, D.C.: Sino-American Publishing Service, 1957.

Ch'eng, Tien-fang. *History of Sino-Russian Relations.* Washington, D.C.: Public Affairs Press, 1957.

Chiang Kai-shek. *Soviet Russia in China: A Summing-up at Seventy.* New York: Farrar, Straus, and Cudahy, 1957.

Chiang, Yung-ching. *Bao-lo-t'ing yu Wuhan cheng ch'uan* (Borodin and the Wuhan Regime). Taipei, 1963.

Chinese Ministry of Information. *China Handbook, 1937-1945.* New York: Macmillan, 1947.

Chow, Ching-wen. *Ten Years of Storm; The True Story of the Communist Regime in China,* tr. Lai Ming. New York: Holt, Rinehart, and Winston, 1960.

Chu, Hsieh. *Yueh-nan shou hsiang jih chi* (Diary of Accepting the [Japanese] Surrender in Vietnam). Shanghai: Commercial Press, 1947.

Cole, Allan B., ed. *Conflict in Indochina and International Repercussions: A Documentary History, 1945-1955.* Ithaca: Cornell University Press, 1956.

Curl, Peter V., ed. *Documents on American Foreign Relations, 1950-1954.* New York: Harper, 1951-1955.

Dai, Shen-yu. *Peking, Moscow, and the Communist Parties of Colonial Asia.* Cambridge: Center for International Studies, Massachusetts Institute of Technology, 1954.

Daniels, Robert V., ed. *A Documentary History of Communism,* 2 vols. New York: Vintage Books, 1962.

Das, S. R. Mohan. *Ho Chi Minh: Nationalist or Soviet Agent?* Bombay: Democratic Research Service, 1951.

Devillers, Philippe. *Histoire du Viet-Nam de 1940 à 1952.* Paris: Editions du Seuil, 1952.

Donnell, John C. "North Vietnam: A Qualified Pro-Chinese Position," in *The Communist Revolution in Asia: Tactics, Goals, and Achievements,* ed. Robert A. Scalapino. Englewood Cliffs, N.J.: Prentice-Hall, 1965.

Bibliography

Douglas, William O. *North from Malaya*. New York: Doubleday, 1953.

Du Bois, Cora. *Social Forces in Southeast Asia*. Minneapolis: University of Minnesota Press, 1949.

Durand, Maurice. *Text et Commentaire du Miroir Complet de l'Histoire du Viet*. Hanoi: Ecole Française d'Extrême-Orient, 1950.

Dutt, Vidya Prakash and Vishal Singh. *Indian Policy and Attitudes Towards Indo-China and S.E.A.T.O.* New York: Institute of Pacific Relations, 1954.

Eden, Anthony. *Full Circle; The Memoirs of Anthony Eden*. Boston: Houghton Mifflin, 1960.

Eisenhower, Dwight D. *Mandate for Change: The White House Years, 1953-1956*. New York: Doubleday, 1963.

Elegant, Robert S. *China's Red Masters*. New York: Twayne, 1951.

Emerson, Ruppert. *From Empire to Nation*. Cambridge: Harvard University Press, 1960.

Emerson, Ruppert et al. *Government and Nationalism in Southeast Asia*. New York: Institute of Pacific Relations, 1942.

Eudin, Xenia J. and Robert C. North. *Soviet Russia and the East, 1920-1927: A Documentary Survey*. Stanford: Stanford University Press, 1957.

Faber, E. *The Mind of Mencius*, tr. Arthur B. Hutchinson. Boston: Houghton Mifflin, 1882.

Fall, Bernard B. *The Viet-Minh Regime*. New York: Institute of Pacific Relations, 1954.

———. *Street Without Joy: Indochina at War, 1946-54*. Harrisburg: Stackpole, 1961.

———. *The Two Viet-Nams: A Political and Military Analysis*. New York: Frederick Praeger, 1964.

———. *Viet-Nam Witness: 1953-1966*. New York: Frederick Praeger: 1966.

———. *Hell in a Very Small Place: The Siege of Dien-Bien-Phu*. New York: Lippincott, 1967.

———, ed. *Ho Chi Minh on Revolution*. New York: Frederick Praeger, 1967.

Feis, Herbert. *The China Tangle*. Princeton: Princeton University Press, 1953.

————. *Japan Subdued: The Atomic Bomb and the End of the War in the Pacific*. Princeton: Princeton University Press, 1961.

Feng, Tzu-yu. *Chung-hua-min-kuo kai kuo chien ko ming shih* (A Revolutionary History before the Establishment of the Republic of China). Chungking: China Cultural Service, 1944.

Fifield, Russell H. *The Diplomacy of Southeast Asia; 1945-1958*. New York: Harper, 1958.

Fishel, Wesley R., ed. *Problems of Freedom: South Vietnam Since Independence*. New York and East Lansing, Mich.: The Free Press of Glencoe and Michigan State University Bureau of Social and Political Research, 1961.

Gobron, Gabriel. *History and Philosophy of Caodaism*, tr. Pham-Xuan-Thai. Saigon: Tu-hai, 1950.

Grauwin, Paul. *Doctor at Dien Bien Phu*. London: Hutchinson, 1955.

Guillain, Robert. *La Fin des Illusions*. Paris: Centre d'Études de Politique Étrangère, 1954.

Gurtov, Melvin. *The First Vietnam Crisis*. New York: Columbia University Press, 1967.

Hall, D.G.E. *A History of South-East Asia*. New York: St. Martin's Press, 1955.

Halle, Louis J. *The Cold War as History*. London: Chatto & Windus, 1967.

Hammer, Ellen J. *The Struggle for Indochina*. Stanford: Stanford University Press, 1954.

Hart, Donn V. *Southeast Asia and the United States*. New York: Institute of Pacific Relations, 1954.

Hinton, Harold C. *China's Relations with Burma and Vietnam*. New York: Institute of Pacific Relations, 1958.

————. *Communist China in World Politics*. Boston: Houghton Mifflin, 1966.

Ho Chi Minh. *Selected Works*, 4 vols. Hanoi: Foreign Languages Publishing House, 1961-1962.

Bibliography

Ho Chi Minh. *Prison Diary.* Tr. Aileen Palmer. Hanoi: Foreign Languages Publishing House, 1966.

Ho Chi Minh et al. *A Heroic People.* Hanoi: Foreign Languages Publishing House, 1960.

Ho Chi Minh et al. *Yueh-nan min chu kung ho kuo shih nien lai ti ch'eng chiu* (The Achievements of the Democratic Republic of Vietnam in the Past Ten Years). Peking: *World Culture,* 1956.

Ho, Ying-ch'in. *Military Reports During the Resistance War.* 2 vols. Taipei: Wen hsing, 1962.

Hoai Thanh et al. *Hu pai pai* (Uncle Ho). Hanoi: Foreign Languages Publishing House, 1962.

Hoang Van Chi. *From Colonialism to Communism.* New York: Frederick Praeger, 1964.

Holland, William L., ed. *Asian Nationalism and the West.* New York: Macmillan, 1953.

Honey, P. J. *Communism in North Vietnam: Its Role in the Sino-Soviet Dispute.* Cambridge: M.I.T. Press, 1963.

————, ed. *North Vietnam Today: Profile of a Communist Satellite.* New York: Frederick Praeger, 1962.

Hsiao, Tso-liang. *Power Relations within the Chinese Communist Movement, 1930-1934.* Seattle: University of Washington Press, 1961.

Hsiao, Yang. *Chieh fang chung ti Yueh-nan* (Vietnam in Liberation). Shanghai: Chung lien, 1951.

Hsieh, Alice Langley. *Communist China's Strategy in the Nuclear Era.* Englewood Cliffs, N.J.: Prentice-Hall, 1962.

Hsu, Sung-shih. *Tung-nan-ya min tsu ti Chung-kuo hsueh yuan* (Chinese Blood Relations of the South Eastern Asiatic People). Hong Kong: Ping On Book Co., 1959.

————. *Yueh chiang liu yu jen min shih* (History of the People of the Yueh River Valley). Hong Kong: World Book Store, 1963.

Hu Ch'iao-mu. *Thirty Years of the Communist Party of China.* Peking: Foreign Languages Press, 1951.

Huang, Chieh. *Hai wai chi ch'ing* (Memoirs of Indochina). Taipei, 1958.

Huard, Pierre Alphonse, and Maurice Durand. *Connaissance du Viet Nam*. Paris: Imprimerie Nationale, 1954.

Hull, Cordell. *The Memoirs of Cordell Hull*, 2 vols. New York: Macmillan, 1948.

Isaacs, Harold R. *No Peace for Asia*. New York: Macmillan, 1947.

————. *The Tragedy of the Chinese Revolution*. Stanford: Stanford University Press, 1951.

Jansen, Marius B. *The Japanese and Sun Yat-sen*. Cambridge: Harvard University Press, 1954.

Jen min ch'u pan she. *Jen min shou ts'e* (People's Handbook). Peking, 1953.

Jones, F. C. et al. *Survey of International Affairs, 1939-1946: The Far East, 1942-1946*. London: Oxford University Press, 1955.

Kahin, George McT. *The Asian-African Conference, Bandung, Indonesia, April 1955*. Ithaca: Cornell University Press, 1956.

———— and John W. Lewis, *The United States in Vietnam*. New York: Delta, 1967.

Kai Ming Book Store (reprinted). *Shih chi* (Records of History). Shanghai, 1934.

————. *Han shu* (History of the Former Han Dynasty). Shanghai, 1934.

————. *Hou-han shu* (History of the Later Han Dynasty). Shanghai, 1934.

————. *San-kuo chih* (History of the Three Kingdoms). Shanghai, 1934.

————. *Sui shu* (History of the Sui Dynasty). Shanghai, 1934.

————. *Sung shu* (History of the Sung Dynasty). Shanghai, 1934.

————. *Ming shih* (History of the Ming Dynasty). Shanghai, 1934.

————. *Nan shih* (History of the Southern Dynasty). Shanghai, 1934.

Kautsky, John H. *Moscow and the Communist Party of India*. New York: John Wiley & Sons, 1956.

Kennedy, Malcolm D. *A History of Communism in East Asia*. New York: Frederick Praeger, 1957.

King, John Kerry. *Southeast Asia in Perspective*. New York: Macmillan, 1956.

Kissinger, Henry A. *Nuclear Weapons and Foreign Policy*. New York: Doubleday, 1957.

Kung, Hsueh-sui. *Chung-kuo chan shih chiao t'ung shih* (A History of the Wartime Transportation of China). Shanghai: Commercial Press, 1947.

The Kuomintang, the Sixth Section. "Vietnamese Communism and Vietnamese Problems—Today and Yesterday," in *Studies on Special Subjects*, 2 issues. Taipei, 1955.

Lacouture, Jean. *Vietnam: Between Two Truces*. New York: Random House, 1966.

———. *Ho Chi Minh*. Paris: Editions du Seuil, 1967.

Lacouture, Jean and Philippe Devillers. *La Fin d'une Guerre, Indochine 1954*. Paris: Les Editions du Seuil, 1960.

Lancaster, Donald. *The Emancipation of French Indochina*. London: Oxford University Press, 1961.

Laniel, Joseph. *Le Drame Indochinois: de Dien-Bien-Phu au pari de Genève*. Paris: Plon, 1957.

Le Duan. *Some Questions Concerning the International Tasks of Our Party*. Peking: Foreign Languages Press, 1964.

———. *Kuan yu Yueh-nan she hui chu i ko ming* (On the Vietnamese Socialist Revolution), 3 vols. Hanoi: Foreign Languages Publishing House, 1965.

Le Thanh Khoi. *Le Viet-Nam, histoire et civilisation*. Paris: Les Editions du Seuil, 1955.

Legge, James. *The Chinese Classics*, Vol. II, The Works of Mencius. Hong Kong, 1960.

Levenson, Joseph R. *Liang Ch'i-ch'ao and the Mind of Modern China*. Cambridge: Harvard University Press, 1953.

Li, Cheng-fu. *Chun hsien shih tai chih Annan* (Annam During the Chinese Chun-Hsien Period). Chungking: Commercial Press, 1948.

Li, Chien-nung. *The Political History of China, 1840-1928.* Tr. Ssu-yu Teng and Jeremy Ingalls. Princeton: D. Van Nostrand, 1956.

Liu, F. F. *A Military History of Modern China, 1924-1949.* Princeton: Princeton University Press, 1956.

Liu, Shao-ch'i et al. *Ten Glorious Years.* Peking: Foreign Languages Press, 1960.

Lo, Hsiang-lin. *Chung hsia hsi t'ung chung chih Pai-yueh* (The Hundred Yueh in the Chinese People System). Chungking: Tu li, 1943.

Lu Ku. *Yueh-nan jen min fan ti tou cheng shih* (History of the Vietnamese People's Anti-Imperialist Struggle). Shanghai: Tung fang, 1951.

McLane, Charles B. *Soviet Strategies in Southeast Asia; An Exploration of Eastern Policy under Lenin and Stalin.* Princeton: Princeton University Press, 1966.

McVey, Ruth T. *The Calcutta Conference and the Southeast Asian Uprisings.* Ithaca: Cornell University, 1958.

Mai, Lang. *Chan tou chung ti hsin Yueh-nan* (The New Vietnam at War). Shanghai(?): New Vietnam Publishing Co., 1948.

Mao Tse-tung. *Selected Works,* I, II, III, IV. Peking: Foreign Languages Press, 1961 and 1965.

———. *Selected Military Writings.* Peking: Foreign Languages Press, 1963.

———. *On Guerrilla Warfare.* Tr. Samuel B. Griffith. New York: Frederick Praeger, 1961.

Masson, André. *Histoire de l'Indochine.* Paris: Presses Universitaires de France, 1950.

Mei, Kung-i. *Yueh-nan hsin chih* (New Records of Vietnam). Chungking: Chung hua, 1945.

Morse, Hosea B. *The International Relations of the Chinese Empire.* London: Longmans, Green and Co., 1910.

Mus, Paul. *Viet-Nam, Sociologie d'une Guerre.* Paris: Les Editions du Seuil, 1952.

Nan fang lai hsin (Letters from the South). Hanoi: Foreign Languages Publishing House, 1964.

Bibliography

Navarre, Henri-Eugène. *Agonie de l'Indochine (1953-1954)*. Paris: Plon, 1956.

New China News Agency. *Daily News Release*. Peking, 1949-1961.

Nguyen Duy Thanh. *My Four Years with the Viet Minh*. Bombay: Democratic Research Service, 1950.

Nguyen-Van-Mung and Nguyen-Van-Thai. *A Short History of Vietnam*. Saigon: The Time Publishing Co., 1958.

North, Robert C. *Moscow and the Chinese Communists*. Stanford: Stanford University Press, 1953.

O'Ballance, Edgar. *The Indo-China War, 1945-1954; A Study in Guerrilla Warfare*. London: Faber and Faber, 1964.

Pentony, DeVere E., ed. *China, the Emerging Red Giant: Communist Foreign Policies*. San Francisco: Chandler Publishing Co., 1962.

Pham Van Dong and the Committee for the Study of the History of the Vietnamese Workers' Party. *President Ho Chi Minh*. Hanoi: Foreign Languages Publishing House, 1960.

Purcell, Victor. *The Chinese in Southeast Asia*. London: Oxford University Press, 1951.

Raskin, Marcus G. and Bernard B. Fall. *The Viet-Nam Reader: Articles and Documents on American Foreign Policy and the Viet-Nam Crisis*. New York: Vintage, 1965.

Ridgway, Matthew B. *Soldier: The Memoirs of Matthew B. Ridgway*. New York: Harper, 1956.

Robequain, Charles. *The Economic Development of French Indo-China*. London: Oxford University Press, 1944.

Romanus, Charles F. and Riley Sunderland. *Stilwell's Mission to China*. Washington, D.C.: Department of the Army, 1953.

Rosenman, Samuel I., comp. *The Public Papers and Addresses of Franklin D. Roosevelt, 1944-45 Volume, Victory and the Threshold of Peace*. New York: Harper, 1950.

Roy, Jules. *The Battle of Dienbienphu*. Tr. from the French by Robert Baldick; Introduction by Neil Sheehan. New York: Harper & Row, 1965.

Sainteny, Jean. *Histoire d'une Paix Manquée, Indochine, 1945-47.* Paris: Amiot Dumont, 1953.

Scigliano, Robert. *South Vietnam: Nation under Stress.* Boston: Houghton Mifflin, 1963.

Shaplen, Robert. *The Lost Revolution: The U.S. in Vietnam, 1946-1966.* New York: Harper & Row, 1966.

Shih chieh chih shih she (*World Culture*). *Shih chieh chih shih shou ts'e* (Handbook of *World Culture*). Peking, 1954.

————. *A Chronicle of Principal Events Relating to the Indochina Question, 1940-1954.* Peking, 1954.

Snow, Edgar. *Red Star over China.* New York: Random House, 1938.

Starobin, Joseph R. *Eyewitness in Indo-China.* New York: Cameron & Kahn, 1954.

Stebbins, Richard P. *The United States in World Affairs, 1954.* New York: Harper, 1956.

Su, Tzu. *Chin jih Yueh-nan* (Vietnam Today). Hong Kong: Freedom Press, 1952.

Ta Kung Book Store. *Jen min nien chien* (People's Year Book). Hong Kong: 1950.

Tanham, George K. *Communist Revolutionary Warfare: The Vietminh in Indochina.* New York: Frederick Praeger, 1961.

Teng, Ssu-yu and John K. Fairbank, with E-tu Zen Sun and Chaoying Fang. *China's Response to the West: A Documentary Survey, 1839-1923.* 2 vols. Cambridge: Harvard University Press, 1954.

Thompson, Virginia. *French Indochina.* New York: Macmillan, 1937.

———— and Richard Adloff. *The Left Wing in Southeast Asia.* New York: William Sloane Associates, 1950.

Trager, Frank N., ed. *Marxism in Southeast Asia: A Study of Four Countries.* Stanford: Stanford University Press, 1959.

Tran Dan Tien. *Hu Chih-ming chuan* (Biography of Ho Chi Minh). Shanghai: August Publishing Co., 1949.

Bibliography

Tran Dan Tien. *Glimpses of the Life of Ho Chi Minh.* Hanoi: Foreign Languages Publishing House, 1958.

Tran Hoai Nam. *Yueh-nan jen min ti chieh fang tou cheng* (The Struggle for Liberation of the Vietnamese People). Peking: *World Culture,* 1954.

Tran-Ngoc-Danh. *Two Years' Achievement of the Viet-Nam Nationalist Government.* Paris: Vietnam Information Service, 1947.

Trullinger, O. O. *Red Banners over Asia.* Boston: Beacon Press, 1951.

Truong Chinh. *Hu chu hsi* (President Ho). Hanoi: Foreign Languages Publishing House, 1966.

―――. *The August Revolution.* Hanoi: Foreign Languages Publishing House, 1958.

―――. *The Resistance Will Win.* Hanoi: Foreign Languages Publishing House, 1960.

―――. *Resolutely Taking the North Vietnam Countryside to Socialism through Agricultural Cooperation.* Hanoi: Foreign Languages Publishing House, 1959.

Vandenbosch, Amry and Richard A. Butwell. *Southeast Asia Among the World Powers.* Lexington: University of Kentucky Press, 1957.

Vietnamese Studies, Numbers 7, 8, 9, 10, 11, 12. Hanoi: Vietnamese Studies, 1965-1967.

Viollis, Andrée. *Indochine S.O.S.* Paris: Gallimard, 1935.

Vo Nguyen Giap. *People's War, People's Army.* New York: Frederick Praeger, 1962.

―――. *One Year of Revolutionary Achievement.* Bangkok: Viet Nam News Publication, 1946.

―――. *Dien Bien Phu.* Hanoi: Foreign Languages Publishing House, 1959.

Wang, Chia-hsiang. "The International Significance of the Chinese People's Victory," in Liu Shao-ch'i et al. *Ten Glorious Years.* Peking: Foreign Languages Press, 1960.

Wang, Chien-ming. *Chung-kuo kung ch'an tang shih kao* (History of the Chinese Communist Party), 3 vols. Taipei, 1965.

Warner, Denis. *The Last Confucian.* New York: Macmillan, 1963.

Wedemeyer, Albert C. *Wedemeyer Reports.* New York: Henry Holt, 1958.

Wiens, Herold J. *China's March Toward the Tropics.* Hamden, Connecticut: The Shoe String Press, 1954.

Whiting, Allen S. *Soviet Policies in China, 1917-1924.* New York: Columbia University Press, 1954.

———. *China Crosses the Yalu; the Decision to Enter the Korean War.* New York: Macmillan, 1960.

Wilbur, C. Martin and Julie Lien-ying How. *Documents on Communism, Nationalism and Soviet Advisers in China, 1918-1927.* New York: Columbia University Press, 1956.

Zagoria, Donald S. *The Sino-Soviet Conflict, 1956-61.* New York: Atheneum, 1964.

———. *Vietnam Triangle.* New York: Pegasus, 1967.

ARTICLES FROM PERIODICALS AND NEWSPAPERS

Aurousseau, Leonard. "La première conquête chinoise des pays annamites," *Bulletin de l'Ecole Française d'Extrème-Orient* (Hanoi), Vol. 23 (1923).

Baldwin, Hanson W. "China as a Military Power," *Foreign Affairs,* October 1951.

Benda, Harry J. "Communism in Southeast Asia," *Yale Review,* March 1956.

Bullit, William. "The Saddest War," *Life,* December 29, 1947.

Butwell, Richard. "Communism Liaison in Southeast Asia," *United Asia* (Bombay), VI, No. 3, June 1954.

Buu Loc. "Aspects of the Vietnamese Problem," *Pacific Affairs,* XXV, No. 3, September 1952.

Chang Ch'u-kun. "The New Military Victory of the Vietnamese People," *World Culture,* Vol. 22, No. 17, October 28, 1950.

Chen, King C. "North Vietnam in the Sino-Soviet Dispute, 1962-1964," *Asian Survey,* September 1964.

———. "Peking's Strategy in Indochina," *Yale Review,* June 1965.

Bibliography

Ch'en, Po-ta. "Mao Tse-tung's Theory of the Chinese Revolution Is the Combination of Marxism-Leninism with the Chinese Revolution," *Hsueh hsi* (Study), July 1, 1951.

Clubb, O. Edmund. "Chiang Kai-shek's Waterloo: The Battle of the Hwai-Hai," *Pacific Historical Review*, November 1956.

Crozier, Brian. "The International Situation in Indo-China," *Pacific Affairs*, December 1955.

Dai, Shen-yu. "Peking and Indochina's Destiny," *The Western Political Quarterly*, September 1954.

Durdin, Peggy. "Why Ho Chi Minh Can Win," *The Nation*, November 11, 1956.

Durdin, Tillman. "Life and Death on Hill 135," *New York Times Magazine*, February 28, 1954.

Farley, Miriam S. "Vietnam Kaleidoscope," *Far East Survey*, XXIV, No. 5, May 1955.

Fifield, Russell H. "Communist China's Foreign Policy," *Current History*, December 1957.

Fischer, Ruth. "Ho Chi Minh: Disciplined Communist," *Foreign Affairs*, October 1954.

Gavin, James M. "We Can Get Out of Vietnam," *Saturday Evening Post*, February 24, 1968.

Griffin, Allen. "Must Indochina Be Lost?" *New Republic*, March 31, 1952.

Guber, A. "The Vietnam People in Their Struggle for Independence and Democracy," *Voprosy Istorii*, October 1949, tr. in *Soviet Press Translations*, Vol. V, Nos. 6 & 7, March 15 and April 1, 1950.

Hackett, Roger F. "Chinese Students in Japan, 1900-1910," *Papers on China*, Cambridge: Harvard Regional Studies, 1958.

Hall, D.G.E. "China and Southeast Asia Yesterday and Today," *Far Eastern Economic Review*, June 23, 1955.

Halpern, A. M. "The Foreign Policy Uses of the Chinese Revolutionary Model," *China Quarterly*, No. 7, July-September 1961.

Hoai Thanh and Thanh Tinh. "His Native Village and His Childhood," in Hoai Thanh et al., *Hu pai pai* (Uncle

Ho). Hanoi: Foreign Languages Publishing House, 1962.

Hoan Buu. "Vietnam: Economic Consequences of the Geneva Peace; Structure of a Dependent Economy; Impact of Military Expenditure," *Far Eastern Economic Review*, December 11, 18, 25, 1958.

Hong Ha. "The Vietnam People Progress Steadily on the Line of Economic Struggle," *World Culture*, No. 32, August 16, 1952.

Hu, Wei-te. "New China's International Position," *World Culture*, Vol. 24, No. 11, 1951.

Isaacs, Harold R. "'A Thing Is Good or Bad,' When A Red Straddles Its News," *Newsweek*, April 25, 1949.

Jen Hsiao. "The Great Success of the Land Policy of the Democratic Republic of Vietnam," *World Culture*, February 5, 1954.

————. "Great Achievements of the Democratic Republic of Vietnam in the Financial-Economic and Political Fields," *World Culture*, August 20, 1954.

Jen min jih pao. "Indochina Peace Depends upon Spirit of Compromise," July 19, 1954.

Jumper, Roy. "The Communist Challenge to South Vietnam," *Far Eastern Survey*, December 1956.

Karpikhin, A. "The United States Takes Over in South Vietnam," *International Affairs* (Moscow), April 1956.

Katzenbach, Edward L., Jr. "Indochina: A Military-Political Appreciation," *World Politics*, IV, No. 2, January 1952.

Kennedy, John F. "America's Stake in Vietnam," *Vital Speeches*, August 1, 1956.

Kuo, Mo-jo. "The Korean Armistice and World Peace," *People's China*, No. 16, August 16, 1953.

Le Thanh Khoi. "The Democratic Republic of Vietnam," *Eastern World* (London), December 1954.

Lindbeck, John M. H. "Communist China and American Far Eastern Policy," Department of State *Bulletin*, November 7, 1955.

Liu, San. "When President Ho Chi Minh was in South China," *Wen hui pao* (Hong Kong), September 7, 1953.

Bibliography

Lu, Ting-yi. "The World Significance of the Chinese Revolution," *Hsueh hsi*, July 1, 1951.

Luu Duc Pho (Nguyen Duy Tinh). "Struggle of Vietnam People for Independence," *For a Lasting Peace, For a People's Democracy*, October 7, 1949.

Mus, Paul. "The Role of the Village in Vietnamese Politics," *Pacific Affairs*, September 1949.

———. "Vietnam: A Nation Off Balance," *Yale Review*, June 1952.

Ner, Marcel. "Le Viet-Nam et la Chine de 1945 à 1953," *Les Temps Modernes* (Paris). Vol. 9, Nos. 93-94, October-September 1953.

Nguyen Thai. "The Two Vietnams and China," *The Harvard Review*, II, No. 1, Fall-Winter 1963.

Pham Van Dong. "The Foreign Policy of the Democratic Republic of Vietnam," *International Affairs* (Moscow), July 1958.

———. "The Seventh Anniversary of the Resistance War of the Democratic Republic of Vietnam," *World Culture*, No. 34, August 30, 1952.

Rigg, Lieutenant Colonel Robert E. "Red Parallel: Tactics of Ho and Mao," *Army Combat Forces Journal*, January 1955.

Roberts, Chalmers M. "The Day We Didn't Go to War," *Reporter*, September 14, 1954.

Roy, M. N. "Mao Tse-tung: A Reminiscence," *New Republic*, September 3, 1951.

Sacks, I. Milton. "The Strategy of Communism in Southeast Asia," *Pacific Affairs*, September 1950.

Shabad, Theodore. "Economic Development in North Vietnam," *Pacific Affairs*, March 1958.

Shaplen, Robert. "The Enigma of Ho Chi Minh," *Reporter*, January 27, 1955.

Sharp, Lauriston. "Paradoxes in the Indochinese Dilemma," *The Annals of the American Academy of Political and Social Science*, July 1954.

Singh, Vishal. "The Geneva Agreements and Developments in Vietnam," *Foreign Affairs Reports*, September 1955.

Bibliography

Snow, Edgar. "Interview with Mao," *New Republic*, 152, No. 9, February 27, 1965.

Steiner, Arthur H. "Mainsprings of Chinese Communist Foreign Policy," *American Journal of International Law*, January 1950.

———. "Vietnam: Civil War Again?" *New Republic*, July 18, 1955.

Strong, Anna Louise. "The Thought of Mao Tse-tung," *Amerasia*, Vol. XI, No. 6, June 1947.

Szu, Li. "Restore Peace in Indo-China," *People's China*, No. 7, April 1, 1954.

Taussing, H. C. "North Vietnam's Headaches," *Eastern World*, March 1957.

Ton That Thien. "The Geneva Agreements and Peace Prospects in Vietnam," *India Quarterly*, October-December 1956.

Turnbull, George S., Jr. "Reporting of the War in Indochina: A Critique," *Journalism Quarterly*, Winter 1957.

Vo Nguyen Giap. "The Vietminh People's Army Fights for Freedom, Independence and Democracy," *Ta kung pao*, December 22, 23, 24, 1951, tr. in *Soviet Press Translations*, Vol. 7, No. 6, March 15, 1952.

Way, Tsung-to. "Overseas Chinese in Vietnam," *Far Eastern Economic Review*, January 2, 1958.

Whiting, Allen S. "The Logic of Communist China's Policy, the First Decade," *Yale Review*, Autumn 1960.

Wolf, Charles, Jr. "Soviet Economic Aid in Southeast Asia: Threat or Windfall?" *World Politics*, October 1957.

Yefimov, P. "The Democratic Republic of Viet-Nam Builds A New Life," *International Affairs* (Moscow), August 1955.

Zhukov, E. "The Bandung Conference of African and Asian Countries and Its Historic Significance," *International Affairs* (Moscow), May 1955.

Zhukov, Ye. "China's Revolutionary Victory and Its Influence on the Liberation Movements of the Various Asian Peoples," *World Culture*, No. 38, September 27, 1952.

Bibliography

NEWSPAPERS (RELEVANT PERIODS)

Central Daily News (Chung yang jih pao. Chungking, Kweilin, Kunming, Nanking, Taipei)
Chieh fang jih pao (Yenan, Shanghai)
The Christian Science Monitor
Hsin hua jih pao (Chungking)
Jen min jih pao (Peking)
Kung Sheung Daily News (Hong Kong)
Le Monde
New York Herald Tribune
New York Times
Sing tao jih pao (Hong Kong)
Ta kung pao (Chungking, Hong Kong, Shanghai) and *Chin pu jih pao* (T'ienchin; formerly *Ta kung pao*)
The Times (London)
Wah kiu yat po (Hong Kong)
Wen hui pao (Hong Kong)

INTERVIEWS AND CORRESPONDENCE

Interview with Gen. Chang Fa-k'uei, New York City, October 7, 1960.
Interview with Archbishop Paul Yupin, New York City, February 2, 1961.
Letter from Gen. Chang Fa-k'uei, Hong Kong, June 30, 1961.
Letter from Gen. Shao Pai-ch'ang, Taiwan, July 7, 1967.
Letter from Gen. Hou Chih-ming, Taiwan, March 16, 1967.
Letter from Professor Franklin L. Ho, New York City, July 13, 1967.
Letter from Mr. Nghiem Ke To, Saigon, March 31, 1969.
Letter from Mr. Vu Hong Khanh, Saigon, May 30, 1969.

OTHERS

The Library of Peking. *Ch'uan kuo chung wen ch'i k'an lien ho mu lu, 1833-1949* (United Index to All-China Chinese Periodicals, 1833-1949). Peking, 1961.

Bibliography

The Union Research Institute. *Chung-kuo yu Yueh-nan, 1950-1960* (China and Vietnam, 1950-1960; clippings from Chinese newspapers and periodicals in microfilm). Hong Kong, 1961.

Index

Index

Vietnam, 258. *See also* Sino-Vietnamese relations

China, Nationalist, xif, 17, 24, 27, 29, 32-34, 42, 48, 50, 53, 62, 65, 71, 74, 78f, 84, 92, 95, 97f, 104, 112, 115, 117-19, 121, 123, 126, 131f, 139f, 142, 148f, 161, 180, 186, 198f; and France, 42f, 72f; occupation of Vietnam, 115-54; scandals of Lu Han's army, 138-40; Sino-French clash, 144f; Sino-French financial dispute, 135-38; troops' relief, 360f; policy toward Vietnam, 97f, 115, 118f, 126f, 131f, 334-36; troops retreat to Vietnam, 206-11. *See also* Sino-Vietnamese relations

Chinese civil war, 196-98

Chinese Communist Eighth Route Army, 34

Chinese influence in Vietnam: cultural, 5-7, 10-13; economic, 6, 10, 12; political, 5-9, 12f

Chinese-Vietnamese relations, *see* Sino-Vietnamese relations

Chinese residents: status in Indochina, 140, 142

Chinghsi, 46-48, 50f, 56, 72, 85f, 178, 192

Chou En-lai, 17, 21, 34, 203, 205, 213, 251, 272, 280f, 283, 287, 289, 292, 308-15, 317-19, 327-29, 399

Chu, Hsieh, 117n, 121, 127, 135, 138

Chungking, 34, 37, 58f, 97, 98n, 117, 126f, 132, 134, 140f, 144, 148, 187. *See also* Nationalist China

Churchill, Sir Winston, 91, 282, 301, 304, 314

Chu Van Tan, 87

Cochin-China, Republic of, 150

Collins, Lawton (Gen.), 329

Colonialism, French, xi, 159, 330, 336, 340, 344

Cominform, 173, 191, 221, 225, 285, 287, 292-94

Comintern, 21, 24, 26, 30, 35

Communism: in Vietnam, xi, 33, 82, 149

Condore Island, 169

Confucianism, 11-13

Constans (Col.), 206

Couturier, Paul Vaillant, 29

CPPCC (Chinese People's Political Consultative Conference), 198, 212

Cuong De (prince), 16, 45

Cuu Quoc (national salvation), 250

Cuu Quoc Hoi, 51

Dai Viet Party, 68

d'Argenlieu, G. Thierry (Adm.), 107, 158, 162

Dang Dinh Cuong, 75

Dang Viet Chau, 95

Debès (Col.) 158

Decoux, Jean (Adm.), 42f, 92, 99, 111

De Gaulle, Charles, 73, 91, 110, 117

De Lattre de Tassigny, Jean (Gen.), 210f, 266, 270

Democratic Republic of Vietnam, *see* North Vietnam

Devillers, Philippe, 33, 78

Dien-Bien-Phu, 273, 295, 297, 302-307

Diselev, S. V. (Isuliff), 10

Dong-Khe, 264

Dong Minh Hoi (Viet-Nam Revolutionary League), 60, 61-71, 75, 94-96, 104f, 122, 129f, 148, 150-55, 157, 181

Drum, Hugh A. (Gen.), 71

Drumright, Everett F., 306

Dulles, John Foster, 281, 286, 293, 297, 299-302, 304, 314f

Duong Bao Son, 75

Duong Duc Hien, 95

Duong Thanh Dan, 172

Duong Tu Giang, 75f

Eastern Workers' University (University of the Toilers of the East), 21

Index

Index

Index

Chen, King C   1926–
    Vietnam and China, 1938–1954. by King C. Chen.
Princeton, N. J., Princeton University Press, 1969.

    xv, 436 p. 23 cm. 12.50

    Bibliography: p. 406–427.

    1. Vietnam — Foreign relations — China (People's Republic of
China, 1949–   ) 2. China (People's Republic of China, 1949–
)—Foreign relations—Vietnam.   I. Title.

DS740.5.V5C484   327.51′0597   78–83684
SBN 691–03078–2   MARC

Library of Congress   70 ɾr70d3ɿ rev